EALING WALKABOUT

KATE McEWAN was born and educated in Cape Town, and has lived in Ealing since 1975. Her decision to change careers from Microbiology to the Media led to a variety of jobs in PR, advertising agencies, magazines and newspapers, as well as a number of freelance commissions. She began to take an interest in what was happening in the borough while helping to present a weekly news-programme for Hospital Radio West Middlesex, and started to delve into local history for the *Ealing Gazette* in 1979. She is a member of several local history and conservation societies, and hopes to play a more active role in their projects now that this book — her first — is finally complete. She lives with a professional London guide/tour manager and their son, aged two.

ALAN GILLETT has lived in Ealing all his life, but admits to visiting many parts of the borough for the first time while illustrating *Ealing Walkabout*. His interest in art began at Malborough College and he was Art Editor of *Varsity* at Cambridge, where he added Estate Management to his drawing skills in order to become a chartered surveyor. He enjoys sketching buildings, street-scenes and churches, and is involved in numerous local activities as the Founder Chairman of the Friends of St. Mary's Perivale, surveyor to the William Hobbayne Trust in Hanwell and a former president of Ealing Rotary Club — to name just a few. He is married with five grown-up children.

I

For Peter
who learnt about typewriters at an early age

and Alistair
who learnt to cook

EALING WALKABOUT

Kate McEwan

... Out into the outskirt's edges
Where a few surviving hedges
Keep alive our lost Elysium — rural Middlesex again.

John Betjeman — Middlesex

x

EALING WALKABOUT

Kate McEwan

... Out into the outskirt's edges
Where a few surviving hedges
Keep alive our lost Elysium — rural Middlesex again.

John Betjeman — Middlesex

III

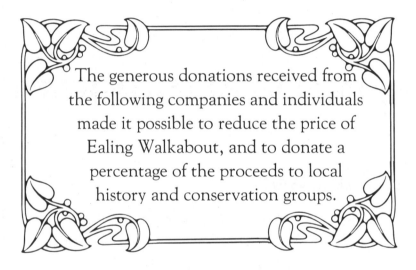

The generous donations received from the following companies and individuals made it possible to reduce the price of Ealing Walkabout, and to donate a percentage of the proceeds to local history and conservation groups.

SPONSORS

Barclays Bank UK
British Home Stores
H.W. Carter — Ye Olde Hanwell Stores
Ciborio Ltd
Cole & Hicks
Mr. J.B. Combes
Cornucopia Wholefoods
Fuller Smith & Turner
Gallaher Ltd
Glaxo
Arthur Guinness Son & Co (Great Britain) Ltd
Hetheringtons
Hoover Ltd
Ind Coope — Taylor Walker
Italvini Ltd
Jones & Co
Kemsley, Whiteley & Ferris
John Laing Development Services
Lyons-Tetley Ltd
Prontaprint
Quaker Oats Ltd
Russell Collins & Co
Mr. Duncan Smith
U.B. (Biscuits) Ltd
Unigate Ltd
Watney Combe Reid & Co
Nick Wheatley Associates
Whitman Read & Co
Wine City

Published by Nick Wheatley Associates
Stanley House
Stanley Street
Warrington
Cheshire

Copyright © 1983 Kate McEwan

ISBN 0 9508895 0 4

Layout and Design by Kate McEwan

Printed by Pulse Design and Print, Warrington.

CONTENTS

 FOREWORD

I think Kate McEwan's book is beautiful and am pleased to be associated with it. I don't think it needs any introduction from me, it is its own introduction and like all good things it speaks for itself.

My own feelings on the changes being made to our environment in the name of Progress are summed up in the following extracts from an article I wrote two years before the Borough of Ealing and other new GLC boroughs replaced the ancient County of Middlesex.

Like many others, I can recall Middlesex High Road before the onslaught of traffic and supermarkets which started in the thirties and has gained pace in the fifties and sixties. There were still chemists' shops, with big coloured bottles behind their *art nouveau* glazing bars, and, inside, the rows of coloured jars on mahogany shelves; there were linen drapers where the change ran in a wooden ball from the counter to the cash desk on a rail among handkerchiefs and lace; dairies, lined with blue and white tiles, were adorned with a polished churn and a china cow; the sweet smell of baking came from bread shops; butchers' shops were open to the straw and dust of the highroad, and along that highroad was the occasional chug of a motor-car, the clop of horse hooves and the hiss and grind of the electric tramcar beneath its overhead wires.

I don't say the High Road was more hygienic than it is now, but I do say it was pleasanter and one could sleep in a house looking over it without the united aid of sleeping pills, ear plugs and double glazing. One knew, too, that between the main roads into London were still a few hay fields, market gardens and dairy farms which supplied London with fodder and fresh food. There were village greens and inns like that which unexpectedly remains, church, inn and all, at Norwood Green near the farmland round Osterley and the banks of the Brent, so near to London that you can see above enormous elms the flashing factory towers of the Great West Road.

Probably there is no turning back and for that reason every acre where there is still quiet and the smell of grass and the sound of brooks becomes more precious and essential for our recreation. Most of the delicate attractions of the county, old brick walls, inns and farm buildings, survive close up to its parish churches. To the local authorities, and those very few landowners who have withstood the blandishments of 'developers', we owe the identity of Middlesex as a county at all. Unless there is public will to preserve and maintain the wild and natural, the old and gentle, then all the Home Counties will suffer the same fate.*

Today there is an even greater need for 'public will to maintain the wild and natural, the old and gentle'. I hope Ealing Walkabout will help to make residents aware of this, before it is too late.

JOHN BETJEMAN
June, 1983

Extracted from 'Middlesex', which first appeared in the Daily Telegraph Weekend Magazine, 12th August 1963.

Outside the Fox and Goose in Hanger Lane, Ealing, during the 1887 Perambulation. (Note the willow wands for 'beating the bounds'.)

X

INTRODUCTION

Respice, Prospice (Look backward, Look forward)
MOTTO of the MUNICIPAL BOROUGH OF EALING (1901-65)
Progress with Unity
MOTTO of the LONDON BOROUGH OF EALING (1965-   )

IN THE DAYS before maps and guide books, stories about people and events in the eight Middlesex villages that now constitute the London Borough of Ealing, were retold over the centuries during the parochial **Perambulation** — an ancient ceremony dating back to Roman times, and reinforced by Elizabeth I. She ordered that once a year, usually in Ascension Week, the residents of every parish were to gather at the parish church (then the centre of village life), and follow the vicar and other local dignitaries in procession around the parish boundaries. Willow wands were distributed for beating the boundary line the whole length of its course (even in the middle of the River Brent), and the exact position of boundary posts and stones was forcibly impressed on succeeding generations of parishioners by bumping their heads against them. Except for these minor inconveniences, the Perambulation offered a jolly day's outing: stops were made at inns and places of interest along the way, there was gossip, lusty singing of hymns, and a free meal provided by the parish authorities. The practice of 'beating the bounds' was thus a relatively painless way of ensuring that land was not sneakily encroached on by neighbouring parishes, and that local legends were kept alive as times and places changed.

Such a simple custom could not survive the massive changes brought about by the 20th century, however. The annual 'walkabout' gradually died out as villages grew into towns; the responsibility for parish administration was transferred from the church to local boards, and wider authorities; and old boundary marks were buried under the spread of suburbia. Thanks to modern administration and communications, residents in today's towns undoubtedly enjoy a higher standard of living than their counterparts of a century ago — the majority of whom suffered bad sanitation, poor education and severe poverty. But, as small rural parishes merged into urban districts, and the districts were in turn absorbed into boroughs, individuality was swept away with the old boundary lines, and community spirit (with a few rare exceptions) was destroyed by the ever-increasing numbers of new residents from other towns, counties and even countries.

On April Fools' Day 1965, the Municipal Boroughs of **Southall, Acton** and **Ealing** (which already included **Hanwell, Greenford, Northolt, Perivale** and **West Twyford**) were amalgamated to form the new **London Borough of Ealing** — one of 32 such administrative units to be created in Greater London by the London Government Act of 1963. Over 300,000 people fell under the jurisdiction of the new borough, making Ealing — in terms of population size — the fifth largest London Borough and one of the biggest urban administrative areas in the whole of England and Wales. Perambulations and *Progress* simply do not go together, and there's no point in bewailing the fact. But the personality of a place depends on the extent to which its legacy from the past has been incorporated into new developments, and by foresaking the old principle of '*looking backwards*' in favour of *Unity* and standardisation, we are in danger of losing something much more important than a few out-of-date boundary lines and the quaint custom that maintained them. If the remaining traces of the borough's heritage are to be preserved, we must first appreciate them; and there is therefore an urgent need for today's residents to understand something of the way in which people and events of the past have influenced the emergence of the towns they live in, and the character of their borough as a whole.

Ealing Walkabout offers a series of leisurely walks around the borough, through which residents (and other explorers) may discover for themselves the distinctive identities and surviving features of these eight ancient parishes, and those neighbours — **Osterley, Syon, Brentford** and **Gunnersbury** — that played a part in their history. To make it easier for you to 'perambulate' today's boundaries, the towns of the borough have been visited in an anti-clockwise direction — beginning with Ealing (the oldest incorporated town), and ending with Brentford. The latter has been included not only because its ties with Ealing and Hanwell go back much further than its relatively short association with Hounslow, but because the town provides access to the River Thames — the most important link in the long chain of events which finally led to the borough being welded to London.

After an introductory chapter highlighting some of these events, each chapter begins with a brief outline of a suburb's development from the time it was first given a name, followed by the story of the parish church around which it grew. The churches (even those no longer used for religious purposes — like St. Mary's, Perivale and St. Lawrence's, Brentford) form the starting point for several possible walks around the area, which will enable readers to build up a picture of village life in generations past — aided by what can be seen today. The names of some prominent citizens feature in several chapters, since wealthy landowners often held land in surrounding parishes — thus establishing a bond between the scattered communities of the borough long before they were officially united.

Many of the historic sites are buried beneath or hidden behind the modern facade of today's town centres; but, wherever possible, built-up areas are enhanced by diversions along canal towpaths, or through the parks and recreation grounds which serve as reminders of the wheatfields, market gardens and country estates that once covered the borough. The journeys are spiced with tales of famous former residents — royalty, politicians, writers and business entrepreneurs, and of the infamous — murderers, forgers, highwaymen and ghosts. And, in the best tradition of the old Perambulation, the walks offer every opportunity for stops to be made at wayside inns.

Readers with long memories may recognise the occasional excerpt from the series of **Weekend Walkabout** articles I wrote for the *Ealing Gazette* several years ago — which many people asked to have reprinted in book-form. But, from the above description (not to mention sheer weight) of this volume, they will have realised that the 'booklet' they have awaited for so long, bears about as much resemblance to my original articles as Frankenstein's monster did to his blueprint. Nevertheless, I hope they will not be too disappointed. I really did set out with the idea of merely adding a few more walks to my newspaper articles, but it soon became apparent that my original investigations into the borough had barely scratched the surface. In the end, my problem was not so much what to put in, but what to leave out.

True local historians (whose own laborious research into the original State and Parish records has made my job so much easier) may not agree with my final selection of facts and fallacies, but I should like to stress that this lengthy-but-lighthearted guide has been written by an ordinary resident for others of the same ilk. It is not a definitive history, but only one interpretation of the wealth of information that is easily available to anyone wishing to put the story of the borough into perspective — given the right amount of time, perseverance, and insanity. Although I have sometimes adopted a rather irreverent attitude towards important people and serious events of the past, I have tried to present the main facts as accurately as possible — without losing sight of the 'story' part of history. The credit due to the work of earlier and contemporary writers is indicated by the length of my bibiliography; while the personal help given to me in researching, writing and publishing the book is gratefully acknowledged in a list at the end.

Apart from discovering that writing a book whilst rearing a baby is not the ideal combination for meeting deadlines, I have learnt a lot during my rambles around the borough. The importance of not taking a place at face-value was the first to emerge. I began with a very confused idea of how to relate all that I'd read of the past, to the present; but, as I explored the towns themselves, I was constantly surprised by how much evidence of their history still existed. Sometimes it was only reflected in the name of a street, pub, school or block of flats; but often it was more substantial. Besides ancient churches such as the one at Perivale, or better-known landmarks like Ealing's **Pitshanger Manor** (the country house built by the famous architect, *Sir John Soane*, which now houses the Central Library), **Twyford's 'Abbey'**, and Southall's **Tudor manor house;** I found that the former home of Greenford's manor lord had been converted into a community centre, as had the old manor farmhouse at Northolt, two cottages in the South Ealing Road were once part of the parish workhouse, several early 19th century "gentlemen's residences" were still used as homes on Norwood Green, while others in Acton had become schools or offices. Every place, no matter how over-developed or modernised, revealed some structural proof of the fact that people have been living here for a long, long time.

There were also less obvious signs — where my early 19th century map indicated brickfields or gravel pits, I found factories and industrial sites; old fishing ponds had been filled in to provide village greens or rest-gardens; well-trodden footpaths and trackways had become modern streets. A definite visual pattern thus emerged, which made it easier to explain how each town had developed and why they were all so different. I hope that I managed to transfer some of the atmosphere absorbed from each place, into the book; and that my discoveries will help readers to appreciate that a town does not have to be attractive in order to be interesting.

Of course, there were disappointments as well — especially among the listed buildings specifically 'preserved' by the Department of the Environment for their architectural and historic interest. Many of these — such as **Berrymead Priory** in Acton, once the home of the celebrated novelist, *Lord Edward Bulwer Lytton*, and some of the outbuildings in **Gunnersbury Park** which date from the ownerships of *Princess Amelia*, George II's favourite daughter, or the wealthy *Rothschild* family — are grossly neglected for want of the funds to restore them. But, even here, there was hope — for where the local authorities had failed to maintain the buildings or were advocating that they be pulled down, local residents had formed themselves into action groups to protest against demolition or, like the **Friends of Gunnersbury Park and Museum,** to raise the necessary 'protection money'. The **St. Lawrence Brentford Trust** has shown how the 'useful lifespan' (to coin a Council phrase) of an old building can be extended, by converting the redundant church into a theatre; while older groups like the **Brent River and Canal Society,** the **Hanwell Preservation Society** and others listed in the book, have also proved what can be accomplished by getting local people involved in conservation projects — and all depend on new recruits for their continued success.

Perhaps the most overwhelming impression gained from this experience, was the speed with which places can change. *Ealing Walkabout* was written over a period of three years — which may have seemed an eternity to the author, but was scarcely a moment in the history of the borough. During that time, just about every chapter has had to be partially rewritten or updated as buildings I'd mentioned in the earlier walks were demolished, factories and hospitals closed, new roads were built, or previously uninteresting sites improved by redevelopment. Since it was not possible to perpetually perambulate the borough right up to going to press, I cannot promise that everything you find en route will be as I last saw it — but I do hope that readers will let me know about any errors and their own discoveries. Many years ago, when the old County of Middlesex was fighting for its life, the Council issued a pamphlet called 'Mind your own Middlesex'. It would be a real sign of progress if *'Mind your own Borough'* could become the unofficial motto of the new Ealing.

Ealing, September 1983.   KATE McEWAN

⌬ ILLUSTRATIONS ⌬

An asterisk indicates tha the picture came from the London Borough of Ealing Library Service's local history collection; the initials A.G. stand for an Alan Gillett original. My sincere thanks to all contributors.

BRENTFORD

 MAPS

(See Key overleaf)

KEY TO ROUTE MAPS

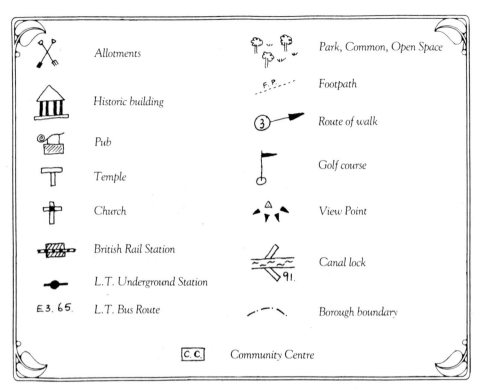

Allotments		Park, Common, Open Space	
Historic building		Footpath	
Pub		Route of walk	
Temple		Golf course	
Church		View Point	
British Rail Station		Canal lock	
L.T. Underground Station		Borough boundary	
L.T. Bus Route			

Community Centre

Scale

Because of the distance covered by some of the walks and the amount of area information that needed to be included, for reasons of clarity most maps are not drawn to scale — but a rough estimate of the length of each route is given in the text.

All route maps have been drawn by *Alistair Chisholm*, and are based on the Ordnance Survey 1:10,000 maps with permission of the Controller of Her Majesty's Stationery Office, Crown copyright reserved.

Never move an old boundary mark that your ancestors established
PROVERBS 22:28 (Today's English Version)

People will never look forward to prosperity who never look backward to their ancestors
EDMUND BURKE (1729-97)

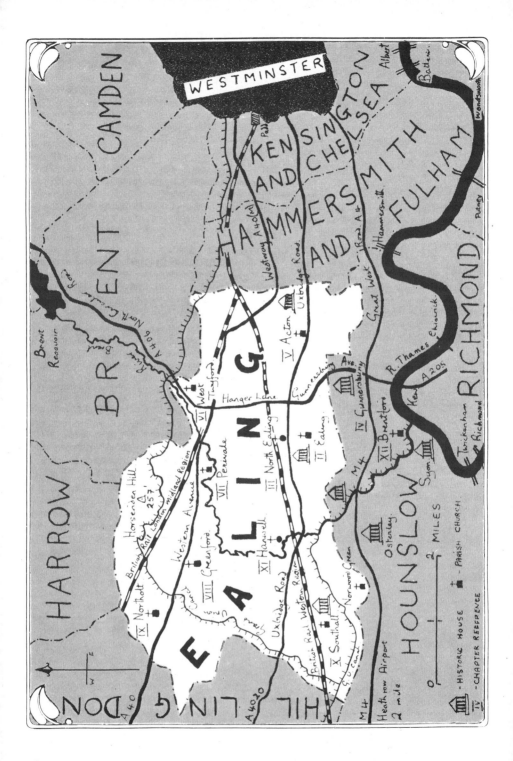

CHAPTER I

One age cannot be completely understood if all the others are not understood. The song of history can only be sung as a whole.

JOSE ORTEGA Y GASSET (1883-1955)

 ƎFORE SETTING OUT to explore individual places in the Borough, it may be worthwhile to pause and survey the district as a whole in order to understand how certain geographical and historical influences common to all these former Middlesex villages have led to their being swallowed up, County and all, by their once distant neighbour — London. This introductory chapter roughly sketches in the story of the borough from the earlies times, and explains many of the customs and terms that recur throughout the book.

FROM DINOSAURS TO DOMESDAY (BC — 1086)
Geology and Geography

The relationship that Ealing and London were to share was determined millions of years before man created them. Geography is the key to history, for it was the lie of the land that dictated where and when people made their settlements. The dark blue **clay** that can still frustrate gardeners in the **northern parts** of the Borough and metropolis, was laid down some 70-40 million years ago at the bottom of a muddy sea which then filled the funnel-shaped depression (now known as the **London Basin**) in the great fold of chalk between the Chilterns and the North Downs. The **gravels** and **brickearth** overlying the clay in the **southern regions,** was deposited long after the sea had retreated — during the interglacial periods which separated the **Ice Ages** of 2 million to 10,000 years ago. As water on the land alternately froze and melted, the level of the sea changed accordingly — causing the vast precursor of the **River Thames** (which was too far south to be frozen permanently) and, to a lesser extent, the **River Brent** to erode deep channels in the clay as they flowed down to the lower sea-level during cold periods; and to flood over wide areas during warm intervals, depositing pebbles and other alluvial debris on top of the clay. A series of stepped gravel **terraces** thus emerged as the process was repeated.

Today, most of the southern part of the Borough lies between 50-125 feet above sea-level, on the second of the three terraces that make up the **Middlesex Plain** of the **Thames Valley.** At **Southall,** parts of **Ealing** and **South Acton,** the gravel has been overlaid by large patches of fertile brickearth. Further north, above the Uxbridge Road, the clay plain rises steeply to the **North Ealing Ridge,** which is topped by the accumulated glacial deposits that formed **Castlebar** and **Hanger Hills.** The relief then falls sharply to the flood-valley of the **Brent** with its minor gravel terraces around **Hanwell, Perivale** and **West Twyford;** and finally rises to the plateau north of the Brent which is dominated by **Harrow** and **Horsenden Hills** — the latter, at 278 feet, being the highest point in the borough.

Ancient Britons

The Borough has revealed traces of practically every stage in Prehistoric Man's progress towards civilisation — making it impossible to do justice to the number of archeological finds and their significance in a few paragraphs. Those of you who would like to learn more about the prehistoric discoveries in the borough are therefore advised to visit the well-explained and displayed exhibits at **Gunnersbury Museum** and the

1

Museum of London, or to get hold of a copy of Mr. C.H. Keene's booklet, *'Field Monuments in the London Borough of Ealing'*. What follows is merely a brief introduction to the primitive peoples who passed through the Borough, leaving their mark here and there, but not — if the dearth of excavated dwelling places is anything to go by — settling permanently in the area until after the Romans had conquered Britain.

Paleolithic (Old Stone Age) **Man** first travelled up the Thames in an interglacial period some 300,000 years ago — in the days when the river still flowed into the Rhine, and Britain was joined to the Continent. He soon found that the Thames gravels provided both prey — mammoths, elephants, hippo, rhino and deer — and flints from which to fashion crude weapons. Finds from this period range from the remains of a **mammoth** and the hand-axes that killed it in Tentelow Lane, **Southall,** to a **flint 'factory'** in Creffield Road, **Acton.** After the last of the ice-sheet melted and the rising sea-level made Britain an island c.7,000 BC, small family groups of **Mesolithic** (Middle Stone Age) **Man** crossed the North Sea in skin boats and dug-out canoes. They lived by fishing in the river, and hunting in the marshes around their riverside camps and in the dense oak forests that covered the higher clay regions. By the dawning of the **Neolithic** or New Stone Age about 3,000 years later, man had learnt to polish his **flint tools** to perfection and began using them to make small clearings on the less-wooded and better-drained gravels — perhaps at **Ealing Common** or **East Acton** where some of these implements have been found. He moved camp frequently to find grazing for his herds of wild sheep, goats, pigs and cattle, or better land for the food he had started to grow. Later, he discovered tin and copper in the West Country, and eventually learnt how to smelt them to make bronze.

The Thames was the main route used for trading with Europe during the **Bronze Age.** By 1000 BC, the West London region around **Brentford** for several miles downstream had become the principal bronze-working area in England, and the number of bronze **swords** found in the river suggest frequent fighting between rival tribes for control of the trade-route. A 'hoard' marking the site of a **bronzesmith's workshop** has been excavated at **Norwood Green,** and Bronze Age **'cemeteries'** (where the ashes of the dead were buried) have been found at Mill Hill Park in **Acton,** and Boston Road, **Hanwell.** However, the district seems to have declined in importance as farming developed into the chief occupation — clearing the forest for arable land having been made easier by the stronger and more readily available metal of the **Iron Age.**

The drawing on the left shows what the Iron Age hamlet excavated at **Heathrow Airport** probably looked like; but, except for traces of an Early Iron Age dwelling at **Brentford** and remains of what may have been an Iron Age **fort** on **Horsenden Hill,** little evidence of settlement during this period has been found in the Borough. The fort could have been built to protect an ancient trackway from the waves of **Celtic invaders** who slaughtered their way across the country from the 7th century BC. They laid out fields of wheat and introduced the first **plough** to Britain, but preferred hunting, fishing, metalwork and fighting each other from their horse-drawn chariots to serious agriculture. The names of both **London** and the **River Brent** are thought to be Celtic in origin, but it is not known whether any ever settled in the region. Each tribe was made up of groups from the same family, who lived in open hamlets or isolated wooden homesteads scattered over a wide area — but all answerable to the chief of their clan. Other clans were considered to be enemies. This fiercely loyal 'kinship' stretched across the sea to help their bretheren in Northern Gaul

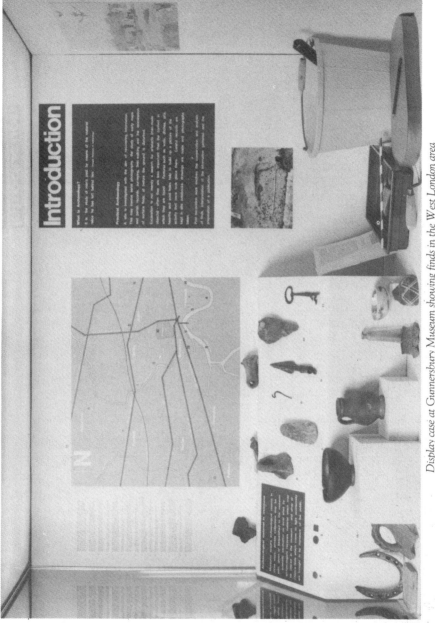

Display case at Gunnersbury Museum showing finds in the West London area dating from Stone Age to Saxon times.

fight the Romans — and was one of the reasons why *Julius Caesar* decided to subdue the Britons.

Romans

At the time of Caesar's second, more successful, invasion in 54 BC, the whole of south-east England was ruled by *Cassivellaunus*, King of the **Belgae** — the most warlike of the Celtic tribes. But his primitive warriors were no match for Caesar's trained armies, and the Belgae were defeated at the lowest natural crossing place over the Thames — generally believed by early local historians to have been at **Brentford,** although firm archeological proof of this has yet to be found. Caesar returned to Rome almost immediately, however, and the final conquest of England only took place a century later in AD 43. As far as the borough is concerned, the most important consequence of the 400-year period of Roman rule was the establishment of **London** as the main commercial port in Britain. The position of the City today was dictated by the site of the **first bridge** across the **Thames.** The Romans built this a little to the east of the present London Bridge, just above what was then the tidal limit — which happily coincided with one of the few strips of firm ground on the marshy, southern side of the river. From London, Roman legions laid out a network of fortified **military roads** to facilitate subjugation of the scattered Celtic tribes. The south-western road to **Silchester** and Bath (from today's Fleet Street, the Strand, through Kensington and along King Street, Hammersmith) skirted the Thames at **Brentford,** which became a small **relay-station** for the horsemen and coaches of the Imperial Post. Archeological finds suggest that there may also have been some sort of Romano-British settlement at **Acton,** which lay close to the junction of the Silchester Road and the north-western road from London — today's Oxford Street, Bayswater Road and Goldhawk Road.

Saxons

Why, c.410 AD, the Romans abandoned Britain to the Teutonic **Angle** and **Saxon** invaders is not certain. What is important is the lasting effect that the Anglo-Saxons had on the borough. To them we owe the first permanent settlements, the origin of local place-names, and the open-field method of farming which survived until the Enclosure Acts of the 19th century. Settlement began on the well-drained alluvial land above the river at places like **Brentford, Norwood Green,** and **Ealing;** and gradually spread northwards into the clay and forest belt around **Acton** and **Twyford.** Easily-defended hill-top settlements were also made at **Northolt** and **Hanwell,** or where the **Brent** served as both a fresh water supply and an obstacle to attackers — as at **Greenford** and **Perivale.**

The administrative system that eventually evolved was based on the tribal idea that land belonged to the community. In the **vills** and townships, all the cultivated land was divided up into **hides.** The amount of land in each varied according to the quality of the soil and the size of the family of **freemen** (freeholders) it had to support, but usually represented an area of about 120 acres. As more of the surrounding forest was cleared for cultivation it was shared out in small strips, so that each family's hide consisted of scattered plots of land in several **common fields** — rather like today's allotments, but all under the same crop. The fields were worked in strict rotation (one always being left fallow), and after harvest they became grazing grounds for the sheep and cattle of the village — pigs having the run of the surrounding heath or forest. The king of the tribe often granted larger holdings to his professional warriors or **thanes,** and it became the custom for the less warlike farmer to work the thane's land in exchange for his protection from marauding tribes.

The freemen of the village framed their laws and customs at the village **moot** or meeting, which was led by their chosen headman or **reeve.** He represented them at the meeting of the **Hundred,** which was made up of a hundred hides or a group of villages.

A number of Hundreds in turn made up a **Shire,** under an elected earldorman (**alderman**) and the king's shire-reeve (**sheriff**) — who were both members of the king's Council or **Witan.** The **Shire of Middlesex** (originally the Province of the **Middle Saxons** — first mentioned in a charter of 704) was divided into six Hundreds, each named after their meeting place. **Ealing, Acton, West Twyford, Brentford** and **Gunnersbury** fell into the **Hundred of Ossulstone,** which met at Oswulf's stone near Marble Arch and included all the villages immediately north and west of the Port of London. **Southall/Norwood, Hanwell, Greenford, Perivale** and **Northolt** lay in the **Hundred of Elthorne,** which met at a thorn-tree near Hayes; while **Osterley** and **Syon** were in the **Hounslow Hundred** (later renamed **Isleworth**). And so they all remained until the use of Hundred divisions died out only a century ago. **London,** itself, seems to have been more or less independent under a **Port Reeve** appointed by the king to oversee trade. Three times a year, the great bell of St. Paul's summoned Londoners to a folkmoot in the corner of the churchyard. In early Saxon times, both London and Middlesex were ruled in turn by the kings of Essex, Mercia and Wessex; and on several occasions **Brentford** was chosen as the meeting place for negotiations between the three rulers, or for Church Councils.

The **Church,** in fact, was largely responsible for this civilised state of affairs. The See of London (with **St. Paul's** as its cathedral) had been refounded under *Bishop Mellitus* in 604 AD — soon after St. Augustine had been sent to re-establish the Roman religion in Britain. The Bishop's diocese included **Middlesex,** which had been divided up into **parishes** by about the 8th century. The first parish priests were usually private chaplains to the thanes, who were responsible for building the original wooden churches on the sites where many of today's **parish churches** still stand. (Northolt's and Hanwell's date from the 8th/9th century.) The Clergy, the only literate men in the Witan, were the Crown's chief advisers, and taught the Anglo-Saxon kings how to make written wills (often in their favour) and to exert their royal jurisdiction by means of charters — some of which provide us with the earliest records of places in the Borough. In order to save their souls, the kings endowed bishoprics and monasteries with vast estates of land — which is how so much of the borough came to be in ecclesiastical hands at Domesday.
Danes

Law and order was further stimulated by the Danes, whose plundering expeditions from the end of the 8th century had the effect of uniting the various Anglo-Saxon kingdoms into one nation under *Alfred the Great,* King of Wessex. **London** and **Middlesex** were ravaged several times during Danish incursions up the Thames, but were saved by the treaty Alfred made in 874, which gave all of north-east England to the **Danelaw** and left London and the south in relative peace under the Saxons. During the next century, while the ancestors of *Canute* and *Edmund Ironside* fought for the conquest of England, many of the Danish administration methods were adopted by the Saxons. The Danish 'burug' system of military garrisons was converted into the English network of fortified 'burghs' (hence **borough**) and large towns like London were defended by their own **burgesses.** The English title of **Earl** comes from the Danish 'Jarl', and the **Danegeld** demanded by the Northmen in exchange for peace developed into the first direct **taxation** — the main reason behind William the Conqueror's Domesday Survey.

The high proportion of Danegeld paid by the wealthy merchants of **London** was to increase their independence and the powerful influence of the City over Saxon, Dane and Norman alike — all of whom made its capture a vital objective of their campaigns. In 1016, **Middlesex** and most of the country chose *Canute* as King, but the **City** chose *Edmund Ironside* and it was only after his death that London made a truce with the Danes. There seems to have been little intensive Danish settlement in Middlesex, however — **Gunnersbury** is the only place-name to date from this period. Some time during the peaceful and prosperous years of Canute's reign, the important positions held by the **Sheriff of Middlesex** and the leading burgess of London became united in the same man — *Tofi the Proud*. His huge land holdings in Middlesex included **Northolt,** parts of **Greenford,** and **Perivale** — all of which passed with his titles to his grandson, *Angsgar*.

As Master of the Stud to *Edward the Confessor*, Angsgar must have overseen the transportation of building materials for the King's favourite (some say only) project — the rebuilding of the **Monastery of St. Peter** two miles upriver, where it had been founded by *King Offa of Mercia* three centuries before. But even more important than the Abbey was the erection of the adjacent **Palace of Westminster** — the magnet that was to draw the City's expansion westwards. The year 1066, the best known date in English history, saw the new Abbey used for three decisive events — the burial of the pious, pro-Norman Edward in January; the subsequent crowning of *Harold*, son of the Earl of Wessex; and, on Christmas Day, the coronation of *William*, **Duke of Normandy,** as King of England by conquest.

Normans
Within a decade of Angsgar leading the best men of Middlesex and London to surrender to William at Berkhamsted, he and his Saxon contemporaries were to have all their land confiscated and their system of administration drastically altered. Under William there was no question of his new subjects having any say in the way they were governed: the King owned all the land, and the grants he made to favoured barons and prelates were strictly in return for their loyalty and military support. The title '**Baron**' comes from the Latin for a freeman but, although the barons were given the right to govern the farmers of their villages (or **manors** as they were now called) through the **manorial courts,** William made sure that their holdings were scattered over the country so that they could not unite against him. He also ensured that the authority of the Church did not interfere with his own by separating the ecclesiastical courts from the lay courts. The **sheriff** now assumed a new importance as he was responsible for collecting the **feudal dues** from the lords in the **Counties** (the old Saxon shires). As tenants-in-chief of many manors, the Norman barons and clergy sublet their land to **knights** in return for their military services, who saw to it that the **villeins** (no longer freemen, but serfs) worked on the lord's **demesne** — the land around his domain or **manor house** — for a certain number of days each week in exchange for the limited rights they now held over their hides in the common fields. The conditions of their holdings were copied into the manorial **Court Roll** — hence the term, **copyholder.** The forests now belonged to the King, and the heath and wasteland to the **manor lord.**

Everybody, from Baron to villein, was taxed according to the amount of land he rented, and it wsa to discover the exact strength of his resources that William had the whole country surveyed. The Survey was worthy of the combined forces of our modern Inland Revenue and Customs & Excise, and its victims called it the Day of Judgement — **Domesday.** When completed, shortly before William's death, its two volumes (which can be seen in the Public Record Office) stated the extent, value, population, state of cultivation, stock and ownership of every manor in the kingdom. From it we know that **Southall/Norwood** were part of the *Archbishop of Canterbury's* Manor of Hayes; **Acton, Ealing, Brentford** and **Gunnersbury** belonged to the *Bishop of London's* Manor Fulham; **West Twyford** was owned by a *Canon of St. Paul's*; and **Northolt, Perivale** and **Stickleton Manor** in **Greenford** were the property of *Baron Geoffrey de Mandeville*.

Considering how little is known of early history, I seem to have devoted a fair amount of space to laying the foundations of law and order, and of the borough itself. I felt this was necessary, however, as these developments have not been properly explained elsewhere in the book. Conversely, the events which led to the overthrow of the Feudal System and the rise of our present form of national and local government, are just too many and varied to be considered here in any but the most superficial way. Detailed accounts of the most important events are given in the chapters on the towns they concern; but for the purposes of *this* chapter, I have added a date-embellished version of the old 'Royal Rhyme' to help you keep track of time as we fly through the ages — touching briefly on the incidents that affected the borough and concentrating particularly on administrative changes, especially at local level.

Norman 1066-1154	Willie, Willie, Harry, Steve,
Plantagenet 1154-1399	Harry, Dick, John, Harry III, One, two, three Neds, Richard II,
Lancaster - 1461	Harry's IV, V, VI, then who?
York - 1485	Edward IV, V, Dick the Bad,
Tudor 1485-1603 (Eliz.)	Harry's twain and Ned the Lad. Mary, Bessie, James the Vain,
Stuart (James I) 1603-1714	Charlie, Charlie, James again. William and Mary, Anna Gloria,
Hanover 1714-1917	Four George's, William and Victoria. Edward VII next, and then
Windsor 1917-	George V in 1910. Edward VIII soon abdicated, and so a George was reinstated. In '52 a QE II, Charles is next, but that will do!

Kings and Queens of England 1066-1983

THE CROWN, THE CITY AND THE CHURCH (1086 — 1547)

At Domesday, somewhere in the region of 6,000 men, women and children lived in Middlesex, which probably then comprised the whole tract of land between the rivers Thames, Lea and Colne. Vast forests filled with game still covered the northern part of the County, and there were no towns — only scattered villages. It will thus not come as too much of a surprise to learn that the manors in the borough were not writ large in the political records of early medieval times. Their subsequent growth and any role they played in national history came about purely and simply because they lay on the doorstep of London. During the conflicts between King, Barons and Clergy which constantly erupted throughout the Middle Ages, London's wealth and political importance secured the City more and more freedom to conduct its own affairs and, consequently, those of Middlesex.

Normans

William the Conqueror may have succeeded in making the barons and clergy accept his supremacy, but even he allowed the burgesses of London to retain their old laws and customs. However, he took the precaution of erecting an impregnable fortress within the City walls — the **Tower of London** — over which he appointed his most trusted baron, *Geoffrey de Mandeville*, as first Custodian. Weaker kings were forced to make greater concessions in order to gain the City's financial support: *Henry I (1100-35)* granted Londoners the right not only to collect their own taxes, but also to appoint the **Sheriff of**

Middlesex (a privilege they were to enjoy until 1888), and sold them hunting and farming rights in the County as well. His nephew, *Stephen (1135-54)* must also have endeared himself to London traders in some way for, in his contest for the Crown with Henry's daughter *Matilda*, the unwavering support of the City helped him to overthrow the treacherous grandson of Geoffrey de Mandeville and confiscate all his land.

Plantagenets

However, the merchants quickly switched allegiance to Matilda's son, *Henry II (1154-89)*, after he issued a charter granting London citizens exemption from tolls throughout the country, and confirming that they were not answerable to any courts other than their own. The Barons did not fare so well. Henry curbed the power of their manorial courts by extending the jurisdiction of the **King's Court** over the whole realm, introduced the beginnings of the **jury system,** and appointed **Circuit Judges** to travel round the country hearing criminal cases at the **Court Leet** which limited the **Court Baron** of the freeholders to petty offences only. He further weakened the feudal system by allowing the barons to pay a **scutage tax** for the hire of mercenaries, instead of personally following him to war. But he was less successful in bringing the Church into the framework of the royal courts, and the quarrels with the Pope which had begun earlier with the eviction of *Anselm*, Archbishop of Canterbury (and manor lord of **Southall**), culminated in Henry's murder of the Archbishop he himself had appointed — *Thomas Becket*. The resultant public outcry forced Henry to concede to the Pope's spiritual authority, and it was to be many years before another Henry (the Eighth) succeeded in reversing the situation.

The 12th century, in fact, saw a fever of church-building — both within and outside the City walls. The lords of **West Twyford** and **New Brentford** founded the first chapels in their manors during this period; **Greenford's** chapel was mentioned in a Papal Bull of 1157; traces of the church erected at **Norwood Green,** and a large part of **Perivale's** are still in existence; and the tithes from **Ealing's** church were granted to a school run by St. Paul's very early in the 12th century. The voluntary payment of tithes (or one-tenth of the parish's produce) towards the upkeep of the Church had gradually become compulsory, and was a constant source of friction between parson and parishioner. The rector usually claimed the **large tithes** of the major crops, while the **small tithes** of eggs, chickens and lesser produce were given to the parish priest. These, combined with the feudal dues demanded by the manor lord, placed an enormous burden on the poorer farmer, yet the **parish churches** and monasteries did much to improve life in the community. Besides catering for parishioners' spiritual needs, they served as hospital, school, almshouse and social-centre rolled into one; but their interest in the instruction and relief of their flock was slowly corrupted by their greed for land and worldly goods.

The Church could not condone the greed of *King John (1199-1216)*, however, and neither did his barons. He gained the temporary support of the City by allowing London citizens to govern themselves by means of a new official, the **Mayor**; but the heavy taxes he imposed on merchants to pay for his disastrous campaigns in Normandy, assured their support for the **Barons' Rebellion** of 1215. The Mayor and *Henry de Bohun* (who was soon to become Lord of the Manors of **Northolt, West Twyford** and **Perivale**) were among the 25 men appointed to make the King stand by the **Magna Carta** — safe conduct through the ravaged battlefield of Middlesex having been granted to all who assembled over the river at Runnymede. John's son, *Henry III (1216-72)* did not present any immediate threat to the City's independence as he was only nine when he came to the throne; but while he was growing up to be a troublemaker, a new force began to emerge in the City.

It should first be explained that only one in three Londoners (chiefly merchants) were entitled to enjoy the privileges of **'citizens'** — foreigners, tradesmen, artisans and the like were not considered worthy. Although John had stipulated that the Mayor was to be annually elected by *all* citizens, the City's leaders (those few closely-related families who dominated the wool, cloth and wine trades) had narrowed down the electorate to 24 aldermen of their number — which was naturally deeply resented by the goldsmiths, fishmongers, grocers and other craftsmen. They seized the opportunity to gain more say in the City's government by alligning themselves with the London rabble in support of *Simon de Montfort*, leader of the **Baron's War** against Henry III in 1263, and succeeded in taking command. In the **Civil War** which followed Simon's rise to power, he found fresh support in the similarly dissatisfied rural gentry — the knights and lesser vassals who had taken advantage of scutage payments to return to the land, but who had little say in the administration of the manors. The famous **Parliament** that de Montfort summoned to **Westminster** in 1265 included Barons, Clergy, two knights from each Shire and, for the first time, two representatives from each of the chief towns and boroughs.

But it was not until 1295 that the Crown found it advisable to follow this democratic example, and summon a Parliament representing all the estates of the realm. *Edward I (1272-1307)* was a strong King and attempted to rule without the support of the City. He transferred its trading privileges to foreign merchants who funded his wars in Wales and Scotland, thus completely undermining the dominant London families. But the financial crisis forced him to turn to other City craftsmen, and his grant of **Boston Manor** to the **Priory of St. Helen** in Bishopsgate was probably made in return for money from the **goldsmiths** whose daughters filled the convent. Finally, in order to raise money from all his subjects, he summoned his **Model Parliament. Brentford** and **Uxbridge** were the only Middlesex towns to be represented in the Commons, and Brentford's growing importance was further emphasised by the **market charter** which the King later granted the town. Edward also began to make use of rural landowners as instruments of government by appointing local **Justices of the Peace,** instead of wholly relying on sheriffs and judges.

The new regime in the City, meanwhile, had once again resolved into a self-elected clique of great merchants (this time representing members of Companies such as the Mercers, Fishmongers and Grocers) who, to demonstrate their newly acquired wealth and status, began to buy or lease property in Middlesex villages. Stone manor houses soon rose above the wooden huts of the villagers, but although some owners — like *Peter le Boteler* of **Northolt,** and the *Shoredych* family, goldsmiths, of **Southall** — took proper interest in their manors, others such as the fishmonger who obtained the lease of **West Twyford** from St. Paul's, were seldom resident.

The outbreak of the **Hundred Years' War** with France soon after *Edward III (1327-77)* came to power, firmly established London as the centre of **government** as well as commerce. Until then the **Exchequer, Courts of Justice** and **Parliament** had assembled wherever the King happened to be at the time, but London's resources and proximity to the French coast made **Westminster** the obvious strategic centre after the war began. Several City officials and merchants sought refuge in the more isolated local manors when the **Black Death** (1348-50) swept through overcrowded towns throughout the country, killing off almost half the population and leaving the surviving lords with vast acres of untilled land. Edward had other problems, too: *Alice Perrers*, the mistress he had lovingly installed at **Gunnersbury,** had such a hold over the King that in 1376 she became the first person to be impeached by Parliament, and was banished after the **House of Commons** (now made up of knights, citizens and burgesses) had presented her case to the **House of Lords** (bishops and barons). The death of Edward's equally beloved son, the *Black Prince* — whose wife, the *Fair Maid of Kent*, had once owned the **Manor of Down** in **Northolt** — hastened the King's own demise, and left his 10-year old grandson, *Richard II (1377-99)*, to sort out the growing social unrest in the impoverished rural areas.

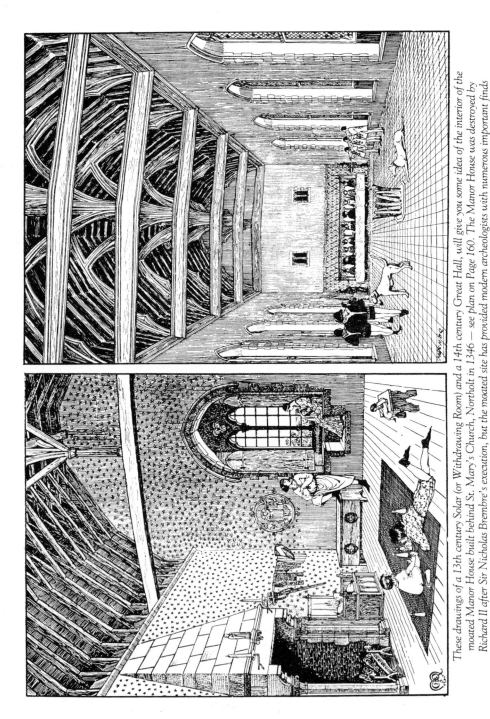

These drawings of a 13th century Solar (or Withdrawing Room) and a 14th century Great Hall, will give you some idea of the interior of the moated Manor House built behind St. Mary's Church, Northolt in 1346 — see plan on Page 160. The Manor House was destroyed by Richard II after Sir Nicholas Brembre's execution, but the moated site has provided modern archeologists with numerous important finds relating to its medieval occupants — as well as those of Saxon times.

10

The imposition of a **poll-tax** on every person over the age of 15 (to raise money for the fruitless war with France) was not the wisest move to make in these circumstances — a point that was swiftly driven home by the **Peasants' Revolt** of 1381. A large Middlesex contingent was among the labourers from Essex and Kent who plundered their way to London to demand their freedom — which Richard granted, together with a general pardon, as a ploy to disperse the mob. Hundreds of rebels were later killed by the army, however, and men from **Greenford**, **Hounslow** and **Chiswick** were among those excluded from the pardon. *Nicholas Brembre*, manor lord of **Northolt** and a friend of the King, was knighted for his part in suppressing the uprising, and later became a key figure in the King's government as **Lord Mayor** of London. It was this preference for the advice of a mere grocer, together with the King's extravagant ways, that stirred up the nobility against him. Brembre was executed, and Richard was eventually forced to resign the throne in favour of his cousin.

Lancaster and York

The reign of *Henry IV (1399-1413)* was marked by the persecution of the **Lollards** — the followers of *John Wycliffe*, who condemned the corruption and power of the Church. *Henry V (1413-22)* followed his father's example and gained further support from the established church by founding **Syon Abbey,** and from Parliament for his victories in France. His son, *Henry VI (1422-61)*, was less successful in battle and managed to lose all the English holdings in France (except Calais) before the Hundred Years' War ended in 1453. He was unable to control his restless barons on their return from France, and the **Wars of the Roses** — the battle for the throne between the rival houses of Lancaster and York — which began in 1445 after poor Henry went mad, delivered the final death blow to Feudalism. By the time they came to an end thirty years later, there were simply not enough survivors of the Old Nobility to continue the struggle between Crown and Barons.

The City, too, had been appeased during the reign of the Yorkist *Edward IV (1461-83)* who was himself a member of the **Merchant Tailors' Company.** Besides creating an atmosphere in which trade could flourish, Edward was very liberal in his bestowal of knighthoods on influential merchants — among them *Alderman Thomas Frowyck*, who owned **Gunnersbury** and several large estates in **Acton.** Meanwhile, in the country, landlords had generally ceased to work their demesne by the forced service of villeins, and instead let it to **tenant farmers.** The landlord provided cattle, seed and implements in return for a share of the profits, and the farmer was able to pay labourers to do the work. Marriage between the rural gentry and traders from the towns had produced a strong new **Middle Class** which was to provide the leaders of the **Renaissance** — men like *Dean John Colet* (son of *Sir Henry*, manor lord of Perivale in 1485), who roundly denounced the abuses of the Church, translated the Lord's Prayer into English, and founded **St. Paul's School.** The stage had been set for an age of enlightenment, peace and prosperity under the **Tudors.**

Of course, there was still the little problem of the Church — but *Henry VIII (1509-47)* soon solved that by declaring himself Supreme Head of the Church of England. In the massive changes in land-ownership which followed the **Dissolution of the Monasteries** and forced sale of Church-owned manors between 1536-9, the Friar of St. Bartholomew's and Dean of St. Paul's lost **Acton** to the King's favourite, *Lord John Russell;* **Northolt, Greenford** and **Hanwell** were given to the new *Bishopric of Westminster;* **Southall** passed from Archbishop Cranmer to **Robert Cheeseman,** one of the Esquires sent by the King to collect his fourth wife, Anne of Cleves; while **Syon** was used to imprison his fifth, Catherine Howard, before removing her head.

PEOPLE, PROPERTY AND POLITICS (1547 — c.1800)

Bewildering changes of religion with every fresh Tudor monarch were accepted by laity and the Church alike — much as a change of Cabinet is accepted today. Neither Parliament nor the Reformed Church were strong enough to defy the Crown's authority. Only towards the end of Elizabeth's reign did the House of Commons begin to show signs of political strength and religious conviction — but it took the gross misrule of the early Stuarts, a Civil War, and a Revolution, before Parliament came into its own under the Hanoverians. As London expanded and the wealthy moved westwards, estates in the borough changed hands frequently and landowners played an ever-increasing role in local and national government. Four centuries were to elapse before the ordinary man-in-the-street qualified for a vote, but the wheels of the Industrial Revolution soon ground down the opposition and cleared the way to political freedom for the masses.

Tudors

The Protestant movement against the power and privileges of the Catholic priesthood, gained strength during the reign of *Edward VI (1547-53)*. Puny and consumptive, the 9-year old King hardly matched the high expectations Henry had envisaged for his only son, and the boy was easily manipulated by his 'Protector' uncle, the *Duke of Somerset*. On Edward's behalf, Somerset generously presented himself with **Osterley, Boston Manor** and **Syon House,** and forced a 200-year lease on **Ealing** and **Brentford** from the Bishop of London — who did not share the Duke's staunch Protestant beliefs. The Bishopric of Westminster was dissolved and **Greenford** and **Hanwell** became the property of the *Nicholas Ridley*, the new Protestant Bishop of London, while **Northolt** was granted to *Sir Thomas Wroth*, the King's tutor. But Somerset's personal greed left him open to attack by the equally ambitious but far more devious *Duke of Northumberland*, who took over as Protector in 1552, did away with his rival and took all his property for himself.

Northumberland was also responsible for having *Lady Jane Grey* proclaimed Queen at Syon, but did not last long after *'Bloody' Mary (1553-58)* stormed into London to claim her rightful place on the throne ten days later. Catholic to the core, Mary might have been persuaded to spare the innocent Lady Jane's life had the girl's father, the *Duke of Suffolk*, not participated in the rebellion led by *Sir Thomas Wyatt* a few months later — when the men of Kent marched on London by way of **Kingston** and **Brentford** to protest against the Queen's marriage to *Philip II* of Spain. But although Mary gained the support of both Parliament and the City on this occasion, her fanatical persecution of the Protestants (some of whom were burnt at the stake on **The Butts** in Brentford) bred a hatred for the Church of Rome which was to prove the one constant element in the years of civil and religious strife that followed.

Elizabeth I (1558-1603) ascended the throne amidst national joy, and retained the loyalty of her people and statesmen throughout her reign. The growth of London mushroomed during the glorious Elizabethan Age. The flourishing **cloth-trade** and discovery of new **ocean routes** produced a new era in English maritime commerce, in which the City handled nine-tenths of the country's overseas trade. People flooded into the Capital in search of work or wealth, creating an enormous demand for food and housing. Accommodation and industry connected with the shipping trade spread eastwards, while the royal court at **Whitehall** encouraged smarter developments to the west — which was kept free of smoke and fumes by the prevailing westerly wind.

As forests were cleared to grow corn for London, **Perivale** and **Greenford** became renowned for their wheatfields and City corn-buyers flocked to place their orders at **Brentford Market**. The **Thames** was choked with ships carrying produce to the City and rivercraft ferrying Londoners in search of fresh entertainment at some of the bawdy

Brentford inns (frequented by *Shakespeare, Ben Jonson* and other writers of the day), or the notorious **Brentford Fair.** More City merchants bought land in the borough as large estates like the *Frowycks'* in **Acton** were subdivided and sold, and members of the New Nobility were well rewarded for their loyalty to the Queen. She granted **Boston Manor** to *Sir Robert Dudley,* Duke of Leicester; **Osterley** to *Sir Thomas Gresham,* founder of the **Royal Exchange; Syon House** to *Henry Percy,* 9th Earl of Northumberland; and permitted the manor lands of **Ealing** and **Brentford** to be leased to London traders.

The power of the **Justices of the Peace** increased considerably in late Tudor times, as they began to take over many administrative functions of the manorial courts. These unpaid royal officials were usually chosen from the local 'squirearchy' of tenant-farmers and freehold yeomen, who appointed other rate-paying landowners in the parish to help them carry out their numerous duties. This committee met regularly in the vestry room of the parish church, and became known as the **Parish Vestry.** Their responsibilities included the maintenance of highways and bridges, the licensing of public houses, the fixing of maximum wages according to 'the plenty and scarcity of the times', and — most important of all — the administration of the **Poor Law.**

Since Henry VIII's time, various ferocious legislative measures had attempted to control the ever-increasing numbers of **vagrants** who had been set adrift by the closure of the monasteries, subsequent sale of church land (in which many had lost their small strips in the common fields) and overcrowding in the City to beg, borrow and steal in order to stay alive. Death was the ultimate penalty among the harsh punishments they had to endure — which included branding, flogging (children included — as Brentford records show), and being kept in slavery for two years. But it was not until 1601 that the problem was tackled in a more charitable way and a new **Poor Law Act** instructed JPs to appoint **overseers** of the poor in each parish, with powers to raise money from the ratepayers for their maintenance. They were only entitled to this benefit if they had been born in the parish, however, and much time and money was spent on returning the poor in outlying counties to their home parishes.

Stuarts

The plight of the poverty-stricken was also taken up by the **Puritans,** a radical group of Protestants, who preached the doctrine that goodliness, not goods, led to Godliness — but stressed at the same time that if a poor man were to develop the qualities of virtue, self-control and discipline, he would inevitably be rewarded on earth as well as in Heaven. Not surprisingly, this theory also appealed to the wealthy, who rather fancied the idea that their riches were evidence of exceptional virtue. The Puritans disapproved of just about everything, but above all they disapproved of the Stuart line of monarchs. They were not alone in this feeling, however, for the autocratic rule of *James I (1603-25)* and his son, *Charles I (1625-49)* completely destroyed the loyalty and goodwill so carefully built up by Elizabeth. The **House of Commons** became increasingly insistent on their rights to have a free say in government, and even refused to give James any more money unless he abandoned his belief in the 'divine right of Kings'.

Charles tried to solve the problem by dissolving Parliament altogether, and ruled for 11 years with the assistance of *Sir Thomas Wentworth,* Earl of Strafford, and *Archbishop William Laud.* Without Parliament there was no money so, to raise a fleet for the war with Spain, Charles took the advice of his Attorney General, *Sir William Noy* (who lived in **Brentford**), and imposed a **Ship Money Tax** on seaports and maritime counties. This proved such a valuable source of income that it was extended to inland towns as well — causing many farmers and Middle Class gentry in towns like **Ealing, Acton** and **Brentford** to be swung over to the Parliamentary cause. The struggles between Upper and Middle Class, Episcopalian and Puritan, Royalist and Parliamentarian led inevitably to **Civil War.**

This mural in a waiting-room at Ealing Hospital was painted by Robert Rees RA in 1979, and depicts scenes from the Borough's history:

1. *The rebuilding of Hanwell parish church in 958 AD*
2. *16th century Brentford/Ealing market gardeners carrying baskets of produce*
3. *Francis Awister and his wife — Manor Lord of Southall in Elizabethan times*
4. *'Taking the waters' at Acton Spa in Queen Anne's reign*
5. *The Duke of Kent holding his infant daughter, Queen Victoria*
6. *Dr. John Connolly, Superintendent of the 'Hanwell Asylum' (now St. Bernard's Hospital), supposedly holding plans for the building, which opened in 1831. (Col. Clitheroe of Boston Manor was actually the person responsible for its planning and erection.)*
7. *Thomas Huxley (1825-95), the Ealing-born scientist*
8. *The Wharncliffe Viaduct at Hanwell — built for the GWR in 1838 by Izambaard Brunel (in foreground)*
9. *1930s horse-dealers at Southall Market — first licensed in 1698.*
10. *High Street Street traders in present-day Southall*
11. *Hospital scenes being filmed at the BBC Studios on Ealing Green*
12. *Ealing Town Hall*

14

It took six years for the rebellion to be resolved, but the final outcome had been decided within the first few months. Despite having observed the ease with which his Cavaliers had overcome the opposition at **Brentford** in 1642, Charles foolishly abandoned his march on London after only a brief skirmish with the Parliamentary army assembled on the outskirts of **Acton** — and never again came so close to winning back the wealth and resources of the City, which ultimately gave the Roundheads their victory. Royalists such as *Sir Edward Spencer* of **Boston Manor** and *John Penruddock* of **Ealing** were forced to flee, and during the years of the **Commonwealth** and **Protectorate** (1640-60), Cromwell granted many of their estates to his supporters. *Sir William Waller* took over **Osterley;** *General Skippon* and *Sir Francis Rous* had houses at **Acton** — where *John Perryn*, alderman and goldsmith, also acquired a large estate; while *Sir John Barkstead*, who had been instrumental in the King's execution in 1649, became the new manor lord of **Ealing.**

It was the death of Cromwell, however, that brought an end to the Puritan Revolution. Without the Protector to control his supporters, the City feared that some of the wild notions circulating among London apprentices and tradesmen (such as the outrageous idea of votes for all men) might come to fruition, and willingly provided loans to pay off Cromwell's army so that the old form of government could be restored under *Charles II (1660-85)*. But the struggle between Crown and Parliament as to who was to have the larger say continued for almost 30 years, and the Restoration failed — just as the Commonwealth had done — to bring about religious toleration.

The vicars of **Ealing** and **Acton** were among the 2,000 nonconformist clergymen forcibly ejected from their livings. Some found employment during the **Great Plague** in 1665, when the Established clergy joined the rush to the less contaminated atmosphere of **Ealing, Hanwell** and beyond. Charles II and his Privy Council met at **Syon** at the height of the epidemic in which one in four Londoners lost their lives, and every parish in the borough suffered severe losses as the disease spread. Once the danger was passed, the shamefaced C. of E. clergy returned to their flock and, in retaliation, promoted the passing of the **Five Mile Act** which forbade their braver Nonconformist counterparts from coming within five miles of London. But the famous Puritan divines, *Dr. John Owen* and *Richard Baxter*, continued to preach at a safe distance from the metropolis, and attracted large followings to their homes in **Ealing** and **Acton.**

A year after the Plague, many government officials, courtiers and merchants were forced to take up permanent residence in **Ealing** and **Acton** — the disastrous **Fire of London** having destroyed their homes and business along with four-fifths of the City. One of the less scrupulous building speculators to make their fortune in the massive rebuilding programme that followed, was *Dr. Nicholas Barbon.* His shoddy houses for the *nouveaux riches* soon began to appear all over London, while he himself lived in style at **Osterley** — which he maintained out of the profits he made from being the first man in England to sell insurance against fire. He died a bankrupt, however.

Antagonism in the religious sphere, meanwhile, had switched from the Nonconformists to the Papists. Fear of a Catholic uprising split Parliament into two parties — the **Whigs,** who wanted to exclude all Catholics from public office (including the King's brother, James), and the **Tories,** who supported Charles in his efforts to save James' rights to the throne. The conflict was temporarily solved by *James II (1685-89)* himself, who followed such an indiscreetly pro-Catholic policy that all parties and classes were united against him. In the **'Glorious Revolution'** of 1688, James was deposed in favour of his daughter, Mary, and her Protestant husband, William of Orange. The Revolution tipped the balance of power firmly on the side of Parliament,and by the **Toleration Act** of 1689 Nonconformists were at last allowed to worship freely.

Throughout the reigns of *William and Mary (1689-1702)* and *Anne (1702-14)*, both political parties shared power evenly — the Crown favouring first one side, then the other — and the whole country was united in the war against *Louis XIV* of France, who supported the exiled James II. William granted **Southall** its first market charter, and encouraged the westward spread of London by taking up residence in the small country town of **Kensington** — where the air relieved his asthma. **Acton's** fame as an inland **spa-resort** began in Queen Anne's time, when the medical properties of the wells on Old Oak Common attracted large numbers of London gentry to Friars Place and East Acton. **Osterley** became the home of *Sir Francis Child*, 'father of the banking profession', and the *Duke of Kingston-upon-Hull* lived at **Berrymead.**

Hanoverians

One of the Duke's daughters later married the *Earl of Mar*, who led the **Jacobites** in their unsucceful attempt to place James II's son on the throne soon after *George I (1714-27)* had reluctantly left his beloved Hanover to ascend it. Mar escaped back to France with the erstwhile James III, but the *Earl of Derwentwater* was less lucky. His widow lived briefly at **Acton House** after his execution. The fact that many Tories sympathised with the Jacobites, encouraged the early Hanoverian Kings to favour the **Whig** party — and it was under their ministry that *Sir Robert Walpole* became the first official **Prime Minister** of England, and the **Cabinet** system was established. Walpole's first task was to restore public credit after the collapse of the **South Sea 'Bubble'** — a scheme whereby the South Sea Company had offered to pay off part of the National Debt in return for exclusive trading rights in the South Seas. (*Sir Joseph Gulston*, a former director of the Company, retired discreetly to Ealing in the aftermath.)

The Parliamentary System of the day was pretty rotten, however. Only the large landowners had the right to vote and, because many of the seats were privately owned, would-be MPs were able to buy their way into the Commons. But the majority of country squires in the Ealing area (mostly Middle Class Londoners) shared the City's wary view of 18th century governments. Parliament therefore chose its **Justices of the Peace** from men much further down the social scale, who were more amenable to bribery. The **Middlesex justices** earned themselves a particularly corrupt reputation — with the exception of the writer and reformer, *Henry Fielding*, who took a house near **Ealing Common** during the reign of *George II (1727-60)*. The King's favourite daughter, *Princess Amelia*, made **Gunnersbury** her summer residence after her father's death, and when her nephew, *George III (1760-1820)*, chose to spend *his* summers at **Kew Palace,** Ealing's reputation as a fashionable place to live was assured. Dukes, earls, lawyers and politicians sought country retreats in the area as London became more overcrowded. The wayward sons of George III, the *Prince Regent* and *Duke of Kent*, found **North Ealing** the ideal place to house their mistresses — discreetly distant from the Court at Kew, yet near enough to pop home for a quick loan when the need arose. **Ealing Common** also achieved a certain notoriety after its most famous resident, Prime Minister *Spencer Perceval*, was assassinated.

The polling place for the **Middlesex Elections** had moved from Hampstead Heath to **Brentford** at the start of the 18th century, and although representation was restricted to only two MPs for the whole County, local freeholders expressed their disapproval of George III's corrupt government by electing members of a distinctly radical nature — such as *John Wilkes* (supported by the then vicar of Brentford, *John Home Tooke*) and later *Sir Francis Burdett*, who had lived in Ealing as a child. The working man had no vote, but did not particularly resent it until the effects of the Napoleonic Wars and Industrial Revolution began to take their toll — making it vital for him to achieve more social and political power.

FROM FIELD TO FACTORY (1801 — 1965)

The Industrial Revolution had, of course, been a continuing process ever since Man first began manufacturing tools from flints. But the speed with which technical developments took place from the mid-18th century onwards offered opportunities — and miseries — of unprecedented magnitude. The Borough did not feel the full impact until the improvements in mechanical transport of the late-19th century, but the future use of much of its land had already been decided by the sweeping changes applied to farming methods during the Napoleonic Wars (1793-1815), and its inhabitants certainly prospered or suffered indirectly as a result of the earlier industrialisation of the Midlands and North.

By the turn of the 18th century, **Acton's** popularity as a spa-resort had declined and most of her large estates had been subdivided into smaller properties, but the small town continued to attract the middle class City gent. If one had a title or two, then one naturally moved further west and took a country house at **Ealing** (where the air and one's neighbours were of a better quality), and **Hanwell** was the place to live when one had retired from the rigours of war, politics and making money. Further north, the tiny farming communities of **West Twyford, Perivale, Greenford** and **Northolt** nestled among the wheat and hayfields that covered the clay region as far as Harrow; while at **Southall,** although the cattle market had encouraged a small settlement on the Uxbridge Road, the gentry preferred the rural villages of **Southall Green** and **Norwood Green** — social standing increasing with proximity to **Osterley,** where Lord and Lady Jersey now resided.

Southall's market had never achieved the same importance as the one at **Brentford,** however — which was the only proper town in the district and boasted several thriving industries. In 1801, labourers in Brentford's breweries, mills, potteries and brickworks formed a large percentage of the Borough's total population of 8,700 — but within 50 years this figure had doubled, was to jump to over 55,000 by 1881 (by which time Brentford was no longer part of it), and reach 165,000 by 1911. Numerous factors contributed to this rapid increase, and its consequences were to bring about a complete change in the district — not only in the appearance of its towns and villages, but also in the way they were administered. Some of these causes and their effects deserve closer examination.

Land Enclosure and the Poor

In **Ealing** and **Brentford,** the open field method of strip farming had begun to disappear from the 16th century onwards, as arable and pasture land on the fertile brickearths and gravels in the south were gradually enclosed to meet London's demand for fresh fruit and vegetables. By the time Napoleon set about cutting Britain's links with the Continent, **market gardening** was the chief occupation in this area and there were

17

few open fields left, but the compulsory enclosure of land, which followed the increased demand for homegrown food during the French wars, had greater effect elsewhere in the Borough. In **Northolt, Greenford** and **Perivale** it merely hastened the swing from wheat to **hayfarming**, and by 1816 almost all the cultivated land had been turned over to grass to fuel London's horses. Farming died a rapid death in **Hanwell,** however, and **houses** soon began to appear on Hanwell Heath and in the former common fields. Most of **Southall's** farmlands gave way to **brickfields,** and although **Acton's** four open fields survived until the Enclosure Award of 1859, thereafter they were swiftly buried beneath **laundries, brickfields** and **housing** for the workers. (Acton accounted for 17,000 of the 1881 population figure.)

While the more efficient use of land and its consequent rise in value benefited the landowner, the loss of their common grazing rights and small strips of land was disastrous for the poorer members of the community. They now had to hire themselves out as labourers in a market where the cost of living rose as wages fell — or face the **workhouse.** These institutions (such as the one's at **Northolt, Ealing** and **Brentford**) dated from the early 18th century, and were deliberately made as uninviting as possible in order to encourage people to seek work elsewhere, and thus reduce the Poor Rate. Unfortunately, they also encouraged farmers and other employers to decrease wages drastically — knowing that the poor would accept work at any price in order to stay free. Because local crops commanded a ready market in London, wages in the area were comparatively high (though still not good), but neither the poor rate nor conditions in the workhouses and cholera-ridden slums of Brentford were alleviated by the influx of labourers from other counties and Ireland, whose plight had been worsened by the Corn Laws.

Introduced by the Tory Government in 1815 to protect their fellow-landowners from the importation of foreign corn, the **Corn Laws** prospered the farmer by keeping the price of homegrown corn artificially high. But labourers, already deprived of the right to grow their own bread, now found they could not afford to buy it either, and abandoned their home towns in the hope of finding work in the better-paid farming communities and rising towns of Middlesex. The men were often able to maintain themselves (except in 1830 when the hay-crop failed and many starved to death), but their families were usually confined in the workhouses. The allotments and almshouses provided by the Vestries, and the charitable bequests left by wealthier residents could only support a limited number of indigenous poor, and parish records show that many local authorities tried to solve the problem of overcrowded workhouses by sending women and children to work in the mines and cotton-mills of the North.

It is interesting to note that although most Middlesex landowners supported the Tories, they share the same suspicious view of new-fangled machinery as the farm and factory workers who feared their own displacement by the inventions of *Meikle, Hargreaves* and *Boulton & Watt.* Only one threshing machine was to be found in the Ealing area in 1846 and when its owner proudly displayed some of the corn and grain it had produced at a local farmers' meeting, he was almost drummed out of town for using 'an invention so injurious to the labourer'. This apparent disregard for increasing their turnover by more efficient means earned Middlesex farmers a reputation for 'backwardness', from their counterparts in outlying counties — who no doubt envied the easy profits to be made on the London market. But, bearing in mind that local farmers were usually retired businessmen, it is far more likely that their 'backward' philanthropy stemmed from recognition of the advantages of abundant, cheap hand-labour over expensive machinery.

Transport and Communications

Rivers: For centuries, the **Thames** (the southern boundary of the old County of Middlesex) served as the main communication link between London and the West. The control of the river below Staines had passed from the Crown to the **City** at the end of the 12th century, and river traffic carrying goods and passengers to and from Oxford increased steadily as London expanded — causing a running dispute between boat-owners and the fishermen, basket-weavers and mill-owners on the riverbanks. It is because of the Thames that **Brentford** developed into such a thriving commercial centre — the town relied on boats to transport its market produce down to London, and later to supply coke to its steam-powered mills, factories and gasworks. Barges were drawn by gangs of men called 'halers' until a towpath fit for horses was completed in 1819. The City reluctantly handed their jurisdiction over the tidal river to the **Thames Conservancy Board** in 1857, but by the time this was succeeded by the **Port of London Authority** in 1908 the use of barges had given way to new roads and railways. Today the river is chiefly used for recreational purposes.

The tidal limit of the Thames, incidentally, has moved some 19 miles upriver (from Southwark to Teddington) since the Romans built the first London Bridge. South-east England is thought to be subsiding at the average rate of nine inches a century as melting ice in the Arctic Circle causes the sea-level to rise — but it is hoped that the recently completed tidal barrier at **Woolwich** will at last put an end to the kind of floods that have practically submerged Thameside towns in the past. Although equally damaging, the frequent flooding of the unnavigable **River Brent** has also had a positive influence — as it deterred early developers from building in the valley. Rising at Mill Hill in Hendon, the Brent flows down to the **Welsh Harp Reservoir** (built by the Grand Junction Company in 1838) at Kingsbury, then runs beside the North Circular to enter the Borough at **Perivale**. The land on either side of its meandering route through **Greenford, Hanwell** and the canalised section from **Southall** to **Brentford** now forms the **Brent River Park** conservation area — the only continuous stretch of open land in the Borough. Since the late 1970s, the GLC have been widening and dredging the river to prevent further flooding.

Perivale Lane (looking south) during the Brent floods in 1905

Canals: In 1793, *George III* approved an Act of Parliament which enabled the **Grand Junction Canal Company** to build its canal from **Brentford** to **Braunston** in Northamptonshire — thus shortening by 60 miles the distance boats had to travel to reach Birmingham and the Black Country via the Thames and Oxford Canal. The opening of the first stretch from Brentford to Uxbridge in 1794, followed by the arm from Southall to **Paddington** in 1801, encouraged further industry at **Brentford** and exploitation of the brickearth lining the canals at **Southall, Northolt** and **Acton** — but had little immediate effect on the rest of the Borough. Farmers resented the competition they now had to endure from outlying counties, but gradually began to make use of the canal to transport their own hay to London — from whence it returned in the form of fertiliser. The daily **passage boat** service from Paddington to Uxbridge proved extremely popular, however, and Londoners delighted in this novel way of seeing how the other half lived in rural Middlesex. Except for the dyeworks established at **Greenford** in the 1850s, there were few canalside factories on the **Paddington Arm** until after the First World War — when the sale of farmland and munitions factories in North Acton led to the development of the vast **Park Royal Industrial Estate.** Traffic on the canal declined steadily with improvements in rail and road transport after 1945 — although boats continued to carry rubbish from London until the disused arms of the brickfields in Northolt and Greenford were filled in. In 1929, the Grand Junction's canals were incorporated into the **Grand Union Canal Company** (nationalised in 1948) and since 1963 have been administered by the **British Waterways Board** as recreational cruiseways.

Roads: Many of the roads in the Borough have developed from the meandering **Green Lanes** that connected the earliest settlements. Little more than footpaths, the condition of these rough tracks did not encourage long journeys and their regular use for the transportation of goods did not really begin until the 16th century. **Tolls** for road and bridge repairs were extracted from wayfarers on the 'highway' from London to **Brentford** in medieval times, while others in the Borough were usually the responsibility of the individual manor lords until the Parish Vestries took over in 1555. During the 17th century, **Turnpike Trusts** were set up to improve the main highways for **coach** travel. Their name came from the gate topped with iron 'pikes' (to discourage horsemen from jumping it) that blocked the road until travellers had paid at the tollhouse. Farmers greatly resented the added cost of getting their goods to London — especially as road conditions were still far from perfect. For most of the winter of 1797, the road from Tyburn through Uxbridge had 'only one passable track, less than six feet wide and eight inches deep in fluid mud', while the road from Hyde Park through Brentford and Hounslow was 'equally deep in filth, in spite of the King travelling it several times a week'. The heavy loads drawn by teams of six to eight horses were chiefly responsible for this decay of His Majesty's highways, and several royal proclamations tried to restrict the number of horses driven by farmers' wagons — but many carriers got round this by adding oxen to their teams.

Houses selling liquor to travellers had to be licensed by the local J.P. after 1552 but, as the rumbling of carriages grew heavier and profits in the catering-trade increased, many Justices opened up inns for themselves — the more corrupt granting licences to anyone who agreed to pay them a regular share. **Highwaymen** and footpads were also eager to part travellers from their money and infested the commons or lay in wait for revellers leaving the alehouses late at night. *Sir John Fielding* (Henry's brother) enrolled the first **Bow Street Runners** to put down the pest in 1753, but law and order only began to triumph after the most dangerous heaths were enclosed and *Sir Robert Peel* established the **Metropolitan Police Force** in 1829. Within a few years, police stations had replaced the stocks and cages maintained by most Parish Vestries. Local inns with extensive stabling became important staging points as the Coaching Age progressed — especially after mail coaches were introduced in 1784. But, despite the improvements in road surfacing brought about by *John MacAdam* at the beginning of the 19th century, the Turnpike revenue dropped steadily after inns like the **Feathers** in Ealing and **Viaduct** (formerly the Coach and Horses) in Hanwell began serving railway passengers. In 1864, the Uxbridge Road was freed from tolls and transferred back to the parishes.

Gentlemen still drove between their country houses and London businesses, however; and the houses that began to spring up all over the **North Ealing** hillside towards the end of the century were strictly for those who kept their own carriages. But the days of the horse were numbered. The **tram route** from **Acton** to **Southall** was electrified in 1901, and a line between **Hanwell** and **Brentford** was opened a few years later. Until 1896, any mechanically propelled vehicle had to be preceded by a man on foot carrying a red flag, but by the time *Edward VII (1901-10)* became the first monarch to own a motor car, the legal speed-limit had reached a dizzy 20 mph.

The pace of industry also quickened as existing lanes were improved and new roads pushed through farmland — creating space for the car manufacturers and electrical suppliers that were to change Acton's name from 'Soapsuds Island' to 'the greatest industrial area in the south of England'. Between the wars, the hayfields of **Perivale** and **Greenford** were gobbled up by the 'ribbon development' of housing estates — chiefly for workers in the factories that sprang up along the new **Greenford Road** and **Western Avenue.** Hoover and A.E.C. increased the population of **Perivale** and **Southall;** the **North Circular** and Guinness Brewery came to **West Twyford;** and jazz-age factories lined the 'Golden Mile' on the **Great West Road** through **Brentford.** Only **Ealing** managed to escape the industrial onslaught, but modern shop-fronts soon disguised the 19th century facade of the **Uxbridge Road** from **Southall** to **Acton,** and Ealing's skyline changed rapidly with the rise of uninspiring (but profitable) office blocks in the 1960s.

Today, travellers from Heathrow Airport whizz along the M4 oblivious of the historic places to be glimpsed behind the factories; while the Borough's clogged arterial roads bear witness to the fact that Ealing boasts the highest industrial acreage of any London Borough. Road-works to improve Western Avenue have been creating traffic jams for years, and conservationists are at present trying to prevent the GLC from turning the North Circular into a six-lane highway between the Hanger Lane Gyratory System and Gunnersbury — which would not only destroy numerous houses and the pleasant avenue of trees that survive from the original lane, but remove a large chunk from Ealing Common as well.

Railways: The 'Iron Road' had the greatest influence on the urban development of the Borough. Villages did not turn into towns overnight, but wherever stations opened the 'relentless march of bricks and mortar' followed. Cheap Irish labour had facilitated the building of canals, now it swelled the workforce on railway cuttings, embankments, tunnels and viaducts — enabling the **Great Western Railway** (or "God's Wonderful Railway" as it was affectionately known) to open its main line from Paddington to the west in 1838, with stations at **Ealing, Hanwell** and **Southall.** 'A remarkable change for the worse' is said to have taken place in the retired neighbourhood of **Southall Green** where the railway 'spread immorality and dissatisfaction among the poor, the place being inundated with worthless and overpaid labourers'. But this was only the beginning — building speculators rubbed their hands with glee as the **GWR, South Western,** and **District** Railways opened up the most rustic and inaccessible corners of the Borough, and people of every class poured out of London to the new suburbs.

Passenger services were too poor to begin with as the railway companies preferred the more profitable long-distance transportation of goods — hence the extension of the GWR line from **Southall** to **Brentford Dock** in 1855, to provide river barges with a direct rail link. This suited **Ealing,** which wanted to maintain her reputation for being a 'good-class residential suburb' (the *'Queen of the Suburbs'* in fact), but while City gents enjoyed flexible working hours, the working-class chap in **South Ealing, Acton** and **Hanwell** had to be woken by his local police constable at an unearthly hour in order to walk the 4-6 miles to Shepherd's Bush to catch an early workmen's train to London. But, by the end of the century, most of **North Acton** had disappeared under railway junctions for the lines that criss-crossed the Borough, and **Third Class Fares** for the bulk transport of less privileged human beings had made life considerably easier for the people living in row-upon-row of terraced houses below the Uxbridge Road. (Much more imagination was shown in the 'Garden Suburbs' of **Brentham** and **Bedford Park** — created for the working and middle classes by private planners.) Many had only a short distance to travel because of the number of new industries beside the railway, and demand for servants in the posher suburbs of **Ealing** and **Hanwell.**

Although the GWR's loop-line from **West Ealing** to **Greenford** had opened in 1905, the northern areas were slow to develop as water was scarce and the heavy clays difficult to drain. The cost of carrying out the required road works and arranging for main water and drainage to be provided thus deterred builders until the opening of the new arterial roads led to the large, uniform housing estates that now cover the area. **Northolt** remained virtually untouched, however, until the extension of the **Central Line** along the old GWR route after the Second World War furthered the Council's plan to turn the rural village into a sprawling **'dormitory suburb'.** By the 1960s, not only Northolt but the whole of Middlesex had become one vast dormitory for London. Today, so many commuters have taken to the roads that British Rail has been forced to announce the pending closure of some of its suburban links — such as the delightful diesel service from Ealing Broadway through Hanwell to Greenford.

Parliamentary Reforms

Most of the new industrial areas and towns that arose in the first half of the 19th century had no Parliamentary representation whatsoever — despite the fact that every working man was affected by the heavy taxation of the times. Appeals by radical reformers for Parliament to legislate on fair wages and hours of work, and give all male taxpayers a vote went unheeded by the Tory government of *George IV (1820-30)* — although the *'Iron Duke' of Wellington* did finally concede to pressure for another long-overdue reform. In 1829, **Catholics** were allowed to enter Parliament for the first time since James II — but the law against the sovereign being of the Popish faith has yet to be repealed. (Parliamentary predjudice against **Jews** was not lifted until 1858 when Lionel Rothschild of Gunnerbury became the first Jewish M.P.)

The new **Liberal Party** — chiefly Whigs and a few enlightened Tories — came into power under *William IV (1830-37)*, and swept away the 'rotten boroughs', redistributed seats to give fairer representation, and extended the franchise to middle-class landowners and tenant-farmers. The working-class radicals were no better off, however; and although the Liberals introduced the first Acts towards restricting women and child labour, and providing an elementary education for everyone, their new **Poor Law Act** of 1834 was definitely a two-edged sword. While it transferred the burden of paying Poor Relief from individual parishes to a **Union** of several, and substituted local workhouses for larger Union ones (the poor of **Ealing, Acton** and **Brentford** being sent to Isleworth from 1836, and **Northolt's** to Hillingdon), it compelled those who were unable to keep themselves to live in the new workhouses (which were even more forbidding than the old ones), and refused relief to the able-bodied — whether or not they were able to find employment.

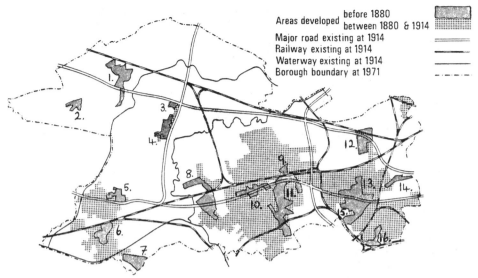

The Borough in 1880 and before the First World War

1. *Northolt Village & Wood End*
2. *West End*
3. *Greenford Green*
4. *Greenford Village*
5. *Southall Town (Northcote)*
6. *Southall Green*
7. *Norwood Green*
8. *Hanwell*

9. *Haven Green*
10. *West Ealing*
11. *Ealing Town and Village*
12. *West Acton*
13. *Church/Town Acton*
14. *East Acton*
15. *South Acton*
16. *Acton Green*

Urban growth before and after the Second World War

23

In 1846, *Sir Robert Peel* (the liberal-minded leader of the **Conservative Party** — as the Tories now called themselves) brought an end to the **Corn Laws,** but it was not until 1867 and the Conservative government of *Queen Victoria (1837-1901)* that **farm-workers** and **industrial labourers** obtained the right to vote. In 1885, the Liberals extended the household vote to counties outside the metropolitan areas, and **Middlesex** was divided into seven single-member constituencies. The **Ealing division** was made up of Ealing, Acton, Chiswick, Greenford and Perivale; while Southall/Norwood, and Hanwell were included in the **Brentford division.** Both usually returned a Conservative member, and it was many years before the Trade Unions' new **Labour Party** (which gained 42 seats in the 1910 elections) made any inroads in the Borough. **Women** over 30 had to wait until 1918 before they gained any say in national affairs, but **universal suffrage** was finally given to everyone over 21 in 1928 — the age limit being lowered to 18 forty years later.

The first Old Age Pensions and Labour Exchanges were introduced by the Liberals in 1909, followed by their Ministeries of Health, Labour and Transport after the First World War. But the abuses of the **Poor Law** system remained basically unchanged until 1929 when County and Borough councils were given the right to administer poor relief through Public Health Committees. These were absorbed into the **Welfare State** created by Labour after the Second World War, when the **National Health Service** and National Insurance were established — the latter being succeeded by Labour's Ministry of Social Security in 1966.

Local Government

Middlesex: The **Parish Vestries** found it increasingly difficult to cater for the needs of their rising numbers of parishioners as the 19th century progressed. Their powers were limited as almost any improvement made with public money required the sanction of an Act of Parliament. The **Public Health Act** of 1848 empowered districts outside the London area to set up Local Health Boards to improve drainage and sanitation; but although the Upper Side of **Ealing** fought hard to establish such a body, the Lower Side (which represented the much larger town of **Old Brentford**) resisted strongly — as anything that improved living conditions for the workers would probably reduce profits for the factory-owner. The roads in both towns (except the Turnpikes) had been maintained somewhat inadequately by an elected **Highway Board** since 1767, which was also responsible for drainage (or rather, the lack of it) and street lighting — although only Brentford enjoyed this privilege until the gasworks began to supply Ealing and Acton in the 1850s. (Electricity took another 30 years.) Numerous **committees** were formed to cope with other public services such as education, fire-brigades etc, while the householder was called on to pay a whole variety of rates to cover their cost.

Ealing finally won its case in 1863 and established the first **Local Health Board** in the district. **Acton's** was formed in 1866, and **Hanwell** and **Southall** followed after the rapid expansion of the 1880s. During this period, various Acts of Parliament gave the Local Boards powers to control the sizes of new houses and width of streets (hence the bye-law housing typical of the period in Southall, Acton, South Ealing and Hanwell) and to remove slums and build tenements and cottages for the working-classes. All the Local Boards were swept away by the establishment of **Middlesex County Council** in 1888, followed by the creation of **Urban District Councils** (Acton, Greenford, Ealing, Southall and Hanwell) in 1894-5. Greenford Urban District also included Perivale and West Twyford, while the **Parish of Northolt** formed part of Uxbridge Rural District. The local councils could legislate under the Housing and Sanitary Codes, but as yet had no direct control over town planning.

The year 1901 was one of mixed feelings in the town of **Ealing** for, while its inhabitants mourned the death of the Queen, it was difficult to disguise their jubilation at being the first town in Middlesex to achieve **Borough** status — their's being the first **Charter of Incorporation** to be signed by *Edward VII*. By the time **Acton's** commercial importance was similarly recognised in 1921, Town Planning Acts had made it obligatory for large local authorities to prepare **planning schemes** for building development on suburban land. The **First World War** had temporarily interrupted the spread of development, but the tremendous industrial and urban expansion of the '20s and '30s had changed the northern face of the Borough (all of which had been absorbed into Ealing by 1928) before any of these draft planning schemes had achieved ministerial approval.

In 1936 despite the plight of 2 million unemployed, *Mosley* (who, incidentally, had a house in Greenford) and the Fascists, the Spanish Civil War and the threat of Hitler on the Continent, the relationship between *Edward VIII* and the twice-divorced *Mrs. Simpson* formed the one topic of conversation throughout England — especially in **Southall,** which had its **Charter of Incorporation** signed by the King shortly before his abdication. Attention was to focus all too soon (and too late) on Hitler, however, and planning schemes were forgotten as the Borough joined in the battle for Britain. During the 1914-1918 War, the nearest bomb to Ealing had fallen in Whitestile Road, Brentford, but no part of the Borough escaped bombing in the 1939-45 raids. The first, ironically, fell on Greenford Park Cemetery, but the numerous war memorials in the Borough commemorate more effective attacks. The munitions factories in the Greenford/Northolt area attracted no less than 223 bombs, and a column on Western Avenue near Northolt Airport is dedicated to the 546 Polish pilots who were killed in action while assisting the R.A.F.

With the end in sight in 1944, the need for large-scale reconstruction after the Blitz brought forth several planning proposals for the London region — the most important being *Professor Patrick Abercrombie's* **Greater London Plan.** The main features proposed a restraint on the overall growth of population and industry to counteract the uncontrolled spread of the inter-war period. This was to follow a programme of 'decentralisation' and resettlement through a scheme which divided the London Region into four 'rings' and encouraged movement from the **Inner Ring** (which included much of **Acton**) to the **Outer Ring,** leaving the **Suburban Ring** (including **Southall** and most of **Ealing**) and the **Green Belt Ring** (parts of **Northolt**) more or less as they were in the middle. The Labour government's Town and Country Planning Act of 1947 gave local authorities a comprehensive legislative framework to enable the Plan to be put into operation. For the first time in planning history, the owners of land and buildings were required to obtain permission from the Local Planning Authority (in our case, Middlesex County Council) not just to develop but to make *any* changes to their property, and were no longer entitled to compensation if refused.

Unfortunately, this legislation came too late for many of the Borough's open spaces and fine old houses — their loss being made worse by the undistinguished quality of the buildings that had replaced them. Nevertheless, the **County of Middlesex** duly submitted its first development plan to the Minister of Housing and Local Government in 1951, and eventually received approval for its proposals to relieve congestion in both Middlesex and London by limiting the density of prescribed industrial, business, residential and shopping areas. The population total for the three municipal boroughs obediently fell by the required level, and stood at just over 300,000 by the time a review of the plan was approved in March 1965 — a few days before the Middlesex County Council was replaced by the **Greater London Council,** and **Southall, Acton** and **Ealing** were amalgamated to form the new **London Borough of Ealing.**

London: The capital's population had reached 4 million by the time London acquired its first directly elected local authority in 1888. The new **London County Council** has jurisdiction over the whole town (except the City, of course) as well as the urbanised areas it had absorbed from **Middlesex** (including Westminster, Kensington, Chelsea and Hammersmith), **Surrey** and **Kent.** Neither the City nor Parliament had been particularly keen for London to have a proper government — the former because it resisted anything that might encroach on its own powers, and the latter, perhaps, because it feared that a London Council would prove as dangerous an institution as medieval kings had found the City. The Liberals had been pressing for London's administration to be controlled by an expanded City Corporation for some time, and it was to prevent such a thing happening that the Conservatives created a Council that initially had little more power than the ineffective **Metropolitan Board of Works** it had replaced.

The first elected Councillors included a number of **Fabian socialists** who believed that London should be governed in the communal interest to counteract the slums and poverty of the times. In bringing London's gas, electricity and water supplies under municipal control, they aroused the deepest suspicions of the Conservative Prime Minister, *Lord Salisbury*. His denouncement of their 'socialist experiments' in 1897, produced a cartoon in Punch which showed the 'Salisbury Frankenstein' addressing the 'Municipal Monster' with the words: "Sorry I ever put you together, you great horrid booby! But just you wait. I'll soon take you to pieces again." And sure enough, in 1899 the Conservatives reorganised the County's 42 almost powerless Parish Vestries and Local Boards into 28 **Metropolitan Boroughs** (one of which later became the **City of Westminster**) — establishing a two-tier system of government that made it even harder for the LCC to exert its authority over the sprawling capital , especially as far as property developers were concerned.

In 1965, the Conservatives followed a remarkably similar strategy in replacing the LCC with the Greater London Council, and enlarging still further the size and planning powers of its constituent boroughs — so much so that critics of the GLC began to wonder what the thousands of employees at County Hall found to do.

The London Borough of Ealing: The new administrative area of **Greater London** covered an area of 610 square miles which embraced the whole **County of Middlesex** and parts of **Hertfordshire, Essex, Surrey** and **Kent.** The Metropolitan Boroughs and local administrative units formerly in these counties were amalgamated and re-divided into 32 new **London Boroughs** — each with its own Mayor and Council, and each a Local Planning Authority and Educational Authority in its own right. All, however, were subject to the planning authority of the GLC, and could not formulate plans for the future development of their respective districts outside the GLC's strategic framework for Greater London as a whole. The **City of London** continues to be administered separately by its City Corporation, but also enjoys the same powers as the London Boroughs and shares four seats on the GLC with the City of Westminster.

Ealing Borough Council is made up of the **Mayor** (elected annually by other Councillors) and 70 **Councillors** — elected every four years by the public. The Councillors appoint a number of **Committees** to manage particular aspects of their responsibility for local planning, health, educational, social and welfare services; and both Council and Committee meetings are open to the public. Besides comprising three **Parliamentary Constituencies (Ealing Acton, Ealing North** and **Ealing Southall),** the Borough has also been divided into four main **districts** for statistical purposes: **Ealing** (including Hanwell), **Acton** (including West Twyford), **Greenford** (including Northolt and Perivale) and **Southall.** These are further divided into 24 **wards** — each of which

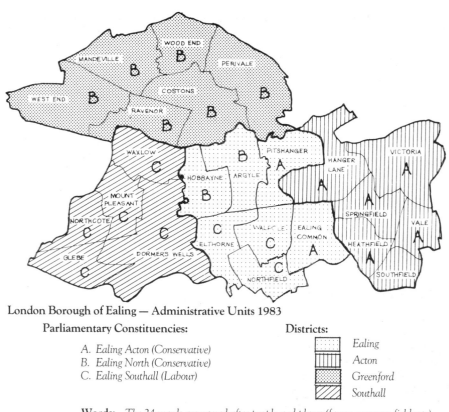

London Borough of Ealing — Administrative Units 1983

Parliamentary Constituencies:

A. *Ealing Acton (Conservative)*
B. *Ealing North (Conservative)*
C. *Ealing Southall (Labour)*

Districts:

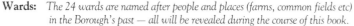

Ealing
Acton
Greenford
Southall

Wards: *The 24 wards are named after people and places (farms, common fields etc) in the Borough's past — all will be revealed during the course of this book.*

elect three Councillors, except Victoria and Vale which elect two. Since the last local elections in 1982 (and for some years before that), the Council has been predominantly Conservative and the Borough also returned a Conservative majority in the 1983 General Election.

The **Greater London Council** is run on similar lines. Its 92 Councillors are elected by residents of all the London Boroughs every four years — each Parliamentary Constituency returning one GLC member. In the 1981 GLC elections, Ealing North and Southall elected a Labour GLC Councillor, and Ealing Acton a Conservative. The overall result of the election produced a predominantly Labour GLC. The regional services provided by the GLC include the fire service, main drainage and flood prevention, main traffic and road planning, and (since 1970) London Transport. The relationship between the GLC and London Boroughs is meant to be one of partnership — it does not control or supervise their activities in any way except to ensure that their local planning policies fit into the strategic plan for the Greater London region — which has to be approved by the Secretary of State for the Environment.

PLANNING FOR THE FUTURE? (1965 — 1984-and-all-that)

It will have become apparent during this gallop through history that not only does every type of government and political party have its faults, but that the uniformity of certain housing estates, the predominance of industry, and the conflict between traffic and shoppers in the town centres of the Borough are just as much a legacy of the past as the green oases of Horsenden Hill and the Brent River Valley. What is being done to ensure that developments in our towns are better planned in future?

In 1965, the development plans for Middlesex, London and places formerly in other Counties were amalgamated into what became known as the **Greater London Development Plan (GLDP)** — which was finally approved in a modified form in 1976. In accordance with the new two-tier local development plan procedure, Ealing Council then set about incorporating the relevant GLDP guide-lines into a **Statutory Land Use Plan** — which reflected their own ideas for future improvements, redevelopment and new development in the Borough. The **Draft Borough Plan** was completed in January, 1982 and the Council went to great lengths to ensure that residents were given a chance to express their opinions on the proposals that would affect planning decisions for the next 15 years.

Employment, housing, transport and shopping were among the many policies considered, and emphasis was also placed on improving the 'Urban Environment'. Here, the Council aimed to enhance the individual identity of local towns by protecting certain buildings (through renovation and adaption rather than redevelopment), safeguarding trees and townscape features, and preserving ancient monuments, archeological sites and the natural heritage of the Borough. Suggestions were also made for adding to the seven designated **Conservation Areas** which had come about as a result of the Civic Amenities Act of 1967. After a Public Enquiry, the Draft Plan is to be officially adopted in 1984 — around the time that a revised GLDP is due to be submitted to the Secretary of State.

So far, so good. But, the final phase of Lord Salisbury's prophesy is about to come true, and the government's recent announcement that the GLC is to be abolished by 1986 has caused certain doubts about future planning procedures. The government proposes handing over many of the GLC's present responsibilities to the Boroughs themselves, while three Joint Boards of appointed Borough Councillors will oversee Police, Fire and Public Transport services for the Greater London area — supervision of the latter, together with major road works, being shared with the Department of Transport. Each of the 32 London Boroughs will prepare their own strategic plans for the

G.L.C. — R.I.P.?

28

approval of the Secretary of State, who will be advised by a nominated (chiefly Tory) **London Planning Commission.** This body, like the others, will have no legislative powers at all, however — overall authority for Greater London being vested in the Secretary of State for the next three years.

In 1883, the writer of an illustrated guide to the town of Ealing (pop. 17,000) ended his introduction with the words: "In these days when the growing tide of population presses more and more closely upon us, we can sympathise in some measure with those who deplore the quietude and rusticity thus rudely broken up for ever. Change, however, is inevitable, and progress or retrogression must be the order of the day ... it is satisfactory to note that the change in Ealing has without doubt been a beneficial one." Most of these observations still hold true but, in summing up my introduction to the Borough of Ealing (pop. 273,000) in 1983, I cannot state with equal certainty that the physical changes of the last century have been particularly beneficial — at least from the point of view of today's residents.

However, neither can I share the delightfully pessimistic view of the future held by the present Chairman of the GLC Planning Committee. He recently described the government's proposed changes in planning and local government as 'a recipe for chaos' in which London would return to the 'muddle, inefficiency and corruption of being run by boards and vestries ... the Secretary of State would take on a new role as London's overlord ... the Boroughs would be reduced to serfdoms ... and the last to benefit would be the people of London whose future and that of their capital City is at stake.'

At this stage, with accusations and recriminations flying from Left to Right and back again, it is difficult to judge how Borough residents will be affected by what appears to be merely another Conservative vs Labour bid for power. But two things are certain — Londoners have come a long way since the bad old days of the JPs; and 'going back' does not necessarily have to mean 'retrogression'. It has, after all, taken us nearly a thousand years for us to formulate a system of government that incorporates the freedom and fairness of Saxon administration — maybe it is time we also re-adopted the tribal notion that land belongs to the community?

The powers-that-be have at last begun to actively encourage public participation at every stage of the planning procedure — the old scheme of fitting people to places in an effort to reduce the overcrowding of the post-war years having been rather too successful. With phrases like 'Inner City decline' ringing in our ears, and the migration from the centre to the Outer Ring causing the population of suburban areas like Ealing to drop much faster than was ever expected, Councils have recognised that their careful 'zoning' of land for residential, industrial or commercial use does not always fit in with what residents would choose for themselves.

It is obvious that there will have to be some overall strategic plan for the London area (and no doubt there will be) but, in the meantime, if residents of all the London Boroughs exercised their right to have a say in the plans and schemes devised by their elected Councils, then I think the towns of the Capital might yet have a future worthy of their past.

The following books have proved invaluable in the preparation of this chapter:
Middlesex — **Michael Robbins** (Collins, 1953)
A History of London — **Robert Gray** (Hutchinson, 1978)
A Shortened History of England — **G.M. Trevelyan** (Penguin, 1976)
An Illustrated History of England — **John Burke** (Book Club Associates, 1974)
A People's History of England — **A.L. Morton** (Lawrence & Wishart, 1979)
Outlines of English History — **George Carter** (Ward Lock, 1978)
Background to Ealing — report by **Town Planning Division of Ealing Council** (1973)

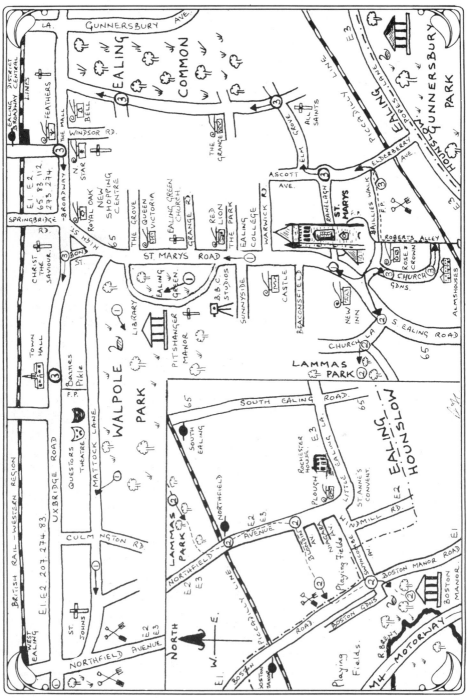

CHAPTER II

'In olden days when Ealing had not put on her smart suburban
dress and manner . . . there were bright cornfields and wild roses,
shady pools and clear bubbling streams in her midst, and groups
of ancient elms with flocking rooks making noise in the branches,
as busy as the children at play on the pretty village green.

EDITH JACKSON, Annals of Ealing (1898).

  began as a straggling
village around the
parish church of St.
Mary's but by the 19th century had developed into one of the most
fashionable residential areas west of London, numbering dukes,
bishops, generals and even a princess among her eminent residents.
As communications improved and the town expanded, Ealing
assumed a prosperous middle-class character and adopted the title
'Queen of the Suburbs' to show that her social standing had not faded along with the
country estates. Their ideas may have been rather grandiose but thanks to the far-
thinking policies of these early town planners, Ealing managed to avoid the
manufacturing industries which destroyed the identity of neighbouring suburbs, and
many of her parklands, commons and stately homes can still be enjoyed by residents
today.

No doubt the Romans were familiar with the forested area stretching up from
the natural ford over the Thames at Brentford; but it was the Saxons who gave a
name to the clearing in which they had made their settlements. Ealing was first recorded
in a 7th century charter when Ethelred, King of Mercia, gave 'Gillingas' (meaning 'of the
tribe of Gilla') to the Bishop of London. Later, the Bishop was granted an even larger
tract of land at Fulham and he probably combined the two estates, as Ealing is not given
a separate mention in the Domesday Book.

The name appears again in an early 12th century grant in which Bishop de Belmeis
appropriated the 'tythes of Xelling' to augment the salary of the Master of St. Paul's
School. Ealing residents seem to have been fiercely independent from a very early stage,
however, and by the 16th century had managed to break away from the Manor of
Fulham denying that they had ever been part of it. In subsequent records, the spelling of
the name varies from 'Yelnge', to 'Gillynge' and 'Zealing', but 'Ealing' seems to have been
adopted from about 1700 onwards.

The ancient Manor of Ealing extended to the Thames and included the town of **Old
Brentford** as well as a detached, triangular portion of land to the east (now part of
Bedford Park) and several subordinate manors such as **Coldhall, Pitshanger** and
Gunnersbury whose stories are told elsewhere in these chapters. Ealing Manor House
stood a little beyond Gunnersbury Park until it was demolished by road-works in 1929.
The original demesne, or manor lands, stretched north up to Hanger Hill and south
down to the Thames covering an area of about 600 acres. In the early days, most
settlements were made on the arable land south of the Uxbridge Road and the northern
region remained largely undeveloped until the 19th century. To do justice to all the
different faces of Ealing without completely overwhelming the reader with facts and
figures, I have devoted this chapter to **South Ealing** and will concentrate on North
Ealing in the next.

The earliest existing parish records begin in 1582, and little is known of Ealing's history before then except that it appears to have been relatively peaceful. The open heath and rich woodlands which had covered Ealing at the time of the Conquest continued to be used as hunting grounds by wealthy Londoners until the 13th century, when clearing of the forests began to make way for the fields and farmlands that were to provide London with most of her produce from the Middle Ages onward. Ealing village grew up around the church at the centre of the parish and there were smaller hamlets to the west at **Ealing Dean** and **Little Ealing,** and a large farm connected to the Manor House at **Ealingbury** in the east.

From the 14th century, the Bishop of London leased the manor to various farmers who acted as Lord of the Manor on his behalf. In 1547, bad Bishop Bonner (whose persecution of the Protestants had made him thoroughly unpopular) leased Ealingbury to the *Duke of Somerset* for a period of 200 years. Somerset was the oldest brother of Jane Seymour, the only one of Henry VIII's wives to give him a son. As Edward VI became king when he was only nine years old, Lord Somerset virtually ruled the country as his nephew's 'Protector'. His power was shortlived however, and after his execution in 1552 Ealing came into the hands of the Crown. Towards the end of Elizabeth's reign, the manor was granted to *Simon Willis* for the remainder of the lease and he in turn divided the estate in two, letting the northern portion to *Thomas Fisher* and the rest to *Thomas Penruddock.*

The Penruddocks were a staunchly royalist family, supporting the monarch even when he made himself as unpopular as did Charles I by imposing heavy and often illegal taxes to raise a fixed revenue. His Ship Money Tax was particularly resented by inland towns like Ealing and an entry in the state papers for 1638 shows that tax evasion is a very old problem as tax collectors reported great difficulty in collecting money in 'Ealing alias Zealing' because 'many of the inhabitants are gone away by reason of taxation'. The fact that the Lord of the Manor was Catholic and therefore in sympathy with the Queen did not do much to further the peace in Ealing during the **Civil War** which followed — especially as Acton and Brentford were both held by Puritan parliamentary forces.

In the Parliamentary Survey of 1650, Ealing Manor House is described as 'ruinated and lying open since the plundering thereof in the beginning of the last troubles'. There are no records as to exactly when this happened, but Cromwell is said to have slept at the Manor House shortly after losing the Battle of Brentford (in 1642) and he is unlikely to have done so by invitation nor to have left things neat and tidy when he left. Sir John Penruddock was later executed for a final rebellion against Cromwell, but the Manor of Ealing had already been confiscated from the Bishop of London and passed through the hands of several of Cromwell's supporters during the Commonwealth years. *Sir John Barkstead,*a member of the Court which had condemned Charles I to death, bought the manor in 1659, but Charles II was reinstated the following year and Barkstead lost his head along with his fellow regicides. The new King restored all confiscated land to their rightful owners and Edward Penruddock thus resumed the lease of Ealing manor.

Neither Ealing nor her overlord had much time to recover from the devastation of war before they were struck by that unseen enemy, the **Great Plague.** The infection seems to have been brought into the neighbourhood by two soldiers quartered at Old Brentford and the epidemic raged throughout 1665, tolling 286 deaths in the parish. Despite the general distress, a local joke concerning Ealing's name was prevalent around this time and perhaps provided some lighthearted relief for the stricken parish. According to the story, the richer folk who fled from the disease in London found the fine air in Ealing extremely beneficial although not as therapeutic as Hanwell, which seemed to provide complete immunity. The grateful evacuees in the latter town are said to have affectionately called it 'An(d)well', while the convalescents in Ealing borrowed the discarded letter to advertise the 'H-ealing' advantages of their retreat.

An Historical **MAP** *of the* **PARISH** *of* Ealing.

A magnifying glass will make it easier to examine this ancient Town Plan —
regret that it was not possible to reproduce map any larger.

Prosperous times were to come as Ealing recovered and expanded to keep up with the demands of the London markets. Cultivation of grain crops and cattle-breeding had been the main occupations during Elizabethan times, but during the 17th and 18th centuries landowners turned to the more profitable pursuits of market-gardening and dairying. Rural Middlesex also served as a pleasure ground for London and there was no further need for royal proclamations exhorting 'persons of livelihood and means' to stay in their country residences and not add to overcrowding in the capital — as rulers from Elizabeth to Charles II had been forced to issue. Londoners were only too pleased to 'go West' and Ealing's country atmosphere, combined with proximity to the Court at Kew, made the town a popular home for the retired nobility and gentry whose handsome mansions began to ornament the parish during the 18th century.

The Manor House remained uninhabitable for many years after Cromwell's destruction, but was rebuilt sometime after 1735, when the Bishop of London granted new leases for North, South and Little Ealing. You can read more about subsequent Lords of the Manor in the chapter on Gunnersbury, but by this time the title had ceased to be of much importance as the power of the old manorial court system had gradually been transferred to the Parish Vestry, which met at the **Old Cross House** near St. Mary's church. Roads were managed by the **Highway Board** from 1767 onwards,· which was made up of residents from the village of Ealing and town of Old Brentford.

But the centuries-old tie between the **Upper and Lower Sides** as they were called, threatened to strangle the prosperity of both towns — each having progressed in such different ways. Rural Ealing was regarded as a rather insignificant extension of Brentford which, besides being an important commercial centre, was also the County Town of Middlesex. Brentonians naturally found it irksome having to travel to Ealing to vote on parish matters, while Ealing residents equally resented being out-voted by the larger town on matters they felt would improve their village.

Almost a century was to pass before Ealing gained her independence — a period of great change which saw the passing of the Coaching Age with the building of the **Grand Junction Canal** in 1801, and the arrival of the Great Western Railway at **Ealing Haven Station** in 1838. Old Brentford had been formed into a separate ecclesiastical parish when St. George's Chapel was built in 1828, but the Highway Board still governed both towns. Despite its name, the roads and paths were in a deplorable condition — continually flooded in winter, dusty and dirty in summer; and the situation was aggravated by their being plunged into darkness at night as the only lamps were along Brentford High Street for the benefit of royal personages who passed that way.

To the many new residents who came to Ealing in the 1850's, a policy of self-rule seemed the only way of improving their district. After years of trying to get the proposal approved by Brentford, a special committee applied directly to the Local Government Board to form an independent district under the Public Health Act. The resulting public inquiry led to the formation of **Ealing Local Board** in 1863, although it was another seven years before they were able to shake off the restraining influence of the old Highway Board, and a further three before the area north of the GWR was incorporated.

Once they were given the go-ahead however, the Local Board wasted no time in putting their plans into action and within a few years Ealing had been transformed under the guiding hand of the Town Surveyor, *Charles Jones*. He provided Ealing with the first proper drainage system in the Thames valley, built new roads and paved and lit the old ones, designed the Town Hall and numerous other buildings, and acquired Walpole and Lammas Parks for public use. (What a pity he did not live long enough to save the Manor House.)

The extension of the GWR's service to **West Ealing** and the opening of the **District Railway's** stations at Ealing Common and Ealing Haven during the 1870's, helped develop the rural areas and promoted the growth of a new town centre along the Uxbridge Road. Building Societies (described by Jones as 'those curses of modern civilisation') began to buy up large quantities of land and took exception to the policy that all new roads had to be kerbed, channeled and finished with flint before houses could be erected; but this stringent road programme resulted in a phenomenal increase in the value of property ensuring that only the 'better classes of society' were attracted to the area, and 'undesirable new-comers' made their homes elsewhere!

During the 1880's the **Beaconsfield, Grange** and **Windsor Road** estates spread over southern Ealing and much of the land surrounding country estates at Little Ealing was sold for building after South Ealing station opened in 1883. The population had been a mere 5,000 when the Local Board took over but, by the time the Urban District Council was created in 1894, the modest rates, private schools and absence of industry had attracted over 30,000 people to Ealing. In 1901, on the merits of having consistently done its work as a suburban district far in advance of its times, Ealing was the first town in Middlesex to be made a Municipal Borough. It was joined by Hanwell, Greenford, Perivale and West Twyford in 1926; Northolt in 1928; and in 1965 amalgamated with Southall and Acton to make the London Borough of Ealing.

Today, small businesses and office blocks flourish where crops once grew and many of the large houses have been converted into flats and bedsits, but the Council tries to ensure that new developments blend with the environment and Ealing remains a village at heart — as you will discover for yourselves on any walk through the town.

Charles Jones (1830-1913), first Surveyor to Ealing Local Board.

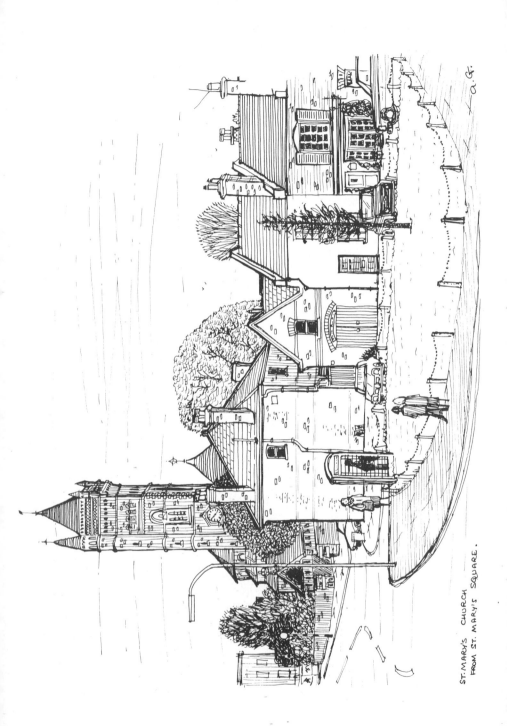

ST. MARY'S CHURCH
FROM ST. MARY'S SQUARE.

A. G.

The Parish Church of St. Mary stands in the centre of old Ealing Town on the same site as its 12th century predecessor. It is not known exactly when the first church was built, but it was obviously in existence by 1127 when the Bishop of London granted its tithes to the Chancellor of St. Paul's School, who also served as rector of St. Mary's. The first vicar was appointed in 1308 and was given £10 p.a. as well as a house, glebe and all the small tithes and offerings; but the rector retained the large tithes and the moated rectory house near the church. A complete list of vicars and rectors is displayed on the west wall of the church.

The patronage of the Bishops of London no doubt helped protect St. Mary's from the plundering and violence of the Reformation, for the inventory taken by Edward VI's commissioners in 1552 showed an ample list of church property. But the parish birth registers (which begin in 1582) reflect the growing influence of Puritanism in the parish, as sound Anglo-Norman names like William and Henry give way to Gideon and Amos in the years leading up to the Civil War. The local population thus seems to have been firmly on the side of Cromwell despite the Royalist leanings of Ealing's overlords, the Penruddocks, and the fact that the vicar, *Robert Cooper*, had been appointed by Archbishop Laud, one of Charles I's ill-advisors.

Following Laud's execution and the sale of the manor to Cromwell's henchmen, Cooper was evicted by the Puritans and replaced by one of their own. His successor, *Thomas Gilbert*, had the tables turned on him when Charles II was restored to the throne, as he was the first Puritan minister in the country to be ousted from office. Describing himself as the 'proto-martyr to the cause of non-conformity', Gilbert joined the Pilgrim Fathers in America, Cooper was re-instated at St. Mary's, and the Bishops of London have appointed all vicars ever since.

The old church deteriorated steadily during the years of war and sickness from the Plague and by 1673 it was in such a ruinous condition that, according to the vestry minute books, it was considered unsafe for use. The impoverished parish was not able to afford more than the most urgent repairs, however, and in 1719 the steeple had to be taken down. The rest of the church remained in a dangerous condition and was closed a few years later when services were transferred to a temporary wooden 'tabernacle'. This building had to serve the parish a lot longer than intended as in 1729, the old church 'fell down bodily' after more than six centuries of constant use.

Few relics of the ancient stone church survive for, while the lengthy business of fund-raising for a new place of worship was being accomplished, the handsome mouldings and carvings which had adorned the old church were left to lie about amongst the rubble in the churchyard for any unscrupulous person to help themselves. Someone even managed to steal one of the great bells, which was converted into a giant punch-bowl at a celebration for the marriage of Frederick, Prince of Wales. This neglect of the ruins prompted a donation from an unexpected source, for when the fund-raising committee paid a courtesy call on *Jonathan Gurnell*, a wealthy Quaker landowner, they were surprised to be told: "Thee knows, friends, that I am not in the habit of giving money to build up steeple-houses, but here's a hundred pounds to help thee take away the old one!"

Some of the rubble formed the foundations of the new St. Mary's which opened on Trinity Sunday, 1740. Built in the classical Georgian style, the church is said to have resembled a large red-brick barn with a square embattled tower and plain glass windows. Pews for the gentry crowded the main floor of the plain white interior as well as the three side galleries, while poorer members of the congregation had to sit on uncomfortable window seats round the edges. Pupils of Great Ealing School occupied peculiar 'pigeon hole' galleries under the roof as the west end. The five remaining bells from the old church were recast to make a peal of eight bells which still ring out over Ealing today.

The old Church of St. Mary's as rebuilt in 1740.

This straight-forward style of architecture was considered much too plain by Ealing's Victorian community however, and in 1866 a wooden tabernacle was once more erected in the glebe field while £20,000 was spent on remodelling the church to the design of S.S. Teulon. The result was the elaborately ugly St. Mary's you see today, embellished with flying buttresses, coloured brickwork and Byzantine decorations round the plain 18th century windows, which were reglazed with stained glass. At the opening ceremony in 1872, Bishop Tait described the transformation as 'the conversion of a Georgian monstrosity into a Contantinopolitian basilica'; but I prefer the words of a contemporary critic who, when writing about another of Teulon's 'Byzantine' restorations at Sunbury, compared the result to 'an elephant with a few feathers from the tail of a peacock'!

According to the burial registers, just about everyone who was anyone in Ealing was buried in St. Mary's churchyard until South Ealing cemetery opened in 1863; but the profusion of gravestones shown in the etching of the old church disappeared, for the most part, when the churchyard was raised in 1801 to make more room. The memorial plaques inside the church thus give a better idea of departed Ealing gentry, whose stories are told in this and the two following chapters. The church is open from 10 - 12pm on Tuesdays and Thursdays, if you want a quiet look-round during the week, and a complete list of the inscriptions and positions of the monuments is available from the warden on duty. A few of the names to look out for are briefly mentioned below.

The brass to *Richard Amondesham*, or Aunsham (on the **west wall**) is the oldest memorial in the church. The date of his death has been obliterated but it is assumed to be not long after he bought Coldhawe Manor in 1496. The porch on the west side contains plaques to *Alexander Copeland* of Gunnersbury House; *General Wetherall* of Castlebar House; *Sir Johnathan Miles* of Castlebar Park; and *Dame Jane Rawlinson* who founded St. Mary's Girls' School. Working your way up the **south aisle,** you will find the names of *Anne Goodenough* whose husband ran a school at Goodenough House; *John Horne Tooke*, the eccentric humanitarian who resigned as assistant minister at Brentford, to support the radical John Wilkes in the Middlesex elections; and the *Walpole* and *Perceval* families who donated the semi-circular baptistry and font. Behind the reading desk in the **chancel** is a marble plaque to *John Bowman*, Chancellor of St. Paul's and Rector of St. Mary's from 1615-29, and on a pillar near the altar an alabaster tablet with skull and crossbones over an hourglass is dedicated to *Richard Tavener*, whose death in 1638 led to the appointment of Robert Cooper as vicar. The *Perceval* family appear again in the **north aisle,** as do the *Woods* of Hanger Hill, *Peter Thorn* of Ealing Manor, and the architect, *S.S. Teulon* whose last work was the restoration of St. Mary's. A window in the warden's **Vestry** commemorates the *Rev. William Bevridge*, vicar during the Great Plague; and **upstairs,** names along the walls of the galleries include *Joseph Gulston* of Ealing Grove, *Major Morison* of Gunnersbury House and *John Loving* who built Place House (later known as Ealing Park) in Little Ealing during the 17th century.

The circular **stair turret** to the tower (which gives the whole structure a slightly unbalanced appearance) was added in 1874, but is no longer open to the public. Back in the churchyard, the **lych-gate** stands as a memorial to *Rev. Relton*, the vicar responsible for remodelling St. Mary's. (The word 'lic', incidentally, is Old English for 'corpse' — hence its being applied to the roofed gateway where the coffin traditionally awaited the clergyman's arrival). Two stone slabs in the wall beside the footpath to the north-east of the church, commemorate the **Old Cross House** and its successor, where the Parish Vestry and later the Local Board used to meet. The Cross or Church House was listed in the inventory taken by Edward VI's commissioners as 'the gift of Master Frowyck, for to kepe a drynking for the relyefth of the Pore'. *Sir Thomas Froyck* died at Gunnersbury House in 1485, but the Cross House featured prominently in the parish records until the old building was replaced by a Vestry Room in 1840.

The drinking fountain in the wall outside the north gate to the churchyard, was erected in 1874 as a memorial to *Lady Jane Walpole* and to maintain the thirst-quenching tradition of Frowyck's gift — although today it would not relieve the poor or anyone else, as the water supply has long since been disconnected. The **Vestry Hall** was built in Ranelagh Road in 1880 but was sold to the Council when the new parish centre or Polygon was erected in 1977, and is now used by Ealing College.

The three walks around South Ealing that follow, cover a fair bit of ground and a lot of history, both ancient and modern. Although the noisome traffic has dispelled forever the aura of genteel grandeur in which Ealing once revelled, by describing the homes of the rich and sometimes famous personalities who have lived here, I hope to give you at least some idea of what Ealing was like in her heyday.

(St. Mary's to Ealing Dean via Walpole Park — 1¼ miles) The first part of this walk, along what used to be the only road between Brentford and the Uxbridge Road, was called 'Zealing Towne' in the old rate books but is known as Ealing Village today. There were no inns and few houses in the area until the 1600's, but by the 18th century buildings stretched the length of St. Mary's Road and shops, serving the many fine residencies and private schools, had begun to establish themselves in the High Street. As the town centre moved away from the church to the Uxbridge Road, the old village settled back into quiet retirement and little change has taken place since the 1930's. Groups of 18th and 19th century houses still survive and the route from the church to Ealing Green is now a Conservation Area.

Directly opposite the church lych gate, stands part of the old **Parish Workhouse** — although the two pretty cottages you see today (Nos. 72-4) bear little resemblance to their original bleak setting. The workhouse was built in 1727 with accommodation for 55 inmates who were employed at spinning and casual labour, such as sweeping the streets and levelling the Commons. Their work was never profitable however, as tools were lacking and women and children far out-numbered the men. As the village expanded, the number of poor people in search of work increased and, in the words of the assistant overseer at the time, the workhouse became 'rather confined' — a classic understatement as the vestry minute books record 175 occupants, sleeping three or more to a bed! An application was later made to Parliament for more commodious accommodation on Ealing Dean Common, but the plan had to be abandoned because of some disagreement between the Upper and Lower Sides, and it was not until 1812 that sufficient funds were raised to enlarge the existing building to house 150 people. Most of the workhouse was demolished in 1839 after the Brentford Poor Union had opened a new institution in Isleworth, and the remaining blocks were converted into the ivy-covered cottages you see today, their gardens covering the old paved courtyard. The stocks and a watchman's box stood nearby, until replaced by a Police Station in the High Street in 1836.

Across the road from the workhouse, lay a different world altogether — **Great Ealing School,** one of the leading private schools in the country. It was established in 1698 in the old moated **Rectory House** and by the 19th century, had gained a reputation second only to Eton and Harrow under the headship of the *Rev. Dr. David Nicholas.* The site of the school is now covered by **Ranelagh Road,** and the houses and shops as far as Warwick Road stand on the former playing fields which included a 'fives' court, swimming pool, tennis courts and football and cricket pitches. Following Dr. Nicholas' death in 1829, the school was run by his sons, the *Rev. George* and *Rev. Francis Nicholas* — the latter being headmaster in 1846 when the school moved to new premises further up St. Mary's Road, after dry rot had forced them to vacate the Old Rectory.

Many pupils of the Great Ealing School later achieved fame in a variety of careers. Among the eminent clergymen the school produced were *Zacchary Pearce,* Bishop of Rochester; *Cardinal Henry Newman;* and *Bishop Selwyn,* in whose memory Selwyn College, Cambridge, was founded. Writers included *William Makepeace Thackeray,* aged 11, who later parodied Dr. Nicholas as 'Dr. Tickle-Us' in the 'Thackeray Papers'; *Captain Frederick Marryat,* of 'Mr. Midshipman Easy' and other swashbuckling stories; and *Charles Knight,* the author and publisher of popular editions of serious literature. The 19th century composer, *Sir George MacFarren* attended the school (where his father taught dancing), as did *W.S. Gilbert* before joining up with Sullivan. *Thomas Huxley,* the biologist and philosopher who coined the term 'agnostic', was another pupil. He was born nearby in a large house behind the present butcher shop in Church Place, and his father taught mathematics at the school. (I wonder what he would have thought of the 'Brave New World' depicted by his grandson, Aldous.)

The Old Rectory, home of Great Ealing School from 1698-1846.

Bearing in mind the period during which the school flourished, it is not surprising that it provided its fair share of military heroes who battled for the Empire from El Obeid in Egypt to Lucknow in India. Amongst the more famous soldiers were the *Lawrence* brothers, *Sir Henry Rawlinson,* and *William 'Hicks Pasha'* whose parents lived in one of the newly-converted workhouse cottages while he was at school here. *Louis-Philippe,* who later became the 'citizen' King of France, taught mathematics and geography at G.E.S. in the early 1800's. He and *General Doumouriez* (about whom you can read more in route 2) were both denounced as traitors by the revolutionists in France and fled to Europe, eventually settling in Twickenham and Ealing, respectively, until the fall of Napoleon allowed them to return to France.

Back on the west side of St. Mary's Road, the grounds of **St. Mary's Place** cover the site of the **Hall of Variety,** or Assembly Rooms, which were Ealing's only venue for public entertainment until the Lyric Hall was built on the Uxbridge Road in 1887. A corridor connected the Assembly Rooms to the **New Inn,** which was probably 'new' in the 17th century — some parts were found to be over 200 years old when the inn was rebuilt in 1897. The New Inn was an important coaching stage-post in the early 1800's when the Ives family ran a coaching service to London several times a day from here and coaches bound for other parts of the country also made use of the inn's extensive stable-yard — now part of **St. Mary's Court** next door. Recent renovations have tried to recapture some of the rustic, 'spit-and-sawdust' atmosphere of a bygone age and the long beer-garden at the back is very popular in summer. The pub also has an excellent little theatre upstairs, with regular evening productions and occasional lunch-time performances on weekends.

Ealing Court Mansions, the large block of flats on the corner of **Beaconsfield Road,** was built in 1867 as an Industrial School for Girls, founded by Lord Shaftesbury. Here, homeless and destitute maidens were trained for domestic service in the arts of washing, cleaning and cooking — successfully, it would seem, as by 1901 Ealing was reported to have a higher proportion of female servants than any suburb except Kensington and Hampstead. The school moved to Esher during the 1930's and the old building was converted to provide more pleasant accommodation. Further along, the **Castle Inn** also did a brisk trade during the coaching era and was the meeting place for Ealing's 'Court of Tenants' in the days when residents were struggling to get the Highway

Board to do something about the roads. Higher up the road, **Cairn Avenue** and Nicholas Gardens are built on the site of **The Owls** — the second home of Great Ealing School from 1846 to 1908.

Ealing College, on the opposite side of St. Mary's Road, had its beginnings in some art classes held at Ashton House in 1876. Physiology and hygiene were added to the curriculum when the classes were moved to the new Town Hall, but chemistry was tabooed as it was 'too smelly' and the fumes found their way to the reading room of the adjacent library. Classes were later transferred to The Hall on Ealing Green and in 1929, new college buildings were opened in Warwick Road, behind the old **Vicarage.** The College has expanded steadily ever since, new wings have been added over the years and in 1966 they also took over the former Girls' County School in The Park. (The school moved to Queen's Drive and is known as Ellen Wilkinson High today.) The absence of science and technology courses precludes the College from being designated a polytechnic, but its excellent reputation for degree courses in a variety of other subjects has gained international recognition.

St. Mary's Vicarage was pulled down in 1969, having occupied the same site since the original 'house and glebe' was granted to the first vicar some six centuries earlier. The gardens of the house used to cover a 5-acre stretch between Warwick Road and The Park, but were gradually absorbed by the College and today only the bulging garden wall on St. Mary's Road remains.

Warwick Road appears as 'Guys Lane' on early maps and is one of the oldest streets in this area — probably built to provide access to the ancient mansion of Hickes-upon-Heath on Ealing Common. In the early 19th century, an inn called **The King's Arms** stood on the corner next to the Vicarage, until *Sir Herbert Oakley* (vicar from 1822-34) deemed it 'an undesirable neighbour' and had the pub removed to the remote and unfrequented Grove. It gradually recovered trade and the 1897 version is still flourishing there today.

The Park was laid out as a smart residential side-street in 1846 by the architect, *Sydney Smirke,* who had redesigned the Rothschild's mansion at Gunnersbury Park a few years earlier. Only the cottages in Park Place and the row of fine houses further down the north side of the street date from this period, however; the rest were built much later. Between The Park and the Red Lion stand three large Regency-style houses (Park, Acacia and Ness House) which were erected c.1830 on the site of an old mansion called **Ealing Grove.**

If you refer to the 1822 map of Ealing reproduced earlier in this chapter, you will see that the estates of Ealing Grove and its northern neighbour, **Ealing House** (then rented by Richard Gray Esq), extended as far as Ealing Common and covered nearly all the land between today's Warwick Road and The Grove (formerly called Love Lane). Both houses were built in the early 1600's and their various owners and tenants formed the backbone of Ealing society for over two centuries. So, although nothing remains of the estates today, I think a few of their more famous residents deserve a brief mention.

Ealing Grove, the larger of the two, was leased by *Sir John Maynard* (Cromwell's lawyer) before he acquired Gunnerbury House, and, a century later, *Richard Savage* (the last Earl Rivers) scandalised the neighbourhood by setting up home here with his mistress, *Elizabeth Colleton* — of whom you can read more in the Perivale chapter. The estate passed to their illegitimate daughter, Bessie, *Countess of Rochford,* and subsequent owners included *Joseph Gulston* (one-time director of the disastrous South Sea Company), the *Dukes of Marlborough* and *Argyll,* and the *Earl of Oxford.* After the Civil War, **Ealing House** was bought by the lord of the manor, *Sir John Barkstead* (the Manor House having been ruinated by Cromwell's troops) and, in later years, became the country residence of *Slingsby Bethel,* Lord Mayor of London, and the *Earl of Galloway.* In 1834, *Lady Noel Byron* (wife of the poet) established an industrial school for boys at Ealing House, which incorporated some of the grounds and outbuildings of the then recently demolished Ealing Grove. When Lady Byron moved away from Ealing a few years later, she handed the school over to the headmaster, *Charles Nelson Atlee,* who remained in charge until its closure in 1852, and then opened a new school, **Byron House,** in The Park. This closed during the First World War but the buildings are still standing (just behind the College) and are now used as flats.

Ealing House gave way to **Grange Road** in the 1860's, but the **Red Lion,** which came between the two estates in the mid-18th century, is still going strong. During the coaching age, the inn was noted for its gardens and bowling-greens but achieved fame of a different sort in the 1930's when it was popular with young filmstars-in-the-making at **Ealing Studios** across the Green. Today, those actors (whose signed photographs decorate the walls of the pub) are household names and their films have become ever-popular 'golden oldies'. The off-licence nearby was a grocer's shop in the old days and, tucked away behind it, stand a group of cottages which probably housed gardeners and workmen on the surrounding estates when they were built in 1824.

Modern housing developments (named after the old houses they replaced) now line the next stretch of this road; but over on the western side of **Ealing Green,** the beautifully preserved cottages look much as they did in the early 1800's — with the exception of **The Lawn,** the first large house in the row, which is only partly occupied and has been allowed to fall into a sad state of decay. The large ponds which once lay at either end of the Green have been filled in, but otherwise the Green has changed very little since the 19th century when, for many years, it was the scene of the annual 3-day **Midsummer Fair.**

Ealing Green at Fair-time with the old Horse and Groom in the background.

19th Century posters advertising the Fair and Ealing Dean pony races (see Page 47).

At Fair-time, stalls and booths selling all kinds of things were set up outside Pitshanger Manor and gypsy caravans and tents crowded the lower end of the Green. Richardson's Travelling Circus came to town for the occasion and entertained the crowds with antics by the Acrobat, the Performing Poodle and the Learned Pig — not to mention the large lady and the gentleman who weighed 30 and 40-stone apiece! As you can see from the poster, there were plenty of races and competitions for locals to enter — which must have been highly amusing to watch. The Fair failed to meet with the approval of the staid Victorian community, however, who described it as an occasion of 'vice and moral laxity' and boarded in the iron railings around the Manor to keep the riff-raff from the refined. The Local Board finally appealed to the Secretary of State, and the Fair was abolished in 1880.

But it was not too long before a more sophisticated form of entertainment was being manufactured on the Green. Although Ealing is internationally famous for the comedy films produced here after the Second World War, the town's role in cinema history began long before the Ealing Studio days. In 1904, *W.G. Barker*, one of the pioneers in the film industry, bought a house called **West Lodge** which then stood behind the Girls' School on the Green, built studios (said to be the largest in England) in the grounds and began manufacturing a series of topical news-films. He later produced what film-buffs will know as the 'first really important British film' — an adaptation of Sir Herbert Beerbohm Tree's stage production of 'Henry VIII'.

In 1931, the studios were bought by *Basil Dean* of Associated Talking Pictures. He added sound studios and enlarged the site by joining Barker's West Lodge estate to a house on the Green. This became the main entrance to the studios and was converted into offices which are still used by the **BBC** today. Stars such as Gracie Fields, Ivor Novello, Gloria Swanson, George Formby and Lawrence Olivier were given their first big chance by Basil Dean; but it was under the fatherly direction of his successor, *Sir Michael Balcon*, that **Ealing Studios Ltd** was established and the classic Ealing Comedies were made. Old favourites like Alec Guiness, Stanley Holloway and Jack Warner still pull the crowds to see 'Passport to Pimlico', 'The Lavender Hill Mob' and 'Kind Hearts and Coronets' (to name just a few) . . . albeit round the television set on a Sunday afternoon.

Real-life Ealing featured in many of these films and 'Hue and Cry', in particular, is filled with shots of the town in the post-war era. Ealing is still a popular location for television films made by the BBC, who took over the studios in 1956. The old police station in the High Street, for example, was often used in the series 'Dixon of Dock Green', before the site was sold to Sainsbury's in 1970. The stages at Ealing Studios have also featured in many other well-known BBC television series and, in recent years, have played a part in films like 'Colditz', 'Porridge', 'The Chinese Detective' and 'Shoestring'.

As you make your way from the studios towards Pitshanger Manor, you will pass the old **St. Mary's Girls' School** buildings, now used by Jehovah's Witnesses as their Kingdom Hall. The school was founded by *Dame Jane Rawlinson* (Sir John Maynard's granddaughter) in the early 1700's and rebuilt, as you can see from the inscription, in 1861. The forge which once stood in the little lane next to the school (leading to West Lodge) is now a garage, and the Flextol factory, on the opposite corner, replaced an old mansion called Rock House during the pre-conservation era of the 1930's. It's 18th century neighbour, **St. Mary's-on-the-Green,** has managed to withstand the march of progress however, and is now used as the headquarters of the GPO Sorting Office.

Ealing Green High School (formerly Ealing County Boys') was built in 1913 on the site of **The Hall** — the home of the Rt. Hon. **Spencer Horatio Walpole,** one of Ealing's leading citizens during the 19th century. Three-times Home Secretary and also Chairman of the GWR Company, Walpole moved into The Hall soon after marrying his cousin, Isabella — one of the daughters of the ill-fated Prime Minister, *Spencer Perceval*, whose story is told in Route 3. It is thanks to the generosity of Walpole and the foresight of his close friend, *Charles Jones* (the Town Surveyor), that Pitshanger Manor and its beautiful gardens were acquired as a public park for a mere £40,000. The Walpole family had bought the Manor in 1844 for Isabella's five unmarried sisters, and the only proviso Walpole placed on his agreement with Jones was that his sisters-in-law were to remain in occupation until their deaths. Frederica, the last surviving sister, died in 1900 and Ealing residents have enjoyed **Walpole Park** ever since.

Pitshanger Manor has been the home of **Ealing Central Library** since 1902, but the history of the Manor goes back much further than that. Before delving back in time however, take a look through the trees to the eastern side of the Green, where another of *Charles Jones'* legacies stands in the shape of **Ealing Green Church.** Originally called Ealing Congregational, the Gothic-style church and adjacent manse were designed by Jones in 1859, when the estate of Ealing House went up for sale. The church had been founded some thirty years earlier in a small chapel in The Grove (now used by St. Saviour's First School) which soon became too small for the ever-increasing congregation. The present church changed its name in 1972, when it united with members of Ealing Broadway Methodist.

To the left of the church, on the corner of **The Grove,** stands another time-honoured institution — the **Queen Victoria** pub, established almost two centuries ago as the Horse and Groom. Further south, on the corner of **Grange Road,** a fine old Victorian house provides a pleasant setting for **The Drama School** which was founded by *Peter Layton* in 1966 and offers post-graduate courses for experienced actors to refine their art.

Bond Street, at the northern end of the Green, was built in 1906 over the site of **Ashton House,** where *Mr. John Allen Brown* first established the **Ealing Free Library** 100 years ago. Many readers may remember an equally popular source of entertainment which once stood higher up Bond Street — the **Walpole Picture Palace** which, from 1912 to 1972, displayed the wonders of the silver screen in a converted ice-rink. This was recently demolished and offices are now being built on the site, but nostalgia-lovers will be pleased to know that the facade of the old cinema has been preserved and will be incorporated into the back of the new buildings.

The east end of **Mattock Lane** was first built up during the 1860's on part of the Ashton House estate, and many of the grand old houses are still standing — although most have been converted into flats and bedsits. All these changes have been quietly observed by the four statues with which *Sir John Soane* ornamented his 'country villa' when he rebuilt **Pitshanger Manor** at the beginning of the 19th century. The architect had bought the Manor from *Thomas Gurnell* (son of the wealthy Quaker who contributed towards the rebuilding of St. Mary's church), but was already well-acquainted with the house as he had helped to design it some thirty years earlier.

In those days, the recently established Royal Academy was barely aware of the young man who was to become one of their most distinguished members. The son of a mason, Soane was hired as an errand-boy by the architect, *George Dance Jnr.* (a founder member of the Royal Academy) who soon recognised his creative talents and, as a trial project, allowed him to assist in the plans for the Gurnell's home on Ealing Green. (As you will discover in the next chapter, the actual Manor of Pitshanger from which this house took its name, lay to the north of Ealing and also belonged to Gurnell.) The Academy later granted Soane a travelling scholarship to Italy and, on his return, he was commissioned to design a new Bank of England — since rebuilt within Soane's outer walls.

Fame appears to have changed Soane's taste in architecture for, on acquiring Pitshanger Manor, he pulled down most of the house, preserving only Dance's upper and lower rooms in the south wing — which today are used by the Reference Library. Soane originally bought the Manor for his son, who had shown every sign of following his father's profession but lost interest after his marriage which, according to a letter Soane wrote to a friend, followed "an excursion to one of those watering places where young ladies are found who are in haste to get married"! Bitterly disappointed, Soane sold Pitshanger Manor and retired to his town house in Lincoln's Inn Fields — now the fascinating Sir John Soane Museum.

Pitshanger Manor (Ealing Central Library)

Today, the frontage of the south wing and central block of the Manor are much as Soane left them, but the north wing has been rebuilt to house the Lending Library and many changes have been made to the interior. Fortunately, these are only of a temporary nature as the Manor is a protected building and, if things go according to plan, the rooms should be restored to their original splendour once the Library moves to the larger premises it so desperately needs, in the new Town Centre.

The names of the Ealing residents who lost their lives in the two World Wars are inscribed on either side of the wrought-iron gates leading into **Walpole Park,** where you will find well-laid out lawns, flower gardens and lily ponds, and many places to sit and enjoy the surroundings. A bronze bust and commemorative plaque to Charles Jones stands on the path to the north of the house, and to the south-west, a small playground has been provided for youngsters near the 'farmyard' of goats, rabbits, guinea-pigs and the most belligerent gang of geese I've ever come across. From here, a long avenue of trees (each dedicated to a Mayor of Ealing) leads down towards Lammas Park; while another path takes you west, past the duck-pond, to the Mattock Lane exit.

The Questors Theatre in Mattock Lane is not actually on our route (it lies a few hundred yards to the east of the Park gates) but, as one of the finest amateur theatres in the country, it is well worth a short detour for those who are not already members, to do something about joining. The theatre, which celebrated its Golden Jubilee in 1979, has expanded from a redundant chapel (affectionately known as the 'tin hut') into the splendid playhouse you see today, opened by the Queen Mother in 1964. Questors' high standards of acting, direction and design have earned the theatre an international reputation. Their experimental and ambitious programme (currently 25 productions a year) has always included plays by new writers, many of whom — such as *Tom Stoppard* and local writers, *James Saunders* and *Michael Green* — are now established names in the business. Some of today's most successful TV and film directors gained their early experience with Questors, and a number of actor-members have worked their way through Questor's excellent drama courses to achieve fame on the professional stage. *Sir Michael Redgrave* is president of the theatre and award-winning actress, *Judi Dench*, vice-president. Financially, Questors depends on the annual subscriptions from their 4,000-strong audience members, which entitles them to a free seat at many major productions throughout the year. Why not join their ranks and see what you've been missing?

Our walk winds its way to a close by turning west into Mattock Lane, towards Northfields Avenue and **Ealing Dean** — as this area was called during the 19th century. On your left lies the site of the **King Edward Memorial Hospital,** demolished in 1981 (despite strong local protest) after its services had been taken over by the new Ealing Hospital on the Uxbridge Road. A housing estate is planned for the site. **St. John's Church,** higher up the road, was built in 1876 but severely damaged by fire in the 1920's, when the fine steeple it once boasted was replaced by the present square clock-tower. **West Ealing** (formerly Ealing Dean) **Baptist Church** in nearby Chapel Road, pre-dates St. John's building by ten years and was one of the first developments on this side of Mattock Lane.

Ealing Dean Common, which once lined the southern side of Mattock Lane, was more popularly known as 'Jackass Common' in the days when pony races were held there at holiday times. Both the nickname and the custom were considered 'vulgar' by the vicar of St. Mary's and like-minded citizens and in 1830 part of the land was divided up into allotments — the rent being used to repair the old almshouses. 'Steeplechases' continued to take place on the remaining common, however, until it was built over by new streets and houses in the late 1870's. One of the houses in this group of roads (No. 16 Somerset Road) later became the birthplace of the novelist, *Nevil Shute.*

West Ealing in 1881, looking east down the Uxbridge Road towards the Northfields Avenue junction. The gabled shops on the left are still standing, but the 'Pound' for stray animals (on the right) has been absorbed into the present recreation ground.

Allotments still line both sides of **Northfields Avenue** at its junction with Mattock Lane, although some were taken away to form **Ealing Dean Gardens,** at the top of the road, earlier this century. The cinema opposite continues to be known by its former name of **The Lido** by long-established residents. It was built in 1913 on the site of **Ealing Cottage Hospital,** which had served the medical needs of the community for over 40 years until replaced by the King Edward.

The shopping centre of **West Ealing** has been considerably modernised in recent years, but several old buildings survive behind new shopfronts. The district around **Drayton Green Road** was called **Stevens Town** until rebuilt in the 1960's, and was virtually a slum area a century ago. The fact that some 8,000 people were crowded into a mere 700 cottages was a great source of worry to the Local Board, who felt that such an obviously working-class area would 'lower the general tone' of Ealing! Further west, the **Green Man,** an 18th century inn which once provided stabling for over 100 horses when it stood near the tollgate on the Uxbridge Road, was demolished in 1981 to make way for a new W.H. Smith — but its name lives on in **Green Man Lane.**

Fortunately for today's thirsty travellers who would like to end their walk in an historic hostelry, two even older inns survive in a more substantial form on the far side of the shopping centre. The **Old Hat,** the first one you come to, is reputed to have been in existence over 400 years ago and, according to local tradition, was connected to the ill-famed Hanwell Heath by an underground passage — although, considering the distance involved, this seems rather unlikely. It was the first stage-post out of London for the mail-coach to Oxford during the 18th century, when pigeon-shooting and cock-fighting were among the delights it offered to travellers. A second inn, also called Olde Hatte, was built further west during the early 1700's; but its name was later changed to the **Halfway House** — as it is still known today. Both inns have since been rebuilt.

(St. Mary's to Boston Manor via Lammas Park and Little Ealing — 1¾ miles). **St. Mary's Square** formed the southern boundary of the 18th century village of Great Ealing, and assumed a more triangular appearance when St. Mary's Road was widened in later years. Ne'er-do-wells in the old village would have been very familiar with the Square, as this was the site of the 'cage' where miscreants were confined until they could be removed to a more permanent prison. The **Old Fire House,** on the eastern side of the Square, is another reminder of the days when all public services centred round the church. The first engine house on the site was built in the mid-1700's, and all fire-fighting equipment for the Upper Side of the parish was stored here until the Local Board erected a new fire station behind the Town Hall in 1888. The old one was then rebuilt, in it present form, as a small sub-station for the South Ealing Volunteer Fire Brigade, who manned its manual engine and curricle until 1908 (see picture on Page 36).

The 'horsepower' for the old fire-engine was housed in the **stableyard** at the inner corner of the Square — later used as a dairy, and now a workshop for Morgan cars. The humble predecessors of the cottages on the Square today, once formed part of Sir Charles Lockyer's Coldhall estate and were described as being 'much dilapidated' in 1817 — when, incidentally, their combined value, including the stables, was estimated at £430. They were later rebuilt and two more added to the south of the Square — the latter serving as business premises for the local bootmaker and shopkeeper at the turn of the century.

North of the Square, in the curve of St. Mary's Road, stands **Westfield House,** built in the early 19th century for the *Butlin* family and now occupied by the **Conservative Club.** Looking down the busy South Ealing Road today, it is difficult to imagine that just over a century ago Westfield House was the last dwelling on this side of the road, and that nothing but farms and market gardens covered the rest of the way to Brentford.

Church Lane has always been a fairly busy thoroughfare as, until 1861 — when South Ealing was supplied by water from the new Kew Bridge pumping station —

Church Lane in 1903 as seen from No. 17. The cottages in the foreground were bombed during the war but No. 1 (just beyond the gas lamp) is still there, and the building with a pub sign is now a book-shop.

villagers in this part of the parish depended on the well in Church Lane (or Frog Lane, as it was then called) for their daily needs. The country atmosphere has long since gone, but two of the cottages that lined the lane during the 18th century still survive as Nos. 1 and 17. The former bears what I assume to be an old fire-mark high up on the wall i.e. a plaque bearing the number of an ancient fire insurance policy. (Fire insurance was first introduced after the Great Fire of London and people who took advantage of the scheme often fixed these numbered plaques to the walls of their houses). Next to No. 17, another cottage bears the proud inscription 'Circa 1600' which shows that its history has been delved into at some stage — although, judging by its present appearance, the original cottage has probably been quite extensively rebuilt over the years.

The lane curves round into **Culmington Road** (once a footpath leading to Ealing Dean) where you'll find an entrance into **Lammas Park.** The name comes from Loafmass Day, the harvest festival celebrated on the 1st August, which marked the start of the season when villagers were allowed to graze their animals on certain open fields and commons (known as Lammas Lands) until Candlemas (2nd February). The Local Board bought out the Lammas rights to these particular fields in 1880 and preserved them as a public park which, today, makes a pleasant open space in an otherwise built-up area. Playgrounds for toddlers and older children have been provided and all the tree-lined paths eventually lead to the exit in **Northfield Avenue,** where you turn left towards Little Ealing.

Northfield Avenue has undergone a tremendous change in the last fifty years — largely as a result of the growth of Little Ealing which began to spread out along the winding lane during the 1920's. By the outbreak of the Second World War, this once-quiet lane (which for centuries had formed the eastern boundary of the Great North Fields) had become the centre of a busy shopping and residential area that covered the open fields in all directions.

Northfields Station was opened by the District Railway in 1908, and rebuilt when the Piccadilly line was introduced some thirty years later. The District service finally ceased in 1964. Opposite the station stands the 1930 **Spanish-style cinema** which was

Northfields Avenue in 1903, looking north from The Plough.

saved from demolition in 1981, when the head of the Coronet group fell in love with its unique architecture. A rather different form of entertainment is provided by the **Log Cabin Playground,** across the road, which aims to give handicapped children an atmosphere of freedom in which to experiment with new activities. The Playground (founded by Councillor Margaret Lorde during her mayoral year in 1977) offers a climbing tower, giant slide and shallow pool, all accessible to children in wheelchairs. A League of Friends has been formed to help with fund-raising for the Log Cabin and membership forms are available from Northfields Library next door.

The shops between **Julien Road** and the Plough were the first to be built in the area, following the opening of the station. At that time, they faced the original **Niagra House** (the name now given to the large block of flats and shops on the opposite side of the road) where *Charles Blondin*, the famous French rope-dancer, lived from 1886 until his death in 1897. He retired to Ealing after crossing the Niagra Falls in as many ways as it is possible to do so — given only the aid of a tightrope. Not content with merely getting to the other side in one piece, Blondin varied his terrifying act by crossing blindfolded, on stilts, and with a wheelbarrow; but not, needless to say, all at the same time. Niagra House was demolished during the 1930's, but **Blondin** and **Niagra Avenues** still commemorate this celebrated resident.

The area between Windmill Lane and the railway line (including the site of Niagra House) once formed the main estate of the **Manor of Coldhall** which, until the mid-19th century, included a long strip of land (known as the Lower Horse Leys) along the eastern side of Northfields Lane, as well as several scattered properties in the vicinity of Great Ealing Village. The first record of this ancient manor occurs way back in the 14th century, in the will of a city merchant; but the names of its early owners are not of any particular interest, except that of *Richard Amondesham* who bought the 250-acre estate in 1496, and whose brass plaque is the oldest memorial in St. Mary's Church. Coldhall was later bought by *John Loving Junior*, owner of the neighbouring Place House, who sold the manor to *Sir Charles Lockyer* in 1728, together with a nearby house called **The Hollies.**

Lockyer, an MP for Ilchester in Somerset, never married and left the bulk of his possesssions, including Coldhall, to a woman named *Elizabeth Hodgson* with the proviso the she and her husband changed their name to Lockyer. She was, perhaps, the mother of his illegitimate son who had inherited most of Lockyer's Somerset estates. Much of the land belonging to the manor had been sold to various individuals by 1840, but to get some idea of their extent as well as an excellent picture of Ealing in the 18th century, I would recommend Hector Smith's delightful booklet, '*A Perambulation at Ealing in 1766*', which is based on a survey of the Lockyer estates.

Residents of Coldhall Manor had no close neighbours until **Place House** was built by *John Loving* in the early 17th century. Other houses began to appear around the junction of Windmill and Northfield Lanes, and by 1650 the tiny hamlet was known as **Little Ealing.** For the next two centuries, the dusty lanes from Brentford and the Uxbridge Road echoed with the rumble of carriages belonging to the rich and famous who made their homes in this secluded corner of the parish. Place House was the largest of these fashionable estates, its grounds stretching from Windmill Lane, along Little Ealing Lane, to the lodge gates in South Ealing Road.

John Loving, Teller of the Exchequer to Charles II, was succeeded by his son and namesake who, in 1729, sold Place House to the baronet, *Sir William Ellis* — the first in a long line of titled owners. The most noteworthy of these was the *Earl of Warwick* who lived here from 1760-5 and often entertained his great friend, *Alexander Pope*. The house was rebuilt towards the end of the 18th century and renamed **Ealing Park.** It became widely renowned for its beautiful gardens during the ownership of *Sir William Lawrence*, a leading Victorian surgeon, and formed the backdrop for numerous 'high society' parties.

Rochester House in the 18th century — now the Institute for Industrial Engineers.

Rochester House, on the opposite side of Little Ealing Lane, also attracted many high-ranking visitors. It was built c.1712 for a London distiller, *Thomas Pearce,* and later named after his son, the **Bishop of Rochester,** who died there in 1774. During the early 19th century, Rochester House was the home of the exiled French General, *Charles Dumouriez,* whose 'pleasing manner and delightful conversation' made him numerous friends. The Duke of Kent and Dr. Nicholas (headmaster of Great Ealing School) often joined him for a game of whist, and his fellow-exile and future King, *Louis-Phillipe,* was naturally among his most frequent visitors.

Behind a high wall, between the eastern end of Windmill Lane and Ealing Park, lay several more substantial houses including **Pickerings** (built for *Mr. William Pickering,* proprietor of a London coffee-house in the early 18th century), **Gumley,** and **The Hollies.** The latter was bought from Sir Charles Lockyer by *Mr. King Gould,* a distinguished lawyer, who seems to have owned half the properties in Ealing before his death in 1756. His son, Charles, inherited all his real estate as well as his father's legal talents, and became Judge Advocate-General and a well-trusted advisor to King George III, who knighted him for his services. The old saying about the rich getting richer certainly seems to have applied in his case, as he married *Jane Morgan* of Tredegar, an heiress so wealthy that he changed his name to hers and, as *Sir Charles Morgan,* moved to live on her estate in Monmouthshire. The Goulds, or rather Morgans, continued to hold property in Ealing for several generations, however, and later leased the Hollies to *Mrs. Hogarth,* sister-in-law to the author, *Charles Dickens.*

But for all the prestige of its inhabitants, Little Ealing remained essentially rural and still retained all its olde-worlde charm at the turn of the present century. The roof-garden of the old village inn was described as being 'ablaze with blossom', ivy mantled Rochester House, and noble cedars overhung the walls around Ealing Park (then a convent for the Ladies of Nazareth). But, ominous signs of the changes that were to take place in the next twenty years were already evident in Little Ealing Lane which, denuded of its shady trees, had recently been 'trimmed into a most respectable roadway'.

THE PLOUGH - 1980

Today, only two of the old houses survive and little of their original setting remains to stimulate the imagination. The **Plough Inn,** rebuilt c.1905, is a mere shadow of its 18th century predecessor, which boasted 3 acres of bowling-greens and pleasure-grounds and was reputed to have been one of *Dick Turpin's* favourite haunts between forays on Hounslow Heath. The adjacent **Rochester House** was occupied by Mrs. Robinson's Academy for Ladies after General Dumouriez' departure in 1818, and now houses the **Institute for Industrial Engineers.** The large gardens and fish-pond behind the house were sold in 1904 and the site was soon covered by **Little Ealing First and Middle School.**

Across the way, the gates of **Ealing Park** now lead to **St. Anne's Convent School** which was founded in the grand old house by the Sisters of Charity in 1903. Sir William Lawrence's son sold the major portion of the estate to the British Land Co. in 1882, and effectively signed the death warrant for Little Ealing. Soon housing was encroaching on the quiet hamlet from all directions and by 1920, the only open space lay to the west of Niagra House. 'Gumley' and 'The Hollies' were swiftly reduced to street-names off Windmill Lane; and 'Pickerings', like the later 'Laurel Court', have been transposed to large flat and office blocks.

Before setting off for Boston Manor, I'd like to tell you about just one more ancient mansion (if you can bear it!) which stood opposite the entrance to Little Ealing Lane, on the corner of today's Pope's Lane and South Ealing Road. Because it formed part of Sir Charles Lockyer's extensive estate, this house was erroneously thought by early historians to have been the Manor House of Coldhall (the true site of which we will be passing later in this walk), but its chief interest lies in its connection with *Dr. William Dodd,* who earned himself the dubious distinction of being the last man in England to be hanged for forgery.

Such an ignominious end hardly seems fitting for a man who was chaplain to King George III but, despite his large income, Dr. Dodd's expensive habits drifted him steadily into debt. He rented the house in question in 1769, and started a school for 'high class boy pupils' — among them *Philip Stanhope,* the future *Lord Chesterfield.* When, for various reasons, Dodd's name was struck off the list of chaplains, Lord Chesterfield came to his rescue and presented him with the living of Wing in Buckinghamshire. Sinking hopelessly into debt, Dodd sold his chapel and, in February 1777, presented a stockbroker with a bond for £4,200 on which he had forged the signature of his benefactor. Despite the efforts made by Dr. Johnson and others to secure him a pardon, Dodd was sentenced to death.

His school at Ealing was taken over by the *Rev. Samuel Goodenough* (later Bishop of Carlisle) whose pupils included the future Prime Minister, *Henry Addington;* the *Earl of Elgin;* and the soldier, *Sir Robert Walpole.* **Goodenough House,** as it became known, was demolished in 1858 and replaced by another called **The Limes** which survived until early this century.

And now . . . back to the present and on to Boston Manor! It can be approached via a semi-rural route by retracing your steps to either **Blondin** or **Niagra Avenues,** at the end of which you will find an entrance to **Northfields Recreation Ground.** This open space is formed from land surrounding the old **Manor House of Coldhall;** or, to be more precise, it was the site of the main residence on the estate at the time of the 1766 survey of Lockyer's land — whether the original 14th century Manor House also stood here, nobody (as yet) has discovered.

If you head across the football pitch, towards the railway line, you will come to another path that leads west alongside a hedge, and then past a large allotment ground, to emerge in **Boston Manor Road.** A little way south, on the opposite side of the street, you will see a side-gate into the grounds of **Boston Manor** itself, which once belonged to the ancient parish of Hanwell, but now lies on the Brentford side of the borough boundary.

In contrast to other manors and large houses in and around the borough, Boston has had relatively few owners, most of whom will be fairly familiar to readers — or should be by the time you finish this book The earliest mention of the Manor occurred in 1157 when it was called 'Bordestone' and belonged to the Abbot of Westminster, lord of the manor of Hanwell. It was later leased to *Ralph Brito* of New Brentford but in 1280, King Edward I separated the Manor from Hanwell and granted it to the *Priory of St. Helen's* in Bishopgate. The nuns retained the estate until the dissolution of the monasteries when, like most religious houses in the London area, Boston (or 'Burston' as was then called) was given to the *Duke of Somerset.*

After the Duke's execution, the Manor was confiscated by Queen Elizabeth who presented it to her favourite, *Sir Robert Dudley,* Duke of Leicester. He sold Boston almost immediately to *Sir Thomas Gresham* of Osterley, and it eventually passed to Gresham's stepson, *Sir William Reade.* His widow, *Lady Mary Reade,* inherited the estate and built the present Boston House in 1623, before marrying *Sir Edward Spencer* of Althorp, an early ancestor of Lady Diana Spencer — the new Princess of Wales. Sir Edward was a devoted Royalist in the Civil War that followed, and Charles I is said to have watched the Battle of Brentford from the roof of Boston Manor; but this kind of rumour is as difficult to substantiate as the number of beds that Queen Elizabeth slept in, or pubs frequented by Dick Turpin.

In 1670, *James Clitherow,* Sheriff of Middlesex, purchased Boston House and its 230 acres of land for the grand price of £5,136/17s/4d and it remained in his family for over two centuries — the Clitherows thus becoming Brentford's longest established and best respected citizens. King William IV and Queen Adelaide paid tribute to their standing in the community by dining with Colonel Clitherow and his sister at Boston House one memorable evening in 1834, much to the delight of the 'natives' who gathered to watch the royal arrival.

The Clitherows sold most of their land (which extended as far as Windmill Lane on the Ealing side) for building in 1923, but Brentford District Council bought Boston House and 20 acres as a public park. The house suffered some damage during the war but was repaired and occupied by an infant's school until 1961, when it became clear that more extensive restoration was urgently needed. A plan costing £35,000 was put into operation and the restored house was opened by the Queen Mother in July, 1963.

The house was later carefully divided into flats for a charitable organisation and closed to the public for many years, but some of the rooms (including the Jacobean **drawing room** with its magnificent panelled ceiling inscribed with Lady Reade's initials and the year, 1623) have recently been reopened and can be viewed on Saturday afternoons from 2 - 4.30 p.m. during summer months. Entrance is free and information sheets about what you can see are available at the door, so I won't go into details here.

James Clitherow planted many of the beautiful cedar trees that still grace the lawns to the south of the house — although I'm sure he never imagined that their spreading branches would one day help to screen the unlovely view of the M4 motorway. The grounds are open all year round and offer tree-lined paths, sloping lawns and a large lake filled with a variety of waterfowl. There is also a children's playground to the east of the house.

Although the canal runs close by, you cannot reach the towpath from this side; but if you walk through the adjacent London Playing Fields (entrance in Boston Gardens) and down towards the motorway, you'll come to the **weir** over the Brent at its junction with the Grand Union. **Gallows Bridge** lies a little way further west but, frustratingly, is fenced off fom the playing fields so you cannot gain access to the towpath. There are plans to correct this silly situation some time in the future, however, and Boston Manor will then make an excellent starting-point for a canalside walk to Brentford.

Boston Manor House

(St. Mary's to The Broadway via Ealing Common — 1¾ miles). The **Rose and Crown** in Church Place was described in 1823 as the first inn on the road from Brentford, but it was probably in existence long before that date. Today, the pub offers a good pint and excellent toasted sandwiches — as well as a sunny beer garden in which to enjoy them. **Church Gardens,** nearby, was built on the site of a 5-acre orchard which belonged to Sir Charles Lockyer's estate in the 18th century. At the end of the road stand **St. Mary's Church Homes,** a group of half-timbered almhouses which were opened in 1900 to replace their dilapidated predecessors on the Uxbridge Road.

You can return to Church Place by turning left into **Roberts Alley** — once a private footpath from the church to a large house called Village Park (then owned by Edward Roberts Esq.) in Pope's Lane. The **Grange Schools,** to your right, were founded in 1925 and further up, at No. 11 Church Place, stands the new Vicarage of St. Mary's which was built on part of the old burial ground in 1969. Continue to follow the footpath through the churchyard until it branches off to the right, into **Baillies Walk.**

Baillies Walk

This is all that remains of the ancient footway from the church to Gunnersbury — the southern end now being covered by Elderberry Road. Despite evidence that the path is a popular haunt of the local canine community, it is worth the occasional navigational hazard to escape the traffic for a while. The allotments lining the path make a pleasant change from rows of houses, and serve as a reminder of the acres of arable land that once stretched across to the Common and down to Gunnersbury and Ealing Manor House. A *James Baillie* lived at Ealing Grove for several years before his death in 1793, and was buried in the churchyard; but I have not been able to discover why the path should have been named after him — if, indeed, it is. Whatever the reason behind its name, for over a century Baillies Walk formed the southern boundary of the grounds of Great Ealing School, which extended from today's Warwick Road to **Ascott Avenue** — where the path emerges.

An old engraving of Elm Grove and Ealing Common.

Here you turn left, then first right into **Elm Grove Road,** named after a large house which once occupied the site of All Saints Church. **Elm Grove** had its origins in an ancient estate called **Hickes-upon-Heath,** which was carved out of the Common during the 15th century. *Sir William Trumbull,* Secretary of State to William and Mary, and *Dr. John Edgerton,* Bishop of Durham, were just two of the famous 'men of their times' who owned the house during its long history; but it is as the home of *Spencer Perceval,* the only British Prime Minister to be assassinated, that Elm Grove is best remembered.

Perceval bought the estate in 1808, in the hope that Ealing's healthy reputation would be beneficial to his ailing wife. Four years later, in the lobby of the House of Commons, he was shot by a bankrupt Liverpool businessman called Bellingham, who felt that the Government had not paid sufficient attention to the list of grievances with which he had been bombarding MP's for weeks. The attention he received after his crime was perhaps not quite what he'd had in mind: within the space of a week, he was brought to trial and hanged at Newgate.

Elm Grove passed to Perceval's widow (whose health seems to have responded remarkably well to Ealing's 'fine air' — she later remarried and, as Lady Carr, lived to be over 90) but was sold after her daughters moved to Pitshanger Manor, and demolished in 1894, when *Leopold Rothschild* bought the 35-acre estate for development purposes. *Frederica Perceval,* the youngest daughter, must have inherited her mother's longevity as she died at the ripe old age of 95, leaving a bequest in her will for a church to be erected in her father's memory. Rothschild generously donated the site of the old house, and **All Saints Church** was opened in 1905.

The triple line of ancient elms on **Ealing Common** which gave the house its name, have given way to splendid chestnut trees (planted by Charles Jones) which today provide Ealing school boys with thousands of conkers every autumn. The Common was the scene of the public reception to celebrate the granting of Ealing's Charter of Incorporation as a Borough on the 10th July, 1901 — the same day that the Shepherd's Bush to Southall Tramway opened. Crowds gathered to hear the Town Clerk read the unique charter which was the first this century, the first to be signed by Edward VII, and the first to be granted to any district in Middlesex. Over on the south-eastern side of the Common, a large grass-covered depression serves as a reminder of less pleasant historic events — bombing raids in 1940. Forty-two years later, this corner of the Common and houses in Elm Avenue are once again threated with extinction — this time by the Department of Transport who plan to widen the North Circular to four lanes from the Uxbridge Road to Gunnersbury Lane.

Fine houses began to line the west side of the Common after **Ealing Common Station** opened in 1879, and many survive today — although several large blocks of flats appeared on some of the prime sites in the between-war building boom. The **Grange Hotel,** on the corner of Warwick Road, took over the licence from an earlier inn called The Cricketer in 1873. Recently redecorated in the elegant style of an Edwardian gentlemen's club (complete with potted palms and comfy armchairs), the pub has a delightful atmosphere which is further enhanced by the absence of any juke-boxes or dreadful 'space-invader' machines. A good selection of hot or cold meals is always available and you'll find a large paved beer garden through the side entrance in Warwick Road, where food is served in a splendid wrought-iron-and-glass conservatory.

"THE GRANGE", EALING COMMON

From the windows of the Grange, you can look across the Common to the site of another home of the famous, **Fordhook,** which used to stand on the north side of the Uxbridge Road, almost opposite the station. *Henry Fielding* bought the house as a country cottage in 1752 — perhaps with the profits from his novel 'Tom Jones', which had been published several years earlier and was not, as is popularly believed, written at Fordhook. He, too, had been attracted to Ealing because 'the air was the finest in Middlesex', but only stayed here for short periods — the last just a month before setting sail for Lisbon, where he died from dropsy a few weeks later. (The efficacious effects of Ealing's air were obviously not infallible, although, as made clear by the writer of a 19th century guide-book, the renowned improvement in general health was only assured if visitors were 'in good condition — and not absolutely ill before coming'!)

Fielding had also been a magistrate on the Middlesex bench — a position he took very seriously. A strict disciplinarian, he tried for many years to get a County poor-house erected at Acton Vale, which was to include a House of Correction for vagrants, with dungeons and fasting-rooms. Fortunately for the poor vagrants, this scheme never materialised. After his death, Henry's work was continued by his blind half-brother, *Sir John Fielding* (popularly known as the 'Blind Beak of Bow Street'), who was responsible for enrolling the first Bow Street Runners — the predecessors of our modern police force.

Fordhook later became the home of **Lady Noel Byron,** the founder of Ealing Grove School, but better known as the wife of the poet, Lord Byron. Their marriage only lasted a year as they separated soon after the birth of their daughter, Ada, whose own wedding took place at Fordhook in 1835. Lady Byron moved away from Ealing a few years later, but the gardens she had planted on the estate continued to attract attention until the old house was abolished c. 1910.

You could end your walk on the Common, or make your way up to the **Uxbridge Road.** A ramble through Ealing's main shopping centre may not be your idea of recreation, but I should like to round off this chapter by telling you about some of the buildings in the Mall and Broadway — perhaps the information will come in useful the next time you're stuck in a queue for a cash-dispensing machine, or waiting for a bus.

A little over a century ago, shops lined the High Street and The Grove but this section of the Uxbridge Road was almost empty except for inns like the Bell and the Feathers, which served the carriage trade. Brickfields and a market garden covered most of the south side of the Broadway and, on the opposite side, a large rosery extended from North Common Road as far as the Bell. But, within a year of the Local Board taking over from the ineffectual Highway Board, new residences had sprung up along the newly kerbed and macadamised Uxbridge Road and, by the 1880's, many of these had already given way to promenades of shops and business premises. Today, the busy shopping centre on along the Mall and Broadway has the biggest turnover in the borough, and will no doubt become even more popular once the new Town Centre is completed in 1984.

The *Wood* family must have made a fortune as Ealing expanded and property values rose. They owned all the land north of the Uxbridge Road from the present Town Hall to the eastern boundary; but, like the Rothschilds, they were generous with their wealth and played a large part in Ealing's early development. **St. Matthew's Church** in North Common Road was built between the large detached houses on land donated by *Edward Wood* in 1883, after the small iron church in Grange Park had become too cramped for this fast-growing part of the parish.

Most of the large Victorian houses on the south side of **The Mall** have been converted into flats or offices and are beginning to show their age but, further along, two early-19th century houses (Nos. 42 - 3) have been well preserved and give a better idea of how smart this area must have been in the days when the alleyways between the houses led to their private stables, rather than the present series of small industrial firms.

T. Bryant's Cycle Shop on The Mall in 1886 — now Crispin's Wine Bar.

Crispin's Wine Bar was once a cycle shop (see photograph) and beyond, on the corner of Florence Road, **The Bell** presents a very different picture from the quaint bow-windowed inn of the 1750's. Every morning, the wooden benches outside were crowded with market-gardeners having an early breakfast before taking their produce through to London, while their horses waited patiently before laden carts and wagons outside the rosery across the road. The Bell was just as busy during the the early 19th century, when it was an important stop on the London to Worcester coach run. The 'Royal Mail' coach called here twice daily, as well as the 'Paul Pry' and 'Blenheim' coaches on their way to Cheltenham and Oxford. In 1812, the proprietor was one *William Williams*, who also served as coachman to *Spencer Perceval* and had driven him to the House of Commons on that fateful day. Despite the sad circumstances, one cannot help thinking that Williams' link with the unfortunate Prime Minister must have been very good for business. During the 1960's the Bell was rebuilt and incorporated into new office buildings on the eastern half of its former site, and today you'd have difficulty parking a car, never mind a laden cart, anywhere in the vicinity.

The Bell as it looked in the 18th century.

The **Ealing Gazette** used to have offices at 57 The Mall, before moving to larger premises in West Ealing. The paper was founded in 1898 to compete with Ealing's first newspaper, the Middlesex County Times, established 1863. Both publications were very successful and, between them, had bought out most of the local papers from Uxbridge to Acton, before merging in 1941.

The houses in **Windsor Road** should soon be restored to their former grandeur (at least from the outside) if the rash of building activity taking place at the moment is anything to go by. **Ealing Broadway Methodist Church** is practically the only building in the street that is not swarming with workmen — more's the pity. The church, with its distinctive spire, was built in 1868 with accommodation for 1000 people, but became redundant in 1972 when the congregation joined Ealing Green Church. Now, like so many listed buildings in the borough, it quietly rots away while waiting to see whether any money can be found in the Council coffers, to develop the church for community use. The adjacent **Windsor Hall** (now administered by the Samaritans) was rebuilt on the site of the old school buildings and temporary chapel, designed by *Charles Jones*, which burnt down in 1893. (Incidentally, the Great Man himself lived at No. 5 Windsor Road in the 1870's.)

Back on the Mall, the parade of shops to the west of Windsor Road was built in 1902 on the site of the old **almshouses,** which were maintained by rent from the Ealing Dean allotments. Princess Amelia (of Gunnersbury) is said to have paid for the original almshouses to be built in 1783. Across the road, the talents of Ealing's first Surveyor manifest themselves once more in the buildings of the **National Westminster Bank** — designed by Jones in 1874 as offices for the Local Board.

The Feathers marks the start of the **Broadway** and has been in existence since at least 1746, when *Samuel Verrey* (see Perivale Chapter) was attacked by footpads near 'the sign of Ye Feathers'. The pleasure gardens at the rear of the inn did a thriving trade during the coaching age, when the pub was run by the former head-gardener to the Duke of Kent. This land was later bought by the GWR for Haven Green Station. The present version of the Feathers dates from 1891, although it was considerably 'modernised' during the 1920's.

The North Star nearby is another long-established watering-hole, and used to have a forge at the back when it was first built in the early 1800's. Behind the modern facades of the shops between the Midland and Barclays Banks, you can see the original frontage of the **London and South Western Bank,** which opened on the site of the former brickfields in 1883. Supermarkets now cover the market garden which once stretched back to **The Grove,** where the £50 million **Town Centre** is rapidly taking shape after a rather slow start. Plans for the 11-acre site were first put forward during the 1950's and approved by the Council in 1969; but building only began in 1980. The Centre has been designed by John Laing Development Services to match Ealing's Edwardian architecture and will include shops, offices, flats, car-parks and squash courts around a tree-lined 'town square' with a fountain and terraced cafes. A colonnade of red-brick shops will flank the High Street and the Central Library will be rehoused above Safeway.

W. H. Smith, on the opposite side of the Broadway, has been trading in Ealing since 1866, although the present premises were built during the late 1950's on the site of the **Palladium Cinema.** The Palladium replaced the old **Lyric Hall** in 1899 and was originally called Ealing Theatre and later, Ealing Hippodrome. The large hole left by the old below-stage machinery is now filled by W.H. Smith's basement book department. On Sunday evenings during the 1920's, the Palladium provided a less decadent form of entertainment when it was used by former members of Haven Green Baptist Church who had left the congregation after a disagreement with the minister. The services were conducted by various popular preachers, supported by an orchestra and soloists, and attracted large audiences for many years.

Gas lamps along The Broadway in 1893, looking west from The Feathers.

Bentalls occupies the premises of an old firm of family drapers, **Eldred Sayers and Son,** who began trading in the distinctive domed building over a century ago. At the time of writing (1982), there are Council-approved plans to relocate Bentalls in the new Town Centre and build a 7-storey office block on its present site. The suggestion is being strongly opposed by local conservationists and has already been vetoed by the GLC, but Bentalls has appealed against the decision and a public enquiry is to be held in the near future. (If the proposed office block bears any resemblance to the characterless buildings that line the approach to West Ealing, one hopes the appeal will be turned down.)

Ealing's other big department store, **John Sanders,** grew from a small outfitting business which used to stand next to a pub called the **Bricklayer's Arms,** (on the corner of the Broadway and High Street) in the 1860's. Sanders bought the site when the inn was demolished and built their present store in 1891. This suffered severe damage during the Second World War and been quite extensively rebuilt. The **Royal Oak,** nearby, was constructed from bricks that came from the Duke of Kent's former home on Castlebar Hill after it was sold piecemeal in the 1820's. **New Broadway,** the stretch of road between the High Street and Town Hall, was developed at the same time as **Bond Street** (c. 1905) and parades of shops soon replaced most of the old houses that once stood there.

The history of Christ Church is told in the next chapter, and we now jump to the **Town Hall** — built to who-else-but Charles Jones' design in 1888. This prime site fronting the Uxbridge Road and stretching back to the railway, was once meadowland belonging to the Wood family and was procured by the Local Board for a mere £300, thanks to Jones' negotiations and Edward Wood's generosity. The latter also donated a further £500 (as did Lord Rothschild and Sir Montague Nelson) towards the building of the **Victoria Jubilee Hall,** which was opened by the Prince of Wales at the same time as the new public offices. The Town Hall has been extended and altered many times since then, but still looks fairly imposing — especially since the years of grime were recently scrubbed off its walls.

Around the corner in **Longfield Avenue,** you'll find new offices going up behind the Town Hall on the site of the former **Public Baths.** When they were first built in 1884, the three pools were designated First, Second and Third Class to ensure that the gentry were not contaminated by poorer residents who, until then, had enjoyed the freedom of a natural bathing pond near Ealing Common, formed by a stream that rose in the grounds of Elm Grove. The 1888 **Fire House,** nearby, has so far managed to survive the demolition experts, although its services were transferred to the new Central Fire Station on the corner of St Leonard's Road in 1933.

The northern side of the Uxbridge Road, from the Town Hall to West Ealing, only began to be developed after the First World War and was largely rebuilt during the 1960's when the ugly blocks of Council offices first made their appearance. The cinema opposite the Town Hall still offers a bit of Thirties quasi-Egyptian style and next-door to it (should you want to escape from the Age of Progress altogether), a narrow alleyway called **Barnes Pikle** leads down to Walpole Park — giving me the opportunity to end this chapter with a final piece of fascinating information: namely, that the path once formed the western boundary of a small field, or 'pikle', belonging to a Mr Barnes.

The opening ceremony of the Shepherds Bush to Southall Tramway outside Ealing Town Hall on 10th July 1901.

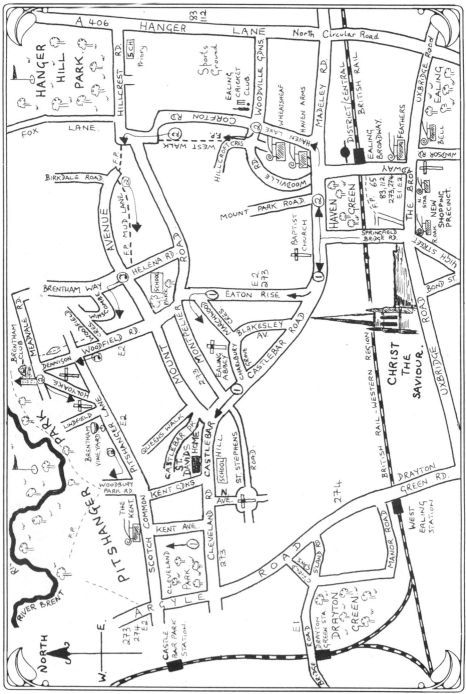

NORTHEALING 64

CHAPTER III

'... lanes that were themselves retired and lonely, led to green
sequestered meadows through which the humble Brent crept
along its snake-like way.'
from 'My Novel' by LORD EDWARD BULWER LYTTON, describing a walk through North Ealing in the 19th century.

 clung to its meadowland and country lanes long after its southern counter part had begun to sprout houses instead of crops. The hillside became quite fashionable after the Duke of Kent took up residence there in the early 1800's but development was slow, even after the opening of Haven Green station, and the area was considered 'too rural' to be incorporated by the new Local Board in 1863. Once this omission had been corrected however, the excellent system of drains constructed by Ealing's surveyor, Charles Jones, swiftly transformed the hilly, clay-covered north into the most desirable residential area in the 'Queen of the Suburbs' — a position it still holds today.

Early settlers were not attracted to the heavy clay land covering North Ealing, although a road following the same course as the present Argyle Road had been in existence since pre-Roman times. This ancient trackway from Perivale provided access to settlements in South Ealing and Brentford, and was protected by a 'castelburh' (the old name for a 'fortified place') along the high ridge of ground known as Castlebar Hill today. Fragments of Romano-British burial urns were found when excavating the reservoirs west of Hanger Hill in the 19th century, but the earliest record of anyone living on the hillside occurs in 1222, with the 'Putelshanger' or *Pitshanger* family.

By the 15th century, the farmlands of **Pitshanger Manor** extended northwards from Hanger Hill to the Brent, and were quite independent of the manor of Ealing. A small hamlet of about a dozen cottages had grown up at **Drayton Green** to the west, and there was another freehold estate called **Absdonsland** south of Castlebar Hill, but otherwise the northern portion of Ealing manor was populated chiefly by the stag and wild boar which roamed the open heath and forest on Hanger Hill — 'hangra' being the Anglo-Saxon for 'a wooded slope'.

The abundance of game was no doubt appreciated by *Thomas Fisher* when he was granted the lease of North Ealing in 1601, for the new overlord was a skinner by trade. He did little or nothing to cultivate the manor lands however, and except for the construction of a kiln for tile-making to the east of Hanger Lane, few changes occurred in the basic community during the 17th century. **Drayton House** was built at the north end of Drayton Green by the *Walter* family, **Castlebar Park** appeared on Absdonsland towards the middle of the century, and there were three houses on Pitshanger Manor; but no new estates were formed until the 1700's when some of the woodland on Hanger Hill was cleared for a mansion west of Hanger Lane.

Mr. King Gould had bought or leased most of these estates, including the manor lands, by the mid-18th century, and he was also responsible for building the fore-runner of the Duke of Kent's house on Castlebar Hill. After his death in 1756, the lands passed to his son, Charles, who sold Pitshanger Manor and a large farm at Drayton Green to *Thomas Gurnell* of Ealing. *Richard Wood* took over the lease of the manor lands on Hanger Hill in 1775 and began to acquire more of the surrounding land — a practise which was to make his family Ealing's largest property-owners in later years, when they bought the freehold of the manor lands in North Ealing.

By the beginning of the 19th century, pastures and commons had replaced many of the open fields as sheep and stock-farming were then the main occupations. Houses had begun to appear on the north side of **Haven Green,** a so-called **Manor House** had been built to the west of Drayton Green (although Drayton was never a manor), a **new Drayton House** to the east, and the *Duke of Kent* was not short of neighbours on Castlebar Hill. But, compared with the prosperous and populous area south of the Uxbridge Road, North Ealing had a long way to go.

The arrival of the GWR at Haven Green (the first stop on the Paddington to Maidenhead line), put an end to the days when a partridge or hare might be bagged on the green; but although the railway brought many visitors to unknown Ealing, several decades were to pass before any new roads or houses began to encroach on the 'gentlemen's residences' on the hill. Even then, the first attempt at a large-scale housing scheme (devised by *Henry de Bruno Austin* in the 1860's) was a dismal failure.

And so things remained until North Ealing was finally brought under the jurisdiction of the Local Board in 1873, and Charles Jones was able to improve drainage and roads. During the 1880's, the country estates of Dukes and Generals began to give way to rows of 'high class villas' which soon extended over the Wood's farmland north-east of Haven Green. Many schools and churches were built in the massive building boom between 1890 and 1903, which saw the spread of cheaper semi's towards Drayton Green, and the start of a new concept in smart housing for ordinary working folk, the **Brentham Garden Estate,** on the farmlands of Pitshanger Manor. The last of the Wood family's 750-acre estate was later developed by the Prudential Assurance Company and by 1908, Drayton House had been replaced by Drayton School and the remaining 4-acres of green were almost surrounded by new housing. Drayton 'Manor House' however, managed to survive until the 1920's.

The fact that most residents kept their own carriages, probably accounted for the lack of public transport in the area north of Haven Green. Stations opened at Drayton Green and Castlebar Park in 1904, but people living in Brentham were fairly isolated until a suburban service, linked to the GWR's Birmingham line, was provided from **Brentham Halt** (now Hanger Lane) in 1911. Buses travelled up Eaton Rise and Montpelier Road during the First World War, but it was another thirty years before the service was extended to Woodfield Road and Pitshanger Lane. (See photo Page 73.)

Between the World Wars, building covered most available plots and was carried to the edges of the district, except where open spaces had been preserved on Hanger Hill and beside the Brent in **Pitshanger Park.** Farming was virtually extinct by 1930 — **Cotching's Farm** at the south end of Hanger Lane being one of the last to go when it was taken over by United Dairies in 1928. Expensive blocks of flats appeared beside Victorian houses and on neglected strips of land — such as the 1934 **Ealing Village,** near the railway in the south-east corner. The railway and Western Avenue made North Ealing an obvious target during the Second World War and many roads and houses had to be rebuilt in the aftermath.

Today the treelined streets are not quite as exclusive as they once were but, although many of the fine houses have been divided into flats, a large proportion are still owner-occupied, private schools abound, and the area retains a distinct aura of properous respectability.

CHRIST THE SAVIOUR, EALING BROADWAY

The church of **Christ the Saviour,** was built in 1852 to cater for the rapid increase in Ealing's population following the opening of the Great Western Railway. The expansion northwards had shifted the town centre away from the parish church of St. Mary's, to the Uxbridge Road. The Broadway was thus the obvious location for the new church and a site was chosen on land formerly belonging to the Wood family. The building was entirely funded by a wealthy parishioner, *Miss Rosa Lewis,* who commissioned *Sir George Gilbert Scott,* then the leading architect in the Gothic revival, to design Christ Church as a memorial to her father: 'Gentleman' Lewis, a Liverpool actor who had lived in Ealing for a time and grown very attached to the town. He was buried in Christ Church, Liverpool, which probably explains Miss Lewis' original choice of dedication. The stone church is a fine example of the early work of Gilbert Scott (his later memorial to Prince Albert in Kensington Gardens is slightly better known!), and its graceful spire is a familiar Ealing landmark. The church was damaged during the Blitz but was restored in 1952 , when it was united with St. Saviour's (formerly in The Grove until destroyed by bombing in 1940), and the name changed accordingly. The first Vicar, the Rev. William Lambert, was suspended for 'immorality' (the case would hardly have made headlines today...he was unmarried, but she, unfortunately, was); but his successor, *Joseph Hilliard* was the very model of a moral parish minister. He raised funds for the four 'daughter' churches (St. John, St. Stephen, St. Saviour and St. Peter), and established the adjoining Boy's and Girl's Schools (built in 1870 and 1885 respectively) which now form **Christ Church Middle School.** Rev. Hilliard died in 1895 and his memorial cross outside the church, was designed by Gilbert Scott's son.

(Haven Green to Castlebar Hill and Pitshanger Park — 1½ miles). We begin in **Springbridge Road,** alongside the church, which leads onto the west side of **Haven Green.** The clear spring which gave the road its name is now covered by housing from its source on Castlebar Hill, and the railway runs along part of the old course to Little Ealing and the Thames. On reaching Haven Green or 'Ealing's Haven' as it was once called (see Perivale chapter for one explanation), you might like to pause for a few minutes on one of the shaded benches, and consider the changes that have occurred here during the last century or so. The buildings that surround the green today, do not detract from its charm (only the BBC's high-rise 'Villiers House' looks out of place), but in the early 1800's, you would have had a clear view up Castlebar Hill.

Only two roads then led off the north side of Haven Green: to the left, the very old and dusty lane which zig-zagged up Castlebar Hill to Perivale; and to the right, Haven Lane, which had a row of cottages on one side, then ended in a footpath leading up to Hanger Hill. Eaton Rise was built c.1865, but all the other roads only appeared after 1880. Four cottages occupied the site of the present Baptist Chapel; then came a large house called 'The Laurels' where the 1930's Haven Court now stands; a pond lay at the entrance to Woodville Road; and Madeley Road was covered by a dairy and orchard.

The parade of shops on the east side of the green replaced the house and gardens of 'an ancient time-worn edifice, in which the lord of the manor or other great man of the parish, might be supposed to have lived' — or so the writer and policitican, *Edward Bulwer Lytton* described the boarding school he attended in the early 1800's. The school was run by the *Rev. Charles Wallington,* who by all accounts, was not much of a scholar and had difficulty explaining Ancient Greek to his pupils even with the aid of an English 'crib'. However, he no doubt rose in their estimation when he purchased 'Black Bess', the favourite horse of King George III and specially trained for the King's protection to trample anyone who tried to seize her bridle while she was being ridden. Queen Charlotte sold the horse as soon as the King's increasing bouts of insanity made horse and rider a somewhat dangerous duo, but whether the Rev. Wallington ever had reason to be grateful for the horse's training, we do not know.

Haven Green in 1880 showing the new District Railway Station (left) and Great Western Railway Station (right), with spire of Ealing Broadway Methodist Church in background. The position of the cab-rank is the same today.

The opening of the Great Western Station, Haven Green, in 1838 brought few immediate changes to the green. The Town Hall has a delightful picture, painted in 1840, which shows an old steam locomotive trundling into the station, watched by a herd of unperturbed cows in a nearby field; but as you can see from the photograph reproduced here, taken the year after the District Station was built, houses have replaced the fields in the background, and the fine trees which shade the green today had then been recently planted. The District station was rebuilt in 1910 and its name changed to Ealing Broadway, the service being greatly improved by the opening of the Central line ten years later. Over 100,000 children passed through the station in the first four days of September 1939, when **Ealing Broadway** was one of the main interchange stations between London Transport and the GWR for children evacuated from London. The Great Western and District stations merged when the present Ealing Broadway station was built in 1964, but you can still see the old District booking-hall behind the shops to the left.

Castlebar Road (or Perryfield Lane, as the northern bit was called on early maps) may have been a secluded lane in Bulwer Lytton's time, but I suggest you try to avoid some of its 20th century traffic by turning aside into Eaton Rise; just past the splendidly ugly Victorian pile of **Haven Green Chapel,** which celebrated its centenary in 1981. The exterior of the church is in complete contrast to the symphony in wood and glass within: the west side has been replaced by a modern glassed-in vestibule, but the light oak pews and galleries (seating 800) are original and the chancel and organ date from 1928. **Eaton Rise** is a mixture of Victorian houses and modern flats, none of any particular interest except that *Henry Dobson*, the poet and biographer of Henry 'Tom Jones' Fielding, lived in the original No.75 at the turn of the century, before it was replaced by a block of flats.

Marchwood Crescent to your left, winds down into **Charlbury Grove** and back to Castlebar Road again, but before going any further I think I should explain that 'Castlebar' and 'Castle Hill' featured prominently in the names of many of the old residences I am about to describe, and that they live on in street-names today — a combination which makes for rather confusing reading. The only consolation I can offer is that the names have been confusing historians for years, but I have tried to make things as clear as possible!

Ealing Abbey in Charlbury Grove was built as a church for the Benedictine monks of Downside Abbey in 1899, after they had acquired the Castlebar House estate a few years earlier. The church later became independent of Downside and achieved Abbey status in 1955. It was extensively rebuilt in the original Perpendicular Gothic style in the 1960's to restore war damage, and the Chapel of St. Boniface in the right-hand aisle was funded by the West German Government. The church also serves the adjoining **St. Benedict's School,** which was established by Father Sebastian Cave in 1902. Girls have recently been allowed to join the sixth form.

Castlebar House was built in 1790, and became the home of *General Sir Frederick Wetherall* from 1817. He had served as aide de camp to the Duke of Kent in Gibraltar, and accompanied him to Ealing in 1801, later becoming a godfather to the Duke's daughter, the infant Queen Victoria. After the Duke's death in 1820, Castlebar House was let to *Archibald Constable*, friend and publisher of Sir Walter Scott. In a letter to Scott, Constable wrote: 'I am at last fixed here in an excellent house, standing in a field of 20 acres, nearly one third covered by fine elms, two centuries old, gardens etc . . . The situation is said to be healthy'. General Wetherall died in 1842, in his 88th year, and is buried in St. Mary's churchyard. His 'excellent house' was occupied by various orders of nuns after it was sold to the Benedictines, and from the 1930's it was used by a Catholic Men's and Youth Club. War damage and old age took its toll however, the house had to be demolished in 1973, and the gates in Castlebar Road were finally sealed up.

Castlebar House shortly before demolition in 1973.

Back on Castlebar Road, the tower blocks on the north side of **St. Stephen's Road** stand on the estate of another, even older mansion **Castlebar Park.** This house had already been built on the ancient **Absdonsland** when it was bought by *Sir William Bateman* in 1650, and remained in the family for two centuries. In 1752, it was leased to *General George Augustus Eliott,* whose heroic defence of Gibraltar against the Spaniards earned him the title Baron Heathfield. Later tenants included *Isabella Cunningham, Countess of Glencairn, General Wetherall* (before moving across the road), and *Sir Jonathan Miles.* Francis Swinden bought the estate in 1854, when the house was near to falling down, and demolished it a year later when he leased some of the land to Henry de Bruno Austin. St. Stephen's Road had been laid out in 1874, but no houses were built on the land for at least ten years. Many locals will still remember the house called **The Grange** which was built on the site of the old mansion in 1891, and only demolished in 1963.

Montpelier Avenue, further up the road on your right, was the scene of a very nasty double murder in the not too dim and distant past. The victims were 'Lady Menzies' and her daughter Vera, who ran a nursing home at No.1 Montpelier Avenue during the 1950's. The daughter was married to *Donald Merret, alias Ronald Chesney,* who, at the age of 18, was acquitted of murdering his mother for money, but went on to a career of forgery, blackmail and fraud after he had spent his inheritance. He dabbled on the black market in Germany after the war, but ran out of funds and slipped back into England in 1954, to relieve his wife of some of her's. After robbing her, he drowned the poor woman in her bath to make her death look like an accident, but was seen by his mother-in-law and had to kill her too. An international alert was put out for him and his body was found near Cologne a few days later, with a self-inflicted bullet-wound in the head. Fibres and hair, linking him to Lady Menzie's death were found on his clothing. Predictably, the agonised screaming of a woman is rumoured to be heard in the area on dark nights, although the house has long since been demolished.

That cheery tale should have brought you to the top of Castlebar Road, where I shall try to transport you back to more pleasant happenings at the turn of the 18th century. Here, on either side of what is now the road called Castlebar Park, stood the lodges of the main entrance to the Duke of Kent's home, **Castle Hill Lodge.** To your right, a narrow lane led through the fields to the low wooden buildings housing the soldiers who guarded these gates. **The Barracks** kept their name long after the Duke had departed, and were demolished when **Mount Avenue** was built in the 1860's. The little group of cottages beyond Park Gate marks the site today.

The Duke's home stood about half-way down today's **Castlebar Hill** road, overlooking the well-wooded pastures and gleaming cornfields of the Brent Valley and his own extensive 'pleasure gardens'. The house and estate had grown from a cottage and orchard which changed hands several times in the 18th century. Extra bits of land were either leased or bought to enlarge the estate, before it was sold to a Francis Burdett c.1773, whose son, then aged three, was to become *Sir Francis Burdett*, the popular radical politician who took part in the Middlesex Elections. The house was considerably improved by both Burdett and its subsequent owner, the MP *Henry Beaufoy*, and was bought by *Mrs. Maria Fitzherbert* in 1795, shortly after her marriage to the Prince of Wales (later George IV) had been annulled. The future King's younger brother, *Edward, Duke of Kent*, took over the lease in 1801 as a discreet country retreat for *his* mistress, Madam de St. Laurent. Unlike brother George, Edward was unencumbered by wife and child, and so was able to live with Madame quite freely.

The tendency of the sons of mad King George III to live beyond their means, provoked the Duke of Wellington into describing them as 'the damndest millstones about the neck of any Government that can be imagined'. Nevertheless, Edward was highly thought of in many places, especially in Ealing. He lived here, on and off, for about 12 years — having been recalled as Governor of Gibraltar in 1803, after his martinet discipline had caused several mutinies. From then on he was officially 'unemployed', which did not help his financial situation, but he devoted himself to patronising and supporting charitable institutions despite having only £7,000 a year to live on. This might seem a perfectly adequate figure for that day and age, but the Duke had very expensive tastes: he employed the architect, *James Wyatt*, and gardeners from the Palace at Kew to turn Castle Hill Lodge and its 38 acres of parkland, into a right royal residence; good mistresses did not come cheaply in those days either; then there were all the servants . . . evidently the Duke satisfied his thwarted military aspirations by holding a dress parade for his servants every day, and a hairdresser was even provided to ensure that the liveried retainers had not a hair out of place!

The Duke of Kent's Castle Hill Lodge — since replaced by St. David's Home.

M'lord and Madame eventually had to flee to Brussels to escape their creditors. The house, valued at £50,000, was put up for sale but at such a price no buyer could be found in the economic depression following the war with Napoleon. By this time, George had become Prince Regent and the death of his only child put pressure on the princes to produce a legitimate heir to the throne. Edward married the widowed daughter of the Duke of Saxe-Coburg in 1818, and a year later they returned to England for the birth of Princess Victoria. The need to sell his only asset was now even greater, but Parliament refused his suggestion to dispose of the Lodge by public lottery which was a shame as, considering the Duke's popularity, it could have been the answer to all his problems. The situation was still unresolved when the Duke died, eight months later, leaving the whole mess to be sorted out by his old friend, General Wetherall, as Executor and Trustee of his Will.

Two of the unsuccessful attempts to sell Castle Hill Lodge in 1827.

And what a millstone the house turned out to be for the Wetherall family! The contents of the house were sold by auction in 1820, but the house and grounds failed to reach the reserve price and were put up for auction again in 1827, when creditors were hounding the Duchess of Kent. This was also unsuccessful and Chancery then ordered the house to be demolished and sold piecemeal for building materials. A buyer was found but he went bankrupt without even paying a deposit for the materials he had carted away (some of which were used to build the Royal Oak pub on the Broadway). Finally, in desperation, General Wetherall bought the estate himself in 1829, but creditors had to wait for their money for another ten years because, it was suddenly discovered, a large part of the estate still belonged to the Isleworth Charity trustees, from whom it had been leased all those years ago. But, by 1839, all the litigation has been sorted out, the creditors were happy, and the long-suffering Wetheralls finally owned the estate they had not really wanted in the first place.

Their land roughly covered the area between today's roads of Castlebar Hill and Pitshanger Lane, and, Kent Gardens and Queens Walk. You can still see one of their boundary marker stones, with the initials 'FW', set in the brick wall on the left hand side of **Queens Walk**. After the general's death, his eldest son, George (who had also led a distinguished military career), built a new house on the site, which appeared in the rate books for the first time in 1845. While Sir George Wetherall was away in Canada, he leased the house to *Miss Rosa Lewis*, the benefactor of Christ Church; and in 1856, **Kent House** became the home of the ambitious architect, *Henry de Bruno Austin*, whose plans for developing a huge housing scheme between the GWR and the Brent, fell through after he got into financial difficulties. In 1870, the Wetheralls sold the house to *Thomas Harrison* (the one-time associate of those engineering pioneers, Stephenson and Brunel), and most of the surrounding land was bought by Ealing's surveyor, Charles Jones, who divided the former pleasure gardens into building lots. Kent House is still standing on Castlebar Hill, although considerably rebuilt and extended, and appropriately has been used as **St. David's Home** for disabled ex-servicemen since 1918.

Considering the brief time that the Duke of Kent actually lived here, the number of 'royal' street-names in the area seems a little overdone: Kent Avenue and Gardens, Queens Walk and Gardens, Sovereign Gardens, Princes Drive etc; but as Queen Victoria was celebrating her Golden Jubilee around the time that these roads were built, it was only natural for the council to emphasise her father's connection with Ealing. The Wetheralls were one of Ealing's oldest families but only **'Wetherall Cottage'** at the top of Castlebar Hill seems to have been named after them. Other houses of interest on the hill are **Courtfield Lodge** on the left, which served as a hostel for Belgian refugees during the First World War, some of whom helped to carve the rood screen in St. Stephen's Church; No.10 was given to what is now the **Royal National Throat, Nose and Ear Hospital** by *Sir John Smith Young* in 1932, and Nos.6 and 8 were later acquired by them as a hostel for deaf children; and at the bottom of the hill, the **Notting Hill and Ealing High School for Girls** was established in 1931, taking over the buildings and some of the pupils from another old school for girls, Girton House.

A B-type LGOC bus trundling up Castlebar Hill in 1914.

The junction of Scotch Common and Argyle Road in 1902, then known as 'Fiveways'.

Kent Gardens and **Cleveland Road** were the only part of de Bruno Austin's 190-acre proposed 'Castle Hill Estate' where houses were actually built in the 1860's. His plan (which is displayed at Ealing Reference Library) covered land he had leased from Pitshanger in the north, Drayton Green Farm in the south, and Castlebar Park and Castle Hill Lodge. The 20 or so houses that were built have now been replaced by modern flats and maisonettes, but most of the roads there today, follow his basic design. It also seems to have been his idea to build **St. Stephen's** on an island in the middle of a crossroads — you can see the church by looking down **North Avenue,** from Cleveland Road. The church was built in 1876 to replace the iron church in North Avenue, where St. Stephen's was founded nine years earlier. The tower, with its flying buttresses and spire, was added in 1888 to *Sir Arthur Blomfield's* design. The fate of St. Stephen's hangs in the balance at the time of writing: the cost of maintaining a church this size has proved too much for today's congregation and the church, which is a listed building, was declared unsafe and closed for worship in 1979. Services continue in the hall next-door until sufficient funds can be raised for more permanent accomodation. One of the proposed plans is for a smaller church to be built at the base of the old tower.

Further on, **Cleveland Park** gives you a chance to catch your breath for a while, so that you have enough energy to totter over the portals of **The Kent** pub (or Kent Hotel as it was called when it opened in 1929) on **Scotch Common.** The Cleveland estate was begun in 1924 and takes its name from Cleveland Lodge, one of the old mansions that stood on the east side of Drayton Green, above Drayton House. **Argyle Road** follows the line of the ancient 'Green Lane' from Perivale, which once crossed Drayton Green before continuing down Northfield's Lane, to Little Ealing and Brentford. It is still called Green Lane on the 1822 map. Sheep still grazed on Scotch Common well into this century, and the common itself has been absorbed into **Pitshanger Park,** which adds a nice rural touch to the end of this walk. The Kent, incidentally, boasts one of the biggest beer-gardens in the borough, with plenty of room for kids to enjoy themselves without being a nuisance to adults.

(Haven Green to Hanger Hill and Brentham — 2 miles) There are still cottages in Haven Lane, where this walk begins, although not all the original ones. The **Wheatsheaf** pub was in existence in 1851, and the **Haven Arms** in 1860 — but the latter was destroyed by fire and rebuilt in 1872. It was here that Ealing Tenants met to discuss their plans for Brentham. Cricket has been played at **Ealing Cricket Club** on the corner of Corfton Road, since 1871, although there is a record of a 'Grand Cricket Match eleven of a side Southall and Norwood People, against Ealing' as early as 1774. The present cricket pavilion was opened in 1900. If you turn left into Woodville Road and then first right, you will find **West Walk,** the modern version of the old footpath up to Hanger Hill. This quiet, paved path leads along the backs of houses built on the Wood family's farmland up to **Hillcrest Road.**

Until the 1970's, two reservoirs stood on either side of this road, a point known as **The Mount** in the 19th century. Mount Castle (an old, possibly Elizabethan, watchtower) was a popular resort in Victorian times, with tea-gardens below and a view as far as Windsor from the top — which you had to pay a penny to see. Sadly the tower was demolished to make way for **Fox's Reservoir,** named after *Edwin G. Fox*, chairman of the Grand Junction Waterworks, who opened it in 1888. The reservoirs held a total of 53 million gallons but were no longer needed when the Metropolitan Water Board took over, and the site was acquired as an 'open space' by Ealing Council in 1949. Very little has been done to it since beyond filling in the reservoirs, but plans are being considered to turn the area into a district park with a nature reserve at the northern end, and gardens and playing fields linked by footpaths to the adjacent **Hanger Hill Park.**

Mount Castle in 1880, before Fox's Reservoir was built on the site.

Fox Lane, to the left of the park, was a continuation of the old footpath from Haven Green to the Fox and Goose — one of the very few inns to feature on the 1777 map of the parish. The modern version is still standing on Hanger Lane (just south of Vicar's, or Alperton, Bridge) but is considerably less accessible to this part of Ealing since the amazing Hanger Lane Gyratory System was constructed in 1979. The *Wood family* owned most of the land on both sides of Hanger Lane from 1775 onwards. One of their houses, The Elms, at the end of Hillcrest Road, was bought by St. Augustine's Priory in 1914, and the Convent of the Augustinian Ladies' School was built on adjoining property a year later. Almost opposite Hillcrest Road, on the other side of Hanger Lane, stood the entrance lodge to Hanger Hill House, which was built for the Woods c.1790. *Sir Edward Montague Nelson*, chairman of Ealing Local Board and later of the District Council, leased the house from 1874, after Edward Wood had moved to Shropshire. Hanger Hill House was used as the headquarters of Hanger Hill Golf Club from 1901, but was demolished after the golf course was built over during the 1930's, and the site is now covered by the Tudor-style, Hanger Hill Garden Estate a Conservation Area.

*Hanger Hill c.1910 with a solitary motor car foreboding the
Gyratory System seventy years ahead.*

As you can see from the photograph, **Hanger Lane** has changed a little from the leafy lane it once was when (dare I say it?) passersby could hardly see the Woods for the trees. It became part of the North Circular in the 1930's, and today the thunder of heavy goods vehicles makes this one of the most unpleasant roads in the borough. Get away from it all by retracing your steps along Hillcrest Road through to the Mount Avenue cul-de-sac. On your left, opposite Birkdale Road, lies **Mud Lane** which, despite its name, is a pleasant tree-lined shortcut to **Helena Road,** reminiscent of the narrow lane leading to The Mount before Mount Avenue was built in 1865.

The site now occupied by **Montpelier Primary School** and the municipal park behind it formerly belonged to one of the leading public schools for girls, **Princess Helena College.** The college was first established near Regent's Park in 1820 as a memorial to Princess Charlotte, the only child of George IV. It was then known as the 'Adult Orphan Institute' and served as a training school for governesses and the orphaned daughters of military and naval officers. It was renamed in 1876 when Princess Helena (the third of Queen Victoria's daughters) became president of the governing body. The school moved to larger premises in Ealing in 1882, and was opened by Edward, Prince of Wales. The college moved to Hertfordshire in 1936 and the old school building was destroyed by bombing during the war. However the original gate-posts of the main entrance can still be seen at the southern end of Helena Road, and Ealing schooldays are fondly remembered by a number of ex-pupils who still live in the district.

Princess Helena College, Montpelier Road, 1882-1936.

This end of Montpelier Road was the scene of several other macabre happenings that have passed into local folk-lore. Elgin Court, (to your left as you come round the corner from Helena Road) stands on the site of an old Victorian house called **Eberslie Towers.** In 1887, twelve-year-old *Anne Hinchfield* killed herself by jumping from the high tower that gave the house its name. During the course of the next 50 years, no fewer than nineteen people committed suicide in the house, culminating in the case of a nurse who threw a child from the tower before leaping to her own death. The house lay empty for several years after this, until it was requisitioned by Ealing Town Council in 1944 as a store for furniture removed from bombed houses and shops in the area. Council workmen complained that a terrible smell pervaded the place, and refused to work there. Later residents were also bothered by the smell, not to mention inexplicable noises, invisible forces and the like. The ghostly face of a little girl at one of the windows was also seen on several occasions and was even photographed by parapsychological consultant, Andrew Green, who later published the photo and story in his book 'Our Haunted Kingdom'. Thanks to the close-up of this photo which appeared in an Ealing Gazette article, I could see the apparition quite clearly — although it did occur to me that the child must have been extremely tall for her age, as her shadowy features appear to fill the upper half of the window. But perhaps I'm seeing things!

EALING TENANTS PLAQUE WOODFIELD CRESCENT

Let 'invisible forces' move you back down Helena Road to where the 1934 block of flats, Mount View, marks the southern approach to **Brentham.** The Garden Estate owes its origin to *Henry Vivian*, a Liberal MP, who believed that ordinary working people should be given a chance to live in the sort of houses usually enjoyed by the more wealthy. He encouraged a group of local men to form a tenants association in which prospective residents could buy shares, thus enabling the company to purchase land and build houses. **Ealing Tenants Ltd.** was founded in 1901 and, with the support of many influential sympathisers (such as *Leopold de Rothschild*), sufficient capital was raised to begin building in Woodfield Road a few months later. The estate was the pioneer in the co-partnership housing movement which larger suburbs like Hampstead were to follow.

The absence of individual ownership encouraged a strong community spirit; and the careful design of the streets and houses added to the unity of the neighbourhood by avoiding the regimented, back-to-back terraces that predominated elsewhere. The estate was completed in 1915, and the resulting blend of gardens, houses, tree lined streets and communal recreation grounds, produced an area of special charm which it has retained to the present day, although only a sixth of the properties are still let to Ealing Tenants Ltd. In 1969, Brentham was designated a Conservation Area, and the **Brentham Society** was formed to foster awareness of the estate's history, and to preserve its character.

The tour of Brentham begins in **Brentham Way,** one of the last roads to be completed. The road curves round to the right, but we turn left into **Winscombe Crescent,** where the distinctive Nos. 1-7 are part of *Barry Parker* and *Raymond Unwin's* design for the 1907-11 phase of building. **Woodfield Crescent** to the left was built 1901-6 and you can see the Ealing Tenants plaque above Nos. 24 and 25. Turn right at the end of the road into **Woodfield Road,** where Nos. 71-87 **(Vivian Terrace)** were the first houses to be built on the estate. The parish church of **St. Barnabas** on the corner of **Denison Road** (named after F. Denison Maurice — one of the pioneers of the co-operative movement) was completed in 1916 as a somewhat belated addition to the estate. Rather surprisingly, no place of worship was included in the original plan, and St. Barnabas grew from a temporary church built in 1906, on the corner of Pitshanger Lane and Castlebar Park, to relieve some of the strain on St. Stephen's. This building was afterwards used as a parish hall, until damaged in the last war.

ST. BARNABAS CHURCH · PITSHANGER LANE ·

Pitshanger Farmhouse in 1902.

At the far end of Denison Road, stands the **Brentham Club,** or **Institute** as it was first called. It was built in 1911 as a social centre for tenants — the original plan provided for a hostel and second hall, but these extensions were never implemented. Strict rules of conduct were laid down by the Society, including a ban on alcohol and Sunday games — the latter being lifted in 1922, but no drinking was allowed until 1935. However, by the Second World War the old co-operative system had dissolved, and the Institute became a private sports club in 1947, with membership open to non-residents as well. The club has produced several well-known sportsmen, such as tennis-champion *Fred Perry* and cricketer *Mike Brearley*. The traditional children's May Day procession starts from here every year, and winds through the estate led by a 'Jack o' the Green' who returns his followers to the club grounds for dancing round the Maypole and the crowning of the May Queen. The site of the old **Pitshanger Manor Farm** on which the whole estate was developed, lies about half-way down **Meadvale Road,** and was used by Ealing Tenants for woodwork classes until demolished in 1908 to make way for the cricket pavilion and 5-acre sportsfield.

Holyoake Walk was severely damaged during the war and many of the houses have been rebuilt. It leads to Pitshanger Lane and the **Brentham Vineyard** on the next corner, where you do not have to be a member to enjoy a glass of wine and sample their excellent lunch-time snacks. The building dates from 1910, but in those days you could not have bought anything stronger than a bottle of milk on the premises, as they then belonged to United Dairies. The congregation of **Pitshanger Methodist Church** nearby, met in the Brentham Institute until the church was opened in 1913.

Pitshanger Lane was called Dog Kennel Lane in the 18th century, after one of the fields belonging to the farm; Wood Field, Barn Field and Fowlers Hill live on in some of the Brentham street-names. Sheep and cows grazed peacefully in the surrounding meadows in the early 1900's, and there was only one shop in the Lane in 1906. Progress was swift as Brentham developed however, and many shops lined the Lane by 1908. Today it forms a very pleasant shopping-centre, and **Pitshanger Park** close by offers benches for the footsore, and plenty of treelined space for children and dogs to let off steam. There is an entrance to the Park in **Barnfield Road,** (where you will find a gaily decorated toddlers' play-centre), and another at the west end of Pitshanger Lane, down **Woodbury Park Road.**

'Woodbury' was the name of another large farm on the site now occupied by **North Ealing Primary School.** The school was built in 1911 and replaced the rather primitive St. Stephen's school in Pitshanger Lane. As North Ealing was originally designed for those who 'kept their own carriages', the children of these wealthy residents were usually educated privately, and there was little demand for a public school. **St. Stephen's School** was founded in 1867 for the poorer children who lived in **Castlebar Mews,** where their fathers looked after the carriage-horses. Appropriately, the school's first home was in a stable at Kent House, until it moved to the red-brick building in Pitshanger Lane on the site of today's Co-op.

If you follow the footpath leading north-west across the Park from the Woodbury Road entrance, you will eventually come to the wooden bridge over the Brent at Perivale. But before taking up the tale of this tiny village, we return 'down south' for a closer look at one of Ealing's former sub-manors.

The Co-op Stores at 40 Pitshanger Lane in 1918.

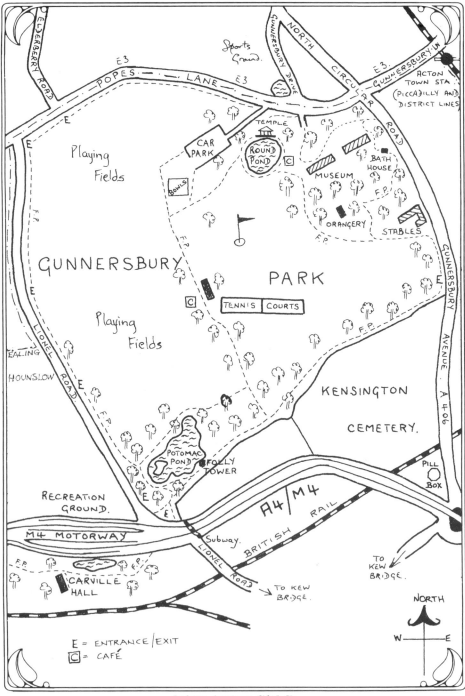

GUNNERSBURY   82

CHAPTER IV

'Some cry up for Gunnersbury,
For Syon some declare,
Some say with Chiswick's Villa,
None other can compare.'

Attributed to WILLIAM PULTENEY EARL OF BATH (1684-1764)

GUNNERSBURY is the best recorded of the several subsidiary Manors which once lay within the ancient parish of Ealing. It is also the only place in the old county of Middlesex to have a Danish name — a legacy from the Vikings who subdued London in 1016. The original name of 'Gunyldesbury' means 'fortified dwelling' and the popular theory that it was named after King Canute's aunt, Gunhilda, has never been authenticated. Like Ealing, the Manor of Gunnersbury was held by the Bishops of London during medieval times.

The first lady of the house to be mentioned in old records, was *Alice Perrers* or Peirce — a formidable lady indeed; if the stories about her are true. She began her career as maid-servant to Edward III's wife, Queen Philippa, and worked her way up to become the King's mistress in 1366. Edward was apparently so bewitched by her, that his attachment 'led him to the commission of many things highly unbecoming to his dignity' — a reputation he could ill afford as his standing in Parliament was already rather shaky.

After the queen's death, Alice's power knew no bounds. She insisted on sitting in the public courts of justice wearing the late queen's jewels (which Edward had signed over to her) and so interfered in state affairs that Parliament, who had watched their King deteriorate from a staunch old war-horse into a drooling lap-dog, forced her to take an oath 'never to return to the King's presence'. Despite this, she seems to have been present at his death-bed, and to have actually stolen the rings from his fingers!

But in 1378, Richard II banished her and confiscated her estate which by this time, thanks to the late King's generosity, consisted of most of the land between Ealing and Hammersmith, including Gunnersbury. Two years later however, the irrepressible Alice succeeded in getting her sentence revoked and she even managed to return to Gunnersbury in 1380 — this time as the wife of Lord Windsor, to whom the Manor was granted by Richard II.

After this somewhat turbulent period in its history, Gunnersbury passed through a series of ownerships more befitting its fine grounds: the 16th century cartographer, Norden, described the estate as being 'well scytuate for wood, ayre and water'; and we know from the survey taken soon after Alice Perrers was banished that it comprised some 228 acres of arable land, pasture, wood and meadow. During the 15th century, it was held by *Sir Thomas Frowyck*, an Alderman of the City of London, who donated the Church House (later called the old Cross House) to St Mary's parish church. He was buried in the churchyard after his death in 1485, and his eldest son, Henry, inherited Gunnersbury. There are sadly no detailed records of this early Gunnersbury House. It seems likely that it became very dilapidated over the years as it was completely rebuilt during the latter half of the 17th century, for *Sir John Maynard*.

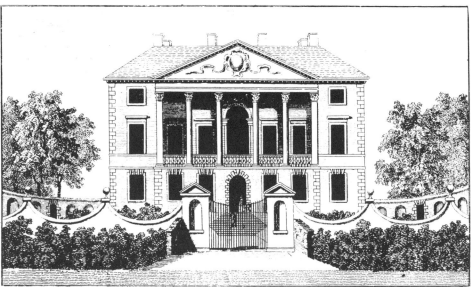

This 1759 engraving shows the formal gardens of the first Gunnersbury House (c. 1658 - 1801), which John Webb designed for Sir John Maynard.

Described as being 'the ablest advocate and soundest lawyer of his time', Maynard's remarkable life spanned almost 90 years — his career as a lawyer and politician covering the Civil War, Commonwealth, Restoration and 1688 Revolution. He began his legal career as a pupil of Sir William Noy, Attorney-General to Charles I, and entered parliament at an early age, conducting the evidence, in 1640, against those obnoxious ministers to Charles I, the Earl of Strafford and Archbishop Laud. In 1647 he was committed to the Tower on a charge of using seditious language and for presuming to question Parliament's attitude towards Charles I; but in spite of this, he was made Sergeant-at-Law (or Counsel) under Oliver Cromwell for the Commonwealth. During this time he silently used his position to influence the re-instatement of Charles II, and after the Restoration continued in office as King's Counsel. He similarly served James II and their majesties King William and Queen Mary — the latter appointing him one of the Lord Commissioners of the Great Seal at the ripe old age of 87.

Maynard moved to Gunnersbury in 1663, shortly after being knighted for his services to Charles II. He was extremely rich and spared no expense in building his new house. He employed *John Webb* (pupil and son-in-law of the famous Inigo Jones) to design the house in what was then an outstandingly modern style of Palladian architecture, with the grand saloon on the first floor opening onto an inset balcony behind a portico of Corinthian columns. Maynard died at Gunnersbury House in 1690 (aged 88) and lay in state in his beautiful mansion before being buried at St Mary's with great pomp and ceremony, after a funeral costing £1,300.

There are some lovely stories concerning this great man, who retained his keen wit to the end. It is said that when he welcomed William of Orange to England, the Prince remarked that the old man had probably outlived all the men of law with whom he had started his career — to which Maynard replied: "If your Highness had not come over, I should even have outlived the law itself." And on another occasion, when the infamous Judge Jeffreys taunted him with being so old that he had forgotten all his law, Maynard snapped back: "True, Sir George, I have forgotten more law than you ever learnt."

After the death of Maynard's widow, Gunnersbury passed to the Earl of Buckinghamshire who sold it to *Henry Furness*. He was mentioned in the parish Vestry Minutes of 1743 for the donation of a piece of his meadow adjoining the south side of the old churchyard, which enabled the burial ground to be enlarged. However, it is unlikely that Mr Furness felt the loss of this piece of his estate, if the following description of his house in 1753 is anything to go by: 'Gunnersbury House is situated between the two great roads and stands on an eminence, the ground falling gradually from it to the Brentford road, so that from the portico in the back front of the house, you have a fine prospect of the county of Surrey, the river Thames, and the borders for some miles, and also in clear weather a good view of London.'

In 1762, Gunnersbury House became the summer residence for another of the royal personages associated with Ealing: *Princess Amelia*, favourite daughter of her eccentric father, George II. She bought the house for £9,000 and is said to have spent twice this amount on improving the estate and plantations, before her death in 1786. While her nephew, the young George III, resided just over the river at Kew Palace, Princess Amelia entertained royalty and fashionable celebrities on a lavish scale at Gunnersbury. *Horace Walpole*, novelist, politician and man of many letters, was a frequent visitor from his house, Strawberry Hill, near Twickenham.

On one occasion, after a hard night playing cards with Princess Amelia, the Prince of Wales and Lady Barrymore (the legitimate daughter of bad Earl Rivers whose exploits are related in Chapter VII), Walpole's yawning was noticed by the Princess who insisted he write some verses about Gunnersbury as penance for his bad manners. Walpole sent her the following stanzas the next morning, excusing their poor standard on the grounds that he was 69, half-asleep and wrote them almost extempore — and by command!

'In deathless odes for ever green,
Augustus' laurels blow;
Nor e'er was grateful duty seen
In warmer strains to flow.

Oh! why is Flaccus not alive
Your fav'rite scene to sing?
To Gunnersbury's charm could give
His lyre immortal spring.

As warm as his my zeal for you,
Great Princess could I show it;
But though you have a Horace too —
Ah, Madam, he's no poet.'

Gunnersbury House as it looked in Princess Amelia's time, from the Horseshoe Pond.

Princess Amelia however, was delighted and in her reply wrote: 'Your yawning yesterday opened your vein for pleasing me, and I return you my thanks my good Mr Walpole, and remain sincerely your friend, Amelia.'

In accordance with her will, Gunnersbury House and ground were sold after Amelia's death (realising £12,000), and after passing through two further ownerships, was bought in 1800 as a business speculation by a *Mr Morley* who demolished the Webb house, divided the estate into two, sold the land, and presumably lived happily ever after making floor-coverings with the profits. (He obviously shared the same feeling for architecture as the fellow responsible for knocking down the Firestone Factory in 1980.)

For almost a century, the Manor remained divided and two new houses were built on either side of the original site. The eastern half of the estate was sold to *Stephen Cosser*, but it was possibly not until a *Major Morrison* took over from him in 1807 that the 'small mansion', also named **Gunnersbury House,** was built. The architect, *Alexander Copeland*, bought the remaining 76 acres of the estate and designed and built the 'large mansion', **Gunnersbury Park,** where he lived until its sale to Nathan Rothschild in 1835.

Nathan Mayer Rothschild was the son of a German financier who established the London branch of his father's bank in 1805 and built it up to become first among the banking houses of the world. The Battle of Waterloo caused the downfall of Napoleon, but made Nathan Rothschild a millionaire overnight: he staked his fortunes on the success of Britain in her duel with Napoleon and was the first to hear of her victory, using this knowledge on the Stock Exchange to a very profitable advantage.

His son, Lionel, who did so much for the civil and political emancipation of the Jews in Britain, inherited the property and engaged the architect *Sydney Smirke* (designer of the Carlton Club and the west wing of the British Museum) to make alterations and additions to Gunnersbury Park. Lionel died in 1879 and the estate passed to his son *Leopold de Rothschild*, who followed in his father footsteps as a generous supporter of causes.

Ten years later, the old Manor was once more united when Leopold purchased the adjacent Gunnersbury House (then the property of *Thomas Farmer*) for the use of friends and relatives. He further enlarged the estate by buying up some of the surrounding land, and the beautifully landscaped gardens became well-known throughout England. There is an amusing story concerning the Japanese Garden, a favourite of Leopold's, which he was showing with some pride to the Japanese Ambassador one day: after inspecting this charming spot, His Excellency is said to have remarked: "It is really very pretty and artistic, and I can honestly say that I have seen nothing like it anywhere in Japan!"

The estate was gradually dispersed after the death of Leopold de Rothschild in 1917; and in March 1925, the remaining 186 acres of land and both houses were bought for £125,000 by the then municipal boroughs of Acton and Ealing; with the help of Brentford and Chiswick. The park was formally opened to the public by the Rt. Hon. Neville Chamberlain in 1926. As a result of the alteration of borough boundaries in 1965, **Gunnersbury Park** (as the whole estate is now called) became part of the Borough of Hounslow which administers it, sharing the ownership with the Borough of Ealing. The 'large mansion' now houses the local history Museum and offices for the Park; while the 'small mansion' is used as a Teachers' Centre. Both buildings provide premises for the West London Parks' Training Centre, and residential flats for staff.*

*The Teachers' Centre closed in 1982, and future use of the building is still under discussion.

Sir John Maynard (1602 - 1690)

Princess Amelia (1710 - 1786)

Nathan Mayer Rothschild (1777 - 1836)

Leopold Rothschild (1845 - 1917)

Any walk through Gunnersbury Park is delightful, whatever the time of year, so instead of outlining a particular route round the estate I shall simply talk about the buildings and places you can see in the grounds, and leave you to discover them for yourselves. A word of warning however ... the condition of some of these buildings may come as more of a shock than a surprise in view of their historical value. Although all the buildings in the Park are Grade II listed, many have been allowed to fall into a state of decay because the Gunnersbury Park Joint Committee does not have sufficient funds to maintain them. Vandals have taken full advantage of this neglect and it seems somewhat ironical that the Councils concerned bothered to 'preserve' these historic buildings, when they are being left to rot anyway.

The **Museum** in the Rothschild's former home celebrated its Golden Jubilee in 1979 and, despite a small budget, is doing an excellent job to help residents find out more about the history, life and development of the Boroughs of Ealing and Hounslow. The collections cover local and social history including archeology (many items excavated from the site of Northolt Manor), topography, transport, laundry (from the old 'Soapsud Island' days of Acton), costume, toys and dolls. There are naturally many items connected with the Rothschild family in the Museum, although it is no longer furnished in the style of the period. Two of the Rothschild's 19th century coaches form part of an interesting collection of early forms of transport; and visitors can see the Rothschild motto ('*Concordia, Integritas, Industria*' — Peace, Integrity, Hard Work) and monogram painted over the drawing-room doorway.

This wide range of exhibits and information all began with a small collection of items of local interest which the then Borough Surveyor of Acton, Mjr. Frederick Sadler, had assembled over the years prior to taking up a post in South Africa in 1927. A committee of local people managed to purchase the Sadler Collection for £500 and it was displayed to the public for the first time in a room in the large mansion in 1929. Gifts, loans and purchases of many items gradually necessitated the expansion of the Museum into its present form (although still nowhere near being large enough for all the exhibits to be displayed), which today is run under the Curatorship of Miss Ann Balfour Paul. The Museum offers many other services to the public in the form of special exhibitions, guided tours and talks, identification of objects and help with student research — not to mention guide books on Ealing! Entrance is free and the Museum is open every afternoon from 1-5pm (2-6pm on weekends), March to October; and 2-4pm from November to February.

GUNNERSBURY PARK, 'LARGE MANSION

Overlooking the **Round Pond** to the west of the Museum, stands the **Temple** or garden pavilion — the only complete 18th century building still standing in the Park. Two pilasters and columns support the stone pediment which has an attractive design of leaves and scrolled ornamentation. The walls of the interior are lined with bas-reliefs of classical Greek scenes and the two fireplaces were added when it was used as a billiard room during early Rothschild ownership. The Temple was recently restored with the help of a contribution from the GLC and provides an appropriate setting for some of the musical concerts and other special activities run by the Museum. It is also being used for craft demonstrations.

The clay lining of the **Horseshoe Pond,** which used to stretch in front of the south terrace, was damaged by a bomb during the Second World War and, as a result of water escaping, the clay dried out. Post-war finances dictated that the pond be partially filled in, but the basin of the ornamental water gardens on the west side still exists — although there's no water there today.

South front of the present Gunnersbury House ('small mansion'). The extension on the left was added by the Farmer family who lived here from 1827 - c. 1889.

The handsome **archway** leading into the gardens at the west end of the terrace, dates from Princess Amelia's occupation; and to the south-east of the small mansion is a **bath-house,** said to have been Amelia's — but an awfully long way from her house, if so. The walls of the pavilion which later enclosed the bath-house, used to be decorated with shells and inset paintings, but are now daubed with graffiti. The archway and detached length of wall near the Gunnersbury Avenue entrance are similar in style to the bath-house, although it is not known exactly when they were built.

The **orangery,** south-west of the house, and **stable-block** (carved with the Rothschild coat-of-arms) with its attractive clock and bell, were designed by Sydney Smirke c.1836 and the main lodge at the Pope's lane entrance also dates from this time. The stable-block was the subject of a recent controversy when the GPJC proposed leasing them to a development company for conversion into offices, in an effort to raise money for use in the Park. This scheme would have conflicted with the pre-sale covenant placed on the land and buildings by the Rothschilds, which restricted their use to leisure and recreation. Thanks to the storm of protest raised by local people, the proposal was defeated but it remains to be seen whether any of the alternative adaptations of the stables put forward to the Committee, are ever put into operation.

One of the most appropriate suggestions was that the stables could profitably be used as a small riding school for children, and at the same time provide some much needed space for the Museum to display part of its collection of transport and agricultural machinery. The recently formed **'Friends of Gunnersbury Park and Museum'** (FROGS for short), hopes to raise funds for this and other projects in the Park. If you would like to see more public involvement in the running of the Park, join the FROGS and help them keep Gunnersbury one jump ahead of vandals and decay.

THE STABLES GUNNERSBURY PARK.

The **mock ruins** near the stable-block, were built to mask the stables from the view of the Farmer family at Gunnersbury House. They employed *W. Pocock* to do the job and he was also responsible for building the east lodge at the Gunnersbury Avenue entrance and adding the extension to the house.

Further south, near the 19th century battlemented gatehouse at the Great West Road entrance, stands Lionel Rothschild's **'folly' tower** used as a boathouse on the Potomac lake or fishing pond. The lake was formed by flooding a former clay-pit which was part of the land bought by the Rothschilds during the 1860's. A licence to fish in the pond (stocked with roach, tench, perch and eels) may be obtained from the Park Superintendent.

The **gardens** remained formal (see 1759 engraving) until Princess Amelia's occupation when, in the quaint words of a contemporary writer, they 'were greatly improved by her Royal Highness, to which many additions were made by Plantations, additional Grounds and elegant Erections.' Many of the trees you see today, were planted in Amelia's time.

Numerous modern sporting facilities are available to the public at Gunnersbury today: tennis, hockey, football, lacrosse, netball and rugby are all catered for; and there are also two miniature golf-courses, bowling greens and a boating pond for adults and children. Refreshments are available from two cafeterias during the summer months, and the lawns are perfect for picnicking. The Park is open from 7.30am till dusk, all year round.

Ealing Manor House, which had stood almost opposite the **Popes Lane entrance** to the Park since the 15th century, was demolished (c.1936) when Gunnersbury Avenue was re-routed from what is now Gunnersbury Drive, to become part of the new North Circular. Following Cromwell's destruction, the house was not rebuilt until the 18th century, probably by *Richard Long* who, in 1756, leased the largest share of Ealing manor. This included **London Stile Farm** (south of Gunnersbury) as well as the 245 acres between the Manor House and Ealing Common. After his death, the estate was divided into several smaller farms until reunited by *George Robinson*, who managed a tile kiln and brickfield on part of the land. These were converted into the **Potomac Lake** in Gunnersbury Park when *Lionel Rothschild* bought the freehold of Ealing manor in 1861. Most of the other land, including the Manor House, was later sold by the Rothschilds, although the *Gledstane* family retained the tenancy of the old mansion from the 1850's onward. The **Manor Farm,** on the north side of Gunnersbury Lane, was developed for housing during the 1920's.

Gunnersbury Lane was notorious for highwaymen and footpads during the 18th century. In 1774, *Dr. William Bell,* chaplain to Princess Amelia, was held up here by the infamous highwayman, John Rann, better known as *'Sixteen-Stringed Jack'.* Swift action by the Bow Street Runners brought Jack to justice two days later and huge crowds lined the route from Newgate to the gallows at Tyburn where Jack was hanged, wearing the pea-green suit with eight silver strings at each knee for which he was renowned.

Should you wish to continue your walk by the river, the **Lionel Road** exit from the Park provides easy access to Kew Bridge and Brentford. In the middle of the busy network of roads to the west of the lodge-gate stands **Carville Hall,** built in the late 1800's on the site of one of the many potteries which flourished in this area last century. The house, with its statue of Queen Victoria, was spared when the A4 cut through the estate in the 1950's, and it has been converted into flats for the Hounslow Parks Dept. but only a small portion of land has been preserved as a recreation ground.

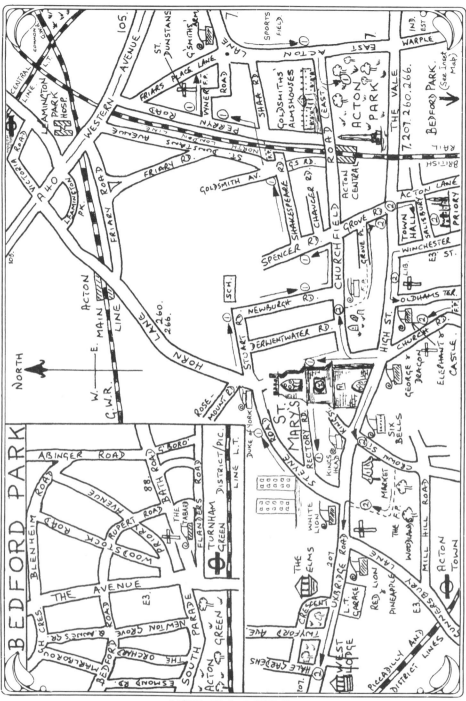

ACTON 92

CHAPTER V

Give over all the busy care
of gain and with despatch repair
To Acton for untainted air . . .
Why hardly breathe in stench and noise
When Paradise is in your choice?

Extracts from a poem to a wealthy friend by DR. EDWARD COBDEN (Rector of St. Mary's, Acton, 1726-64).

  today, would make the good Dr. Cobden turn in his grave. The town that he so enthusiastically recommended to his friend was then enjoying brief fame as a fashionable spa-resort, having been a popular summer retreat for well-to-do Londoners since the previous century. But by the 1860's, Acton's social status was on the decline as country estates south of the Uxbridge Road were sold for cheaper housing — attracting large numbers of laundry workers to the area, which was soon dubbed the 'Washtub of London'. The advent of the railway and availability of work in a variety of trades led to a spectacular population explosion during the latter half of the century, and building speculators gradually abandoned their plans for hard-to-let middle-class housing (with the notable exception of the elegant 'garden city', Bedford Park) to meet the demand for cheaper estates. The growth of engineering and other industries was accelerated by the First World War, and by the 1930's Acton had earned itself a new reputation as the biggest manufacturing town south of Coventry. Virtually all the town's historic houses were swept away in the name of progress, but enough parks and open spaces survive to prevent the commercial aspect from being too overwhelming.

Archeological digs in the Acton area have produced evidence of all the main prehistoric cultures — a Stone Age flint 'factory' was unearthed in Creffield Road, Bronze Age burials were found at Mill Hill Park, and Iron Age coins near Bollo Lane. But the names of these early settlements were buried with their occupants and it was not until the Dark Ages that Anglo-Saxon settlers gave their clearing the name of Actun, the 'settlement by the oaks'. Early in the 8th century Acton was given to the Bishop of London as part of the Manor of Fulham, so it was not mentioned separately in the Domesday Survey of 1086 and the first record of the name appears almost a century later, in St. Paul's Domesday.

Woods of oak and elm covered the northern half of the parish throughout the Middle Ages, and provided feeding grounds for the Bishop of London's swine. But although the Bishop controlled the wastes, commons and rights of hunting and fishing until the 17th century, he had no demesne in Acton and most of the land was rented out to local farmers for their own use — everybody holding a share in the five open fields of arable land. The main medieval settlement of **Church Acton** lay around St. Mary's at the 5-mile post on the highway from London to Oxford — the only proper road through the parish until the 18th century. A footpath connected the church to a smaller collection of cottages and farmhouses lining the green at **East Acton;** and another track led to a few houses in the extreme south of the parish on **Acton Green Common** — although these were linked more closely with the village of Turnham Green until the 1800's. The ancient freehold estates have a slightly more complicated history, but if you refer to Mr. Rowland's excellent map of Old Acton (reproduced on page 95) you should get a clearer picture of the places mentioned below.

It seems that some time before the Norman invasion, over a third of the parish had been granted to a knight called *Fulchered* in exchange for his military services. Modern historians believe that his estate covered most of the land west of Horn Lane and the Steyne, as well as the Berrymead/Mill Hill Park area below the Uxbridge Road. By the 14th century, the estate had been divided into smaller sub-manors — the major landowners being the *Dean of St. Paul's* (who held a 'mansion house' and about 200 acres — traditionally believed to have been in the **Berrymead** area) and the *Prior of St. Bartholomew's*, Smithfield, who occupied a moated 'manor place' (probably on what was later called **Friars Place Farm**) within a slightly larger estate, which stretched north of today's Rosemont Road up to the Willesden boundary. Both religious bodies were forced to relinquish their estates to Henry VIII at the dissolution of the monasteries, and he granted them to his court favourite, *Lord John Russell*, the first Earl of Bedford.

By the time Queen Elizabeth came to the throne, another of Acton's large freehold estates — belonging to the *Frowycks* of Gunnersbury Manor — was in the process of being divided up and sold. Two families, the *Vincents* and the *Garraways*, acquired the bulk of the property (which lay around the Steyne and eastern side of Horn Lane, as far as Friars Place) and it was they who built the forerunners of the large mansions such as **Acton House, Orger House** and **Bank House** which, together with Acton's proximity to London, encouraged courtiers and lawyers to summer here in Jacobean times. East Acton also attracted its share of the nobility during this period, several large houses having been built here during the 16th century — but none so fine as the one called **Fosters,** which *Sir Richard Sutton* bought c.1610 and turned into his country seat.

But while the bigwigs were conducting all these property deals, the ordinary citizens of Acton (who, because of epidemics like the Black Death, never numbered more than about 400) were quietly raising their sheep, cattle and pigs, and growing wheat on the small strips alloted to them in the open fields. Country life was to be rudely interrupted by the Civil War, however, when Acton was garrisoned by Parliamentary troops. Their commander, the *Earl of Essex*, is said to have made his headquarters at **Friars Place** and, in November 1642, he and *Major-General Skippon* led the attack against Royalist forces under *Prince Rupert* at the **Battle of Turnham Green** — which actually took place on Acton Green Common. Skirmishes from the battle spilled over as far as Acton High Street, but the Roundhead defence proved too much for the King's Cavaliers and they were forced to abandon their march on London.

Acton thus remained a Parliamentary stronghold until the Restoration, and it was on Acton Hill that a train of 300 coaches, headed by the Lord Mayor and aldermen of London, met Oliver Cromwell on his triumphant return from defeating Charles II at the Battle of Worcester. Many large estates were taken over by Cromwell's supporters — *General Skippon* came to live at **Acton House;** *Sir Francis Rous*, Speaker of the Little Parliament, bought **Bank House;** and the former Russell estate, which had passed by marriage to *Henry Somerset*, the Earl of Worcester, shortly before the outbreak of war, was confiscated by Cromwell and not returned to the Somerset family until 1660. Land also changed hands in East Acton when Fosters 'Manor' was bought by *John Perryn*, an alderman and goldsmith of London. He died in 1657, leaving the 200-acre estate to the **Goldsmith's Company.**

GROWTH OF ACTON

Roads made in 1860 under the Enclosure Commissioners' Award
of 1859

Entirely new thoroughfares . . . .
Re-formed from footpaths . . . .
Railways . . . .

Scale approx.
4″ to 1 mile.

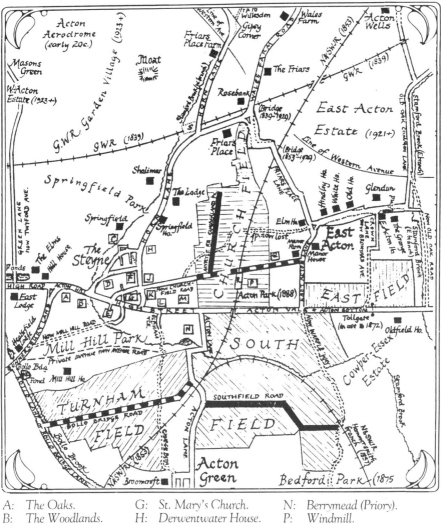

A:	The Oaks.	G:	St. Mary's Church.	N:	Berrymead (Priory).
B:	The Woodlands.	H:	Derwentwater House.	P:	Windmill.
C:	Steyne Mills.	J:	Acton House.	R:	Acton Stn., N&SWJR (1853).
D:	Bank House.	K:	Orger House.	S:	Acton Stn., GWR (1868).
E:	Cock & Crown Yard.	L:	Lichfield/Suffolk House.		
F:	The Rectory.	M:	Grove House.	Devised by R.N.G. Rowland

After the king was reinstated, normality and the nobility returned to Acton and the horrors of war and the Plague were soon forgotten in the powdered, patched and painted era of fashion that followed. The discovery of the medicinal properties of the springs on Old Oak Common gave the hamlets of **Friars Place** and **East Acton** a new lease of life as the gentry flocked to take the waters — which were renowned for their purgative powers. By 1746, Acton water was being sold in large quantities in London, although it was obviously better (for the soul, at least!) to be seen drinking it at the springs themselves — especially during May and June when the public breakfasts and assemblies were held. But, fashion being a fickle thing, high society moved on to other spas and Acton's race-course and assembly rooms (now covered by **Wells House Road**) were being put to more mundane uses by 1790.

Professional and military men continued to buy and build houses at Acton well into the 19th century. The 800-acre Somerset estate had been sold to *Benjamin Lethieullier* in 1736 and, towards the end of the century, had passed to his nephew, *Sir Henry Fetherstonhaugh*, who began the piecemeal sale of the estate to a new breed of middle-class landowners in the early 1800's. Large houses like **Mill Hill House** and **West Lodge** soon appeared in south and west Acton, and Acton Green also became increasingly popular; but Acton's society days were definitely over, and the few mansions contrasted sharply with the majority of houses. Agriculture and pig-farming were still the main occupations although the brickfields near Masons Green, the Steyne Mills carpet factory, and inns along the Uxbridge Road also provided employment. But a rapid switch to industry and trade took place in the large-scale development which followed the 1859 enclosure and sale of Acton's four remaining medieval open fields — **Church Field** and **East Field** above the Uxbridge Road, and **Turnham Field** and **South Field** below it.

Several new roads had to be built across these areas as a condition of the Enclosure Award, and the surrounding land was snapped up by speculative builders like the British Land Company, which had already purchased the Mill Hill estate. Rows of terraced and semi-detached houses began to cover **Mill Hill** and **Turnham Field** and, as fast as they were built, laundresses and their families from overcrowded Notting Hill flooded in to occupy them. Many set up their own **hand laundries** — encouraged by low rentals, soft water, and the fact that their husbands could find work in the new brickfields near the canal, and in the former East Field and South Field.

South Acton rapidly developed into a mixed industrial and residential district as although the newly established **Local Board** (which had taken over from the Parish Vestry in 1866) maintained strict control over the small builder, it lacked the firm hand of someone like Ealing's Charles Jones with the large land companies, whose building was virtually free from restrictions on use. By the end of the century, there would be over 170 private laundries in the area — their steady growth playing a large part in the town's phenomenal population increase from 3,000 to 17,000 in the first 20 years after enclosure.

There were naturally many attempts to promote more exclusive and expensive housing estates in the northern part of town — especially after the North London Railway extended its Kew/Richmond passenger service from **Acton Central Station** (opened in 1853) to Broad Street in 1865, and the GWR finally opened **Acton Main Line Station** in 1868, having run non-stop through the town for years. But despite public transport being further improved by a tramway service along the Uxbridge Road in 1874, the stigmatic tide-mark surrounding South Acton's nickname of *Soapsuds Island* proved difficult to wash from the minds of the class-conscious, and the supply of middle-class houses at **Leamington Park** and on the **Goldsmiths' Estate** continued to outstrip demand — the latter finally abandoning their plan for low density housing in the former Church Field, and selling the site to the Local Board for **Acton Park.**

Slightly better success was achieved during the late 1870's with the sale of new houses in the **Springfield Park** area (formerly Springfield Farm), and on a private estate laid out in the grounds of **Mill Hill House** by the builder *Walter Willett* (who also invented 'daylight saving'); but *Jonathan Carr's* carefully designed **Bedford Park Estate** on Acton Green was the only new 'classy' suburb to really come up to expectations. Cheaper housing continued to spread, however, and by 1901 Acton's population had reached 37,000 — most of whom were employed in the transport, building or laundry industries.

The early 20th century saw a new phase of industrial expansion as electrical and mechanical engineering firms began moving out to Acton from more crowded central areas. Many of the remaining country estates were sold off as factory sites: companies like CAV, *Wilkinson Sword*, *Bronnley Soap* and several motor car manufacturers took over the former **Cowper-Essex** estate south of the Vale where *D. Napier and Sons* produced the first commercially succesful 6-cylinder car engine at their works in **Stanley Gardens;** *T. Wall and Son* turned **Friars Place** into a sausage factory; and, during the First World War, the farmlands of North Acton were covered by munitions factories and **Acton Aerodrome,** where the *Alliance Aeroplane Company* made de Havillands and later developed their own 'Seabird' long-distance aeroplane — winner of the 1919 Acton to Madrid air race.

Acton's growing commercial importance was recognised in 1921 when, having been an Urban District since 1895, it was made a Municipal Borough with a population of 61,000. The post-war industrial growth of North Acton became closely linked with that of Park Royal, and the area was almost completely covered with factories by the Second World War. Since then, the Council has been the main builder — and demolisher — and had filled in any remaining spaces in the north and south, as well as redeveloping an area of 180 acres in and around the Town Centre. By 1965, when Acton was incorporated into the London Borough of Ealing, the population had steadied at around 70,000 and the town provided employment for some 40,000 non-residents.

Today, only a scattered handful of the many fine houses which graced the town a century ago survive — the best preserved being the **Goldsmiths' Almshouses** in East Acton, while **The Elms** and **West Lodge** are still intact but no longer used as residences. The refronted east wing of **Mill Hill House** is now No. 11, Avenue Crescent; **The Friars** has been incorporated into Leamington Park Hospital; and **Barrymead Priory** is clinging to survival under a patchwork of corrugated iron behind the Town Hall. For people who have lived in Acton all their lives and can remember the Way Things Were, the town still retains its identity; but the casual visitor will require a keen eye and vivid imagination to conjure up a picture of this once grand town from the few clues that remain — although I hope that this rather extended introduction has given you at least some idea of what went before.

ST. MARY'S PARISH CHURCH ACTON

The **Parish Church of St. Mary** stands at the heart of modern-day Acton, within a triangle formed by King Street, Market Place and the High Street. The clutter of surrounding buildings prevents it from achieving the same prominence which the first church on the site must have had when it was built c.1220 — but then the tiny village of Church Acton has changed a little since medieval times. The original flint and soft stone church was rebuilt in 1550 and remodelled again in 1836 — the latter result moving the Bishop of London to describe it as the ugliest church in his diocese. Fortunately this unworthy building proved much too small for the sudden increase in congregation which followed, and in 1886 it was replaced by the present red-brick version, designed by architects *H. Francis* and *S. S. Teulon*. For some years it presented an incongruous apppearance with the medieval tower standing alongside the new chancel, nave and south-east chapel, but a bequest from the *Ouvry* family enabled the distinctive, turreted **bell tower** to be added in 1876.

The new church had a seating capacity of 1000, but some of the pressure on its pews was relieved by the creation of separate parishes for South Acton (where All Saints was built in Bollo Bridge Road in 1872), East Acton (St. Dunstans) and Acton Green (St. Alban the Martyr), and the erection of numerous other mission churches to cope with Acton's rapid expansion. A number of items from earlier churches can still be seen in the present St. Mary's and include a 12th century **altar table** of black marble from Ashford-in-the-Water, Derbyshire; a **brass** of one *Humphrey Cavell* who died in 1558; and several 17th century **monuments** and mural tablets dedicated to former Acton residents such as the goldsmith *John Perryn, Viscountess Conway* (whose husband was Secretary of State to Charles I), and the wives of *Francis Rous* and *Major-General Skippon*. The silver-gilt **church plate** (including a large flagon, chalice and patens) was donated by *Lady Alice Dudley* in 1639.

Many famous Old Actonians are buried in the **churchyard,** but age and weather have made their tombstones illegible for the most part. Departed dignitaries like *John Perryn*, and his contemporary, *Sir John Godolphin*, who was a judge of the Admiralty Court during the Commonwealth, share the graveyard with less distinguished residents like the wheelwright, *William Aldridge*, who died in 1698 at the ripe old age of 114 — an excellent advertisement for Acton's once 'untainted air'! The actress *Elizabeth Barry* was buried here in 1713, having retired to Acton after a very successful London stage career during which she had played the leading role in many plays by the controversial writers, William Congreve and Thomas Otway. The churchyard was nearly full by the end of the 18th century and additional space was made in the former Church Field in 1863 — which we will be passing through in the course of Route 2.

The **rectors** of St. Mary's make more interesting reading than faded tombstones. The first on record was *Walter de Stubhere* who came from Stepney to take up his post here in 1228. He lived in a nearby house belonging to *Peter Fitzwilliam*, then the owner of Fulchered's estate, until the Bishop of London presented the parish with a **rectory house** just north of the church. Early rectors led a fairly peaceful existence compared with the the outrages suffered by *Dr. Daniel Featley*, who was rector at the time of the Civil War. His firm support of the King and strict adherence to the Book of Common Prayer aroused the wrath of the rebel troops, who converged on St. Mary's after the Battle of Turnham Green and broke into the church — where they smashed windows, pulled down the font and burnt the altar rails; then plundered the rectory, setting fire to several outbuildings. The fated Featley managed to escape, but was hunted from place to place until caught and imprisoned. He was eventually released but died soon afterwards, a broken man, having lost all his personal goods, property, and position to his Puritan successor, *Philip Nye*.

Nye had been a commissioner for Cromwell in his negotiations with Charles I, and became prominent in the ecclesiastical politics of the Commonwealth after the King's execution in 1649. The Independent religious beliefs of Nye and his successor, *Thomas Elford*, do not appear to have been shared by the residents of Acton, however, as only two out of the entire parish were admitted to communion during their ministries. Most of the congregation no doubt welcomed Elford's swift ejection and replacement by the Royalist, *Dr. Bruno Ryves*, after Charles II came to the throne; but some residents must have been won over to Puritanism, as the famous Nonconformist divine, *Richard Baxter*, gained quite a large, though illegal, following after he came to live in Acton in 1663.

Although he had held a chaplaincy in the Paliamentary army, Baxter's opposition to the execution of Charles I led to his appointment as King's chaplain at the Restoration; but his refusal to accept the 1662 Act of Uniformity (which compelled the Puritan clergy to conform to or leave the Church of England), forced him to forsake London and the established church. His choice of Acton was a happy one, as the subsequent Five Mile Act banned Nonconformist ministers from going within five miles of any corporate town where they had ever preached; but as Acton was exactly this distance from London, Baxter was able to continue living in his house near the church, to which many came from neighbouring parishes to hear him preach. After these private meetings, he always led his followers into St. Mary's for public worship — much to the annoyance of the legal incumbent, Dr. Ryves, whose complaints eventually led to Baxter's prosecution and departure from Acton in 1670.

More evidence of the backlash against Acton's time as a Parliamentary stronghold can be seen in the **parish registers** (which began in 1538), where the entry for the marriage of Major-General Skippon's daughter has been mutilated — perhaps by Bruno Ryves — and the word 'traytor' inserted in place of Skippon's rank. But peace and prosperity brought a series of less militant rectors to St, Mary's — such as the poetic *Dr. Edward Cobden,* who held positions at several other churches (including the archdeaconry of London) in between writing eulogies about the glories of Acton; and the *Rev. William Antrobus,* who was also rector of a church in the City but played a very active role in parish affairs during his time at Acton (1797-1852).

Meetings of the Parish Vestry had been held monthly in the church (or, more often, at the King's Head) since 1586, their chief concern being the maintenance of the poor; but from Antrobus' time onwards, the Vestry began to take over many functions of the manorial court. The affluent Antrobus subscribed a generous amount to the founding of **St. Mary's National School** in 1816, and had enough left over to later buy **Springfield Farm** for his sons. They also owned a house called **Springfield** to the west of Horn Lane, but sold both estates for the building of Springfield Park in 1877. Blocks of flats now mark the sites of the two old farmhouses, but **Antrobus Road** in South Acton serves as a lasting reminder of the former rector, and there are many memorials to his family inside the church.

The following walks give you the choice of heading east from St. Mary's to the old hamlet of East Acton and Acton Park, or making a loop round Central Acton and then taking in the sights of either West Acton or Bedford Park. Before going any further, I should like to acknowledge the tremendous amount of research and foot-slogging put into this chapter by my Man-in-Acton, *David Gordon,* who also devised the routes for the first two walks.

ROUTE ONE *(St. Mary's to Acton Park via The Steyne and Goldsmiths' Estate — 1½ miles.)*
Although none of the buildings shown around St. Mary's on Mr. Rowland's 1860 map survive in their original form (or any form at all in most cases), for the sake of posterity let us make a short diversion around The Steyne area before setting off eastwards — just to see where some of the houses of the great once stood, and learn a little of their history.

The confused junction of roads at the eastern end of the churchyard was no less busy a century ago; for, as the name **Market Place** implies, this road was Acton's main shopping centre — the stores lining the eastern side today, having then been recently built on the site of **Orger House,** which had burnt down in the 1850's. Formerly part of the *Frowyck* estate, this fine Jacobean mansion had been acquired in the early 17th century by one *Thomas Thorney* — a man who was either very dexterous or extremely clumsy as his occupation was the somewhat alarming combination of a 'barber-surgeon'.

It was evidently fairly profitable anyway, as he bought up several other Acton properties, leaving them and his London business to his nephew, Peter, who sold Orger House to *Sir John Trevor*, a gentleman of the Privy Chamber, in 1659. Many influential, but not particularly interesting, owners held the house between then and the fatal fire, after which the site became a sort of fair-ground crowded with hawkers' stalls, roundabouts and coconut-shies, until it was auctioned in 1877. 'Orger', incidentally, is possibly a corruption of *Lord Gerald Aungier*, a Irish peer who was married at St. Mary's in 1638 and may have been a tenant of old Mac-the-Knife Thorney.

At the risk of lead poisoning from traffic fumes, pause a little longer on the corner of Market Place and King Street and look across to the northern corner of Churchfield Road, where **Acton House** stood until late last century. Built by *Sir Henry Garraway* shortly before he became Lord Mayor of London in 1639, the house and 40 acres was bought by *Major-General Philip Skippon* in 1653 and remained in his family for several decades. Subsequent owners rented it out to wealthy visitors to Acton Wells during the summer season; but the *Countess of Derwentwater*, the tenant in 1716, stayed here under less happy circumstances — to attend the trial of her husband, *James Radcliffe*, the 3rd Earl of Derwentwater, for his part in the unsuccessful Jacobite uprising of the previous year. Although he pleaded guilty to high treason and threw himself on the mercy of George I, Derwentwater was beheaded on Tower Hill, and his widow moved to Brussels soon afterwards.

Almost a century later, the Countess' stay in Acton was commemorated by the then owner of Acton House, *Nicholas Selby*, who built **Derwentwater House** in the grounds north of his own home in 1804 and leased it to a fellow-Catholic, *Peter Kelly*. Between them the two families maintained a priest, whose cottage (in an orchard on the corner of Horn Lane and King Street) was used as a private chapel — although services were also attended by Irish labourers from the market gardens at Acton Green. The growth of religious freedom eventually led to the building of a more substantial church, **Our Lady of Lourdes,** in the High Street in 1892; but by that time the Selby's had left Acton, and Acton House was knocked down for shops two years later. Derwentwater House survived a little longer but, after a brief spell as Acton Liberal and Radical Club, was replaced by the Kinema cinema in 1909 — which in turn was converted into the present offices/warehouses during the Sixties.

Derwentwater House — built 1804, demolished 1909.

The discovery of hundreds of buried deer horns is said to have given **Horn Lane** its name in the 18th century, but the trackway existed long before that and is thought to have been the ancient highway towards Harrow which was recorded as Stone Lane in 1377. The gravel for this early road probably came from the banks of Stamford Brook near The Steyne (Old English for 'a stony place', locally pronounced as 'steen') which you reach by walking northwards up the modern version of Horn Lane, and turning left into **Rectory Road.** The present St. Mary's **Rectory** stands on practically the same site as the one donated by the Bishop of London in medieval times, and was built in 1925 to replace the grand, but decaying, parsonage erected by the *Rev. William Hall* 200 years earlier — which, if its reputed 3-storeys, 4 reception rooms and 14 bedrooms is anything to go by, certainly reflected the opulence of the clergy of that period.

The car-parks flanking the approach to Steyne Road cover the site of another of Acton's humble little mansions, **Bank House,** which the *Garraways* sold to Cromwell's Speaker, *Francis Rous,* in 1655. The name had nothing to do with money, however, but stems from from the fact that the house was built on the eastern bank of Stamford Brook, which now flows underground. The *Wegg* family (whom you can read more about in Route 2) inherited the recently rebuilt house in the late 18th century, but sold it some years later and it was used as a school prior to being demolished in the 1870's. The gardens, which had extended down to the High Street, were then built over with the cottages of **Nelson Place** (demolished in the 1960's redevelopment) and new offices for the Local Board at the High Street/Steyne Road junction. (See photograph on page 111).

According to 16th century records, **The Steyne** was originally a small piece of enclosed arable land that eventually gave its name to the whole area in the hollow between Horn Lane and Stamford Brook. Turning right into **Steyne Road,** you will pass the site of the 1887 **Jubilee Almshouses** which lined the opposite side of the road until their demolition in 1972. They were the last in a series of Almshouses which, for nearly 250 years, had provided a home for some of Acton's less fortunate residents. Rearing their not-very-pretty heads in the background are **Rufford** and **Moreton Towers,** named after the country seats of the *Savile* family (former owners of Berrymead) and built on the site of Acton's first industry — the early 17th century **tanyards** belonging to *William Finch.*

East Row on The Steyne c.1905 — as seen from Horn Lane. Replaced by today's Steyne House flats in 1939.

The tannery and mill-house were known as **Steyne Mills** when they were taken over by *William Gee's* dyeing and scouring works and rug manufactory in the early 1800's — later becoming the Empire Steam Laundry, and finally a Co-op jam and pickle factory. The state of the numerous small mill-workers' cottages which began to cover The Steyne during the 19th century, had practically reduced the area to a slum by the 1920's; but it was not until the late Sixties that the maze of crowded backstreets was cleared by Ealing Council for the present flat-blocks. If you follow Steyne Road round to Horn Lane, you'll find the only two institutions to have escaped this redevelopment — the **Blue Anchor** and **Duke of York** pubs. Both were rebuilt towards the end of the last century, but their predecessors provided a spot of cheer for many of Mr. Gee's mill-workers — although they would have known the Duke of York as the **Labourers' Arms** in those days.

A little way up on the eastern side of Horn Lane, **Springfield House** flats mark the site of the old Springfield Farm residence; while across the road from Springfield Park recreation ground, **Rosemont Court** in Rosemont Road shows where the Antrobus' second large house once stood. Other off-route, vanished properties in this area which local residents may like to know about (but not worth making any detours) include the 16th century **Butlers Farm,** which passed through the *Frowyck/Vincent/Thorney* chain to be rebuilt as **Acton Lodge** on the corner of the present Highlands Avenue and Horn Lane, and made way for the **Highlands Estate** in 1902.

Most of the houses west of Horn Lane from the railway line upwards, were built early this century on the land of **Friars Place Farm,** the one-time home of the Prior of St. Bartholomew's. After the break up of the Fetherstonhaugh estate, the farm and another 14th century moated site further to the west (now covered by North Acton playing fields) were bought by the *Wood* family of Ealing, who rebuilt the farmhouse in 1818. *Joseph Narroway* ran a home of rest here for 200 horses at the turn of the century, and the moat was filled in when it later became **St. Gabriel's Vicarage**; but the house was still standing as a private residence (called **Hamilton House**) at No. 367 Horn Lane until a couple of years ago. It had been empty since a disastrous fire in 1975, however, and was eventually pulled down.

But now let's leave the past behind and find some places that can actually be seen today. As there is no direct through-route from here to East Acton, you have to return to **Churchfield Road** — the quickest way being to double back down Horn Lane. But if you're a bit fed up with the traffic, carry on a short distance up Horn Lane, turning right into Stuart Road and then down Derwentwater or Newburgh to Churchfield Road — the first three streets (and near by Derwentwater School) all being built in the back-gardens of Derwentwater and Acton House c.1905. Continue eastwards along Churchfield Road, the first road across the medieval field in 1860, and just before turning the corner into **Spencer Road,** glance across the way to the **Sherborne Laundry** — one of the few survivors of those 178 establishments which gave Acton its 'Soapsuds Island' nickname in the 19th century. Spencer and **Shakespeare Road** take you through Acton's 'Poet's Corner' (developed in the 1870's after the opening of the City train service from Acton Central Station) and roughly follow the same line as the old footpath across the fields from East Acton to St. Mary's.

You enter the **Goldsmiths' Estate** at Goldmith Road/Avenue, where you'll find a footbridge over British Rail's North London line a little way up on the right. Emerging in **Perryn Road** (named after the man who began it all in 1656), you turn left towards Vyner Road which winds through what was once the orchard of Cotching's Farm to **St. Dunstan's Church** in Friars Place Lane. *Shaa, Vyner* and other roads in this area bear the names of celebrated 16th and 17th century goldsmiths — most of whom seem to have become Lord Mayors of London. The 200-acre estate which John Perryn left to the Goldsmiths' Company was greatly added to over the years and, prior to 19th century sales to railway companies and Acton Local Board, consisted of the area east of today's North London line (bounded by Western Avenue, First Avenue and The Vale), and another strip to the west incorporating Goldsmith Road, St. Dunstans Avenue and Friary Road. But after the sale of a large stretch for Western Avenue in 1921, the estate was gradually broken up for housing and by the Second World War only the site of the Manor House had not been built on.

St. Dunstan, a craftsman in fine metals who became Archbishop of Canterbury in 959, is the patron saint of the Goldsmiths' Company — which financed the building of this fine Early English-styled church in 1879. The proximity of the church to the Prior of St. Bartholomew's former estate is thought to account for a strange phenomenon which gave St. Dunstan's much unwanted publicity in the 1940's, when about a dozen monks wearing hooded, brown habits were regularly seen walking in procession up the centre aisle of the church. However, the present vicar of St. Dunstan's assures visitors that no ghostly habits have been glimpsed in recent years; and the ultra-modern changes currently being made to the church interior should encourage any lingering spirits to move on to other haunts.

While on the subject of ghoulies and ghosties, I can't resist repeating Mr. Rowland's delightful story about St. Dunstan getting people into hot water. The legend goes that he was working in his forge in Mayfield, Sussex, when the Devil appeared to tempt him in the guise of a beautiful maiden. Dunstan wasn't fooled for a minute, however, and seized him by the nose with the red-hot tongs he was wielding, whereupon the Devil rushed off across country until he found a cool spring in which to plunge his fiery appendage — and the waters of Tunbridge Wells have been hot ever since!

For the benefit of regular commuters from North Acton Station, I digress once more from the main route to include some information on places to be seen in that direction; but those of you who are just out for a stroll can turn right down Friars Place Lane to the Goldsmiths' Arms pub — and I'll meet you there in a minute or two. **Friars Place Lane**

A 19th century view of Friars Place — demolished 1902. (Now site of T. Wall & Sons' 'Friary' factory.)

has been in existence since the 17th century and used to connect East Acton with the mansion of Friars Place — occupied by the *Earl of Essex* during the Civil War, and later by *Richard Cromwell*, the Protector's son. The family of *Robert Tubbs*, a London horse dealer, owned the estate for most of the 18th and early 19th century, and the surrounding land began to be built up during the 1880's. The 'beautiful villa' had decayed by the time it was demolished in 1902, and the site was bought for a sausage factory (called **The Friary**) by Walls in 1919. Since the 1950's, the Friary factory has concentrated on ice-cream and it was from here that the famous 'stop-me-and-buy-one' tricycles were first introduced to the public.

Western Avenue now cuts across the line of the old Friars Place Lane, which was joined by *Wales Farm Road* in the early 1700's when the medicinal springs at **Acton Wells** began to attract attention. These lay to the north-east on **Old Oak Common** and after their popularity waned c.1800, the assembly rooms became a boarding school, and then a farm — demolished in 1906 for Wells House Road. **Leamington Park Hospital,** originally for isolation cases only, has stood at the junction of Western Avenue and Wales Farm Road since 1902, and incorporates as its administration block the only surviving 18th century goldsmith's house — a 3-storey building once known as **The Friars.** Cricket fans may be interested to know that the famous *Dr. W. G. Grace* once lived at No. 1 Leamington Park Road — diagonally across from the hospital; while residents of Rosebank Way, a little further south, are living on the site of a large Victorian villa called **Rosebank,** the one-time home of the Misses Henrietta and Mary Tubbs. **North Acton Station** was built in 1923 for the Ealing & Shepherds Bush Railway — now London Transport's Central Line.

And now back to the 1910 version of the **Goldsmiths' Arms** (first built in the 18th century), which still retains something of a country atmosphere with its long garden overlooked by a restaurant and a variety of bars. The same cannot be said of the old **East Acton Green,** however — the oversize traffic island at the junction of Friars Place and East Acton Lanes being all that remains of it. The village store and post office beside the pub made way for a car-park in 1964; the old Horse and Groom inn and Forge on the west side of the green disappeared even earlier this century; and apart from a few small houses like the **Beeches** and **Ivy Lodge** to the south, and the **Orchard Place** cottages at the eastern end, all the Victorian dwellings have gone. The fields north of the village became the links of **Acton Golf Club** in 1896, but these were also swept away when the Council bought the land for housing in 1919.

If you continue south down **East Acton Lane,** you will soon pass the site of East Acton **Manor House** on your left. Known as **Fosters** when built by *Sir Richard Sutton* c.1610, the mansion formed the nucleus of the estate bequeathed to the Goldsmiths by *John Perryn,* and was rebuilt in the 17th century. But by the late 1800's, it had become difficult to let and was demolished in 1911 — some wainscotting and a carved wooden overmantle being transferred to the Goldsmiths' Hall, London. The only clues to its existence today are the **gateposts** at the entrance to the **Sports Club** which took over the grounds. Further down on the right lies **Goldsmiths Close,** built in 1956 on the site of **Manor Farm.**

Turning right into **East Churchfield Road,** you will find Acton's most attractive historic buildings — the **Goldsmiths' Almshouses,** built by the Perryn Trust in 1811 and still in an excellent state of preservation . . . which makes a nice change! They overlook **Acton Park** which stretches down to the Vale (once known rather rudely as Acton Bottom), but in the old days the occupants would have been able to see as far as the boats on the Thames at Chiswick. Half of the 24-acre park lies on lands acquired by the Goldsmiths' Company at the enclosure of the Church Field, and sold to the Local Board in 1886. .

To your right as you enter the park stands an **obelisk** commemorating the *Earl of Derwentwater* — erected, according to the inscription, by his widow in the grounds of Derwentwater House, and moved here after the house was demolished. The fact that Derwentwater House was built almost a century after the Countess left Acton has only recently come to light, and its history was often confused with Acton House by 19th century historians. We must therefore assume that the obelisk originally stood in the those grounds north of Acton House which later became the gardens of its neighbour.

And with that bit of one-upmanship, I leave you to wander at your leisure through Acton Park which offers tennis courts, bowling greens and a childrens' playground for those who are still standing; and refreshments from the cafe or pavilion, and easy access to public transport for the rest of us.

GOLDSMITHS' COMPANY ALMSHOUSES ACTON

ROUTE TWO *(St. Mary's to West Acton via Berrymead and the High Street — 1¼ miles.)*
This walk also begins in **Churchfield Road,** but you turn off to the right just before the **Mechanics' Arms** (built in the 1860's) into the old cemetery — now, appropriately, a Rest Garden for present as well as past Acton residents. This land once belonged to Acton House but was sold to the Ecclesiastical Commissioners in 1863 when the churchyard at St. Mary's was becoming a little cramped. *Dr. John Lindley,* the well-known botanist and former resident of Bedford Park, was buried here in 1865. I read somewhere that the gardens were to be connected to the High Street shopping precinct, but could find no evidence of any such thing — so, unless you fancy scaling the 10 ft. wall at the end, I suggest you take the exit into **Grove Place** and work your way round to the High Street via **Grove Road.**

Between these roads lies **Acton Technical College,** built in 1928 on the site of an 18th century mansion called **Grove House.** The grove it took its name from may well have been the one mentioned in 13th century deeds for **Berrymead Priory,** which stands (but only just) behind the Town Hall in **Salisbury Street.** The list of Berrymead's distinguished residents puts all of Acton's other great houses firmly in the shade. I have already traced the estate's early history (from the Dean and Chapter of St. Paul's to Lord John Russell and the Somerset family) in the introduction to this chapter, so shall pick it up again at the Restoration when Berrymead was separated from the rest of the Somerset's recently restored estate and sold to *Sir John Trevor* of Orger House in 1661.

He was followed by *George Savile*, the first Marquis of Halifax and later Lord Privy Seal to William and Mary; and in 1708 *Evelyn Pierrepoint*, Duke of Kingston-upon-Hull, bought the house as a summer residence. His eldest daughter eloped from here to become *Lady Mary Wortley Montague* who, on her return from Constantinople where her husband was ambassador, introduced the inoculation for smallpox to England; while his younger daughter (married more sedately at St. Mary's), became the wife of John Erskine, *Earl of Mar*, who led the Jacobite uprising in 1715 and escaped beheading by fleeing to France with the would-be king.

The house was rebuilt in the mid-18th century, and embellished with Gothic-style battlements and turrets c.1802 when it was renamed **Berrymead Priory.** *Lord Edward Bulwer-Lytton*, the novelist and former Ealing schoolboy, bought the house for his wife in the 1830's, but lived here alone after an unhappy divorce — eventually moving to his mother's Knebworth estate in Hertfordshire. The only known religious use of the so-called 'Priory' occurred a few years later when the *Nuns of the Sacred Heart* resided here for a time before going to Roehampton. They were followed by an altogether more colourful and far less reputable occupant — the 'dancer and adventuress' *Lola Montez.* Her intimate

Berrymead 'Priory' after the 1802 Gothic restoration. The boating-lake in the foreground was supplied by water from the western branch of Stamford Brook, which ran through the grounds.

relationship with the Bavarian King, Louis I, is said to have precipitated the Bavarian uprising of 1848 — after which she came to England and married Berrymead's new owner, *Lt. George Heald*. However, only a month after the marriage she was charged with bigamy, and the couple had to flee the country!

In 1882, Berrymead was purchased by the Berkshire Estates Company who broke up the estate (which then covered the area between today's High Street, Acton Lane, Avenue Road and Oldham Terrace), selling the Priory to the Conservative Party as a Constitutional Club, and the rest of the land for new street and housing developments. The Council bought a large section of the land and, in the early 1900's, erected the **public swimming baths** in Salisbury Street (supplied by water from an artesian well), and the **Magistrates' Court** and Council offices in Winchester Street. Excavations for the Courthouse revealed the foundations of an 11th century building which was possibly part of the original mansion. After the Second World War the Priory was sold to the adjacent **Nevill's Bakery** and used as their administrative block until 1977, when the bakery was demolished and the house taken over by Ealing Borough Council.

The Council did nothing with their historic acquisition for several years, by which time it had deteriorated to such an extent that in 1981 they felt justified in publishing plans for its demolition as a 'dangerous structure' — despite the fact that the Priory is a listed building. But once again local conservationists rallied round and, in the resulting Public Inquiry conducted by the Department of the Environment, won their case for preserving Berrymead. Where the money is to come from for the mammoth task of restoration, is quite another matter — but let's hope it will not be too long before the old Priory presents a less battered face to the public.

Berrymead today.

Continue along Salisbury Street and up **Winchester Street** to the Uxbridge Road. To your right lies the **Town Hall** (built in 1939 on the former King George V Gardens) and, turning left, you will pass **Acton Library** — named after J. *Passmore Edwards*, the local philanthropist who paid for it to be built in 1900. He had also funded the building costs of Acton Hospital which opened in Gunnersbury Lane in 1898 on land donated by *Lord Rothschild*.

A little further west, on the opposite side of the High Street, a plaque to the left of Woolworths marks the site of the **public conduit** erected by our old friend *Thomas Thorney* in 1612. At that time it stood in the grounds of the **Bell Inn** which he had acquired, together with Orger House, the previous year. In his will he stipulated that some of the rent for the adjacent Conduit Close should be used for the upkeep of the spring, but in 1755 *Samuel Wegg* of The Elms had to take the persons concerned to court for refusing to pay the rent charge. *Rev. Antrobus* later used some of the money to replace the conduit with a new pump, but this had to be sealed in 1874 because of pollution from the graveyard in Churchfield Road. It is now stored at Gunnersby Park Museum.

Many residents will remember the two houses which replaced the Bell Inn in 1729, as **Lichfield and Suffolk House** were not demolished until the early 1960's. Once the homes of the nephews of the celebrated Drury Lane actor, *David Garrick*, the houses were fronted with shops and the **Globe Cinema** (later renamed the Gaumont) during the 1920's — all of which made way for the present shopping precinct.

Back on the southern side of the High Street, you pass the church of **Our Lady of Lourdes** before turning left into **Oldham Terrace** just before the **Elephant and Castle** pub. Oldham Terrace is part of the ancient footway to Acton Green, although its name is much more recent — the terrace of cottages which stood here until the 1972 redevelopment having been built by *Martin Oldham*, landlord of the George and Dragon in the 1840's. To your right as you turn the corner, you can see part of the 1837 **St. Mary's Infant School,** now used as offices by Acton Chamber of Commerce and other firms. The Employment Exchange, further down the road, was built in the 1930's on the site of St. Mary's Junior and Senior Schools, which moved here from their original premises in the churchyard in 1852. This southern portion of the lane was known as Love Lane in the days when it formed the western boundary of Berrymead, and a stretch of the Tudor wall around the estate can still be seen on the left — although the original brick has been much repaired with modern building materials.

A footpath on your right will take you down some steps on the far side of the Health Centre, and into **Church Road**. Here you turn right up to the High Street once more, passing the distinctive white frontage of the 1864 **Baptist Church** on the way. Acton's oldest building, the **George and Dragon Hotel,** stands a few hundred yards west along the High Street. Although most of Acton's early inns were either demolished or rebuilt during the 19th century, the George looks much the same as it did in 1620 — when it was probably built as two houses.

The D.I.Y. store just past the far corner of **Mill Hill Grove** was built in the 1960's on the site of another 17th century building — **Mitre House,** once the home of *William Lloyd*, Bishop of Peterborough and Norwich, who was deprived of his office for refusing to take the oath of allegiance to William III. A little further along (roughly on the site of today's Midland Bank), stood the house of the Nonconformist, *Richard Baxter*, which can be seen (together with Mitre House) in the adjacent photograph, taken shortly before its demolition in 1900. In his autobiography, Baxter says that he found near his house the charred remains of books burnt in the Great Fire of 1666.

Celebrations for Queen Victoria's Diamond Jubilee on The Mount in 1897. The famous Nonconformist Divine, Richard Baxter, lived in the first house on the right during the 17th century.

Both houses faced the triangular area known as **The Mount** in front of St. Mary's — which is shown as an open space in the picture, but had been covered with shops and cottages a few years earlier. The **village stocks** used to stand in front of the present Barclays Bank building — built for the London and South Western Bank in 1887. Carry on towards the **Six Bells** pub which was rebuilt in 1910 when the new Crown Street replaced the notorious slum of **Cock and Crown Yard** — a hangover from the 17th century Cock Tavern.

Before turning down Crown Street, have a look across the road at some of the buildings in King Street. **The King's Head** pub on the corner (where the vestry used to meet in the 1670's) was set further back when the High Street was widened in 1894. Next to it, the offices of the *Acton Gazette* stand on the site of the old **village forge.** Acton's first newspaper, the 'Acton Press', was founded in 1869 and won acclaim for printing criticism of the new Local Board. It folded a few years later, however, and was replaced by the 'Acton Gazette and General District Advertiser' — which, with various changes of name, has been published weekly ever since. Further up the road, the 1930's **Odeon Cinema** is now a large DIY store.

A short distance down **Crown Street,** you will find a stairway on the right leading to Acton's **Open Market,** where stallholders display their wares every Thursday and Saturday. Similar markets have been held in the village since 1232 — the year the Bishop of London first granted the right for a market to be held in his Manor of Acton on Mondays. A stroll through the market will bring you out into Crown Street again and, almost immediately on your right, there is a gate into an unexpected little park with plenty of benches for the weary, where we pause for a while to consider the varied academic history of the surrounding buildings.

This 'pleasure ground' (as the Council is fond of calling its open spaces) was made in 1903 in the gardens of a recently-demolished Victorian mansion called **The Woodlands.** The rest of the extensive grounds were taken up by **Acton County Grammar School,** the first purpose-built grammar school in Middlesex, which moved to larger premises near Heathfield Lodge in Gunnersbury Lane in 1939. (It now forms the comprehensive,

HIGHBURY/ ISLINGTON

GRANTBRIDGE ST N1 4 storey 4 bed e/t house, with self cont flat, garden. OIRO £440,000. F/H 0171 704 0648.

NORTHOLME RD N5 Large Victorian 5 bed house period feats. Ch. Gdn. F/H £385,000 Warmans 0171 226 2233.

N1 Spacious 2 bedroom flat in exclusive block in Canonbury. Lse/s.o.f. £155,000 Warmans 0171 226 2233.

RHIEDOL ST, N1. 4 beds, 3 bath, reception, kitchen, dining rm, gardens. Immaculate, f/hold £439,000. Tel: 0171 352 0245

BARNSBURY N1

An attractive light and sunny upper maisonette retaining many period features. 2 bedrooms, bathroom, reception room, kitchen/dining room. West facing roof terrace. Long forward Leafy views.
£215,000 L/H inc shr F/H

HOTBLACK AND COMPANY
0171 226 0160

ISLINGTON ANGEL N1

Charming period house set in this much favoured residential street close to the Regents Canal.
The property is bright and spacious and the unusual layout incorporates 4/5 beds. Bathrm. Shower rm. Kit/Dining rm. Recep with W/facing roof terrace. Garden rm. Pretty garden.
Price: £420,000 Freehold
Sole Agents: Hotblack & Co
0171 226 0160

HIGHGATE

SAVILLS

HIGHGATE, N6

A delightful detached family house, built in the arts and craft style in a wonderful semi-rural setting adjacent

KENSINGTON & CHELSEA

3 BED Corner Mews house SW7, Quiet, immac, 2 Rec, 2 bth, F/h. £375K. 0171 373 2589.

BRAMHAM GARDENS SW5 Sole Agents, 2nd flr flt, prd bldg, gdn views, bed, bth, recep, kit, 116 yrs £169,000. Plaza Estates 0171 581 7646

BUYING For Investment? Get the best results by using Senate International. For the highest yields & lowest capital requirement in London: 0171 408 2444 Edinburgh: 0131 226 3638 Cambridge: 01223 300012 Oxford: 01865 556002

CALLOW STREET SW3. Spacious 2 bed pb flat with balc. L/H. £200,000. Harrington Lowndes 0171 736 7272.

CHELSEA SW10 Luxury int. des. garden flat. New refurb, 2 bd, 1 bath, fully fitted kitchen + bathroom. Bright contemporary feel. £165,000. Leasehold J.Murphy 0151 7071050.

nr SLOANE SQUARE
Excellent 1 Double bed 3rd Floor flat, in good condition. Entrance hall, Reception, Fitted Kitchen, Bathroom, Central Heating, Entry Phone, Caretaker, Access gardens. Vacant possesion.
£175,000 Leasehold
Tel/Fax: 01798 873972
0181 891 6225

HomeSearch London

Let Us Search For You.
London's No.1 Specialist Search Company.

Tel: + 44 171 838 1066
Fax: + 44 171 838 1077
http://www.homesearch.co.uk/hom
HomeSearch (London) Ltd.
Knightsbridge, SW3

CHELSEA SW10 Attractive 2 bed flat on ground floor period house - Good condition. Long lease £119,000 Angela Stanley: 0171 352 0079.

CHELSEA, Oakley St, SW3. Investment immac 1 bed flat, u/grnd pkg. Prestigious mod. port blk. £160,000. L/H. 0171 603 4444

CHELSEA SW3 Elegant 2 bed conversion. Long Lease £290,000. Harrington Lowndes 0171 736 7272.

CHELSEA F/H. 5-6 bed family house, 2 receps, garden. £925,000. CKA 0171 823 6923

CHELSEA immac bright 1 bed flat in portered block, 32 yr lease, £98K Tel: 0171 405 4111.

CHURCH CL W8 Newly refurb flt, mezzanine flr, prtd PBB, rec, 2 bed, bth, kit, 985yrs £285,000 Plaza Estate 0171 581 7646

CORNWALL Gdns SW7, an exceptional totally re furbished very large 1 bed flat, 99 year lease. £295,000. Tel: 0831 484398

GARDEN 1 bedroom flat, GCH, offers over £142,000. Tel: 0181 742 7294 (no agents)

HOLLAND PARK Exquisit 4 bed, 3 bth apt 2 rec. Beaut priv gdn. F/H £780,000. 0171 221 9044

W·A·ELLIS

CHELSEA, SW3
Pretty period cottage in popular part of SW3. Ideal as rental investment/pied a terre.
2 BEDROOMS BATHROOM EN-SUITE SHOWER ROOM RECEPTION ROOM KITCHEN/BREAKFAST ROOM.
FREEHOLD **PRICE £450,000**
W.A. ELLIS: 0171 581 7654

Period Mews House
Beautifully refurbished & redecorated throughout to the highest standard. 3 bedrooms, 2 new bathrooms (1 ens), handbuilt kitchen & breakfast room, 2 large reception rooms with 12ft ceilings & stripped

IVERNA GARDENS W8. Stylish 3rd flr Apartment with balconies off Principal rooms in res-owned portered blk. 4 beds, bath rm, shower rm e/s, recep and dining rms, kit/b'fst rm. Share in FH. £600,000. Harpers 0171 938 2311.

KENSINGTON. Flat, 3 bed, 1 recep, 2 bath, 2 balconies, magnif. views, qck sale. £399,000. 0171 602 9342.

KENSINGTON, W14. Investment modern 3 bed house, kitchen/diner, OSP, 24 hr porter. £235,000. L/H. 0171 603 4444

KENSINGTON Stunning 4/5 bed refurb hse. Terr, balc, priv pkg £715,000. 0171 221 9044

LONDON HOMESEARCH Prof personal service for purchasers 0171 233 7222

MARY PLACE, Ladbroke Grove, W11. 3 bedrm house, 2 recep rms £175,000 Sole Agt Century 21 Kensington 0171 371 2100

MELBURY RD Spectacular triplex apart. 4 beds, 2 receps, conservatory, gge, 80 ft tiered gdn. 2,394 sq ft. £925,000 Park Lane Apts 0171 629 0763

NEVERN SQ SW5 Lux 2 dbl bed fully furn flat, sth facing, roof terr. £225,000. 0171 835 0380.

PHILBEACH GARDENS SW5 A spacious split level 2 bed, 2 shwr rm, 1 bth, roof ter flat £229,950. 0171 259 2779

POND PLACE SW3 Ex Local Authority 1 bed flat in excellent cond. Long Lease £130,000. Harrington Lowndes 0171 736 7272.

QUEENS GATE SW7 4th/5th flr maisonette, 3 beds, 2 baths, recep, kit+dining area, lift, share F/H £365,000. Druce & Co: 0171 581 3771.

REDCLIFFE SQ. W10, Beautiful 2nd flr flt, 1 bed, 1 rec, kitchen /diner. 53 yr lease. £195,000 No Agents. 0181 788 6602.

REDUCED SW7 Own St ent. GFF 2 dble beds, dble rec, kit/bfast, 999 years Porter, £325,000. Druce & Co 0171 581 3771.

SELECTION SW10 2/3 bedroom flats from £239,000. L/L, Druce & Co 0171 581 3771.

SLOANE SQ. 3 bed top floor flat, roof terr,3 mins tube, £290,000 Details/appt. 0171 730 0399.

SOUTH KEN Tired gdn flt. Full plans & specs to make lge 3bd/2bth. Direct access to comm gdns via small patio. £275,000. 0171 736 4539

SOUTH KEN, Campbell Crt, SW7. Immac 2 bed 1 bath, 1 WC flat. Gdn view. 24hr port, lift, Balc £270,000. L/H. 0171 603 4444

STAFFORD TERRACE W8. 2 spac apts newly dec. 2nd & 3rd flrs each with lge bdrm and recep, K&B. Short Lse. £185,000 & £165,000. 0171 720 4400.

SW7 1 bed mais on grd & 1st floors in period building. £149,000. 0171 9245347.

SW7 well loc cl tube & park 1 bd flt, 6th flr, lift, needs redec £145,000. Tel 0171 373 0033

SYDNEY STREET 1 bedroom basement flat in need of refurbishment. £105,000. Please call 0181 7462255.

W14 Oakwood Ct. 3 bed 2 bath 7th flr flat. Mans blk. £419,000 Westways 0171 792 2167

NEW HOMES

KNIGHTSBRIDGE

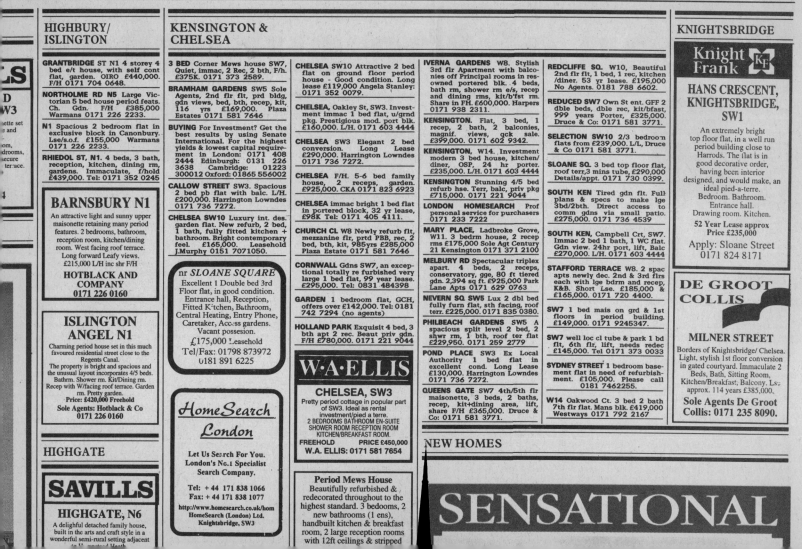

Knight Frank

HANS CRESCENT, KNIGHTSBRIDGE, SW1

An extremely bright top floor flat, in a well run period building close to Harrods. The flat is in good decorative order, having been interior designed, and would make, an ideal pied-a-terre.
Bedroom. Bathroom. Entrance hall.
Drawing room. Kitchen.
52 Year Lease approx
Price £235,000

Apply: Sloane Street
0171 824 8171

DE GROOT COLLIS

MILNER STREET
Borders of Knightsbridge/ Chelsea. Light, stylish 1st floor conversion in gated courtyard. Immaculate 2 Beds, Bath, Sitting Room, Kitchen/Breakfast, Balcony. Lse approx. 114 years £385,000.
Sole Agents De Groot Collis: 0171 235 8090.

SENSATIONAL

Queen of the suburbs

Good communications, beautiful open spaces and houses to suit most pockets — Ealing has it all, says Mary Wilson

EALING is known as the "queen of the suburbs" for its large open spaces and excellent links to central London. Its only real failing is a lack of good restaurants, which is surprising as there are many large houses occupied by the sort of people who like to eat out. There are good pubs, but nice bistros or more expensive eateries do not exist.

The oldest part of Ealing is centred around St Mary's church and many wealthy people built fine estates and houses in the 19th century in this area, although few remain today. In other areas of Ealing, however, there are a good number of houses dating from the early part of this century; these are large properties with equally large gardens, which appeal to families moving out of the centre of London.

The mainline Ealing Broadway station and three Tube lines — Central, Piccadilly and District — serve Ealing, making the area easily accessible from many parts of London. Heathrow is less than half an hour from South Ealing Tube.

"What will really make a difference is the St Pancras to Heathrow express line, which will stop in Ealing," says Kieran Ryan, director of John Spencer (0181-991 5599), a local estate agent. "That will attract a lot of airline people, as well as anyone wanting to be close to the airport. The good thing about Ealing is that it is not on the flight path."

Ryan says that he and other agents cannot believe the prices they are getting for some properties at the moment. "There are a lot of expats and investors who are buying in Ealing," he says.

"We have a large Japanese following because of the Japanese school and the investors like it because it is at the end of the Tube lines and you can easily get into the City."

Hamptons (0171-824 8822) recently took a development of flats by Bellway in Ealing to the Far East and sold 75% of it there.

None the less, there is a large core of people who move into Ealing when they first buy a home and then stay in the locality, moving up through the different price bands and areas as their finances improve. "I would say that about 75% stay within Ealing," says Ryan. "Because there is such a wide band of properties, there is a good mix of people, too."

Ealing, which has three postcodes, W5, W7 and W13, is home to Neil Kinnock and Sir Magdi Yacoub, the heart surgeon. It is blessed with a good selection of schools — both private and public — and many international students, who attend the recently expanded Thames Valley University. This also pulls in tutors, who need a home while they are working there, and parents who want somewhere to stay when they visit their children.

There are no parking restrictions in Ealing, which can cause problems as so many people dump their cars and jump on the Tube. Some of the larger properties are grouped around Walpole Park, the nicest open area made even more attractive by some particularly beautiful trees. The other more expensive areas, all within the W5 postcode, are Montpelier Road, Castlebar Road, Park View Road, Corfton Road and Warwick Dene, by Ealing Common.

A large two-bedroom flat in a conversion costs about £140,000, a little three-bedroom semi-detached almost £200,000 and some of the large six- or seven-bedroom houses more than £1m. Around Ealing Studios there are some lovely Georgian houses, which fetch about £600,000, while the much smaller houses in the Brentham estate, built in the early 1900s east of Pitshanger Park, go for around £200,000.

John Spencer is selling a double-fronted seven-bedroom house in Courtfield Gardens, W13, for £470,000, a six-bedroom detached house with self-contained flat in Woodville Gardens, W5, for £625,000 and a seven-bedroom house with large garden and enclosed heated swimming pool in Chatsworth Road, W5, for £950,000.

Because there is such a wide band of properties in Ealing, there is a good mix of people, too

More Property
page 17

Reynolds High — renamed in memory of the former Mayor of Acton who was Minister of Defence 1965-69.) The old Woodlands school was then acquired for the overflow from Acton Technical College in the High Street, which still uses it today. In 1956, all the advanced science and engineering courses were transferred to two new buildings in Woodlands Avenue to form Brunel College of Technology. This became **Brunel University** after moving to Uxbridge a few years later, and its former premises were taken over by **Thomas Huxley Teacher Training College** — named after the Ealing-born scientist. The college closed in 1980 and its buildings are now used by Ealing Technical College, which had shared the premises for some years.

Having broadened your mind with all these educational details, take the path branching to the right from the centre of the park and follow it through an alleyway, back to the **High Street.** Facing you across the road are the shops of two of Acton's oldest traders — where *Mr A. T. Overall* sold saddles, whips and horse-collars at the end of the last century, you can now buy your holiday luggage; while **Poore's Home Improvement Centre** is the most recent of the stores which have been part of the Poore family's business since 1820.

The building used by the **Luncheon Club** to the right of Poore's also has an interesting history, as it was built to house the Board's new steam fire engine in 1899. A near-disastrous fire at Steyne Mills in 1866 had shown Acton's fire-fighting equipment (which then consisted of chains of men with buckets of water) to be grossly inadequate, and led to the parish acquiring a manual pump which was kept in a shed behind the George IV pub. The advent of steam demanded bigger and better premises, however, and the **High Street fire station** met these requirements until 1938, when it was replaced by the present building in Gunnersbury Lane.

Turning left, you pass the parade of beautifully-designed Edwardian shops fronting the former Woodlands estate and come to the junction where **Steyne Road** meets the High Street at the foot of **Acton Hill.** The western branch of Stamford Brook now runs under the road towards Mill Hill, but the sketch of this corner in 1799 should give you some idea of what it was like when the main highway was some 12 feet lower, and crossed the stream at a ford. Right up to the turn of the present century, this water-splash and the steep hill which followed it were a constant obstacle for waggons passing through

A painting of Acton Hill in 1799, showing the ford over Stamford Brook and archway leading to Bank House in The Steyne.

Acton, and trace-horses always stood by to help heavy loads up the hill. On one memorable occasion in 1899, no less than 22 horses spent four hours hauling a giant boiler to the top.

The Gothic-style offices for the Local Board which once stood on the eastern corner of Steyne Road (after **Bank House** was demolished), were taken over by other firms when the Council moved to Winchester Street in 1910, but disappeared when the junction was widened in the Thirties. On the opposite corner stands the bland grey block of the 1972 **police station** — the most recent in a series on the site since Acton joined the new Metropolitan Police area in 1829, and watchmen ceased to patrol the town.

Moving on up the hill, you pass **Acton Hill Church,** built by the Methodists in 1907, and since 1976 shared by the United Reformed Church. It is on the site of another large Victorian house, **The Oaks.** The original 1857 chapel is still standing around the corner in **Gunnersbury Lane.** The lane itself was widened in 1906, resulting in some drastic changes to the two pubs which had stood side-by-side on the far corner for the last century — the **Pineapple** was demolished, and the **Red Lion** (purveyors of Mr. Turner's Chiswick Ales) rebuilt and set further back. Mr. Turner later joined forces with John Fuller and Henry Smith to create the well-known brewery of Fuller, Smith & Turner who, in a nostalgic moment in 1981, incorporated the old Pineapple's name into that of the Red Lion. The **White Lion** pub across the way, meanwhile, still retains the name it was given when first built c.1520.

Beyond the Red Lion/Pineapple is the London Transport **bus garage** — admittedly not one of Acton's most attractive landmarks, but not without significance. If you peer through the peeling paint on the walls you should be able to make out the words **'London United Tramways Limited'** and, high on the front of the depot, a plaque marks the opening of the building in 1895. Acton had public transport as early as 1764 when the 'Acton Machine' made a two-hour round trip every Saturday from the George to Oxford Street. By 1825, short-stage coaches were making four journeys a day from Acton to the City; and the London General Omnibus Company was running horse-buses from Acton Vale to London Bridge by 1856. The first trams made their appearance in 1874, but only covered The Vale/Shepherds Bush area until the service was taken over

Early bus and electric tram in High Street c.1910. (King's Head on right.)

by London United Tramways in 1895, and extended to the White Hart on Acton Hill. The Acton and Chiswick Gazette wrote an enthusiastic report about the new service, commenting on the trams 'built in the most up-to-date style', and the 'splendid lot of young Irish horses' which worked the cars. The paper was to get equally excited on the 10th July, 1901 when LUT's electric tram service was formally inaugurated, and flags flew all along the new extension 'from Acton, across Ealing Common to Ealing, on to Hanwell and then through almost open country to Southall'. Stirring times indeed . . . but before you're tempted to get carried away by one of the modern buses plying the same route, spare your loins for the last lap of this walk!

Cross over the Uxbridge Road and continue westwards until you come to the large gateposts on the right-hand side of **Twyford Crescent.** Behind them lies **The Elms** — the main block of which was built in the 1720's, shortly before it was sold to *Sir Joseph Ayloffe,* Keeper of the Record Office for George II. The single-storey wings were added some time after 1750 when the house was bought by *Samuel Wegg* — a lawyer, very active in parish affairs and well-known for his charity to less wealthy Actonians. He later moved to **Bank House,** which his wife had inherited, and died there in 1802. The Elms was let to various private tenants in Victorian times (the most noted being *James Shoolbred,* owner of the large Tottenham Court Road stores), and much of the 169-acre estate had been sold for building by the end of the century. Several extensions have been added to the house since it was taken over by **Twyford High School** in 1961.

The **public gardens** beside Twyford Crescent were built in 1903 over two large ponds, which had earlier been drained by popular request because of the unhealthy smell they exuded. You'll find an entrance to the gardens on the Uxbridge Road, and emerge in **Twyford Avenue** — once an old and winding trackway leading across The Elms estate to Masons Green Lane and West Twyford. During the 17th century, it was known as Mill Lane (from the windmill that stood in the grounds of the precursor to The Elms); but had become Green Lane by the time Samuel Wegg straightened out the worst of its bends in 1759. In his memory it was called Wegg Avenue for a time, but in 1901 the road was widened, built up, and given its present name.

That year also saw the demolition of **East Lodge,** which stood on the southern side of the Uxbridge Road, facing Twyford Avenue. The house was one of three built by *John Winter* on land he acquired from *Benjamin Lethieullier* in 1795 — the others being Heathfield Lodge in Gunnersbury Lane, and West Lodge, the only survivor, further along the Uxbridge Road. On Winter's death in 1843, Heathfield and East Lodge were added to the Rothschild's Gunnersbury Park estate and leased out. *Elizabeth Beauchamp* lived at East Lodge in the early 1880's, prior to becoming *Countess von Arnim* and the author of a popular book of autobiographical sketches, 'Elizabeth and Her German Garden'. Interestingly enough (well, I think so anyway!), she later married John, the 2nd Earl Russell, whose ancestors went all the way back to that 16th century John Russell, Earl of Bedford, who was once master of all you survey.

And that just about brings us to the end of this walk. If you carry on through the western half of the public gardens, you will come out into **Hale Gardens** — named after *Sir Matthew Hale,* Lord Chief Justice of England during the reign of Charles II, who lived in Acton for several years before his death in 1676, and was a close friend and neighbour of Richard Baxter. Turn down to the **Uxbridge Road** and, on the far side, tucked away between West Lodge Avenue and the Tudor-style Grosvenor Court flats, you will see the slate roof of John Winter's **West Lodge** — now used as the offices of **Acton Housing Association.** You have now reached the western boundary of Acton which, until early this century, was marked by Fordhook Bridge carrying the Uxbridge Road over **Bollo Brook.** This stream (now piped) rises near Masons Green and flows south under today's Bollo Lane to join Stamford Brook and the Thames in Hammersmith. The name means 'bull hollow'.

(Bedford Park) As none of the approaches to Bedford Park make particularly inspiring walks, I suggest you jump on a south-bound E3 bus near Acton Town Hall which will take you down to Acton Green Common via The Avenue — the first street to be developed on the estate. Alternatively, you could take a District line tube to Turnham Green Station. A walk round a housing estate is not everyone's idea of a 'fun outing' — even if the estate happens to be the parent of England's garden suburbs — so, rather than devising a set route, I shall try instead to present a picture of Bedford Park as a whole which I hope will be of interest to the general reader, as well as providing enough information for the architecturally-minded visitor to make their own way around this one-time home of artists and the literati. (Those who would like a more detailed history of the estate are advised to obtain a copy of Mr. T. Affleck Greeve's *Bedford Park, A Pictorial Survey* from their local library.)

Although the leafy lanes and rather grand houses in Bedford Park add a welcome air of distinction to the predominantly industrial area of South Acton, it is difficult to imagine just how strikingly unusual the scheme appeared when it was first conceived by *Johnathan Carr* in the 1870's. Carr's plan was to provide a completely self-contained housing estate with its own church, schools, shops etc which would allow the newly-educated, but poor, middle classes of the industrial age to indulge their tastes at prices they could afford. The site he chose in the south-east corner of Acton parish, centred around the 18th century Bedford House (then occupied by his father-in-law) and its neighbours, Melbourne and Sydney Houses, on **Acton Green Common.** The estate thus offered all the advantages of a rural setting plus easy access to the City from Turnham Green Station — opened by the London and South Western Railway Company in 1869, and the only station to serve the area until the District line was extended to Ealing Broadway ten years later.

This idea of a sort of cultured commune was in keeping with Carr's radical and artistic family background; but, as a speculative builder, his commercial interests were by no means lacking and he consciously designed the estate to appeal to readers of the popular artistic magazines in which his scheme was widely advertised. At the time there was a growing trend away from heavy Victorian architecture back to more simple, traditional designs; but Carr went even further by reviving the so-called 'Queen Anne' style — neither Gothic nor Palladian — with the help of various distinguished architects such as *E.W. Godwin, E.J. May* and, in particular, *Norman Shaw*, the leading light in the Aesthetic Movement. Their designs produced some 30 different variations on the basic red-brick theme, enlivened here and there by bits of Renaissance, Dutch and Flemish detail.

Bedford House, from which the estate took its name, had recently been vacated by the famous botanist, *Dr. John Lindley*, curator of the Royal Horticultural Society Gardens. Most of the trees he had planted on the land surrounding his home were carefully incorporated into the new estate and a few still flourish there today, although his orchard lives on in street-name only. (A branch of the Russell family, Earls of Bedford, is said to have lived on the site of Bedford House during the 17th century; but, by a strange coincidence, the present house is actually named after its builder — the brothers Bedford). Work on the estate began in 1876 and within a year the first houses in The Avenue were ready for occupation. Woodstock and Bath Road were next to be developed and the estate expanded rapidly as Carr acquired more and more land in the area, including the lease of the triangular, detached portion of Ealing — known as Stamford Brook Grounds — which lay to the east of Woodstock Road.

Street-names reflected people and events of Queen Anne's time, such as that great General, the Duke of **Marlborough** and his two victories over the French at **Ramillies** and **Blenheim.** The latter earned him the reward of the Royal Manor of **Woodstock** where he commissioned Sir John **Vanbrugh** to build **Blenheim** Palace. Joseph **Addision,**

BEDFORD PARK, CHISWICK, W.
THE HEALTHIEST PLACE IN THE WORLD

(Annual Death Rate under 6 per Thousand).

About 500 Houses on the Estate, all in the picturesque Queen Anne style of Architecture.

Close to TURNHAM GREEN STATION

Trains every few minutes.
The Estate is built on gravelly Soil and has the most approved Sanitary arrangements.

A Garden and a Bath Room with Hot and Cold water to every house, whatever its size.
A Kindergarten and good Cheap Day Schools on the Estate, and a School of Art.
Also Church, Club (for Ladies & Gentlemen), Stores, "The Tabard Inn," Tennis Courts, &c.
Several houses now to let at rents varying from £30 to £130.

1881 lithograph by Hamilton Jackson (first Principal of School of Art) advertising Bedford Park. Group of buildings to left of Church includes The Tabard inn.

the writer and poet, and Sir Isaac **Newton** are also remembered, as is **Esmond,** the hero of Thackeray's novel about that period; but, surprisingly, Alexander Pope and Johnathan Swift were not considered worthy of a mention.

William Morris was then just beginning to revolutionise the art of house decoration and Morris wallpaper was another feature of the new houses in Bedford Park. They were also supplied with baths 'fitted for hot and cold water' and buyers were assured of 'the most perfect system of open drainage . . . absolutely preventing any back draught of sewer gas'! The basic plan could be modified to suit the individual and prices were extremely reasonable: 'Inglewood', for instance, the house built in The Avenue for *Moncure Conway* (an American Unitarian minister who wrote enthusiastic articles about the estate for *Harper's Magazine*) consisted of a drawing room, dining room, billiard room, study, 7 bedrooms, kitchen, scullery, larder, cellar, box-room and balcony roof — all for the magnificent sum of £1500 on a 99-year lease plus £24 p.a. ground rent. Today, a Norman Shaw-designed, semi-detached house in Bedford Park sells in the region of £100,000.

Social life centred on the **Club,** designed by Shaw/May and paid for by Carr, which opened in The Avenue in 1879. Carr had earlier served as political secretary to the MP *John Stuart Mill,* one of the first male supporters of suffrage for women, and the Club was completely free of any sexual discrimination. Here women could smoke, play billiards, use the reading room and even enter into debates with male members — who included some of the best conversationalists in the country. The **Church of St. Michael and All Angels,** the **Tabard Inn** and the stores in Bath Road (all designed by Shaw) opened in 1880 and the **School of Art,** east of the inn, was built in the following year. **Bedford Park School** was established in 1884 at **Sydney House** (a large Georgian mansion on the eastern corner of The Avenue) and caused quite a stir in educational circles by allowing boys and girls to attend lessons together, omitting Religious Instruction from the curriculum and holding classes from 9.30-12.30 only, so that pupils could glean more from a richer home-life.

The liberated atmosphere attracted large numbers of creative people who included the painter, *Lucien Pissaro* (62 Bath Road) whose father, the Impressionist *Camille Pissaro,* painted several views of the neighbourhood; the artist *J. B. Yeats* (8 Woodstock Road) and his more famous son, *William Butler Yeats,* who founded the Irish Literary Society at 3 Blenheim Road; the historian, *Frederick York Powell* (2 and later 6 Priory Gardens); the playwright, *Sir Arthur Wing Pinero* (10 Marlborough Crescent); and the architect, C. *Voysey* (7 Blandford Road) who designed the roughcast 'artist's house' at No. 14 South Parade to contrast with its neighbours.

As with anything new and different, Bedford Park had its fair share of critics and to many it symbolised a pretentious way of life. G. K. *Chesterton* portrayed it as Saffron Park in *The Man Who Was Thursday,* claiming that it attracted only the second-rate (although his wife was from Bedford Park!); but in his autobiography he praised the residents for giving something to the community and getting a sense of identity in return. By 1886 however, the boom was over. Letters appeared in the *Acton and Chiswick Gazette* complaining of a 'lower element' creeping into the estate; Carr's Bedford Park Co.

Bedford Park Club in 1881 — now CAV's Social Club. Johnathan Carr's home, Tower House, can be seen in background.

collapsed and was taken over by the Bedford Park Estate Ltd.; changes in parish boundaries together with the earlier transfer of 'Ealing Detached' gave almost half the estate to Chiswick; and, as more of South Acton was developed, Bedford Park gradually merged with the surrounding area and lost the originality which had made it so fashionable.

Sydney House was rebuilt as flats c.1900 — the former Bedford Park School having moved to Priory House in Priory Road a few years earlier. (After various changes of name, the school became Chiswick and Bedford Park Prep. School in 1932, and is still there today.) Bedford House was converted into flats in 1924 when the shops known as Bedford Corner were built around its garden on South Parade. The imposing Tower House, designed for Johnathan Carr by Shaw, which stood near the Club on the western side of The Avenue, was replaced by St. Catherine's Court during the 1930's and the Club itself was closed during the Second World War. The much changed building is now used as CAV's Social Club. About 30 houses were damaged by bombing during the War and the School of Art was completely destroyed. Technical classes had begun there in 1895 and led to the formation of Acton and Chiswick Polytechnic which, by 1908, was the largest poly in Middlesex. Hounslow Borough College now covers the site. The Georgian Melbourne House is still standing (west of Bedford Corner), as are the Church and the Tabard at the eastern end of the common. The pub is decorated with beautiful blue-green tiles made by the ceramic artist, William De Morgan, who had a kiln in Chelsea from 1871 to 1905.

The many undesirable changes to the estate over the years, led to the formation of the Bedford Park Society in 1963 which, under the patronage of Sir John Betjeman, succeeded in getting Grade 2 preservation orders placed on 356 houses. The whole estate is now a Conservation Area, shared by the Boroughs of Ealing and Hounslow. The revival of community spirit is evidenced in the Bedford Park Festival which has been held on the first Saturday in June every year since 1967. Visitors are welcome to take part in the Fair on the Green and various evening entertainments organised by residents, and can learn more about the estate's architecture and past personalities with the aid of Mr. Greeve's new booklet, 'A Guide to Bedford Park in the form of Two Walks', which he published in time for the 1983 Festival.

Beyond the boundaries of the estate, the common widens out and it was here that Prince Rupert and his Cavaliers are said to have camped in retreat from the Roundheads after the Battle of Turnham Green — although it seems rather close for comfort. There are swings and other playthings to keep the children amused behind the 1887 church of St. Alban the Martyr, while adults should find something to their taste at the Duke of Sussex pub. Fairlawn Court, the large block of flats at the western end of the green, takes it name from the former mansion on the same site (demolished 1879) to which Dr. Lindley removed after vacating Bedford House.

Postscript

Readers who are not already familiar with the work of Mr. R. N. G. Rowland, a life-long resident of Acton (from whom the most interesting facts in this chapter have been gleaned), are urged to get hold of a copy of his 'Street-names of Acton' from Acton or Ealing libraries. An enlarged and revised edition of this booklet is due to be published in 1983 (probably under a new title) and should be available from local booksellers as well. Mr. Rowland has also devised a series of Acton rambles for the 1895 Association of Actonians — a rather exclusive organisation when it was first established in 1945, as membership was restricted to those who had been resident in Acton for a minimum of 50 years. Conditions of membership are considerably more relaxed today, however, and any interested resident can join; but the Association's chief aim still applies — to keep alive the story of Acton as it Was for future generations.

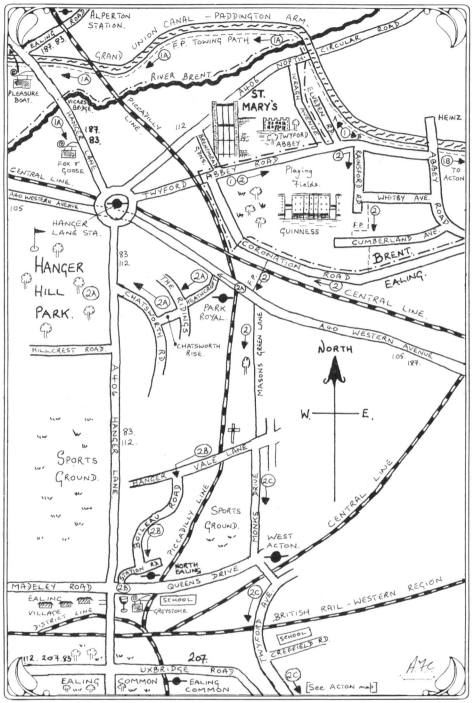

CHAPTER VI

In one of my rambles in the vicinity of the Metropolis,
I was much pleased with the rural simplicity of West Twyford.
The whole place consists only of the church and the manor-
house. . . which is surrounded by a moat.
Extract from a letter to the 'Gentleman's Magazine' (July, 1800)

WEST TWYFORD has undoubtedly had the most uneventful history of any suburb in the borough — which is hardly surprising when you consider that the description quoted above was exactly the same in the 16th century, and did not really begin to change until after the First World War. The last fifty years have more than made up for the centuries of neglect however, and today the 'rural simplicity' of this tiny parish lies somewhere under the North Circular and a mass of housing and industrial estates. Cattle can still be seen grazing in the fields attached to the Guinness Brewery which was built on part of the old manorial estate in the 1930's, but although their grounds greatly improve the landscape, they are strictly private and now lie outside the borough boundary.

The two fords over the River Brent which gave Twyford its Saxon name of 'Tveverde', are no longer even in the parish. They probably corresponded with today's Vicar's Bridge on the Alperton side of West Twyford, and Stonebridge at East Twyford in Willesden. Around 930 AD, King Athelstan presented Twyford to the Canons of St. Paul's who appear as the owners in the Domesday Book. Even at this early stage Twyford is described as two villages, and West Twyford became even more independent after the manor was leased to lay-landowners early in the 12th century, one of whom, *Henry de Capella*, erected a chapel close to the moated manor house for families in the surrounding farms and cottages.

In the mid-13th century, the Capella's married into the *de Bohun* family, descendants of the great Norman baron, Humphrey de Bohun and the Earls of Hereford; and by the time they had finished sorting out their differences with Henry III and Simon de Montford, the village was so severely depopulated that subsequent lords of the manor were able to enclose all the freehold land into their own estate. In 1361, the lease of the manor was taken over by a London fishmonger who paid the Dean of St. Paul's the very reasonable rent of a red rose at Midsummer; but even this rather tenuous link with its former owners appears to have ceased as West Twyford passed through a succession of wealthy London merchants. Thumb-nail sketches of the most memorable Lords of the Manor follow. *John Lyon*, a London grocer and future Lord Mayor, bought the manor for £120 in 1540. He is popularly believed to have been the founder of Harrow School, but modern research shows that he died almost 30 years before his more famous namesake — so West Twyford is denied this link with greatness!

The manor remained in the Lyon family for nearly a century and although they neglected the church and allowed the other properties to run down so that the manor house was the only building left standing, the value of the land must have risen as *Robert Moyle*, a well-known lawyer of the day, paid £520 for the estate in 1637. After his death, his wife married *Sir Christopher Clapham* who was unable to prevent the Willesden parish officers from claiming West Twyford as a sub-parish in 1650 and so had to contribute towards their poor rates which were especially high after the Civil War. It was only after the manor had been sold to the MP, *Sir Joseph Herne*, that a case was successfully brought against the Willesden authorities and West Twyford was re-instated as a parish in its own right. The Herne family retained the manor until the 19th century, but although they

WEST TWYFORD 119

rebuilt the church and replaced most of the 'fine old mansion house' with farm buildings in 1715, the estate was leased to *Henry Lott* from about 1690 onwards.

The year 1800 saw a new century and a new tenant at the manor-house — *Thomas Willan*, a man who was to bring many changes to the parish. Besides being the stagecoach proprietor of the Bull and Mouth Inn near Aldersgate, he also ran a large dairy farm in Marylebone Park (better known as Regent's Park today) and it was probably the lush meadows surrounding West Twyford that first attracted him to this quiet back-water. He liked it so much that in 1806, he bought the estate outright and proudly became Lord of the Manor, running it as 'his little independent sovereignty'. Like all good kings, the first thing he did was to demolish the old manor house and build himself a new castle, complete with battlemented towers (although he had filled in the moat), which he called **Twyford Abbey.** The architect was *William Atkinson*, a pupil of James Wyatt who had designed the Duke of Kent's 'palace' on Castle Hill. Willan later added **Twyford Abbey Farm** to his little kingdom and extended what was then called Twyford Lane from the farm to the newly-built Paddington Arm of the canal, where a third house, **Canal Cottage,** was erected by the Grand Junction Company in 1821.

Willan's eldest daughter, Isabella, continued to live at Twyford Abbey after his death when she and her husband, John Douglas, changed their surname to *Douglas-Willan* so that some of their 14 children would perpetuate her father's name. Twyford Abbey and 19 acres of land was sold to *William Allhusen* a few years before the parish was united with Greenford and Perivale to form Greenford Urban District Council in 1894; but the Douglas Willans retained the major part of the estate, selling some to the Royal Agricultural Society in 1900 for their unsuccessful showground at Park Royal. A station called 'Park Royal and Twyford Abbey' opened in Twyford Abbey Road in 1903, a year after the Abbey had been bought by the *Alexian Brothers* as a Roman Catholic rest home. By 1907, the Brothers and their patients formed half the total population of 95; but factories attracting more residents were soon being built on the failed Park Royal site and although plans for new houses and roads were delayed during the First World War (when West Twyford Farm became part of the Army Service Corp's large horse compound), by 1931 the population had risen to over 300.

The last of the manorial estate was bought by *Arthur Guinness* in 1933, and the final 'face-lift' came a year or two later when the North Circular Road sliced through the parish, removing any remaining beauty-spots. Guinness took over the old railway sidings when Park Royal Station was moved to Western Avenue in 1936, and the Park Royal site gradually extended over Willesden and North Acton to become the leading industrial estate in West Middlesex. Today, Twyford Abbey and Canal Cottage are all that remain of the 'old' parish which became part of the municipal borough of Ealing in 1926. When boundaries were changed in 1935, angry residents found themselves once more transferred to Willesden, but raised such a storm of protest that the authorities swiftly reversed the decision and so West Twyford, whether it liked it or not, was incorporated in the new London Borough of Ealing in 1965.

Old St Mary's and Twyford Abbey.

The fortunes of the little **Parish Church of St. Mary** have been closely linked with West Twyford's lords of the manor. The chapel founded by *Henry de Capella* in 1181 paid tithes to St. Paul's, but was otherwise quite independent. *Gilbert de Cranford*, the first rector, was given a house and 10 acres of land but with the fall in numbers of parishioners towards the end of the 13th century, his successors found it difficult to make a living and the benefice was augmented by payments from manors in Buckinghamshire (where the Capella's owned land) and tithes from Gunnersbury Manor which was then considered part of the chapelry. Rectors were appointed fairly regularly by the lords of the manor until 1439 but as the extra-parochial payments lapsed it is likely that a chaplain was only found on special occasions and the church glebe and tithes were gradually absorbed into the manorial estate along with other freehold land.

In 1575, the parish was temporarily joined to St. Mary's, Perivale when the Bishop of London appointed a rector to hold both positions. This arrangement worked well until 1631 when Twyford was once again left vacant, but as the then Lord of the Manor, George Lyon, lived in Perivale, he was not personally bothered by the oversight. He must therefore have been very surprised when someone took the matter to a higher authority and King Charles I appointed *Charles Lambe* as rector in 1635. Lambe himself was not terribly pleased with his new position and shortly afterwards presented a bitter petition to Lord Coventry, Keeper of the Great Seal, stating that the whereabouts of his parsonage was yet to be discovered; that the Lyons had enclosed the glebe lands and sold them to Robert Moyle as part of their estate; and that he was still waiting to be paid for his services! Robert Moyle died soon after this and perhaps his successors were kinder to their rector, for he dropped the case before it came to be heard.

The old church was rebuilt in 1712 by *Frederick Herne* and the rectors of Perivale preached here once a month throughout most of the 18th century. The name 'Vicar's Bridge' was probably adopted around this time as visiting rectors would often stop off at the Fox and Goose Inn for spiritual refreshment after services at Twyford, before taking a boat or wading across the river back to their own parish. Dr. Nicholas, headmaster of the Great Ealing School, also assisted in services quite regularly. The parish registers begin in 1722 and the births, deaths and marriages of the *Lott* family feature prominently. *Thomas Willan* redecorated the church in 1808 to match the Gothic style of Twyford Abbey, and also extended his gardens over the old farm lane between the church and Abbey to make it look more like a private chapel.

Services ceased after the Abbey was sold to *William Allhusen* in 1890 and the church became very dilapidated and overgrown with ivy. Nevertheless inhabitants protested when the Alexian Brothers tried to use St. Mary's as their chapel in 1902, and the Rural Dean, *Rev. B.S. Tupholme*, then rector of St. Stephen's in Ealing, took the case to the Bishop of London after he was refused admission to the church by the Brothers. As a result, St. Mary's was restored and reopened in 1907 and the curate of St. Stephen's was appointed to the benefice in plurality, by King Edward VII. The church has not looked back since. Services continued throughout the First World War; a church hall was added in 1937; and in 1958, a new church was built to the design of *N. Cachemaille-Day*, incorporating part of the old one as a Lady Chapel.

The oldest monument in St. Mary's belongs to *Adriana Gifford*, daughter of *Richard Lyon*, who died c.1601. Two imposing marble wall memorials to *Robert Moyle* and his son

Interior of the old church (now a Lady Chapel) of
St. Mary's, West Twyford.

Walter, dated 1638 and 1660 respectively, also survive. An exciting discovery was made in 1918, when **church plate** consisting of two flagons, a chalice and paten all stamped with the Moyle coat of arms and dated 1697, was discovered in a crumbling box in a London bank and returned to St. Mary's. It had probably been deposited for safe-keeping soon after it was presented as it showed no signs of having been used. A **churchyard** was recorded as early as 1297 and most of the lords of the manor and their families have been buried here, although few of the very old tombs survive. The churchyard has been extended southwards in modern times, but to the east near the old church you will find many familiar names connected with Ealing's history, such as *Thomas Wood* of the Hanger Hill family; *Samuel Millett* of Perivale; the *Daws* of 'The Grange' in North Ealing; *Rev. B.S. Tupholme*, to whom the church owes so much; the *Goddards* of Twyford Abbey Farm; and, more recently, *Mr and Mrs Basil Holmes*: the former was churchwarden of St. Mary's and the latter wrote the first ever history of West Twyford, which should be read by anyone wishing to know more on the subject.

I have had great difficulty in selecting a walk around West Twyford ... not, I regret to say, because the choice is so wide, but because the few places of interest now stand in a very built-up area and the only open space in the near vicinity lies outside the borough boundaries, along the factory-lined towpath beside the canal. If you do not object to a fairly long walk, a visit to the parish could be combined with one of the routes outlined in the chapters on North Ealing or Acton, and I have devised a rather extended 'short-cut' to enable you to do this. According to the recently-published Borough Plan (which acknowledges that Twyford is suffering from 'a severe local park deficiency'), part of the grounds of Twyford Abbey currently on lease to Guinness, is to be made into public 'open space'. So in the not too distant future, visitors may be able to admire the Abbey at slightly closer quarters without running the risk of trespassing.

Work begins on the conversion of the tree-lined Twyford Avenue into Twyford Abbey Road — April, 1935.

ROUTE ONE *(St. Mary's/Twyford Abbey to the canal, then along the towpath to Ealing or Acton — 1¼ to 2 miles)*
As you can see from the style of the houses surrounding St. Mary's church, **Brentmead Gardens** was built in the mid-1930's. It leads into **Twyford Abbey Road** which was just a shady lane when Thomas Willan erected **Twyford Abbey** in 1808 and landscaped the gardens around his new home. Fine old cedars still flank the central block of his house, although its embattled parapets were removed in 1935 and many other alterations have been made since the Alexian Brothers established their Rest Home here in 1902. Except for the addition of the east wing in the 1960's, most changes have blended well with Atkinson's original design.

Near the entrance to the **Guinness Sports and Social Club** opposite, a peeling red-and-white sign warns traffic to 'Beware Cattle Crossing'. It dates from the days when the cows on the home farm run by the Brothers at the Abbey, were taken over by Guinness, but they changed over to beef cattle in 1963 and the crossing is now seldom used. In the distance stand the three great blocks of the **Guinness Brewery,** designed in 1936 by *Sir Giles Gilbert Scott,* grandson of the architect of Christ Church, Ealing. His many works include the rebuilding of the House of Commons after the Second World War, and Waterloo Bridge; although the Brewery is more in line with another of his industrial designs — Battersea Power Station. Queen's Park Rangers fans may be interested to know that, prior to development by the brewery, the site formed part of Q.P.R.'s old football ground — the kick-off point lying roughly on the site of the racking shed in the buildings to the north. (Guinness, appropriately became Q.P.R.'s sponsor in 1983.)

Aerial view of the new Guinness Brewery — February, 1936.

During the 1930's, the first pupils of **Twyford Junior School** were given lessons in St. Mary's church hall. More permanent premises were later established, and the present school next-door to the Abbey was built in 1967. Most of the land between the school and the canal once belonged to **Twyford Abbey Farm,** where mushrooms were grown for the London market earlier this century. The houses in **Iveagh Avenue** were built by Guinness for workers at the Brewery, as were those in **Moyne Place** and **Rainsford Road** over the borough boundary, on the opposite side of the road.

The canal now runs through the heart of the **Park Royal Industrial Estate,** and both sides of the approach from Twyford Abbey Road are lined with the warehouses and printing works of **Waterlow & Sons** who moved here in 1936. Millions of copies of the *Radio Times* and the *Listener* leave here on their nationwide journey each week, but the canal no longer plays any part in their distribution. Follow the 'Canalside Walk' sign down to the towpath, where a welcome attempt is being made to offset the industrial blight with landscaping. Trees and shrubs have been planted on both sides of the canal and benches are provided at intervals. Factories line the canal in both directions but most have done their bit to landscape their frontages and give workers and members of the public full benefit of the canal view. Brief details of the choice in routes follow, to help you decide whether to walk towards Ealing or Acton. (You have already walked ½ a mile.)

A. West to Ealing Road (just over a mile): Beyond the stile to your left, lies the disused wharf of the Guinness Brewery. Boats filled with barrels of stout were a common sight on the canal in the 'thirties and 'forties, but, according to a report in the *Gentleman's Magazine* for April 1809, some of the intoxicating cargoes carried last century were not nearly so 'Good for You' — and in one case proved fatal. The incident is described as being 'of a novel nature' — which makes me think that the writer must have been really fun at a funeral as the story concerns the sudden and spectacular demise of two boatmen transporting barrels of brandy and rum down the canal late one night. Finding it thirsty work, they bored a hole in one of the barrels and made the nasty discovery that barrels of gunpowder had been included in their cargo. The shock of the explosion is said to have shaken nearby houses like an earthquake and three ricks of hay belonging to Mr. Willan were consumed in the flames. Poor Mr. Willan! This event appears to have been the closest the canal came to making any impact on West Twyford until the Park Royal Estate was developed a century later.

Further on, you come to the **aqueduct** carrying the canal over the **North Circular** where you can peer down at the traffic-jams and feel superior. Some readers may remember the resulting chaos when the aquaduct sprang a leak in 1962. The bridge bears the arms of the former County of Middlesex on one side, but this is more easily seen from the road itself. The River Brent flows through a small tunnel immediately after the aqueduct, and looking along its concrete-lined course towards Vicar's Bridge, it is difficult to imagine that just a century ago, West Twyford's lords of the manor held fishing rights in the river. The canal is very popular with local fishermen however, and you have to pick your way carefully between the buckets of wriggling maggots that line the towpath in summer months.

Well-kept lawns surround the newer factories in the **Northfield Industrial Estate,** but it is a relief to leave the factories behind as the canal sweeps round past the suburban gardens of Alperton. Just before the **Ealing Road,** the Piccadilly Line crosses on an iron bridge high above the canal. Originally named the Ealing and South Harrow Railway, it was the District's first electrified line and opened with a special service to the Royal Agricultural Society's Show at Park Royal in 1903. You will find narrowboats moored next to **The Pleasure Boat** at Ealing Road Bridge, and might be lucky enough to get a ride on one in the tradition of the excursion boat trips that set off from here earlier this century. Otherwise there are plenty of modern forms of transport available nearby, so you should not have any trouble getting home after refreshing yourselves with a glass of Guinness, either here or at the **Fox and Goose** a short walk away at **Vicar's Bridge.**

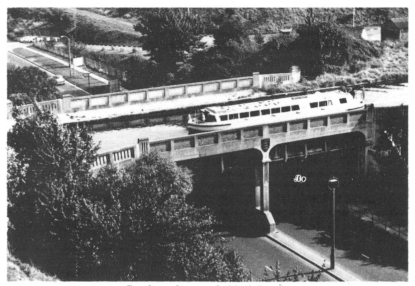

Canal aqueduct over the North Circular.

B. East to Acton or Old Oak Lane (¾ to 1½ miles): To your right, another stile stands beside **Canal Cottage,** built in 1821 by the Grand Junction Company for the lengthsmen that once maintained this section of the canal. From **Abbey Road** bridge, the canopied wharfs of **H.J. Heinz & Co.** stretch along the far side of the canal. The firm opened a small factory for making bottled goods in 1925, but soon expanded their premises after the discovery that 'Canz meanz Beanz' and 57 years and varieties later, the demand for their products is just as strong. Raw beans and tomato purée used to be brought up from the docks by boats which made the return journey laden with canned goods, and its nice to see the old wrought-iron gates and wharves still kept in a reasonable condition even though their days of service are over.

Many of the sheds on the allotments lining the towpath side of the canal look as though they could do with a little restoration work themselves, but a lot of care has obviously been lavished on the rows of flourishing produce. Further on, across the canal in **Waxlow Road,** stands the largest biscuit factory in the world. McVitie and Price were one of the first companies in the area, opening a factory here in 1902. They later amalgamated with McFarlane Lang to form **United Biscuits** and today are second only to Heinz in the number of people they employ. The **canal feeder** from the Welsh Harp Reservoir emerges beneath a little bridge near their works.

The gigantic cooling towers of **Willesden Power Station** now dominate the scenery. The buildings straddle both sides of the canal beyond Acton Lane Bridge, and are connected by a series of walkways. You can turn your back on them at the **Grand Junction Arms,** a pleasant oasis amidst the factories where you can enjoy a pint of real ale in the garden — overlooking the boats moored on either side of the canal.

If you are a railway enthusiast, you might like to continue down the canal to **Old Oak Lane Bridge,** about half-a-mile further on. The old Midland and South Western Railway crosses the canal just beyond the Power Station, and an excellent paved towpath now replaces the rather muddy cinder track to **Old Oak Lane,** where you can feast your eyes on the complex tangle of railway lines surrounding Willesden Junction Station, a little way up the road to the north. The Bakerloo, the old North London freight line and main line from Euston all cross here; and back on the canal just to the east of the bridge, you can look over the wall of the embankment and see the Old Oak Common engine sheds, which were once alive with Great Western steam locomotives.

Buses 187 from North Acton Lane, and 260, 266 or 18A from Old Oak Lane go to **North Acton Station,** which is on the Central Line. Places of interest in this vicinity are mentioned in Route I of the Acton chapter.

('Shortcut' through the factories and under Western Avenue to North Ealing or Acton — 2 to 3 miles)

This route makes use of the public footpath provided by Guinness — not, unfortunately through their attractive and well laid-out grounds where the public once had right of way, but all round the warehouses and old railway lines to the subway under Western Avenue. It would probably be just as quick to skirt their grounds by walking west down Twyford Abbey Road and up Coronation Road — but that road is infested with traffic and not nearly as much fun!

You find the footpath by walking up **Rainsford Road,** past the Bic Factory and left into **Whitby Avenue.** Immediately beyond the first building on the right, a gate (hopefully never closed!) marks the entrance to the footpath. The alley winds past the fleet of Guinness tankers and enters a fenced-in section which emerges at the traffic-lights in **Cumberland Avenue.** A large 'sentry-box' in the middle of the road, guards an entrance to the Brewery, and the footpath continues on the opposite side, next to one of the old single-track goods lines. A footbridge gets you across the railway line to **Coronation Road** where you cross over and turn right. A faded sign saying **'Masons Green Lane'** about 100 yards down on the left means you have found the footpath over the railway to the Western Avenue subway. Here we pause for a short history lesson.

The ancient boundaries enclosing West Twyford's 281 acres were formed by Masons Green Lane to the west, the Brent in the north, and Norwood Lane to the south. **Masons Green Lane** ran from Twyford Lane (now Twyford Abbey Road) through what is now the Guinness estate, then continued as a footpath to Masons Green in Acton (roughly on the site of West Acton station), where it joined Green Lane (now Twyford Avenue) down to the ponds on the Uxbridge Road. The northern end of the lane had disappeared by 1894, long before the Brewery opened, but the footpath remains. **Norwood Lane** ran east from Masons Green Lane towards Harrow Road in Willesden, but was obliterated by the GWR's Birmingham line in 1904 when **Coronation Road** was built to follow roughly the same course. Sometime in the next 15 years, a small 'sitting-out area' (to quote the Borough Plan) is to be created from the scrubland west of Masons Green Lane, between Coronation Road and Western Avenue, but until then you'll just have to plod on regardless.

Having crossed over the Central line and under **Western Avenue,** those wishing to head for Hanger Hill Park should turn left up to **Park Royal Station,** while ramblers bound for North Ealing Station or Acton continue straight on, following the recently-tarred footpath beside the Piccadilly line. (Distances include the walk from the Church.)

Route A. to Hanger Hill Park (just under 2 miles) travels through the final phase of the pleasant Tudor-style **Hanger Hill Garden Estate,** which was built on the site of **Hanger Hill House** in the 1930's. You continue past the station, then left into Hanger Green and up Heathcroft Road, until you reach The Ridings. Here you turn left and first right into Chatsworth Rise, then right again into Chatsworth Road and on to Hanger Lane where you will find an entrance to the Park near Greystoke Gardens (formerly Greystoke Farm). Information about this area is given in Route 2 of the chapter on North Ealing. (A footbridge over Hanger Lane is to be built at some future date.)

The garden of Hanger Hill House c.1895. Sir Montague Nelson
(the first Mayor of Ealing) can be seen in the background, with his wife.

The alternative routes follow Masons Green footpath as far as Hanger Vale Lane. The Warehouses to the east of the path stand on the site of **Acton Aerodrome,** where the **Alliance Aeroplane Co.** constructed de Havilland bi-planes from 1917-20. The huge hangars were taken over by the Ministry of Aviation during the Second World War, and this part of the site was later sold for warehousing, the rest having gone to the first phase of the Hanger Hill Garden Estate in 1925. **Hanger Vale Lane** has developed from another very old footpath which led to the kiln at its western end where tiles were fired during the 17th and 18th centuries. **Tile Kiln House** later became part of the Wood family's farm and they added **Friars Place Farm** in Acton to their large Ealing estates in 1811. Friars Place lay to the east of Masons Green Lane and included the moated site now covered by North Acton Recreation Ground. For many years, the Woods tried to get permission to close the Masons Green and Hanger Vale footpaths, but were successfully opposed by Acton parish vestry.

Route B. to North Ealing Station (just over 2 miles) turns right into Hanger Vale Lane. The clubhouse on the corner was built for early tenants of the Hanger Vale Garden Estate but is now used by the **Church of the Holy Family** nearby, and the sportsfields opposite have been taken over by Ellen Wilkinson High School in Queens Drive. **Boileau Road,** across the railway, is named after *Colonel Charles Boileau Wood* who sold the family's 560-acre estate to the Prudential Assurance Co. in 1906. It leads to

Station Road and North Ealing Station — built on the site of Hanger Lane Farm in 1903 for the Ealing and South Harrow Railway. Most stations were rebuilt during the 1930's when the Piccadilly line was extended to run parallel with the District line, but North Ealing retains its original old-fashioned station-house. In **Queens Parade** you will find sustenance at the **Village Wine Bar** (decorated with stills from films made at the old Ealing Studios) and **The Greystoke** pub. **Ealing Village,** one of the nicer results of in-filling during the 1930's, lies above the District line a little way down Hanger Lane.

Route C. to Acton (just under 3 miles) crosses straight over Hanger Vale Lane and at the end of **Monks Drive,** you will find the remains of **Masons Green.** An *Anthony Mason* was tenant at Ealing Manor House during the 16th century (shortly before it was granted to the Penruddocks) and it is quite possible that he, or his family, held land in this area as well, although I have not been able to trace the origin of the name for certain. **Queens Drive** crosses the Central line at **West Acton Station** which opened in 1923 and was responsible for most of the surrounding housing developments. The estate to the east of the station was built as a co-operative scheme for railwaymen by the **Great Western Village Society** in 1924-31. **West Acton First School,** on the corner of **Noel Road,** followed in 1937, and if you continue over the railway line into **Twyford Avenue** and make a short detour left into Creffield Road, you will see the large building erected for **Haberdashers' Aske's School for Girls** in 1901. *Robert Aske,* a member of the Haberdashers' Livery Company during the 17th century, left his estate and £20,000 for founding a hospital for 'Twenty poor Decayed Freemen of the Company of Haberdashers, and the maintenance of Twenty poor Decayed Freemens sons with Meat, Drink, Clothing and Schooling'. The hospital was founded at Hoxton near London in 1688, but in 1873, the 'decayed freemen' were pensioned off and the building converted into a school for boys with a separate girls' school nearby. The girls moved to Acton when development of the Springfield Park Estate offered the opportunity of made-to-measure premises. While the site of the school was being excavated, archeologists found the floor of a 'factory' where flints had been mass-produced 100,000 years ago. The Girls' School was reunited with the Boy's School in Hertfordshire in 1974, but a foundation stone in the modernised buildings taken over by **Cardinal Newman High,** (named after the famous Great Ealing School 'Old Boy'), commemorates their stay in Acton.

The Springfield Park estate has connections with West Twyford because it takes its name from **Springfield Farm** which stood near Horn Lane when it was bought by *Thomas Willan* while he was still a tenant at Twyford Manor House. The farm was sold after his death and the land was built over during the 1880's. Information about **Twyford Avenue** and its various names through the ages is given in Route 2 of the Acton chapter which this walk now joins at **Twyford High School** which, since 1961, has been housed in the 18th century mansion, **The Elms,** at the end of the road.

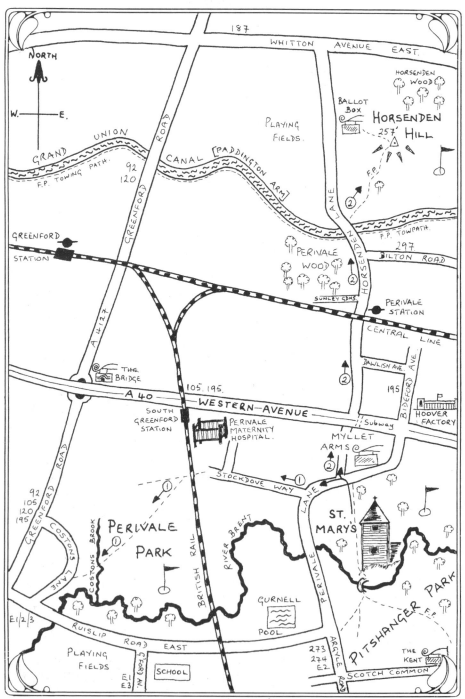

CHAPTER VII

Parish of enormous hayfields
Perivale stood all alone
JOHN BETJEMAN, Middlesex

PERIVALE is the smallest parish in the borough, but what it lacks in size it makes up for in legends and folklore. The little hamlet's proximity to the somewhat unpredictable waters of the Brent (which cut off all access from the south during times of flood), discouraged earlier development so that it was one of the last suburbs to fall beneath the scythe of the 20th century. Although no longer the "parish of enormous hayfields", some of its former rural atmosphere can still be found, especially around the tiny Norman church of St. Mary's.

Perivale appears in the Domesday Book as '*Greneford Parva*', or 'Little Greenford'. Before the Norman invasion, the woodlands and 300 acres of cultivated land which made up the parish were held by a vassal of the Saxon, Angsgar, Master of the Stud to Edward the Confessor; but from 1086, the fifty or so inhabitants found themselves under a new Lord of the Manor: Geoffrey de Mandeville, one of the first great 'feudal barons' created by William the Conqueror for services in battle.

The Manor changed hands many times during the next few centuries, but Perivale itself changed little, except in name. 'Cornhill', 'Purevale' and 'Peryvale' are just some of the variations used in old records. They probably owe their origin to the abundance of 'most excellente good wheate' which covered the fertile farmlands of the Brent Valley and the slopes of Horsenden Hill during the Middle Ages. However, other references suggest that the wine or 'perry' made from the numerous pear trees in the orchards could also have been responsible.

Perivale was at its most populous and prosperous in 1573, when Henry Myllet declared himself 'Lord of the Toune' and built the moated manor-house west of the church. But by 1801, when the Paddington Arm of the Grand Junction Canal pushed its way through Perivale, there were only 28 people living on the five large hay-farms (Horsenden, Apperton, Manor, Church and Grange Farms) which provided most of the hay for London's horses.

Agriculture was still the main occupation and there were less than two dozen houses in the area, when the Great Western Railway passed through Perivale to Greenford a century later. But with the building of Western Avenue during the 1920's, 'progress' finally came to rural Perivale. The tiny parish joined the then municipal borough of Ealing in 1926, and gradually the fields and farmlands gave way to factories and housing estates.

To quote again from Sir John Betjeman's 'Middlesex':

Gentle Brent, I used to know you
Wandering Wembley-wards at will,
Now what change your waters show you
In the meadowlands you fill.

The **Church of St. Mary the Virgin** has seen the great cornlands and hayfields of Perivale come and go. Various additions and changes have been made to the original church during restoration in the 15th and 18th centuries, but a large portion of the building you see today has stood close to the Brent since 1185. The course of the Brent has changed during the last 200 years; it used to flow more than five hundred feet south at this point — which explains why the church was not continually flooded in winter.

Besides being the smallest and oldest church in the borough, its red-tiled roof, wooden tower and churchyard overhung with trees, certainly make St. Mary's one of the most attractive places to visit on any walk through the parish. The church can be approached from the Ealing side via one of the footpaths through **Pitshanger Park,** which will take you past the allotments or across Ealing Golf Course to the wooden bridge over the Brent, with the churchyard beyond.

For several centuries, it was thought that the church had no Dedication. The oldest surviving records date from 1707, but make no mention of its name. However, the patron saint was re-discovered by chance in 1951 when a local historian, Mr. Pugh, was doing some research at Somerset House and came across a copy of the will made by a 15th century parishioner, Isabella Miles, in which she asked to be buried 'in the churchyard of St. Mary of Little Greenford'. On this evidence, a deed was applied for to name the church 'St. Mary the Virgin' and the patronal festival was once again celebrated every year on July 2nd.

To meet the needs of the rapidly expanding population during the 1930's, the Church of St. Nicholas was founded in Federal Road, Perivale. This building became the Parish Hall when a new church, known as **'St. Mary the Virgin with St. Nicholas'** was built on the site in 1964.

In 1976, St. Mary's was declared redundant (although it remains consecrated for the occasional service) and leased to the **'Friends of St. Mary's Trust'** for cultural and community purposes. The Trust has worked hard to restore and maintain the little church and visitors are welcome to look round and have a cup of tea every Sunday afternoon between 2.30 and 5. Why not join the 'Friends' yourself while you are there? A small annual donation secures a copy of their ambitious programme of concerts, festivals and craft fairs, and the knowledge that your contribution is helping to give the ancient church an extra lease of life.

The best-preserved relic of the church is the Early English arched doorway into the vestry, with remains of the Holy Water stoup on the other side. This was the original entrance before the wooden tower was built c. 1510. The weather vane on the tower was rescued from the old Market House at Brentford when it was demolished in 1847, and presented to St. Mary's by the then churchwarden, *Mr. John Farthing.*

When Mr. Farthing took up his post, both the church and rectory had been badly neglected for many years. The vestry minute book of 1836 records that the rector's plea for a new font was turned down 'because there were no christenings for the parishioners of Perivale, nor likely to be any'. However the octagonal font standing in the church today dates from 1490, and was found a few years after this entry, together with the cover, under a pile of useless timber and rubbish in the tower. The cover bears the inscription: 'The Gift of Simon Coston, Gent, March 26th, 1665' and the story of its donor is told later in this chapter.

Not only did Mr. Farthing set about restoring the church, but by interviewing the oldest residents, he put together a history of the parish called 'Pictures of Perivale' (the manuscript has been missing since the beginning of this century) which provided J. Allen Brown with much information for his delightful book, *The Chronicles of Greenford Parva'* (published in 1890) — on which this chapter is based.

One of the characters who proved a valuable source of information to Mr. Farthing, was *Richard Cain*, sexton and parish clerk of St. Mary's. 'Old Cain', as he was known, was a simple but well-meaning fellow who had some difficulty in appreciating the new rector's efforts to encourage parishioners to return to the fold. Every Sunday morning, Cain would stand anxiously scanning the path from Ealing and on one occasion Rev. Hughes, preparing for the service inside, heard the old chap shout: 'Can't see no congregations a-coming along, Sir. May I put the books up?'.

Farming, cattle-doctoring, thatching, carpentry, grave-digging and beer-brewing were just some of Cain's many accomplishments. He threw himself wholeheartedly into leading the singing during services as well, but this enthusiasm was not shared by his listeners. Even kindly Mr. Farthing had to admit that 'without taste, voice or ear, poor Cain grunted forth the most dolorous and unearthly sounds'. Matters were not helped by the toothless condition of the ancient barrel-organ which literally ground its way through the hymns. Desperate to restore harmony, Mr. Farthing finally purchased a new barrel-organ and persuaded Cain to be the organist — thus relieving him of 'leading' the choir. Cain was 83 when he died, and had served the church for almost 50 years. Both Mr. Farthing and Cain are buried in the churchyard.

Reading the plaques and memorials inside the church will give you some idea of the patrons of St. Mary's over the last few centuries. Most of the monuments in the chancel are dedicated to the *Myllet* family and their successors; while under a small carpet on the floor of the nave, lies what is left of the oldest memorial in the church: a group of five brasses, dated 1500, depicting Henry Myllet and his family. Sadly, these survived the plundering of the Reformation and other crises in the church's history, only to fall prey to a modern scourge — the vandals who broke into the church recently. Plans are underway for the brasses to be restored as soon as possible.

The low window filled with dark Victorian stained glass, on the south side of the chancel may have been a 'leper's window' during the 13th century. It looks upon the spot where the altar stood before the chancel was renovated, and would have allowed the unfortunate outcasts a limited view of the service. However, another, less romantic, theory suggests that the window might merely have provided extra light for the officiating priest.

The Churchyard has also suffered at the hands of vandals, but they have not succeeded in spoiling its charm. As you wander along the bramble-strewn paths deciphering the inscriptions on the old gravestones, you will realise that although many personalities connected with the borough's history are buried here, the churchyard has also provided a final resting place for an even larger number of people who had probably never set foot in the parish during their lifetime. Perivale was in fact, a convenient burial place for middle-class Londoners during the 18th and 19th centuries, as the churchyard lay only eight miles from Marble Arch. Legal action was taken againt this practice in 1906, to preserve what little space was left for parishioners.

Some of the names to look out for on the headstones are: *Dr. Nicholas*, headmaster of the Great Ealing School; *George Elliot*, the eldest son of General Elliot of Castlebar Park; *Thomas Cromwell*, said to be related to the Protector; and *Thomas Bowler* of Manor Farm, who was executed at Newgate for adding injury to insult after shooting (but not killing) a neighbouring farmer who had seduced his daughter. His sentence seems to have been particularly severe — possibly because the crime took place in the same year that Prime Minister Perceval was shot. *Elizabeth Colleton*, daughter of a well-to-do 18th century Ealing family, lies in a grave known as **'The Maiden's Tomb'**. The strangely carved stonework of the grave has been pushed aside by what was once a trinity of trees, said to have sprung up in response to the girl's final cry that if there be a just God, trees would grow out of her tomb. Two of the trees have had to be removed owing to Dutch Elm disease, but the remaining one is still there, entwined round a piece of the iron railing which used to enclose the grave. (See footnote at end of chapter).

The parish register also records the untimely end of a previous churchwarden: '*1747. Samuel Verrey, Farmer: He was set upon by two footpads on Saturday night last abount 7 of ye clock near Castle-bear hill, and on making some resistance was shot by one of ym through ye body: of which wound he languish'd till Monday morning and then expired. Bd in Woolen, as per affadavit received*'.

An affidavit stating that the body had been buried in a shroud made of sheep's wool, had to be made to the magistrate or officiating minister as a result of an Act passed by Charles II to keep English wool manufacturers in business after they were forbidden to export their product. A fine of £5 was payable if any other material was used in burials.

As you leave the churchyard and follow the path towards the old wooden **lychgate** (for which a preservation order was recently issued), you will pass the site of the 15th century **Rectory,** to the right behind the church. The half-timbered building had housed the rectors of St. Mary's for over 500 years before dry rot and woodworm caused it to be pulled down in 1957.

A choice of two pleasant walks faces you on reaching the rustic wooden signpost in **Perivale Lane.** (You will find similar signs in all areas covered by the Brent River Park Scheme — see chapter on Hanwell for full details). Depending on how energetic you feel, you can either wander across Perivale Park to Greenford Bridge (1¼ miles); or cross the canal and ascend the heights of Horsenden Hill (1½ miles).

The old Rectory shortly before demolition in 1957.

Turn left and follow the sign towards Hanwell Church. When the lane turns towards the Brent, cross straight over and continue along Stockdove Way, behind the Gurnell Pool. The newly-completed realignment of Perivale Lane will allow work to start on another concept of the Brent River Park Scheme, namely to restore the rural atmosphere of the old lane leading to St. Mary's Church and to create an island sanctuary at Perivale Bridge when the flood control plan has been completed further upriver. The **Gurnell Pool** was opened in July, 1981 and provides swimming enthusiasts with two fine pools, as well as a special one for toddlers.

Follow the footpath behind Perivale Maternity Hospital (once again under threat of closure, at the time of writing) where another sign directs you under the arch of the railway bridge to the playing fields and golf course of **Perivale Park,** which now covers the site of Henry Myllet's moated **Manor House.** Playing fields of some sort have been here for many years. J. Allen Brown described the somewhat sexist rural sports held in the meadows of Perivale during the 1800's: 'The youths,' he said, 'contend in running and other manly exercises, while the maidens vie with each other in the performance of feats requiring skill and dexterity suitable to their sex.'

As you make your way across the park to the main gates in **Coston's Lane,** you will cross the little tributary of the Brent known as Coston's Brook. At the junction of the two streams, the GLC plan to build a large weir to control flooding, which will hopefully be open to the public.

The Legend of Perivale Mill

During the prosperous times of the 17th century, a mill stood somewhere here along the banks of the Brent. If there is any truth in the legend related by Old Cain to Mr. Farthing, it was the scene of many a dastardly deed: It seems that the mill was haunted by the ghost of a miller who had been crushed to death between the millstones, after the local witch had placed a curse on him. After this, the mill remained derelict for many years until an old miser, ignoring the villagers' tales of gloom and doom, decided to take up residence there (rent-free, no doubt!). Shortly afterwards, the miser went missing, and a young foundling, one *Simon Coston*, was the only person brave enough to enter the mill to look for him. There he found that the old man had died a natural death while counting his money. Taking advantage of the strange goings on at t'Mill, the wily lad frightened away the superstitious yokels with the blood-curdling cry: 'Bury me, bury me, 'ere you sleep, in Perivale Churchyard, ten feet deep', then grabbed the money and ran off to Flanders. But not for good; some thirty years later when time had faded the memories of the local folk, he returned with his family (having made a legitimate fortune in Flanders), and bought a large house on an estate nearby. Here he lived to a ripe old age, donating the cover of the font in Perivale Church just before his death. Only then did his executors discover the trick 'Squire' Coston played, but the road around his estate has been known as **'Coston's Lane'** ever since. (Read more about it in the next chapter.)

From the church, cross over to Horsenden Lane South where you might like to refresh yourselves at Perivale's first and only pub, the **'Myllet Arms'**. In 1709, Perivale's reputation for producing barley was eulogised by the poet Drayton in his poem 'Polyolbion':

What barley is there found, whose fair and bearded ear,
Makes stouter English ale or stronger English beer?'

Yet until the 'Myllet Arms' was built in 1936 (on the site of the old Church Farm), the Ballot Box Inn on Horsenden Hill was the only place thirsty local could get a taste of the ale their labours had helped to produce. The Ballot Box used to stand much nearer the canal and is so-named because it was here that the boat-people (the original floating voters) used to cast their votes during 19th century elections.

Before crossing under busy Western Avenue via the subway, take a look at the distinctive Thirties architecture of the **Hoover Factory** across the way. This well-known landmark was recently declared a protected building, to save it from the same fate as the Firestone Factory on the Great West Road. It was built in 1932, three years after **Sanderson's Wallpaper Factory** first introduced Perivale to industry. The latter is now part of a large industrial estate, which lies further up Horsenden Lane, past Perivale Station with it's typically 1940's facade.

Although the woods to the left of the old canal bridge are all that now remains of the great **Perivale Wood** where Lords of the Manor hunted stag and wild boar in the old days, they still provide sanctuary for over 70 species of birds, as part of the **Selborne Nature Reserve,** established in 1902. Here the ferns and wild flowers which once covered the meadows of rural Perivale continue to flourish, and there is a special 'open day' (usually the second Sunday in May) for seeing the bluebells at their best. The entrance to the Sanctuary is in Sunley Gardens.

The "Jazz Age" facade has been well looked after by Hoover over the years, and now fronts their international administrative headquarters.

From the footpath over the **canal bridge**, you can watch the brightly coloured narrow-boats chugging down to Greenford or to Alperton, just around the corner. In the good old days, canal boatmen had a word for people who stood idly by, watching them working the boats. They called them 'gongoozlers'. Today however, there are few professional boatmen left, and 'gongoozling' is quite acceptable.

Over the bridge, the footpath winds through the hedgerow for 277 feet up the slopes of **Horsenden Hill** — the largest open space of natural country in the borough. The hill was probably a fortress in Saxon times, and some traces of ancient defensive work can still be seen on the southern side. On a clear day from the summit, you can enjoy a superb view over the borough and adjoining countryside.

The Legend of Horsenden Hill

A delightful legend surrounds Horsenden Hill, which, besides illustrating the maxim that 'A little knowledge is a dangerous thing', also provides some entertaining reasons as to how this and other places in the borough came by their names: The story concerns a mythical Saxon chief called Horsa, whose wife's nightly revels with elfin folk in the vale below their hillside residence earned it the name of 'Fairy Vale' or Perivale. Their only child, Ealine, was a beautiful girl who, after learning everything her mother could teach her, became something of a child prodigy. She fell in love and married Bren, the handsome chief of a powerful tribe on the banks of the Thames; but, far from living happily ever after, Ealine soon discovered that her new husband preferred carousing with the lads and local wenches to having intellectual discussions with his wife. So, like any intelligent woman, Ealine decided to give him the bird — in the shape of a starling she had taught to speak, and which she sent winging over the fields to tell daddy Horsa of her ill-treatment.

As a result, the armies of the two warriors met in a fearful battle at the ford which still bears Bren's name. He was killed outright and Horsa mortally wounded; but Ealine was carried home in triumph — in time to attend her father's funeral. The mound over the grave where Horsa and his favourite war-horse were buried was named after him, being corrupted to 'Horsenden' over the years. Ealine and her mother retired in their widows' weeds to the forest nearby, where they devoted themselves to study and lived to an advanced age. 'Ealine's Haven' (now Haven Green) commemorates her final resting place.

But some say that Horsa's giant steed can still be heard pacing around his sepulchre, and the shadowy form of the dead warrior has been seen on nights when 'the pale moon illumines the hill, and the white mists curl upward from the vale at its foot'. So if the light is beginning to fade, tarry no longer and head for home!

Footnote
Since writing the charming story of the **Maiden's Tomb,** I have discovered that Ms Colleton was neither quite so young nor innocent at the time of her death. According to the late Hector Smith's recently published booklet, '*A Perambulation at Ealing in 1776*', Elizabeth was the mistress of Richard Savage, the fourth *Earl Rivers*, who set her up in his country house at **Ealing Grove.** He predeceased her by some ten years and outraged his friends by completely ignoring his own wife and child in his will, and making his 'chief wench and bastard' (Dean Swift's forthright description of Elizabeth and her daughter, Bessie) the main beneficiaries after a distant cousin. Bessie, who was probably more of a 'maiden' than her mama, married the Earl of Rochford soon after this; but her mother must have endeared herself to the local people in some way, for the funeral procession which followed her coffin to Perivale was recorded as being over a mile long.

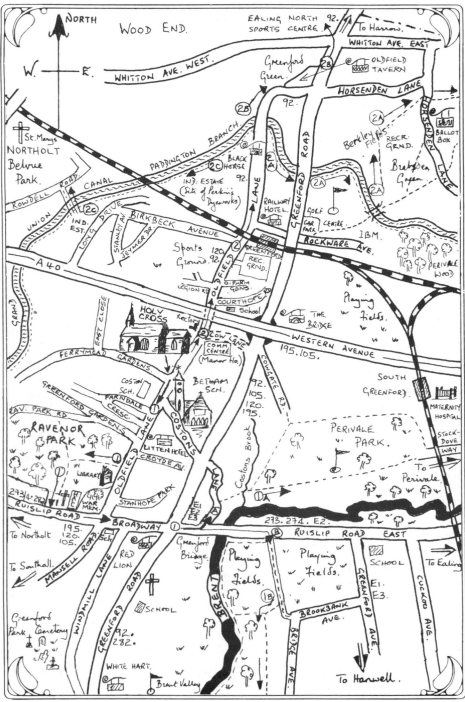

CHAPTER VIII

And from Greenford scent of mayfields
Most enticingly was blown

SIR JOHN BETJEMAN, Middlesex.

GREENFORD was almost entirely devoted to agriculture from the Middle Ages right through to the 1920's. And then, quite suddenly, the seclusion of the straggling village along Oldfield Lane was completely shattered. That might sound rather dramatic, but so were the changes to Greenford. Within the space of ten years, no fewer than three arterial roads had ploughed through the farmlands between the Brent and Horsenden Hill, where previously only rough country lanes had linked the rural community to places beyond the parish boundaries. Besides the Church, only two pre-19th century buildings survived the rapid industrial and residential development that followed; but the distant view of Horsenden Hill and preservation of other open space in and around the town help compensate for the features Greenford has lost.

The name is first mentioned in a Saxon charter of 845 AD when some lands changed hands 'in that famous vill which is called Grenanforda'. It is not known why the green fields surrounding the ford over the Brent should have been so well-known at the time, but perhaps the ford had played an important part in some long-forgotten battle. During the 10th century, King Ethelred granted the manor to the Monastery of St. Peter at Westminster, and the Abbot still held 'Greneforde' at Domesday when some 27 people (including a Frenchman) were recorded as living on scattered farms in the 1,400 acres which then made up the parish. The bulk of the pasture and arable land lay to the south, while pigs had the run of the 300 acres of woodland in the northern part of the parish. Here, several freeholders had made clearings for their farms at **Greenford Green** and on the slopes of Horsenden Hill — in the area later known as **Brabsden Green.**

Although the surrounding parishes could only be reached by muddy cart tracks and footpaths, Greenford had close administrative ties with her neighbours throughout the Middle Ages. The boundary line between Perivale and Greenford (or Greenford Parva and Magna as they used to be called) was never very definite, and landowners frequently held land in both parishes; Hanwell had also belonged to Westminster Abbey at Domesday, and shared Greenford's manorial court and Manor House from the 13th to the 18th century; while the manor lords of Northolt (which was later also acquired by Westminster) had owned a large tract of land south-west of the Brent in Greenford since the time of the Conquest. This formed the basis of the 186-acre submanor of Styclyndon or **Stickleton** (meaning 'village on a steep hill') which Henry de Bohun gave to the Benedictine nuns of Ankerwyk Priory, Buckinghamshire, in the mid-13th century.

When Henry VIII dissolved the monasteries in 1539/40, Stickleton Manor passed into private ownership; and Greenford, Hanwell and Northolt were granted to the new Bishop of Westminster. His bishopric was shortlived, however, and within ten years Greenford and Hanwell were in the hands of the Bishop of London, who leased out the manorial lands almost immediately. By this time, there were about 100 people living in three isolated settlements linked by Oldfield Lane. At the northern end lay the hamlet of **Greenford Green** (part of the manorial demesne since the freehold had been sold in the 14th century); the **Church, Manor Farm** and **Manor House** formed another tiny village in the middle; and to the south, around the junction of Oldfield Lane and the track to Ruislip, stood the farm and cottages of **Stickleton Manor.**

From here, a precursor of **Windmill Lane** meandered southwards through the fields to the Uxbridge Road and on to Osterley. Further east, the Brent was crossed by a rickety structure called **Stickleton Bridge,** built by the Abbot c.1250 to give Greenford farmers access to his windmill on Cuckoo Hill. Today's Greenford Avenue, Cowgate Road and Cow Lane now follow the line of the well-worn footpath from Hanwell, over the bridge, to the Church — from where another path continued westwards to Northolt. Higher up Oldfield Lane, another path led across the hillside to the farm on **Brabsden Green.** Stickleton Bridge appears to have been the only bridge until the new **Greenford Bridge** was constructed near the original ford in the early 17th century.

This pattern of development remained basically the same until the 20th century. The old villages gradually expanded as new settlers like the *Coston* and *Ravenor* families (whose names still feature in Greenford today) acquired land in the area, but agriculture remained the chief occupation — only the crops changed. During Elizabethan times, the woodlands began to be cleared for the vast fields of wheat which swept up to Harrow in golden waves, but hay-farming became the order of the day as the Coaching Age progressed. The farmlands of Stickleton Manor were subdivided and sold from about 1740 onwards, and several new houses were built on the estate; but Greenford's population was still only just over 300 by the end of the century.

The opening of the **canal to Paddington** through the northern part of the parish in 1801 had little effect on this rural way of life until *William Perkin* set up his **dyeworks** near the Black Horse, half a century later. The Enclosure Act of 1814 accelerated the swing from wheat to hay, but although the canal made it easier to transport the haycrop to London, it provoked nothing but complaints from local farmers — who had to drop the price of their hay and straw to keep it in line with the cheaper produce brought by canal from outlying counties. The boats returned with 'mack', a mixture of rubbish, manure and butchers' offal which was rotted down for fertilizer. All work was done by hand, and farming methods were considered notoriously backward by London standards. The lack of drainage on the heavy clay soil added to the farmer's difficulties, yet in 1842 the parish produced 1125 tons of hay from 1500 acres without the aid of any modern machinery.

Besides the traditional trades of blacksmith, wheelwright and publican, few other crafts were practised. By the mid-19th century, about half-a-dozen shops (butcher, baker, cabinet-maker etc) served the needs of the well-to-do families in the main village at the southern end of Oldfield Lane; the rector, schoolmaster and a dentist were the only professional men; and the majority of the 500 or so inhabitants lived in ignorance, poverty and dirt. Although large numbers of labourers on the Great Western Railway found temporary accommodation in Greenford, there was no public transport until the **GWR** opened sidings in Oldfield Lane and South Greenford in 1904. Even then, the lack of water and sewage facilities, and frequent flooding (most of Greenford lies in the lowest part of the Brent Valley) continued to discourage building speculators, and residential development was only just beginning in the south (on the **Greenford Park** and **Ravenor Park Estates**) by the outbreak of the First World War.

However, the canal, railway and large amounts of open land soon attracted new industries to the northern part of town; and from 1924, when the Urban District of Greenford, Perivale and West Twyford (est. 1894) joined the Municipal Borough of Ealing, changes were swift and drastic. In the same year, the new **Greenford Road** sliced through the parish from Harrow, followed by **Western Avenue** a few years later, and in 1935 **Whitton Avenue** completed the transformation from village to suburb. The new roads broke up the unity of the parish, splitting it into four parts and encouraging more factories, so that by the late 1920's North and South Greenford had been further divided by an industrial belt between the railway and canal. This stretched from the **Peerless**

The Scapegoat

By Harlequin

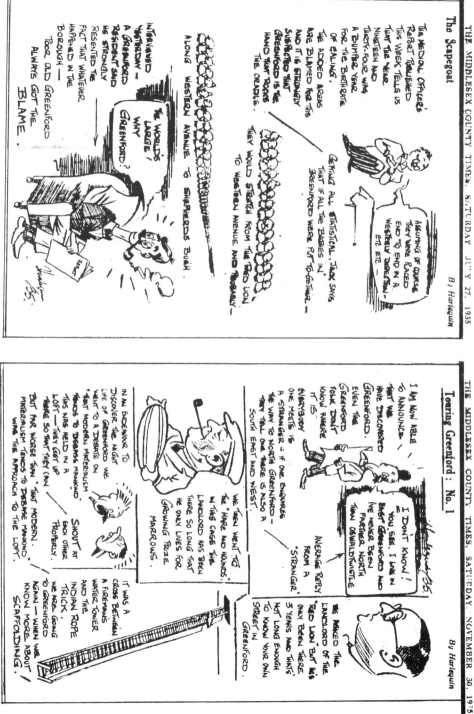

Touring Greenford : No. 1

By Harlequin

Wire Fencing and **British Baths** factories in Long Drive, to **Lyons** tea-blending plant in Oldfield Lane, and across to the **Rockware Glassworks** in the east.

The opening of AEC in Southall and the Hoover factory in Perivale also had an effect on residential development in Greenford, and by 1935 there were so many new roads that the local paper carried cartoons about the number of new residents, and the difficulties encountered by older inhabitants in finding their way around. Housing estates, shopping centres and industrial sites had more or less covered the available open space by the Second World War, and development was completed in the 1950's after the last of the Bishop of London's estates had been sold to the Council by the Church Commissioners. Between 1911 and 1951, Greenford's population increased from just under a 1000 to nearly 47,000.

Although there had been no overall plan to control the haphazard expansion of the town, a reasonable amount of former farmland was preserved as open space or sports fields, and the diversion of the main traffic route to Greenford Road has at least helped Oldfield Lane to retain some of its old buildings and rural character. Many trees still blossom in gardens and despite having to traverse a large built-up area to reach Horsenden Hill or the Brent River Park, you'll find the walk through the town is not without interest.

Two unusual features distinguish Greenford Parish Church from others in the borough — not only is it dedicated to the **Holy Cross** rather than St. Mary, but the tiny medieval church was preserved when the rapid increase of parishioners necessitated the building of a larger one, and the two stand side by side on the same site. The 'Chapel of Greenford' was first mentioned in a Papal Bull of 1157, when Pope Adrian IV confirmed that Westminster Abbey held the advowson. Probably made of wood, this church was rebuilt during the 13th century, and the **old church** you see today is the result of further rebuilding and restoration work between the late-15th and 17th centuries. The design of the **new church** (built 1939-42) was inspired by a 16th century tithing barn in which local farmers once deposited a tenth of their harvest for the use of the rector. The barn, alas, was demolished to make way for East Close, but has a grand memorial in *Sir Albert Richardson's* new Holy Cross.

Both churches have to be kept locked when not in use (a precaution which, unfortunately, does not deter vandals from making their mark on the outside walls), but keys and permission to visit the churches may be obtained from the Rectory. From an historial point of view, the old church is the most interesting as it contains memorials to the Ravenors, Costons, Milletts, Bennetts and many other old Greenford families — which give you some idea of Who was Who in days gone by.

The most ornate memorial was erected by *Simon Coston* on the death of his wife, *Bridget*, in 1637, and dominates the wall opposite the entrance to the **nave.** Carved in the marble are the kneeling figures of his wife (holding their infant son, John) and five daughters, with Simon himself mourning in the background. High up on the south wall near the chancel arch, a brass plaque bears a long Latin inscription composed by Simon in which he describes Bridget as being 'most dear to God and her husband, mother and tireless nurse of a fair brood, and the very best of women'. The **stone font** near the porch entrance was presented to the church by the eldest daughter, Frances, the following year — possible on the anniversary of her mother's death. (More information about this legendary family is given in Route 1.)

At the west of the church, eight large oak posts support the 17th century wooden **gallery** and new **bell-tower,** which was rebuilt in 1913 after a fire destroyed the original.

OLD HOLY CROSS GREENFORD

The **chancel** is thought to have been the oldest part of the church before most of it was rebuilt in early Tudor times. The chancel arch of the original structure survived until the 19th century, but was replaced by the present one in 1871 because it 'obscured the view of worshippers in the Nave'. Most of the glass in the **chancel windows** is pre-18th century. The sketch of Perivale Mill (in the previous chapter) where Simon Coston is said to have made his fortune, is based on the early windmills depicted in the windows on the north wall and above the Ten Commandments behind the altar. Several coats of arms are also displayed among the stained-glass harts and flowers — see if you can spot Mary Tudor's and Philip of Spain's, the lilies of Eton College, and the roses of **Kings College, Cambridge.** Kings College have held the advowson (the right to choose and appoint rectors) since 1700, and donated the painted 14th century **Flemish glass** which features in several of the windows.

Members of the *Millett* and *Bennett* families are among those buried behind the altar rail — which dates from the time of Charles II. Some of the inscriptions are partially obscured by age and carpets, but the latter are easily moved. Several brasses on the north wall commemorate past **rectors.** One (c.1450 — the oldest in the church) shows the top half of *Simon Hart* in his priestly vestments, and, next to him, is a large plaque to *Edward Betham* (rector 1769-83) who paid for the first schoolhouse in the parish (which we will be passing in Route 1) and left a large sum of money to ensure that local children continued to be educated. Descendants of *Edward Terry*, another memorable rector, are buried behind the altar. Before taking up his post at Holy Cross, he had been chaplain to the East India Company, and also to Sir Thomas Roe, ambassador to the Great Mogul Jahangir from 1615-19. Terry's incumbency seems to have terminated during the Civil War, and his son became rector after the Restoration.

While on the subject of rectors (a full list of whom, from 1326 onwards, is to be found under the wooden gallery at the back of the church), I must mention two others who are not buried in the church. *John Feckenham* had been private chaplain and confessor to Queen Mary before becoming Dean of St. Paul's and Rector of Holy Cross in 1554. He was promoted to Abbot of Westminster after the Abbey was refounded, but refused to conform when Elizabeth became Queen and was imprisoned until his death in 1585. *Henry Biscoe* (rector 1890-1912) wasn't quite such a pillar of society, but he made several columns in The Times and Telegraph of 1895 when he appropriated the entire bank stock of the **Betham and Bennett Charities** towards paying off debts of some £2470. The sum was repaid in full by local efforts, however (so he can't have been such a bad chap), and he was acquitted of embezzlement. Details of both charities (but not the scandal!) are inscribed on plaques near the **porch entrance.**

The **stone doorway** to the porch was carved in the Perpendicular style during the late-15th century — some time after the original open timber porch was built. This was incorporated into the present enclosed version during 19th century restorations. Outside in the **churchyard** you'll find many familiar names on the tombstones east and north of the church — including that of poor *Nathaniel Ravenor* who died in 1835 by 'accidentally discharging his gun'. Immediately east of the porch lies the grave of *William Marnham* who in 1710 bequeathed several acres of land to the parish — the rent from which was to be used to teach poor children how to read and be catechised. **Marnham Field** was sold to the Council in 1937, and has been preserved as open space behind Mayfield School in the Brent River Park.

The oldest headstones (dating from the early 16th century) stand on the southern side of the church but, not surprisingly, have been worn almost smooth by age. However, here and there you can make out a name or date, and some have a skull and crossbones carved into them — the emblem of mortality which was meant to encourage the devil to let the departed spirit rest in peace. Behind the fence at the back of the churchyard stands the fine old Victorian **Rectory,** which was built a few yards west of its 14th century predecessor in 1875.

(Holy Cross to Greenford Bridge via Oldfield Lane, and then through the Brent River Park to either Perivale or Hanwell — 2¼ miles)
Less than 50 years ago, **Ferrymead Gardens** was merely a cart track leading to the old **Manor Farm** west of the Church. A footpath at the Oldfield Lane end still led across the fields to Northolt, a few cottages stood opposite the Church and in Cow lane, and the roads south of Greenford Hall were just beginning to be developed. The opening of Western Avenue soon changed things, however, and by 1939 the farmlands had been covered by the **Westridge Estate,** the cottages had given way to the British Legion Club and paved footpath to Greenford Road, and **Greenford Hall** was pending demolition for a new **Community Centre.**

It was only the intervention of the Second World War and subsequent financial restrictions which prevented the Council from putting this plan into action, by which time the Hall itself had proved to be a perfectly adequate Community Centre — and, under the watchful eye of local conservationists, has continued to be ever since. The architectural style of this large, rambling building is difficult to place. The southern part is Georgian (thought to have been built c.1780 for members of the *Betham* family), and the 'gabled' northern half replaced a Victorian structure early this century.

Greenford Hall c.1912 before the present gabled extension was added to the northern side. The gentleman with the proprietorial air may well be Sir George Thurston.

The history of Greenford Hall's predecessors is even more nebulous, but this is believed to have been the site of the original **Manor House** (first mentioned in 1305, and called a Hall in 1538) where the Manor Courts for Greenford and Hanwell were held until the two villages separated towards the end of the 17th century. The Bishop of London's steward or overseer usually presided over these courts, and the Hall probably served as his home until the Bishop sold the Manor House for the grand sum of £3,301 in 1657. It is not known to what extent this decision was influenced by the Civil War but, bearing in mind that the Bishop had been forced to relinquish his Manor of Ealing to Cromwell a few years earlier, and that Holy Cross does not appear to have had a rector between 1649 and 1660, it is likely that the Bishop had little choice in the matter.

The subsequent fate of this house and its owners is not recorded, but several influential families (such as the *Riggs, Harringtons* and *Roys*) have lived in the present Greenford Hall. During the 1840's, the house was occupied by the medical reformer, *Thomas Wakley*, MP for Finsbury and founder of the 'The Lancet', and its last private occupant in the 1930's was *Sir George Thurston*, the famous naval engineer who designed numerous battleships, cruisers and other war vessels. Ealing Council bought the house in 1939 — the same year that Greenford's Community Association was established.

Turning south down **Oldfield Lane,** you will come to No. 164, a building (now carefully converted into flats) which has very definite associations with the Betham family as this was the **school** built by *Edward Betham* in 1780. The rector's endowment stipulated that the school was to provide free clothing, books etc for about 30 pupils from Greenford, Northolt, Hanwell and Perivale, but that a third of these had to come from Greenford. The Latin inscription on the house roughly translates as 'To teach the principles of religion to poor children'. This was the only school in the parish until the Education Act of 1870 compelled the authorities to provide a school large enough to educate all the children in Greenford, which led to the opening of the present **Betham School,** with its distinctive **clock tower,** further down the road in 1878.

By 1926, Betham School roll had increased from 65 children to 216. A small hall had been built to augment the two original classrooms, but rooms had to be hired in the Village Hall across the way to accommodate the overflow until the adjacent **Coston School** was built for 400 pupils in 1928. This, too, was soon bursting at the seams, but the pressure was relieved by the opening of other new schools in the parish (there were nine by 1936) and the expansion of Coston into separate Junior and Senior Schools.

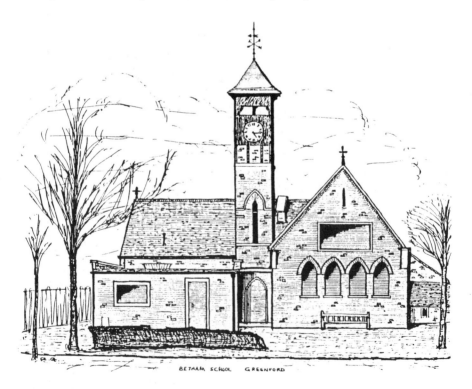

BETHAM SCHOOL GREENFORD

Coston Senior Girls' School was built on the site of the **Village Hall** in 1938. This had developed from a First World War YMCA canteen-hut which residents had converted into a hall for social functions by forming a Company, and selling £1 shares (chiefly to the Rockware factory) to raise the necessary funds. Besides being used for concerts, dances and whist-drives, the hall provided rooms for a child welfare clinic, a small lending library, and the monthly meetings of Greenford Urban District Council — which had previously taken place at Betham School. The latter was requisitioned for Civic Defence during the last War, but reverted to its proper use in the aftermath.

In 1826, the stretch of village between **Costons Lane** and the **Ruislip Road** was described as being 'the residence of many genteel families'. After the break-up of the **Stickleton Manor** estate in the mid-18th century, several large houses had begun to appear on the eastern side of Oldfield Lane — their farmlands extending from the western side as far as the canal. Others were built inbetween at the turn of the present century, but virtually all had disappeared under new housing estates by the late 1930's.

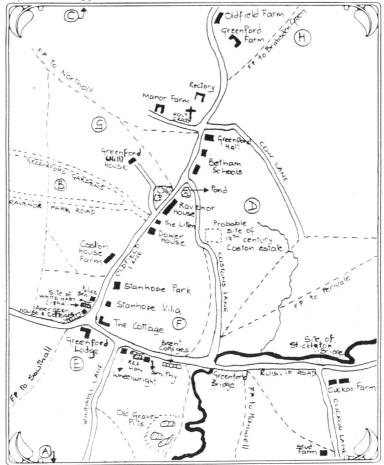

Sketch-map of Greenford early this century — showing subsequent development.

A. Greenford Park Estate — 1908 +

B. Ravenor Park Estate — 1912 +

C. Long Drive Industrial Estate — 1911 +

D. Cowgate Estate — 1920 +

E. Windmill Estate — 1927 +

F. Stanhope Park Estate — 1931 +

G. Westridge Estate — 1935 +

H. Perivale Park Estate — 1935 +

I've drawn a rough sketch map of the main village c.1920, which you can compare with what you see today as you wander down Oldfield Lane. The documented history of the old houses is almost non-existent, but I shall tell you what little I have been able to discover about some of the former occupants whose names live on in those of Greenford streets and schools today.

There is an old saying that when gossip grows old, it becomes myth — and this certainly seems so in the case of the Costons. The fact that **Costons Lane** is named after Squire *Simon Coston* is probably the only truthful element in the *'Legend of Perivale Mill'*, related in the previous chapter. The first mention of the family occurs in 1610 when Simon Coston's father, *John Coston* of London, bought a freehold farm near **Brabsden Green** on Horsenden Hill. This was later sold to *Benjamin Way* (lessee of the Manor Farm) and the family then seem to have moved down south, near the Brent. I have outlined the probable site of their new farm on my map — but, like almost everything to with the Costons, it is open to speculation.

The only certainties are Simon's wealth (manifested by the monument to his wife and other gifts to Holy Cross and St. Mary's Perivale), his six children, and the fact he died in 1665. The parish registers (which date from 1539) would no doubt throw some light on what happened to his son, John, who his five daughters married, and which branch of the family built **Coston House** in Oldfield Lane — but if I'm to finish this book before the year 2000, I dare not undertake any more research. However, the **Greenford Society** are working on it at present — so look out for further revelations from them.

The Ravenors are an even older Greenford family — *Simon Ravenor* being recorded as the Constable of Greenford in 1596. In the days when Greenford and Hanwell were treated as one Manor, each village had their own Constable, Headborough and (the best job of all) Aletaster. But the Constable had the heaviest responsibility as the parish was responsible for all robberies committed in it, unless he was able to apprehend the thieves. Simon Ravenor's name also appears as a member of the Jury at a Court Leet held in 1638 — a service which could only be undertaken by freeholders. His descendants were living at **Ravenor House** when *Nathaniel Ravenor* accidentally shot himself in 1835, but the family seem to have vacated the house soon afterwards and leased it to various farmers.

The autobiography of *Fred Crees*, the tenant from 1897-1900, gives a fascinating account of life in Greenford and Northolt (where he subsequently leased Court Farm) at the turn of the century. Haymaking and dairy farming were his chief concerns at Ravenor House, and the farming methods he introduced from his native Somerset seem to have been far in advance of those in Greenford. He reports that it took him two years to convince his neighbour that hay could be made at half the cost by using machines. Another form of mechanisation surprised his wife, Ellen, who saw the first ever **motor car** in Greenford struggling up the hill one day. The Ravenors later sold the farmlands to a Hanwell land speculator, and **Greenford Gardens** and **Ravenor Park Road** had been laid out by the First World War. Building was slow to start, however, and most of the **Ravenor Park Estate** was developed a few plots at a time by small building firms in the 1930's. **Brookfield Court** flats replaced the old Ravenor House in 1939.

Farndale Crescent had been built along the former driveway to **Greenford(Hill) House** by 1935, and the cottage called **The Litten** was converted into the **Litten Hotel** around the same time. Behind the pub's car-park lies the **Litten Nature Reserve** — a small area of woodland, surrounding a pond, which has been preserved for educational purposes by Ealing Council. Rows of 1930's semi's now line the hill up to the shopping centre, but **Dower House** (previously called Greenford House) was only replaced by the present featureless flat-block in the 1950's. It used to stand a little way north of **Croyde**

Avenue. The **Synagogue** on the opposite side of the road opened in 1959, and Ravenor Park Depot now occupies some of the old buildings belonging to **Coston Farm** — which was bought by Ealing Council in 1928 to create **Ravenor Park.**

Our route now follows the footpath into Ravenor Park but, before turning aside, have a rest on the **Village Green** beside the **War Memorial** while I sum up the changes that have taken place at this end of Oldfield Lane. **Stanhope Park** was built on the site of **Stickleton Manor House** towards the end of the 18th century. *Dr. Samuel Glasse,* rector of Hanwell and chaplain to King George III, is said to have run a school here from about 1775 — assisted, for a time, by a Rev. Dr. Dodd. If this was the same *Dr. William Dodd* of Ealing (see Page 53), former king's chaplain and tutor to *Philip Stanhope,* the Earl of Chesterfield, then it might explain the Stanhope connection; but I have not yet found any firm evidence to support this theory.

There was a strong family link between the owners of Stanhope Park and **The Cottage** for several decades this century, however. The latter was occupied by *Lord Alexander Lawrence* and his wife, *Dorothy Hobson* (a local lass), whose two sisters lived at Stanhope Park — one single, and the other married to a *Mr. Otter.* Lord Lawrence, incidentally, was the grandson of the former Governor General of India, 1st Baron John Lawrence, who had once attended Great Ealing School. The grounds of Stanhope Park were frequently used for village fairs and shows, and when the estate went up for sale in the early 1930's it was intended to preserve the park as open space; but Mrs. Otter later asked for it to be redesignated a residential area to make its sale easier, and by 1934 planning permission was being sought for the first houses in **Stanhope Park Road.** Included in this development was the Otter's **Stanhope Park Farm** (now covered by the parade of shops on the northern side of The Broadway), and the **Dairy Farm** belonging to a *Mr. Wilcox,* which occupied **Stanhope Villa** (also known as the Red House) and the land behind it. The main grazing grounds lay to the north at Wilcox's **Oldfield Farm** but, as you can see from the picture, the cows were driven to the dairy every morning and evening to be milked.

Looking north up Oldfield Lane from Village Green in 1920. The Cottage stands behind the village shop and Post Office, with Stanhope Villa (Red House) Dairy beyond.

The new **Greenford Hall,** on the other side of the green, was built in 1966 on the sites of Aberdeen Cottages (demolished before the Second World War) and **Aberdeen House,** which had served as Council offices for many years. The adjacent **White Hart Inn** (shown on the Ordnance Survey map of 1894) had opened as a beershop in 1845, but had disappeared by 1912 — and I suspect that its license was transferred to the **new White Hart** in Windmill Lane (now Greenford Road), around the time that Greenford Park was being developed. This White Hart had extensive stabling in 1924 when it, together with Aberdeen House and Cottages, was taken over by Watneys from an omnibus company called Sitch & Co. — but the brewers have no record of when it was first built. However, the fact that Oldfield Lane properties adjacent to the original White Hart were included in the sale, suggests that my theory may not be too far from the mark. The present **Police Station** was built early this century (although the Greenford Division of the Metropolitan Police had been established in 1864), and the **Health Clinic** and **Library** opened in 1930 and 1934 respectively.

One thing hasn't changed though, and if you carry on into **Ravenor Park** and look northwards over the town, you will get the same peaceful view of Horsenden Hill that residents following the field-path to Northolt enjoyed in days gone by. Take the southern path through the park to return to reality and the **Ruislip Road,** and then make your way through the busy shopping centre of **The Broadway. Greenford Methodist Church** first opened in 1931, but was bombed during the War and rebuilt in 1957. The old footpath to Southall is now **Mansell Road,** and **Greenford Lodge** was demolished for **Stanhope School** in 1930. The Lodge was last used as a Stud Farm and produced several champions of Greenford's former Trotting Track — which we will be passing in Route 2.

South of the school lies the **Greenford Park Estate,** which began to be developed on the old **Glebe Lands** by private speculators in 1908. The adjacent **Windmill Estate** was planned by Greenford Urban District Council, but building was carried out by Ealing Council from 1927. The **wheelwright** on the corner of **Windmill Lane** became redundant as the farms disappeared, the 18th century **Red Lion** was rebuilt on the corner of Greenford Road in 1930, and the ancient **Smithy** and **Brent Cottages** were demolished at the same time for Burton the Tailor's building — now Playmate. (I was pleased to discover that Women's Lib was alive and well in Greenford as early as 1841, when one *Sarah Hinge* was recorded as being the village blacksmith.) Development of The Broadway/Greenford Road shopping centre was swift. According to Kelly's Directory, between 1929 and 1940 the number of shops in the area had increased from 7 to 123, which included two cinemas in Greenford Road — since replaced by supermarkets.

Beyond the Greenford Road junction, the **Brent River Park** offers you the chance of escaping from the traffic for a while and enjoying a bit of fresh air. At **Greenford Bridge,** you have the choice of crossing over into **Costons Lane** and **Perivale Park** to join up with Route 1 in the previous chapter, or carrying on to the **cycle path** between the playing fields on the southern side of the road. This paved path continues eastwards to Bridge Avenue, but a break in the fencing on the right hand side provides access to the open space around the Brent (the former Lammas Fields), through which you can make your way to **High Lane,** and then across the golf course to **Brent Lodge Park** in Hanwell. High Lane was once called Hay or Mud Lane — and the latter still applies after rain, so be prepared. If it's really muddy, it might be advisable to avoid the open space altogether by following the cycle path through to **Brook Avenue,** and joining High Lane near Mayfield School.

Once the GLC's flood alleviation scheme has been completed, the **Brent River and Canal Society** hope to open up the gate beside Greenford Bridge to give direct access to the Hanwell river path. This part of the river has already been widened and deepened to prevent flooding of the houses in Costons Lane, and an observation area has been built above the Ruislip Road. Tea and refreshments are available at the Golf Pavilion in Perivale Park, and there is a cafeteria in Brent Lodge park (see Route 1, Hanwell). Both these routes follow the line of ancient footpaths.

The old **Stickleton Bridge** lay roughly opposite today's **Greenford Avenue,** then called **Cuckoo Lane.** The bridge was recorded as early as 1339 when the Abbot of Westminster was brought before Edward III for allowing the bridge to fall into such a state of decay that the unfortunate *Rector Iver of Perivale* and two parishioners had drowned whilst attempting a crossing. The Abbot tried to wriggle out of the charge by insisting that the bridge had nothing to with him, as the windmill to which it had once provided access had ceased to exist long before he became Lord of the Manor — but he was ordered to repair it all the same. The first **Greenford Bridge** was built further west near the ford c.1614, and Stickleton Bridge was later demolished. A pub called the **Load of Hay** stood on the south-western side of Greenford Bridge from about 1930 until destroyed by a flying bomb ten years later — the site is now covered by the playing fields of **Cardinal Wiseman School.**

(Holy Cross to the canal via Oldfield Lane, and then along the towpath to either Northolt or Horsenden Hill — 2¼ to 2½ miles)

ROUTE TWO

From the churchyard, turn north up **Oldfield Lane** (note the old sign announcing 'The Rectory', Greenford Magna' on your left) and cross under Western Avenue via the subway. Those in need of early fortification can make their way to the **Bridge Hotel** on the eastern side of the Greenford Road roundabout — not the most ideal setting for a pub, but Real Ale fans will no doubt be grateful that Young's Brewery won their 5-year battle with the authorities (and the Red Lion down the road) to get planning permission for The Bridge, which opened in 1936.

Most of the development immediately north of Western Avenue and on either side of Greenford Road has taken place on land that once belonged to **Oldfield and Greenford Farms,** which ceased production in the early 1930's. The fields around the present **Glaxo Sports and Social Club** had been sold to the Bell Assurance Company (later Sun Life) by 1928, and new housing soon spread down from the railway to surround the farms on three sides. *Mr. Wilcox* and his cows moved out of **Oldfield Farm,** which was sold to a doctor, and **Greenford Farm** became the private residence of *Mr. T. Atkinson* (owner of Peerless Wire Fencing) until it was converted into the present **Conservative Club** in Couthope Road in 1934. The rest of the Greenford estate was bought by the Council to build **Oldfield First School** in 1940. **Oldfield Farmhouse** is also still standing (on the southern side of Oldfield Farm Gardens), but looks very neglected and is only part-occupied.

Community and **Legion Roads** were built after the War on the estate of yet another **Coston House,** which was erected in the late 1920's. The Fascist leader, *Sir Oswald Mosley* is said to have stayed here before his marriage to the Hon. Diana Mitford in 1936 — when the owner, Mr. J. *Shatzow,* converted the house into a factory for experimenting in cinematography. **Birkbeck Avenue** once provided access to Greenford's most popular sporting venue — the **Trotting Track** which had opened in 1919. The pony-drawn 'carts' (two wheels joined by an axle on which the driver balanced) attracted large crowds of locals and Londoners to the track, and betting was especially brisk on bank holidays. Later greyhound and motorcycle racing were also introduced, but the track closed in 1933 and within a few years the houses of **Jeymer Drive** and **Stanley Avenue** had covered the site.

Parents whose children are showing a dangerous inclination to trot into Oldfield Lane, will appreciate the respite offered by the small **recreation ground** opposite the Post Office. If you're heading for Horsenden Hill anyway, and are not too fussed about missing the Black Horse pub, then a shortcut through the recreation ground will enable you to pick up the remains of the old footpath to **Brabsden Green** — and avoid the worst of the industrial traffic. From the park, you cross over **Greenford Road** and continue under the railway bridge to turn right into **Rockware Avenue.** Between the car-park for **Greenford Golf Course** and the **IBM Centre,** a narrow footpath leads down to the bridge over the canal, and the route outlined at the end of this walk. A word of warning, however, in really wet weather this path resembles a muddy stream and is best avoided — unless you happen to be wearing a wet-suit and waders. **IBM** took over the site of **Rockware Glassworks** in 1976 and their computer centre was developed in record time — it was fully operational within a year of the plans being drawn up by world-famous architect, *Norman Soster.*

To return to the main route and Oldfield Lane ... **Greenford Station** first opened in 1904 on the GWR's suburban service from Marylebone to High Wycombe. The present station dates from 1947, however, the year that the Central line from North Acton to Greenford replaced the old GWR's 'push-and-pull' steam engines. The line was extended to West Ruislip the following year, and in 1958 the diesel train service between Greenford and Ealing Broadway began.

From the **Railway Hotel** (built in the 1920's), Oldfield Lane passes through the heart of Greenford's **industrial centre;** but most of the factories on the western side are set back from the road, and their frontages have been landscaped to make this walk an almost pleasant experience — except for the heavy rumble of passing traffic. Many of the larger manufacturing companies (such as British Baths and Rockware) have closed or moved out of Greenford in recent years and been replaced by warehousing concerns like the one in Rockware Avenue, but several long-established firms remain.

J. Lyons and Co. moved their tea-blending department from Hammersmith to a site between the railway and canal in Greenford in 1921, and have been expanding ever since. By 1926 the company were employing a workforce of over 3000 and had begun to build houses for their workers in the Costons Avenue area. Throughout the 1920's and 30's barges transported thousands of tons of tea, coffee, cocoa and chocolate between the Lyons Dock and London every year. The Lyons Maid **ice cream factory** was built on the Bridge Park site in 1958, by which time groceries, frozen foods and instant tea and coffee had also been added to the production line. (The concept of frozen food had been developed at Hammersmith during the War to make use of the refridgeration plant after the manufacture of ice cream had been banned because it was a luxury food.) The parent company was taken over by Allied Breweries in 1978 but, between them, the subsidiary companies of **Lyons Maid, Lyons Tetley** and **Sol Tenco** are still the largest employers in Greenford.

But what of the man who established the very first factory in Greenford? About 50 yards before the canal bridge, a small **blue plaque** on the building belonging to the Road Transport Industry's Training Board commemorates *Sir William Henry Perkin*, who began manufacturing synthetic dyes beside the canal in 1857 — the first such factory in the world, never mind Greenford. The 18-year old chemistry student had accidentally produced the first synthetic dye (aniline purple — better known as mauve) while attempting to synthesise quinine the previous year, and, with the financial backing of his father, set up a small **dyeworks** on a 6-acre site south of the Black Horse on Greenford Green. His father and older brother, *Thomas Dix Perkin*, both left the building trade to help him and, despite the family's inexperience in this type of work, their venture soon proved a commercial success — crowned by the appearance of Queen Victoria in a mauve gown at the Royal Exhibition of 1862.

The new colour fell out of fashion in the next few years, but Perkin had not been idle in his laboratory and used the French discovery of a second aniline dye, magenta, as the base for two new dyes, Britannia Violet and Perkin's Green. (The water in the canal is said to have turned a different colour every week — depending on what dyes were being made at the time!) Alizarin, a red-coloured dye formerly obtained from madder root, was synthesised simultaneously by Perkin and a German company in 1869 — but the Germans beat him to patenting the process by one day, so Perkin was forced to find an alternative method. This proved to be his downfall in the end as, although the factory's

The Black Horse, Oldfield Lane North, Greenford.

profits for 1872-3 were in the region of £60,000 a year, nearly all his income was put back into the business, and Perkin found he could not compete with the large and cheaper quantities of alizarin being produced by the Germans without a large injection of cash to build a more up-to-date factory.

In 1874 he accepted an offer for his business from the dye company of Brooke, Simpson and Spiller, and retired to his house and research laboratory in Sudbury — where he died in 1907, a year after being knighted for his pioneering work. The new dye factory also closed within a few years, and the premises were used by various small industries such as tallow-makers and bone-boilers until **Peerless Wire Fencing** moved a division of their Long Drive factory to the site in the 1930's. **Durasteel** took over when Peerless moved out of Greenford in 1938, and were responsible for restoring the bell which once summoned Perkin's employers to work, and the old gate-keeper's cottage (the original site of the commemorative plaque) for the centenary celebrations in 1957. A number of original buildings still existed at this time, but the bell was later stolen and the last evidence of Perkin's factory was demolished when Durasteel sold the site in 1976.

Perkin had also owned two acres of land on the opposite side of the road, where he had built **Factory Cottages,** a store and a laboratory. These were demolished for Garner's Bakery in 1958 — later taken over by Spillers and, since 1979, occupied by British Bakeries' **Mother's Pride factory.** Over 400,000 loaves of bread are distributed from here every week — not to mention over a million rolls, buns and crumpets. Collectors of useless information may be interested to know that although sliced bread became increasingly popular after the War, the process was not automated until c.1964.

The **Black Horse** pub has been providing sustenance for wayfarers since the early 18th century. Besides good beer and snacks, it offers a well laid-out garden overlooking the canal, where, on a fine day, you can relax in the sun and watch people messing about in boats. The pub became a popular rendezvous for daytrippers after the canal opened — the ride by barge from Paddington into Unknown Middlesex being considered a novel excursion by sophisticated Londoners. The **passage boat** (drawn by horses bedecked with coloured ribands) used to set out at 8 every morning in the summer months, bound for Greenford Green and Uxbridge. Breakfast was provided on board and fares were reasonable — 5 miles for a shilling, ten for 1/6 and the whole journey for half-a crown.

The "clearness of the water, the nut-brown tints of the wavy corn, and the ruddy and healthful tints of the cottagers' children who waited anxiously to see the vessel approach their native shores" were much admired by early-19th century travellers — but it would be interesting to know what the hardworking, though rustic, Greenford farmers thought about the tourists. Stage-coaches and railways gradually took over from the regular canal passenger service, but private boat and bus-loads of visitors from more urban areas continued to assemble at the Black Horse well into this century, for a day's picnicking on Horsenden Hill or country ramble to Harrow.

You have the choice of several walks from the canal bridge — **Route A, along the towpath to Horsenden Hill,** offering the best 'country ramble' in the area today. From the bridge, the canal curves round between sports grounds Glaxo and Mother's Pride, and finally leaves the factories behind at Greenford Road bridge. The firm of **Glaxo** has also expanded considerably since they first began manufacturing baby food and pharmaceutical products beside the canal in 1935. Those of you reared on Ostermilk may like to know that *Joseph Nathan* established the company in New Zealand in 1873 to export butter and cheese, and introduced dried milk to the UK a few years after opening a London-based company in 1899. The slogan '*Glaxo Builds Bonnie Babies*' was soon being widely advertised, and in 1924 the company became the first in Britain to manufacture Vitamin D on a commercial scale. The laboratories went from strength to strength after they moved to their new premises in Greenford — the most important development during the War years being the production of penicillin. Today, Glaxo is Britains' biggest pharmaceutical company and supplies medicine for human and veterinary use all over the world.

Once on the other side of **Greenford Road,** you suddenly find yourself in open country with the fragrant smell of freshly baked bread lingering on the air, and nothing but trees and fields on either side. Cross over the **footbridge** you come to further on, and follow the path through Berkley Fields and **Horsenden Hill Recreation Ground** to the **Ballot Box** pub — an overall distance of about 1½ miles, if you make it to the top of the hill via the footpath through the woods. The half-dozen or so cottages which once made up the hamlet of **Brabsden Green** lay north-west of the pub until demolished for the widening of Horsenden Lane after the War.

For a shorter walk (about ¾-mile), follow **Route B up Oldfield lane to Greenford Green,** and turn north up Greenford Road for a brisk game of squash(!) or a sauna at **Ealing Northern Sports Ground** on Sudbury Hill. Members of the *Perkin* family still lived at this end of Oldfield lane in the 1930's — *Thomas Dix Perkin* having become a country squire at **Greenford Green Farm** after his brother sold the dyeworks. He was Master of the Middlesex Farmers' Draghounds at the turn of the century and his son, *Alfred William,* who inherited the farm, continued the family tradition of contributing something to the community, as a Justice of the Peace and Manager of Betham School. Alfred's widow kept the farm going for a few years after his death, but by 1938 it had been covered by the group of new roads between **Rugby Avenue** and **Wadham Gardens.** The bit of ground around the **Oldfield Tavern** at the top of the lane is all that is left of **Greenford Green** today — the pub itself having been built on the site of an old pond (filled in with rubbish by local residents) during the 1930's.

Route C leads westwards along the towpath (for about a mile) to the footbridge and path leading up to **Northolt Village Green** — which you can find out about in the next chapter.

Passage boat cruising down the Paddington Canal from Greenford Bridge in the 19th century.

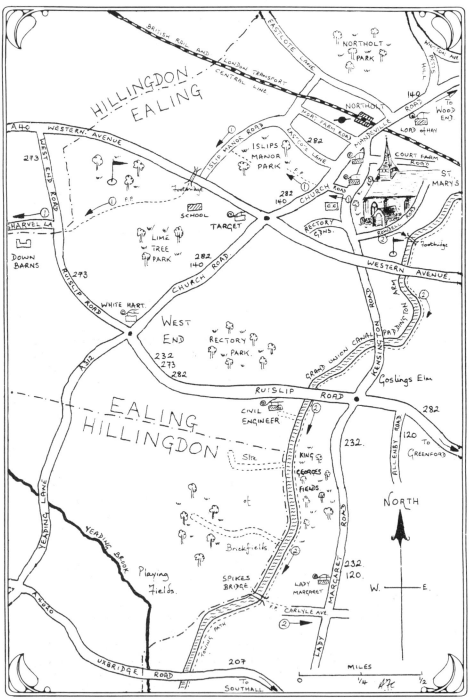

NORTHOLT 158

CHAPTER IX

Recollect the elm-trees misty
And the footpaths climbing twisty
Under cedar-shaded palings,
Low laburnam-leaned-on railings,
Out of Northolt on an upward to the heights of Harrow Hill.

JOHN BETJEMAN, Middlesex.

NORTHOLT was the last suburb in the borough to lose its village identity. In 1845 it was described as one of the remotest areas in Middlesex, and farming was still the main occupation a century later. But the Council's decision to develop Northolt into a sprawling 'dormitory suburb' soon put an end to this rural way of life and, within a decade, the woods and fields of the 18th century farms were covered with houses. Fortunately, the Village Green and two moated Manor House sites of Northolt and Down managed to escape this onslaught but, on the whole, Northolt is sadly lacking in pleasant open spaces to relieve the tedium of housing estates, and no walk can avoid the network of major roads that criss-cross the town today.

Although the earliest record of the old name, 'Nord Healum' (meaning 'at the northern neck of land') occurs in a Saxon charter of 962 AD, archeological discoveries of pagan Saxon burials and dwellings show that the village on the hilltop was occupied several centuries before that date. The first known Lord of the manor was *Tofi the Proud*, standard-bearer to King Canute, and Sheriff of Middlesex - a title that passed, together with his large estates in various parts of the country, to his grandson, *Angsgar*, Master of the Stud to Edward the confessor, who led the London and Middlesex contingents at the Battle of Hastings, and negotiated the terms of settlement with William the Conqueror. But, despite William's promise that "All things in the Kingdom shall be ruled according to the bidding of the Sheriff of the Middle Saxons", Angsgar was soon deprived of his power and his lands presented to William's friend, *Geoffrey de Mandeville*, who appears as overlord of the 2,000 acres and c.150 inhabitants of 'Northala' (the Latinised name) in the Domesday Survey.

The de Mandevilles retained control of what they subsequently called 'Northall', until the 13th century - although, with 120 other manors to play with, it is unlikely that they took much interest in this tiny village, other than to collect the tithes due to them. The most exciting member of the family was undoubtedly Geoffrey's grandson and namesake who, during the tussle for the Crown between Henry I's daughter, Mathilda, and her cousin, Stephen, used his position as Custodian of the Tower to bargain for further privileges from both contestants. Mathilda made him Earl of Essex but he lost everything when Stephen was reinstated as King, and was forced to become and outlaw. He was finally excommunicated by the Pope - so that after his death in 1144, his body lay unburied for nearly 20 years (but fortunately enclosed in a lead coffin) until his son obtained absolution for him, and repossession of the de Mandeville lands.

The bulk of their property (including Northolt, Perivale, and **Stickleton Manor** in Greenford) later passed by marriage to that other great baronial family - the *de Bohuns*, Earls of Hereford. But, from Northolt's point of view, the first Lord of the Manor to have any direct effect on their village was *Peter le Boteler*, a descendant of the butler to King Stephen who had adopted his title as a surname. He leased the manor for the annual rent of one pound of pepper and, c.1300, set the villagers to work at building him a stone

Manor House, surrounded by a moat, on the hilltop north-east of the church - right in the middle of their own small settlement of wooden houses, which then had to be reconstructed in the valley below. This Manor House was rebuilt on a much larger scale about fifty years later for the new overlord, *Simon Fraunceys* (Sheriff, and later Mayor, of London), who probably used it as a refuge during the dreaded Black Death.

By this time, in addition to the main village under the watchful eye of the Lord of the Manor, there were five other distinct areas of settlement in Northolt. The oldest of these was around the Vill or **Manor of Down** (now Down Barns Farm) which lay to the west on the old Roman road from Uxbridge to Harrow. There were also a few houses at **West End,** beside the junction of the road to Ruislip, and Janes Street (now Church Road) - the latter continuing northwards to Frere Place, a 13th century estate which later became known as **Wood End Green Farm.** Nearer the main village, just south of the lane to Eastcote, the Ruislip family held a large freehold estate on the site of the present **Islip Manor;** and, in the south-east corner of the parish, lay the small hamlet later called **Gosling's Elm** — at the junction of the lanes that linked West End and Northolt Village with Greenford (today's Ruislip and Kensington Roads).

Other scattered farms sprang up during the 17th and 18th centuries, but these five medieval settlements remained virtually unchanged until the 1920's. None of Northolt's numerous illustrious overlords seems to have made any lasting impression on this rural backwater - except, perhaps, *Sir Nicolas Brembre* who bought out the Fraunceys family's share in Northolt and, through no real fault of his own, succeeded in getting the Manor House demolished. He fell foul of King Richard II (despite having been knighted for his assistance in suppressing the Peasants' Revolt under Wat Tyler), and was executed on a trumped up charge of treason in 1388. All his property was confiscated by the King, who had the Manor House destroyed - presumably to prevent Brembre's wife from making any claims - before giving the manor lands to *Westminster Abbey* in payment for his tomb there.

After the dissolution of the monasteries, Northolt (like Greenford and Hanwell) belonged briefly to the unsuccessful Bishopric of Westminster, until surrendered to Edward VI in 1550. The boy king granted Northolt to his tutor, *Sir Thomas Wroth,* who soon had to flee the country for his part in trying to make Edward's cousin, Lady Jane Grey, successor to the throne. The manor, however, remained in the Wroth family until 1616, when it was sold to the lawyer and MP, *Sir John Bennett.* His son inherited but, on being fined the huge sum of £24,000 for certain legal malpractices, was forced to dispose of his assets rather rapidly; and *William Pennyfather* of Islips Manor became the new overlord.

James Brydges, the *Duke of Chandos,* took over the manor in the early 18th century; and from his time onwards Northolt was run by absentee manor lords who let their lands to local farmers, and collected their profits from the Manor Court. This was a sound investment as, besides the annual income form the demesne lands, the overlord also held the royalties for 'hawking, hunting, fishing and fowling' throughout Northolt, as well as parts of Greenford, Perivale and Ickenham - which had been under Northolt's jurisdiction since de Mandeville times. The link with these neighbouring parishes gradually fell away, but Northolt's reputation for being the best manor for game in the County of Middlesex continued into the 19th century - and probably explains why this remote parish (which suffered from a notorious lack of fresh water and adequate roads) was never short of eager buyers ... although few chose to live there, themselves.

The Manor was later bought by *Sir Francis Child* of Osterley, and for many years Southall and Northolt shared the same overlord. But in 1827, Northolt was sold to *Sir Lancelot Shadwell* (England's last Vice Chancellor) and remained in his family for the next century. The last of the wide open spaces had been enclosed for hay and dairy farming by the early 19th century, so hunting had become rather restricted; but the earlier opening of the Paddington Canal had provided investors with a new incentive - exploitation of the brick earth deposits lining the canal in the southern part of the parish. By 1861, labourers on the brickfields had increased Northolt's population figure to 658; but the industry soon declined, and with it went most of the new residents at West End.

Poor road and water conditions continued to discourage people from settling in the parish, and in 1894 (the same year that Northolt became part of Uxbridge Rural District) a Parish Council was formed to improve matters. They succeeded in getting a small supply of piped water brought to the village, but their complaints about the state of the roads went unheeded; and although the GWR opened a halt at Northolt in 1907, there was little residential development until 1920, when the Shadwells sold Manor Farm to *Frank Wright*, a Hanwell butcher. But Northolt was not quite ready for the 'garden city' Wright planned for the site, and all that materialised was a few villas in Church Road.

Meanwhile, progressives on the Parish Council were desperately fighting against Northolt's amalgamation with Uxbridge - one of their more successful battles, as in 1928 Northolt was incorporated into the Borough of Ealing with the loss of only a hundred acres in the extreme north-east of the parish, when the old Mount Park estate was transferred to Harrow. During the 1930's, roads through the parish were improved beyond recognition with the opening of Western and Whitton Avenues. Extensive ribbon development followed the widening of Church and Mandeville Roads, and factories soon sppeared in Rowdell Road. The Council's first proper planning scheme was interrupted by the Second World War, but by 1960 over 3,000 new housing units had been built (more than half the post-war total for the entire borough), and today around 35,000 people are living where a mere 500 struggled to make a living from the land at the turn of the century.

A painting of the Village Green in about 1820, showing St. Mary's and the 16th century Church House — demolished c.1838 when a small schoolhouse was built on the site (see Route 1).

The little **Parish Church of St Mary** stands on the hill overlooking the Village Green and presents a pleasantly anachronistic picture in today's new, 'improved' Northolt. Its flint and rubble walls have been covered with whitewashed cement, but the basic structure remains virtually unchanged since *Peter le Boteler* had the village rebuilt almost 700 years ago, and replaced the simple wooden church with one of stone to match his new Manor House. A priest was recorded at Northolt in the Domesday Book, but the first church on the site was probably built over a pagan Saxon shrine during the 7th century, when the last of the Angles became angels.

The **nave** forms the main and oldest part of the church, and its solid construction is a credit to those early citizens of Northolt. The soft sandstone mouldings around the doors and Early English-style windows have crumbled away over the centuries and been repaired with cement; but, except for the addition of some 18th century buttresses to the exterior (when it was feared that the church was slipping down the hillside), the walls of the nave have withstood the passage of time remarkably well. The roof was renewed in the early 1500's — at the same time as the **chancel** was built onto the former east wall, and the wooden **bell tower** and small spire were erected. The south porch and vestry are both modern additions, erected after the Second World War.

Besides the constant battle to maintain a building of this age, the church authorities also have to contend with damage caused by vandals and St. Mary's has to be kept locked when unattended. However, visits can easily be arranged for any non-parishioners interested in exploring this last surviving link with Northolt's past. The most distinctive feature of the interior is the wooden **gallery,** erected in 1703 'for the singers and servant men' and now almost filled by the organ which once belonged to the *Duke of Chandos* — although it was only acquired early this century. The composer, *Handel*, was attached to the Duke's household at Canons in Edgware for several years and it is quite likely that this was the organ played by the 'Harmonious Blacksmith'.

The 14th century **font** is the oldest item in the church and is thought to have been donated by *Sir Nicholas Brembre*, whose shield of arms appears on one of the panels. The Royal Arms of Queen Anne are set in the wall of the nave above the blocked-off north door (which once gave the Lord of the Manor direct access to the church from his moated Manor house) and were probably placed there by *John Cockburn* who was appointed vicar here in 1714, on the Queen's recommendation. Over the main entrance is a hatchment bearing the arms of the three dioceses (St. David's, London and Canterbury) of *Archbishop William Laud* — a former Rector of Northolt. The board was erected in 1945 to mark the tercentenary of his execution on Tower Hill during the Civil War.

Laud was just one of the many famous Bishops of London who were Rectors of St. Mary's between 1231 and 1873. Before that, the church had formed part of the endowment of Walden Priory in Essex (founded by Geoffrey de Mandeville), but the Prior's rights were disputed by the Dean of St. Paul's and it was agreed that a Vicarage be created with the Bishop of London as patron. In 1864, the patronage and rights of presentation were transferred to Brasenose College, Oxford, which later united the offices of Vicar and Rector and has appointed all clergymen ever since.

Even before the church became associated with Oxford, it was noted for the scholarly (if somewhat eccentric) qualities of its vicars — many of whom held important positions outside the rural parish so that the church was often left in the hands of the curate. A small tablet on a wall in the chancel commemorates the most famous of these : *Goronwy Owen*, the Welsh equivalent of Shakespeare and Burns, who is acclaimed as being the founder of the modern Welsh language.

The poet became 'curate in charge' of St. Mary's in 1755 and is said to have written some of his best work during the two years he spent here. He was also the first secretary of the newly formed Cymmrodorian Society of London and never missed a meeting, despite having to walk from Northolt to Fleet Street in order to attend their gatherings. But sadly his drinking problem — he is said to have 'spent more time curing his thirst than in the cure of souls' — and a spot of bother concerning a maid at The Crown, led the Bishop of London to send him to Virginia from whence he never returned.

Memorials to the *Shadwell* family are to be found on the south wall of the nave; and, in the south-east corner, lies the oldest brass in the church which records the death of *Henry Rowdell* in 1452. He owned land near Islips Manor and gives his name to the modern Rowdell Road. In the chancel, there is a fine 16th century brass to *Susan* and *John Gyfforde* of Gyfforde's Farm (another early name for Islips Manor), showing a man in armour, with his wife and two groups of children. According to the Parish Registers (which begin in 1560), Andrea, the wife of William Gyfforde, was indicted for not attending the parish church in 1599 — but as she was the daughter of Richard Lyon, you can see her memorial in St. Mary's, West Twyford.

The **churchyard** has served as a burial ground for almost a thousand years and its gravestones make interesting reading for those who enjoy that kind of thing. The oldest burials are to be found on the south side of the church as, in medieval times, it was considered to be asking for trouble in the after-life if the shadow of the church fell across one's grave. Two notable ex-residents to look out for are *Stephen Demainbury*, who owned a small farm at Wood End and was the first astronomer at Kew Observatory until his death in 1782; and *Edmund Tattersall*, who married the daughter of a farmer at West End, and was the only son of the racehorse auctioneer who founded the Knightsbridge firm of Tattersalls in the 18th century. Some old graves have also been found outside the churchyard in Belvue Park and it is assumed that these belonged to undesirables such as paupers, plague victims and criminals.

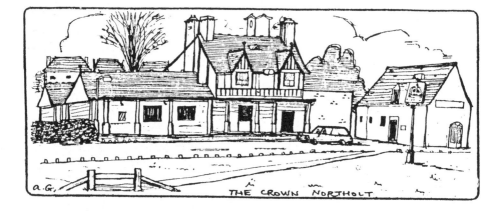

THE CROWN NORTHOLT

(Village Green to Down Barns Farm via Islips Manor — 2½ miles). If you have ever wanted to whisk yourself back into the 19th century, then the **Village Green** at Northolt is the place to do so. The setting is perfect ... nestled in a a small valley around the proverbial babbling brook, lie the village inn, the old schoolhouse and tiny cottages — with the white washed walls of the church gleaming through the trees at the top of the hill. Only the ubiquitous motor-car serves as a sharp reminder of the present, and the traffic rushing by a few yards away on Mandeville Road.

You are unlikely to find a more attractive spot this close to 'civilisation', however, so take your time and savour the scene over a pint at the **The Crown**. First licensed in 1726, the pub has been considerably rebuilt and modernised (as you can see from a painting of the original, inside), but offers good 'pub grub' as well as a proper restaurant and a large rose-filled beer garden. (Don't take any liberties with the serving wenches — remember what happened to Goronwy Owen!)

The annual Village Fair attracted large crowds to the Green during the 18th and 19th centuries, but the frivolities got rather out of hand in later years and the event was

Willow Tree Cottages c.1880.

abolished by the Parish Council in 1897. The occupants of **Willow Cottages** were probably extremely grateful for this injunction, as their homes would have been right in the thick of things. Today the two cottages lead a very peaceful existence as storage sheds in the **Rest Garden** below the churchyard — not, perhaps, the most fitting use for the oldest houses in Northolt (they were built in the early 1800's), but better than the alternative plans that are constantly being proposed for the site, which involve demolition of the cottages. These have been, so far, successfully opposed by local conservationists.

Higher up the hill stands the former **National School** (now called the Memorial Hall) which replaced a smaller schoolhouse at the entrance to the churchyard in 1868. All the local children were educated here until **Northolt Primary School** was built in Church Road in 1907. This stood south of today's Western Avenue and was the only school in the parish for many years; but bigger and better educational facilities were provided as the population increased, and the Primary School finally closed in the 1960's.

Over the wooden footbridge, to the right of the gate into the churchyard, a secluded driveway leads to **Deyntes Cottage** which was built by the Shadwells in 1887. It replaced two earlier cottages — one of which was occupied by *Henry Deynte*, the headborough of the manor, in 1461. The Shadwells also rebuilt the 15th century **Manor Farmhouse** in about 1850, and this survives as the **Village Community Centre** in Ealing Road. But, despite making all these improvements to their Northolt property, the Shadwells never lived here (they owned many other estates outside the parish), and usually stayed with the Vicar in the old **Rectory** when visiting the manor. The houses in **Rectory Gardens** were built on the site of the 17th century Rectory after it was demolished in 1929.

In the old days, the Vicar saw to the spiritual needs of his flock in more ways than one as the **brewhouse** at the Rectory provided beer for the village and church festivals long before any inns were established. Later, the Rectory was to play an even more important part in the villagers' drinking habits when, in 1791, the Vicar sunk a well in the grounds — thus providing the parish with its first and only fresh water supply until a pump was erected on the Green almost a century later. Before then, the village had relied on several large and often unhygienic ponds for their domestic needs.

One of these ponds lay at the northern end of the Green, a little beyond the Village Smithy's premises (on the corner of Court Farm Road) and The Plough. Some two acres in extent, the pond was popular with local fishermen and a well-known landmark — the old **Moat Farm,** across the way, often being referred to as Pond Farm. Improvements to the former Wood End Lane in the 1930's brought many changes to this quiet corner, however. The pond was filled in and partly covered by the new **Mandeville Road,** the rest being grassed over to form **Mandeville Green** where a clock tower commemorating the coronation of George VI was later erected. The Smithy, not surprisingly, went out of business once Northolt was made accessible to motorised traffic; and although Moat Farm, the last of Northolt's 18th century farmhouses, withstood the traffic fumes for a few more years, the estate was finally sold for private housing in the late Fifties.

Northolt Station, higher up Mandeville Road, was merely a halt in the open fields for the GWR loop-line to High Wycombe when it first opened in 1907 — the present station being built in 1948, for the Central Line extension from Greenford to West Ruislip along the GWR route. Housing estates cover almost all the land between here and Whitton Avenue, offering little in the way of quiet walks; but before turning south towards Islips Manor, you might like to take advantage of a seat in **The Plough** (first licensed in the early 1700's, and the last pub on this route) to consider some of the changes that have taken place across the railway line, around the old settlement of **Wood End.**

Although most of the farmland in the parish had been sold off by the 1920's, Wood End was one of the few parts to be developed prior to the Second World War — largely as a result of the new Whitton Avenue and Mandeville Road, and the added attraction of **Northolt Park Racecourse.** Today, the strip of public open space lining Mandeville Road is all that remains of this once famous sporting venue — the rest of the former 2¼ mile track now being covered by Eastcote Lane North, Dabbs Hill Lane and Petts Hill. The Northolt Racecourse Company (backed by the wealthy industrialist *John Wadell*) bought this land from the Shadwells in 1928, with a view to establishing a premier course for London's pony racing enthusiasts.

The track opened the following year but, although crowds flocked to Northolt on race days, it never really achieved the popularity its sponsors hoped for and by 1937, the Company was in the hands of the Official Receiver. Racing continued until the outbreak of War, however, and the Northolt Derby was even televised by the BBC in 1938. During the War, the course and its buildings were used as an ordnance depot and later as a prisoner-of-war camp. Attempts to raise fresh capital and resume racing after the war were unsuccessful, and in 1946 the land was sold to Ealing Council and was soon covered by the tower-blocks and houses of the **Racecourse Estate.** The fact that streets on the new estate were named after racecourses throughout the country, must have been small consolation to disappointed punters.

Should residents living at the eastern ends of Reading Road and Clauson Avenue dig deeply enough in their back gardens, they might find remains of **Frere Place** — the old farm which belonged to the Hospital of St. Thomas of Acon c.1244. Known as **Wood End Green Farm** by the 19th century, it was later bought by *Sir William Perkin,* the Greenford chemist, and sold on his death in 1907. Part of the 90-acre estate was developed by private building speculators shortly before Northolt Racecourse opened, and the rest was completely built over by the 1960's. Not far away, an oasis of open space surrounds the former **GPO Wireless Station** which was built on the site of the old Northall Wood in 1921. The station's once awe-inspiring transmission area of 2,500 miles has been superseded by communication satellites and London's huge Post Office Tower,

Northolt Park Racecourse in 1930 — Dabbs Hill Lane on the right.

and a children's community home is planned for the disused site. The only other building of note in this area — the **Parish Workhouse** — was converted to **The Load of Hay** in 1838, after Northolt had joined the Hillingdon Poor Union. The present pub (which stands almost opposite Northolt Station) was rebuilt on the same site in 1930 .

But to get back to the main route for this walk ... when you leave The Plough, cross over Mandeville Road and continue south past the parade of shops (in 1922 there was only one shop for the whole parish), until you come to the gates and footpath into **Islips Manor.** This ancient estate was established c.1301 by the Ruislip family and it was called Ruislips Place until bought by John Gifford in the 16th century, when it became known as Giffords Farm. In 1629, the estate was sold to the Lord of the Manor, *William Pennyfather,* who used it as his manor house and changed the name to Islips Manor.

The present house was built by the antiquary, *George Harris,* c. 1860. 'Squire' Harris was a man of many parts — sailor, journalist, barrister, judge, anthropologist, psychologist — but, despite this wealth of experience, his autobiography was described by one historian as being 'the classic example of how an autobiography should not be written'! After his death, the house and 123-acre estate passed to his wife, and remained in her family until sold to Ealing Borough Council in 1928. The grounds have been developed for recreational purposes and the house converted into a **Health Centre.**

If you walk in a north-westerly direction across the park, you will come to an exit into **Islip Manor Road,** where you turn left for the **footbridge** over Western Avenue. Curving high above the traffic, the bridge affords a grand panorama of the surrounding countryside ... the view of modern high-rise buildings being offset by the distant green of Horsenden and Harrow Hills, and the rolling fields around Down Barns Farm, which can just be seen to the south, with the shooting tower of the West London Shooting Grounds beyond. Below you, horses can be seen grazing on the open land bordering the busy A40 which cuts through the Metropolitan Green Belt covering this eastern section of Northolt.

For me, the name 'Green Belt' has always conjured up a picture of lush, tree-lined pastures — until I discovered that it usually applies to areas of neglected scrubland which are fighting a losing battle against the illegal dumping of rubbish. Unfortunately, our walk to **Down Barns Farm** passes through just such an area as the tarred path from the footbridge ends at **Northolt First and Middle School.** Ducking through the trees to the right of the path, you cross a rather muddy ditch (much rutted by local 'scrambler' bikes) and, picking your way through various examples of the affluent 20th century's effluent, you ascend the hill to Down Barns. The bulldozers at work on the other side, signal the changes in store for this uninspiring approach, however; and when the proposed **Lime Trees Park Golf Course** is completed, this walk should be considerably more attractive.

It's worth the effort anyway, as once you're over Ruislip Road and into **Sharvel Lane,** the sights and smells of the farmyard soon restore your polluted senses, and herald a mile-long meander along the ridge above the fields and meadows of Down Barns, to the woods beyond the West London Shooting Grounds. Without wishing to dimish the bucolic delights ahead, I feel I should add that Yeading Brook (on the far side of the woods) prevents any further progress in that direction, and you will therefore have to return by the same route. So, if you are relying on public transport to get home, do bear in mind that your nearest bus-stop is back on **Ruislip Road** and conserve your energy accordingly.

DOWN BARNS FARM NORTHOLT

The early history of the **Manor of Down** is not very well documented. Sharvel Lane is assumed to be part of an ancient Roman trackway that may once have followed the clay ridge between Uxbridge and Harrow, and archeological finds in the Down Barns area suggest that a small Roman farming settlement had been established here as early as the 1st century. But there are no records of any subsequent occupants of the site until the 13th century, when a *Roger de la Dune* gave his name to (or, perhaps, took it from) the 300-acre estate of 'La Doune'. These lands achieved Manor status after they were sold to *John De Bohun*, Earl of Hereford and Essex, c.1330. Following de Bohun's death, the Manor of Down was bought as an investment by *Sir Thomas Holland*, Duke of Kent, and his wife, *Joan* (known as the 'Fair Maid of Kent'), who later married the Black Prince and became the mother of Richard II.

Long before Joan tickled the Prince's fancy, however, the Manor of Down was sold to Northolt's new overlord, *Simon Fraunceys*, who built a large moated **Manor House** on the Down ridge, along similar lines to his Northolt home. The moat can still be seen behind the present Down Barns buildings (on the left hand side of the lane), and is usually full of water. An abandoned kitchen garden and small orchard now cover the site of the old Manor House which, like the one at Northolt, was demolished by Richard II before the two manors were given to Westminster Abbey for the upkeep of his tomb (see Page 160 if you have forgotten the details) The Fair Maid of Kent thus, unwittingly, played a decisive role in the fortunes of Down — although it is unlikely that she even visited the manor while it was in her possession.

A new Manor House was built north-east of the moat at Down during Tudor times, and was let to tenant farmers after the manor separated from Northolt in the early 17th century. This was rebuilt into a much larger farmstead in 1754, but the Tudor chimney-stack was retained and was still in use when the house was badly damaged by a flying bomb during the Second World War. The present Down Barns farmhouse was built after the war, and the remains of its 18th century predecessor were finally removed in 1954.

By the mid-18th century, the old highway from Uxbridge to Harrow had ceased to be of much importance and was used mainly by farmers' carts — some sections (like the bit you have just negotiated from Islips Manor Road) already having become part of the cultivated fields. The bridge over Yeading Brook (called Golden Bridge) gradually fell into disuse, and although the eastern section of the road through Hillingdon was re-opened as **Charlville Lane** during the 1930's, what remains of the old Sharvel Lane from Down Barns is still little more than a rutted farm track — and will hopefully stay that way. The road ends just beyond the main buildings of the West London Shooting Grounds, and you reach the woods via a footpath in the large field to your left. (Do make sure that no shooting is in progress before entering the woods, please!)

The later manor lords of Down are of no particular interest except for *Charles Mills*, the banker, who bought the house and part of the estate during the 1850's, and was succeeded by his son, the first *Baron Hillingdon*. Manorial rights ceased early this century, but most of the former demesne lands still belong to Hillingdon as Sharvel Lane now forms part of Ealing's northern boundary. **Northolt Airport** (which can just be seen over the fields and Western Avenue, to the north) actually lies in Ruislip — although, if the following unlikely story is true, it should have been built in Harrow. Rumour has it that during the aerial survey made of the area to find a site for the proposed airfield, the surveyor looked at his map the wrong way round and instead of sticking his pin into Newton Park off the present Alexandra Avenue in Harrow, he sited the airfield off West End Road! In any event the airport opened here in 1915, was used as a training and defensive base during the First World War, and as an important Fighter Command base during the Second. After the War, Northolt became the country's major civil aviation terminal but reverted to an RAF base when Heathrow opened in 1952.

ROUTE TWO

(Canalside walk from Belvue Park to Southall — 2¾ miles) The site of the old **Manor House** was rescued in the nick of time by Ealing Borough Council in 1928, when they purchased the land from from a developer who had planned to build a row of houses right across the moated area. This site and surrounding hillside was made into public open space called Belvue Park, which has now been designated a conservation area. You'll find a gate from the churchyard into Belvue Park opposite the porch door of St. Mary's, and you reach the historic site by turning east and following the fence round the churchyard to where (if it has been raining recently) pools of muddy water mark the outline of the **moat.** At some future date, the Council intend to grass over the area, so that the indentation of the moat will be seen more clearly; but, until then, you'll just have to scramble through the brambles and bushes and do your best to imagine what the site looked like 600 years ago — with the help of Mr. Keene's plan.

When *Simon Fraunceys* rebuilt the Manor House in 1346, he also dug a new, and much larger, moat — using the clay to build up the outer banks and interior, and strengthening this foundation with stone and tiles from the le Boteler house. In those days, it was fashionable for any large house to have a moat — whether or not it was necessary to keep out intruders or provide a water supply. But, in the case of Northolt, the clay site made a moat with a built up interior essential so that the living area could drain into it and be kept reasonably dry. Fraunceys' house was built around a central courtyard and had four large chambers in addition to a hall (about 40 feet square), a huge kitchen (over 100 feet long and 30 feet wide) and a series of outbuildings that were probably used as workshops.

In 1370, Simon's daughter-in-law (who had inherited the house) was hauled before the sheriff for committing 'acts of waste and destruction' at the Manor which involved pulling down all but the kitchen and selling the valuable timber framing, in an attempt to get even in a family dispute. *Nicholas Brembre* repaired some of the damage, but Northolt Manor House met the same fate as Down after his execution and was never rebuilt. The site was later turned into an orchard, although the moat was kept in good repair for many years — the bridge being replaced by a small filled-in section at the eastern corner.

The Abbots of Westminster had no need of a manor house, although there is evidence that they built a house for their bailiff outside the moat on what is now Court Farm Road. This was later called **Northall Court** and was used as a manor house by subsequent overlords until *William Pennyfather* moved to Islips c.1630. Land was taken from Dovehouse Close (on the high ground to the east of the moat) for building **Court Farm** in the early 1700's and this then seems to have taken over as the manor house — the manor court being held here in later years. Court Farm was demolished in 1929 and the houses in Fort, Summit and the northern end of Rowdell Roads now cover the site.

Our walk continues across Belvue Park and down to Rowdell Road. Head towards the large sign for **Gallaher** (the Benson & Hedges company) and, just to the right of the Hoover warehouse, you will find a path to the **Paddington Canal.** The towpath is reached via a footbridge over the canal where moored narrowboats add a splash of colour to the industrialised stretch of water curving round to Greenford. Here you turn west past the green sward of the golf range on the opposite bank, which soon gives way to open scrubland once you've passed under **Western Avenue** — the modern boundary between Northolt and Greenford. As both these parishes are suffering from that urban disease described by the Council as 'a severe local park deficiency', the new Borough Plan proposes that this area be turned into a District Park by extending Belvue Park southwards to include the golf range, which will then be linked by the towpath (under the A40) to landscaped open land on both sides of the canal.

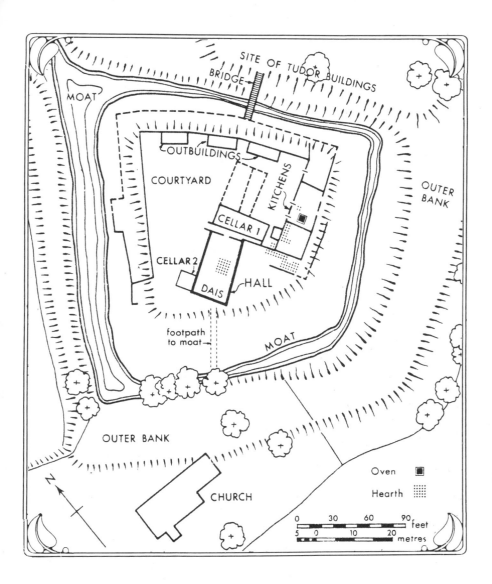

A general plan of Northolt Manor House between 1346 and 1370, after it had been rebuilt by Simon Fraunceys. The two cellars at either end of the great hall each had a ground floor store-room with a solar (living-room) above. The fireplace in Solar 1 was built of London stock bricks, moulded and cut into different shapes, and painted alternately red and white. The floor of Solar 2 was covered with tiles which came from the Penn Potteries in Buckinghamshire. This plan, devised by local historian Mr. C.H. Keene, is based on discoveries made during the 10-year period of intensive excavation carried out in the Fifties and Sixties. The Manor House finds and, more particularly, evidence of earlier Saxon occupation of the site from the 7th century attracted nationwide attention, and Northolt is still considered the most important archeological site in Greater London. A model of one of the Solars can be seen at Gunnersbury Museum.

A fine plan ... but, in the meantime, this section of the canal is dominated by the GLC housing estate which replaced **Smith's Farm** and, judging by the number of boarded up doors and windows, has not proved a particularly popular residential area. The most interesting building on the horizon is the distinctive mosque-like tower of the old Aladdin heating appliance works on Western Avenue. It was renamed the **Sultan Tower** after the premises were taken over by the Turkish firm of Sultan Mondial, but was once more up for sale in 1982. A supermarket chain and DIY company are at present negotiating for the site, and it is hoped that this old landmark will find a place in the new scheme. Although the tower is on the borough's list of local historic buildings, it is not officially protected by the Department of the Environment — despite several applications having been made.

The canal now passes under **Kensington Road** which was once a footpath through the medieval settlement known as **Goslings Elm** and, later, **Elm End.** The old elm-tree has long since passed away, but the various names of the village have been preserved in the surrounding modern streets. A shallow tree-lined cutting brings the canal to **Ruislip Road,** where the offices of **Taylor Woodrow** have spanned the water since the 1940's. (This, I should warn you, is your last escape-route from the canal for the next mile; so the fainthearted may like to take advantage of the pub called **The Civil Engineer** on the western side of the bridge, and read about what they have missed on the bus home!) The shortlived 'boom' of the **brickfields** along the next stretch of canal during the 1830's, resulted in several new houses being built at West End — which lay roughly at the crossroads of today's Ruislip and Church Roads. No further expansion took place for another century and, looking at the modern West End, it is difficult to believe that there were still only three houses and a couple of farms here in 1937. Two years later, Northolt's oldest brickworks, the West End and Middlesex Brick Company, finally closed having, during its finest hours, supplied most of the bricks for lining London's sewers — which was evidently a tribute to their superior quality.

The last fields to be worked out lay on the offside of the canal, just before the sign on the towpath which marks the northern boundary of Yeading; although the three substantial arms of the canal that led off into the old workings further south, continued to be used by the rubbish boats from Paddington for many years. There were incinerators for burning the rubbish at **Yeading Dock,** but these proved inadequate for the vast amounts being brought in by boat which gradually filled in the brickfields and the arms of the canal. Happily, this dumping ground has been grassed over and, together with the playing fields on the towpath side, provides one of the most pleasant aspects of this walk. (Perhaps the buried refuse will provide archeologists with some exciting finds in about a thousand years' time?) **Willow Tree Wharf,** with its narrow-gauge rails, still survives further down on the Yeading bank; and the rusted evidence of a loading bay can also be seen near the former dock to the Durdan Works on the Ealing side.

Yeading, incidentally, was considered even more backward than Northolt by early historians, and was described in 1861 as a place where 'dirt, darkness and ignorance reign supreme' — although the unfortunate inhabitants were 'always found civil'! The canal acts as the borough boundary between Ealing and Hillingdon as far as **Spikes Bridge** (at present the only means of access 'across the border') but it is hoped to narrow this dividing line when the Council's new **Canalway Park Project** gets underway. This scheme proposes, by agreement with the Borough of Hillingdon, to bridge the canal higher up near King George's Playing Fields and incorporate the open space on both sides of the boundary into a district or metropolitan park — thereby improving this stretch of the canal and creating some much-needed recreational facilities for both areas.

A view of the canal c.1920, looking east towards Kensington Road Bridge.

From Spikes Bridge, modern warehouses line the canal to the **Uxbridge Road** where this walk links up with Route 3 in the next chapter. Alternatively, you could leave the canal at Spikes Bridge and make your way to the bus route on **Lady Margaret Road,** where a pub of the same name should help to refresh you after your walk. Both are named after the **Countess of Jersey,** who was Southall's 'leading lady' while she lived at Osterley in the early 1900's and was often called on to open libraries, schools and other buildings in the parish. This north-western section of Southall (which you officially entered at Ruislip Road, by the way), was the last part of the town to be developed but, like Northolt, its country lanes and farmlands were soon buried beneath housing estates after the Second World War. Read all about it in the next chapter ...

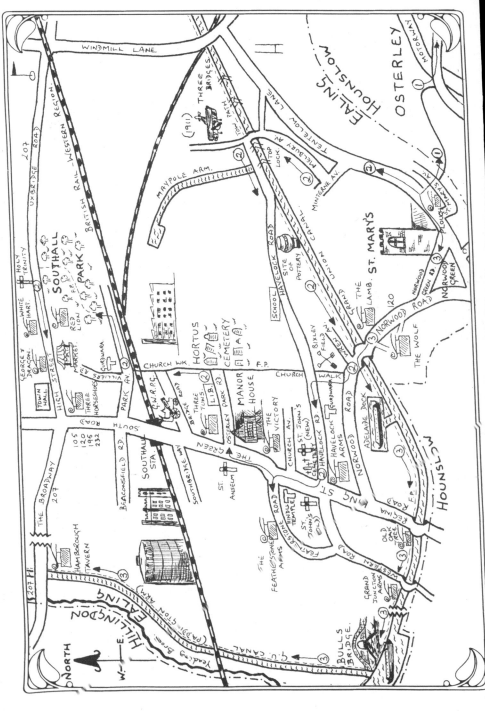

SOUTHALL 174

CHAPTER X

Southall is a busy but not attractive place ... though in some
directions there are green fields, shady lanes and pleasant walks.
JAMES THORNE — 'Handbook to the Environs of London' (1876).

 unlike its
close neighbour,
Norwood, has never
enjoyed a particularly good press. Writers over the last century have
tended to enthuse over Norwood's rural character, with its
handsome houses set around the well-wooded village green, while
Southall has been dismissed as flat and dreary, disfigured by
brickfields, gasworks, factories or housing estates. Taken at face value, these descriptions
still hold true, but what most critics seem to have overlooked is that the rumble of the
railway, the omnipresent view of the gasholder and the large Asian community are as
much part of Southall's history as the quiet walk beside the canal, or birds singing in the
trees on Norwood Green. The overall picture cannot be said to delight the eye, and town
planning leaves a lot to be desired; but in view of the heavy industrialisation and dense
population, it is a wonder that *any* green space survives today, let alone a 16th century
manor house. While Southall will never be a place of beauty, it has a character and
atmosphere quite different from anywhere else in the borough, which compensates for
her blemishes.

The contrast between Southall and Norwood has not always been so apparent of
course: for all their modern differences, the two villages shared the same rural
background until the 19th century. The link between them goes back as far as Saxon
times, when both settlements were part of a large gift of land in Hayes which the Saxon
King Offa of Mercia presented to the Archbishop of Canterbury. Norwood was evidently
far more important than Southall in those days, for this was the name given to the
'Precinct' which was separated from the Parish of Hayes in 832 AD. It comprised all the
land between Yeading Brook and the River Brent — roughly the same area covered by
Southall and Norwood today. A chapel-of-ease was later built at Norwood to serve the
local population, but the Precinct remained under the ecclesiastical jurisdiction of Hayes
Parish for more than a thousand years.

Although both names are Saxon in origin ('Northuuda' meaning the 'north wood'
and 'Suhaull' the 'south corner'), Southall is not mentioned until 1198, long after the
Norman invasion. Both Norwood and Southall had manor houses, but their early
history is a little vague. The original manor house of Southall probably stood to the
north, somewhere near the junction of today's Dormer's Wells Lane and Telford Road,
while Norwood's is thought to have been on Frogmore Green. Until the 16th century,
the Archbishop of Canterbury leased the manors to various noblemen or well-to-do
commoners. The most noteworthy of these were the *Shoredych* family, who had made
their fortune as goldsmiths, and the *Chesemans*: Edward, who was Keeper of the
Wardrobe to Henry VII; and his son, Robert, who was one of the esquires sent by Henry
VIII to meet his fourth bride-to-be, Anne of Cleves, on her arrival from Dusseldorf.
Robert Cheseman became the first lay Lord of the Manor in 1543, when Henry VIII sold
him the manors of Norwood and Southall after receiving them from the Archbishop of
Canterbury in exchange for lands in Kent.

The great house at Dormer's Wells later passed to *Lord and Lady Dacre*, but it
gradually declined in importance once *Francis Awsiter* bought the manors in 1602, as he
preferred to live in his own house on Southall Green, which we know as the Manor
House today. By this time, most of the land in Norwood Precinct had been brought

under the plough, and its woodland cleared for pasture. The few hundred inhabitants lived on scattered farms and in clusters of cottages around the church at **Norwood Green,** the new manor house on **Southall Green,** and at **Northcote,** where quite a large settlement had grown up around the inns on the high road from London to Oxford. The Civil War made little impression on this rural way of life, and local residents do not seem to have taken much part in the battles raging round them.

The Awsiter remained the biggest landowners in the district throughout the 17th century, but their standing in the community was slowly undermined by the son of one of their former stewards, *Christopher Merrick*, whose large estate at Northcote is still preserved as **Southall Park.** In 1698, his heir and nephew, *Francis Merrick*, put Southall on the map by obtaining a charter from William III to hold a weekly market on his land — a privilege usually reserved for the Lord of the Manor. The modern **Southall Market** is on the same site today. By the middle of the 18th century, the Awsiters were in severe financial difficulties and sold the manorial rights to the *Childs*, the wealthy banking family who then owned the great mansion of **Osterley** which *Sir Thomas Gresham* had built on the southern border of the Precinct in the 1570's. George Villiers, the 5th *Earl of Jersey*, inherited the manors together with Osterley when he married Robert Child's granddaughter in 1804.

Great changes were to occur in sleepy Southall before the manors changed hands for the last time, some fifty years later. The census for 1801 records a population of 697, but the earlier opening of the Grand Junction Canal from Brentford to Uxbridge, swiftly followed by the arm from Bull's Bridge to Paddington, soon encouraged more and more people to settle on the Southall side of the canal. Farmlands began to give way to brickfields and the first of many cottages were built for the labourers. Work was also to be found at Northcote where the inns were doing a brisk trade serving coaches on the Turnpike road. The last of the open fields and common land were enclosed by a local act in 1809, and development intensified when Bull's Bridge became the chief depot for the Great Western line from London to Maidenhead, which cut through the middle of Southall. Once the level crossing opened in 1839, the first factories soon appeared and by 1858, when the manors were sold to the banker, *Charles Mills*, the population was approaching 4,000. Manorial rights had long since ceased to be of much significance, however, and the following year the Precinct was finally made independent of Hayes, and the Parish of Norwood became legally responsible for its own affairs.

The year 1859 also marked the opening of the bridge at Southall Station and the goods line to Brentford docks, which attracted more industry to the area. The gasworks opened in 1868 and helped to light many of the new roads between the railway and the Uxbridge Road. Local stock bricks were in great demand during this period of expansion, but the brickfields began to decline towards the end of the century. One of the last projects they helped to build was Otto Monsted's huge margarine factory which is still a local landmark, although now occupied by other firms. The one artistic note in Southall's industrial history was provided by the *Martin Brothers*, who produced their distinctive salt-glazed stoneware at a disused soap factory in Havelock Road from 1877.

The powers of the parish vestry were usurped by Norwood Local Board in 1891, and the Urban District of Southall-Norwood followed three years later. By 1901, when electric trams first ran along the Uxbridge Road from Acton to Southall, the population had reached 13,000 and was to double again in the next decade. The transition from country to industrial town was almost complete in the southern part of the parish, but above the Uxbridge Road, the fields of Waxlow and Dormers Wells Farms still stretched away to Northolt and Greenford. The population continued to grow during the First World War as work was available in the many local factories which had turned to producing munitions. This created a serious unemployment problem after the war until normal business was resumed, and development of the farmlands in the Mount Pleasant and Allenby Road area began to relieve some of the acute housing shortage.

Southall had a population of almost 50,000 when it became a Municipal Borough in 1936 and the name 'Norwood' was finally dropped from the official designation. The charter of incorporation was one of the few granted during the short reign of Edward VIII and the Southall mace is something of a rarity for bearing his royal cypher. The railway, gasworks and factories survived repeated attacks during the Second World War and overcrowding remained the most serious problem in the aftermath, despite a clamp-down on new industries. The sudden influx of immigrants from Commonwealth countries during the 1950's is said to have begun with an ex-soldier from India who sought out his former British officer in Southall after the War and, with his help, managed to find a job in a local factory. He was soon joined by various friends and relatives who, having no immediate claim to Council housing, bought their own homes, set up shops and so began to change the face of Southall yet again.

Immigrants represented about one fifth of the 57,000 people living in Southall when it became part of the London Borough of Ealing in 1965. Today, the figure is more like 50% of a total 65,000, and in the 1982 Borough Plan, Southall is described as a 'specialist centre for Asian goods and services'. The older residents are slowly coming to terms with their new neighbours and although relations between them are not entirely cordial, none of the racial tension in Southall to hit the headlines in recent years has been instigated by the local population. It will take a generation or two to solve all the problems of a multiracial society, but the fact that the old St. John's Church and the new Hindu Temple stand side by side in King Street, shows that a good start has been made.

NARROWBOATS OUTSIDE THE OLD OAK TREE, SOUTHALL

A late-18th century engraving of St. Mary's Church, Norwood Green.

The chapel-of-ease which served the tiny population of Norwood Precinct before the Norman invasion, probably stood on the same site as the present **Church of St. Mary** at the eastern end of **Norwood Green.** The basic structure of the church dates from 1439 when the Archbishop of Canterbury gave money for rebuilding the chapel, but traces of the 12th century building it replaced were found in the walls during more recent renovations.

The wooden porch was added in the late 15th century but was extensively rebuilt after the Parish of Norwood was established in 1864, when many changes were made to the church to celebrate the independence it had been trying to achieve for over 200 years. The records show that when Cromwell appointed commissioners to enquire into the state of ecclesiastical benefices in 1650, they suggested that 'Norwood, being distinct in all duties and parish business from Hayes, should be made a parish church entire of itself'. So much for their recommendation!

The parish registers began in 1654 and the account book which *Christopher Merrick* presented to the churchwarden in 1676 for listing charities and gifts to the Precinct, can be seen in Southall Library. It records his own contributions of a new pulpit and pew for the minister, and a later entry illustrates how the Merricks had eclipsed the Awsiters: they were given the first pew next to the chancel while the Awsiters had to take second place — although both had paid for the new pews to be built!

The red-brick tower was built in 1896 and most of the stained glass is 19th century except for the window in the south wall of the nave (showing the baby Jesus clutching a windmill) which was made in the late 1500's. The font is the oldest item in the church and has been in use since 1439. The small **churchyard** is very pleasant to wander through, but most of the people connected with Southall's early history are commemmorated inside the church. A 16th century funeral helmet and sword distinguishes the tomb of *Edward Cheseman* and his son *Robert*, who both died in the same year as the kings they served: 1509 and 1547 respectively.

The gallery which *Francis Awsiter* donated to the church in 1612 was removed during the 19th century restorations, but the quaint inscription on his memorial brass still acts as a reminder of his generosity:

His soul ascended is,
His body here remaynes;
The churche enjoyes his costs,
The parish had his paynes.

Dr. John Awsiter, the last member of the family to hold the title 'Lord of the Manor', is also buried in the church. According to the inscription on his monument, he claimed to be the discoverer of the beneficial effects of sea-water to which Brighton and other resorts owed their prosperity during the Regency period, but he obviously made no money from the idea.

The *Merrick* family is well represented by a floorslab to Francis Merrick's father who died in 1663, and a life-size effigy of his son and successor, 'John Merrick of Norcut', who enjoyed the privileges granted to his father by William III until 1749. John Merrick had no sons, and the estate passed to his grandson, Francis Ascough, who, according to his monument, lived at 'South Hall' until his death in 1788. His own son, George Merrick Ascough, died a mere 11 years later, but his memorial shows that by then the family home was called **Southall Park.**

As the northern part of Southall has been partly covered by walks in the chapters on Hanwell and Northolt, the routes that follow are concentrated in the area below the Uxbridge Road. Years ago when the railway first split the town in two, locals would say they were going 'over the Green' when they walked south of the railway, or 'over the trams' to the High Street. Our walks all begin at the church on Norwood Green, so these phrases don't really apply — but I thought I would mention it anyway!

ROUTE ONE

(Norwood Green and over the fields to Osterley Park — just over 1½ miles)
The area around the church looks much as it did in the 18th century. Except for the additions to **Vine Cottage** on the corner of Osterley Lane and the construction of **Norwood Terrace** before the First World War, very few changes have been made in this corner of the old village. Next to the church stands the former **Free School** founded by *Elisha Biscoe* in 1767. Biscoe succeeded his father as steward to the then Lord of the Manor, Dr. John Awsiter, and left a large amount of money to see that the education of local poor children continued after his death. The school in fact survived until 1950, a remarkable memorial to Biscoe's philanthropy, and his name has also been given to one of the modern flat-blocks nearby, Biscoe House. **Norwood Lodge** and **Cottage,** on the opposite side of the road, were built in the late 1800's, and the old bowling green which once belonged to The Plough is still being used by **Norwood Green Bowling Club. The Plough** is the oldest pub in Norwood and incorporates the timber-framed building of a 17th century inn — although the first alehouse on the site was probably built much earlier.

A painting of The Plough in 1899 with Biscoe School on the left.

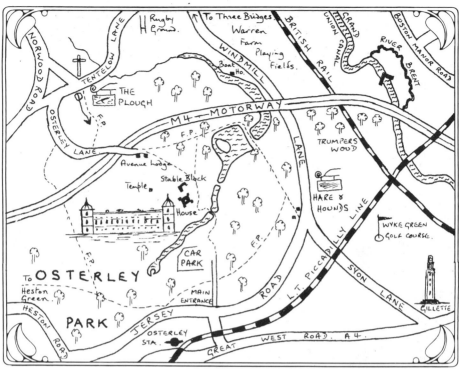

Our walk begins down the little lane between The Plough and the bowling greens, which leads across **St. Mary's Avenue** to the fields of Osterley Farm. From here a track through the cultivated farmlands takes you into foreign parts . . . over the borough boundary into Hounslow! Only a small section of Osterley Park falls within the borough but its past owners have been amongst the biggest landowners in Southall and it holds a very important place in Ealing's history. The walk through the open fields may get rather muddy in winter, but you can always walk up **Osterley Lane** instead, to where the track meets the road near the bridge over the M4 Motorway. Despite the noise of aircraft and traffic, you still manage to appreciate the rural atmosphere, and the urban sprawl of Southall seems very far away. Once over the motorway, the lane leads past Osterley Farm to the lodge-houses at the entrance to **Osterley Park.**

Much has been written about the magnificent mansion built at Osterley during the 16th century, but there was a thriving community here long before Sir Thomas Gresham came on the scene. *John de Osterley* owned land described as being in Heston and Isleworth in the 13th century, and a 'capital messuage' was built on the 500-acre estate in the early 1400's. By 1465 there were at least fifteen other dwellings besides the Manor House, which was granted to the *Abbess of the Order of Bridgettine Nuns* at Syon towards the end of the century. Following the dissolution of the monasteries by Henry VIII, Osterley, like Syon, was given to the *Duke of Somerset* and, after his execution in 1552, passed to his deadly enemy, the *Duke of Northumberland*. The story of how Northumberland came to lose both his lands and his head (not to mention his daughter-in-law, Lady Jane Grey!), is told in the chapter on Brentford; but during these troublesome times, the manor reverted to the Crown.

Osterley was bought by *Sir Thomas Gresham* in 1562, shortly after he had received his knighthood from Queen Elizabeth. His was no 'poor boy made good' story. He was born the son of a wealthy London merchant (and future Lord Mayor), passed into the Mercers' Company after a Cambridge education and became 'kings's merchant' to Edward VI, and later Queen Elizabeth's ambassador at Brussels. After the death of his only son in 1564, Gresham devoted a large portion of his wealth to building the **Royal Exchange** in the City and to creating a 'faire and stately building . . . a house beseeming a prince', at Osterley — or so the cartogropher, John Norden, described the finished product.

Queen Elizabeth was evidently equally impressed when she visited the newly-completed house in 1576, although her stay there was not entirely uneventful. She was 'greatly disquieted' when villagers from Heston and Norwood pulled up the new fence around the park as a protest against what they considered were infringements of their Common rights. Sir Thomas obviously wished to make up for this spot of unpleasantness, for after Her Majesty had casually remarked that she felt the large courtyard would be more handsome if divided by a wall, Gresham waited until she had retired for the night and then summoned workmen from London to put things to rights. Next morning, the transformation elicited several snide comments from the Queen's courtiers — some saying it was "no wonder he could so soon change a building, who could build a 'Change", while those who knew of his family problems, said smugly that "any house is easier divided than united". The Queen however, appeared well pleased.

Osterley Park - The café from the Portico.

The site chosen by Gresham for his new house was close to the original manorial dwelling. This is now incorporated in the large building known as the **Stable Block,** where the path from the lodges emerges. The central part was probably always used for stabling, while the left wing provided the main living accommodation and the right was used for storing grain. Sir Thomas lived here while waiting for his new mansion to be built and his first guest was an unwanted one. She was *Lady Mary Grey*, sister of the unfortunate '9-day Queen', and was kept under virtual house arrest here for offending Queen Elizabeth by secretly marrying the Queen's Royal Sargeant, or porter, without first obtaining permission. Her husband, *Thomas Keys*, enjoyed far less comfortable accommodation in the Tower and eventually died there — after which his poor wife was graciously allowed to go free! The Stable Block has now been converted into a tea-room and on summer afternoons you can enjoy an excellent cuppa in the courtyard, with various home-made cakes and biscuits.

The Osterley House you see today is a much altered and enlarged version of the one built by Sir Thomas Gresham. After his death in 1579, the property was neglected by his widow who bequeathed it (together with Boston Manor) to *Sir William Read*, her son by her first husband. The house later passed out of the family and through various ownerships until it was bought by *Nicholas Barbon* in 1683. He was a builder and speculator and was responsible for much of the rebuilding after the Great Fire of London, as well as being the first to introduce fire insurance to England. He probably made a number of alterations to Osterley before it was sold to *Sir Francis Child* in 1711.

Francis Child was born the fifth son of an obscure Wiltshire clothier, but these humble beginnings did not deter him from becoming apprenticed to a London goldsmith and taking control of the firm by the time he was 39, when he then began to concentrate on the profitable side-line of banking. During the Civil War, wealthy men deposited their money with a goldsmith for safekeeping over a fixed period, and the goldsmiths would then lend out some of this money at interest. Francis Child was the first to abandon his original trade and apply himself exclusively to banking — thus becoming known as the father of the profession. Some of the early clients of **Child's Bank** read like a history book: Charles II, Nell Gwynne, the poet Dryden, the Duke of Malborough, Samuel Pepys and later King William and Queen Mary. It is thought that he bought Osterley for the sole purpose of storing some of the bank's money in the extensive vaults under the courtyard, for he preferred to live in his house at Parson's Green, where he died in 1713.

Osterley passed to his son Samuel whose widow, Agatha, had inherited by 1756 — the year John Awsiter was forced to sell his manors of Southall and Norwood. She no doubt bought the manorial rights for their son, named Francis after his grandfather, who came of age the same year. It is to this *Francis Child* that we owe the present appearance of Osterley. He commissioned *Robert Adam* to remodel the house, adding the Hall and side passages onto the original courtyard and completely encasing Gresham's building in new walls around the four corner towers. Sadly, Francis died before his plans were completed — leaving his young fiancée some £50,000 better off, and Osterley and the bank to his brother, Robert, who thus became the new Lord of Norwood and Southall.

Robert Child lived only fifteen years longer than his brother; his early demise at the age of 43 is said to have been hastened by the elopement of his beloved only child, *Sarah Anne*, with the *Earl of Westmoreland* — although father only had himself to blame if there is any truth in the story behind their marriage. It seems that Westmoreland, aware that Child had rather grand ideas of a match for Sarah Anne, asked what he would do if he were in love with a girl against her father's consent. Perhaps Robert had partaken rather liberally of the after-dinner port, for he replied very rashly: "Why! Run away with her, to be sure!". The Earl's nickname was not 'Rapid Westmoreland' for nothing, which is how Sarah and her lover came to be wed in an alehouse on Gretna Green, and why the heart-broken Child changed his will so that his fortune was to be left to the second son or

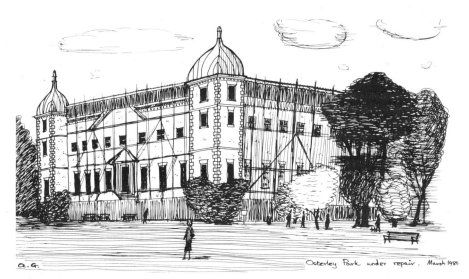

Osterley Park under repair. March 1980

eldest daughter of Sarah Anne's future children — thereby ensuring that Westmoreland would not benefit financially from the runaway match.

Osterley thus passed in due course to *Sarah Sophia*, Lady Westmoreland's second child, who married *George Villiers* in 1804, the year before he added the *5th Earl of Jersey*, to his title of Lord of the Manors. In 1858, Villiers sold Norwood and Southall to *Sir Charles Mills*, a senior partner in the banking firm of Glyn, Mills & Co. which later merged with Child's Bank to form the bank we know today as **Williams and Glyn's.** Osterley however remained in the family until 1949, when the 9th Earl of Jersey gave the house and grounds to the National Trust. During the First and Second World Wars, the Home Guard was stationed in the grounds, and many young recruits had their first taste of army life in the Osterley training camp. Today the park is maintained by the Department of the Environment, while the house itself is administered by the Victoria and Albert Museum.

Unlike the mansions at Gunnersbury and Boston Manor, Osterley still boasts much of its original decor in an excellent state of preservation, and contains all the furniture that was designed by Adam to stand in the principal rooms at the time. The house is thus a marvellous example of how the gentry lived during the 18th century. I am not going to attempt to describe the various rooms as the guidebook on sale at the door gives far better information than I can do justice to here, but I hope that this brief background to Osterley's past owners encourage you to look around their home because it really is worth a visit. Extensive renovations are still being made both inside and out and it is hoped that when these are completed, the upstairs apartments will also be open to the public. The house is open for viewing every afternoon from Tuesday to Sunday, and Bank Holiday Mondays — opening times are listed at the back of the book. There is an entrance fee for the house, but the grounds are free and open all year round. You can visit Robert Adam's semi-circular **Garden House** (near the old kitchen gardens behind the stables), or just wander by the lake, admiring some of the huge cedar trees which were planted by Robert Child to celebrate the birth of his daughter, Sarah Anne.

Had the 1962 proposal to build a World Exhibition Centre within the grounds of Osterley Park been successful, much of these beautiful gardens would today lie beneath exhibition halls, car-parks, flats and hotels. Osterley's proximity to road and rail links with Heathrow made the Park a prime site for a scheme; but thanks to vigorous local opposition the application was turned down and the £20 million plans were later adapted to form the National Exhibition Centre in Birmingham.

If your walk has made you thirsty for something stronger than tea, a footpath to the east of the main drive to the car-park, takes you via a pleasant route to the **Hare and Hounds** in **Windmill Lane.** The 18th century inn was rebuilt in 1904 and offers good beer, snacks and a small children's playground beside the beer-garden. **Wyke Green** nearby, takes its name from a medieval sub-manor of Isleworth which was taken over by the Earl of Jersey in the early 18th century. **Wyke Garden Cottage,** near the path to Osterley, was once part of Wyke Farm and was being restored by a market gardener in 1981. The farmlands used to extend to **Wyke House** in **Syon Lane** which had been restored by Robert Adam, but the house was allowed to deteriorate in modern times and after being set fire to by vandals, was declared a dangerous building and demolished in 1977. As the house stood in the Green Belt, Hounslow Council had intended to leave the grounds as 'open space', but an application to build a housing estate on the site was accepted in 1982 so we can expect a 'new look' for the area in the near future. **Wyke Green Golf Course** behind the Hare and Hounds, formed part of Southall Sewage Farm in the 19th century . . . and on that high note, we end this walk!

A typical scene at Norwood Top Lock in the old days.

ROUTE TWO *(Norwood Green to Southall Park via the canal and King Street — 3 miles)*
This 'City Tour' is not recommended for those who like talking to the trees as most of Southall's historic sites lie in the busy, built-up area of King Street and Southall Green. The walk begins and ends in greener pastures however, and can always be combined with the weekly shopping as the main streets are alive with sound and colour, even on Sundays.

East of the church, the 19th century cottages in **Tentelow Lane** give way to more modern houses and shops. Some years ago, Tentelow Lane yielded evidence of Southall's earliest residents when workmen, digging a deep trench for the main drainage system, found the 35,000-year old bones of a mammoth. Flint implements buried near the skeleton indicated that the animal was probably killed by paleolithic hunters. Cars and lorries are the most dangerous beasts you have to contend with in the lane today, however, but you can avoid the worst of the traffic by turning left into **Minterne Avenue** which, like the large field opposite, was open grazing land for horses and cattle until the area was built up during the 1940's. The many different styles of houses in **Melbury Avenue,** to your right, skirt the sportsfield of the George Tomlinson First and Middle Schools and around the corner, you will find the British Waterways maintenance yard and the bridge over the canal at **Norwood Top Lock.** This is the last of the eleven locks up from the Thames and the start of a long lock-free pound to Cowley, near Uxbridge.

In 1911, the first aeroplane ever to land at Southall made an impromptu descent into one of the fields behind the lock (now part of Ealing Borough nurseries), when a Bristol-Biplane, competing in the 'Standard Flying Race', developed engine trouble soon after take-off. Repairs took two days to complete but, to the crowds who gathered to watch, this strange new-fangled machine was no doubt just as much a source of wonder on the ground as in the air. The Martin Brothers were quite possibly among the first on the scene of this historic event, as their pottery was then one of the few buildings in **Havelock Road;** but before you reach the site, both the towpath and Havelock Road rise sharply over the old **Maypole Arm** of the canal which was built in 1913 to serve Otto Monsted's margarine factory, half a mile away. The Quaker Oats factory took over the arm after Monsted's closed and it remained very busy for years, but today its only use is as a winding-hole for boats on the Grand Union. It is possible to walk the length of the bramble-strewn towpath but there is no proper exit from the nicely landscaped section at the other end (unless you fancy crawling through a hole in the fence!), so I suggest you continue along the main towpath towards **Wolf Bridge.**

A little further on, a modern council estate now stands on the canal bank where the *Martin Brothers* had their pottery. Just before the first of the houses, you will find a very pleasant grassy field with benches overlooking the canal, where you can digest your sandwiches and the story of Southall's most celebrated citizens. Wallace Martin founded the firm at Fulham in 1872, but after he was joined by three of his younger brothers, they began to look for larger premises. The derelict soap factory they discovered in Southall seemed ideal, and they moved all their equipment here by barge in 1877. For all their talent, they never became rich and most of their wealthy sponsors were repaid with samples of their work — which is how some of the great collections of their pottery came to be formed. *Wallace* was the chief designer in the team; *Walter* worked the wheel and specialised in the chemical aspects of the business; *Edwin* decorated the finished items; and *Charles* was a very bad salesman. He managed a small shop for their wares in Holborn but never sold very much as he was so fond of the pieces he was reluctant to part with them! His death in 1910, followed by Walter's two years later, made things very difficult for the remaining brothers — especially as Walter had left no record of the special chemical formulas he had used to produce their characteristic salt-glazed stoneware. Edwin gave up his fight with cancer not long afterwards, and although Wallace continued to do modelling, there was no more firing until his death in 1923. You can see a wide range of their work at Southall Library, where a permanent exhibition is maintained; and a Martinware fountain is still in use in the grounds of the Manor House.

Havelock Road now disappears from view until you rejoin it via the **Church Path,** which you will find by leaving the canal at **Wolf Bridge** and turning right into the little lane just beyond **Wren Avenue.** The original Church Path ran from the Uxbridge Road to St. Mary's at Norwood, but the railway altered its course higher up and drastic changes are about to occur on the remaining section when the long-planned relief road to

Charles Martin, the reluctant salesman, in the Holborn shop.

King Street is finally completed in 1983. The new road will run parallel with the path as far as Bridge Road, diverting most of the traffic from the town centre. At the time of writing however, **Bixley Field,** as the allotments to the right of the path are called, has not yet been poisoned by exhaust fumes, so let us talk of cabbages and kings . . . the allotments, you see, were once part of the brickfield that stretched all the way to the Martin brother's pottery, and it was in this vicinity (in 1826) that the Earl of Jersey granted the architect, *John Nash,* a licence to dig the brick earth which supplied him with most of the bricks for remodelling no less a royal residence than Buckingham Palace! 'Bixley', incidentally, comes from an old Saxon name meaning 'a box-tree clearing'.

As one of the oldest roads in the parish, **Havelock Road** also has an interesting past. It was called Fedder Lane until the 1850's, when it was renamed after a man who would perhaps not be as popular in Southall today: *General Henry Havelock,* one of the heroes in the Relief of Lucknow, the battle which terminated the Indian Mutiny. If you look east down Havelock Road as you leave the Church Path, the neatly landscaped lawns of the new **Havelock First School** mark the site of **Southall Greyhound Stadium** (1933-77); and the Council estate further to the right was once **Langdon's Farm and Nursery.** The estate was built in 1953 and all the roads are named after members of the successful Mount Everest Expedition. The western end of Havelock Road, which you now turn into, has not been modernised to quite the same extent. The houses in Church and Marlow Roads were built in the late 19th century with local stockbricks, and **Havelock Road Cemetery** was consecrated by the Bishop of London in 1883, when the tiny churchyard at Norwood was finally closed for burials. Opposite the cemetery, a row of old labourers cottages has been replaced by **Havelock Court,** but the buildings once used as a dairy depot for Norwood Farm are still standing, although they now belong to the **Sikh Gurdwara,** established in 1967. Ten years later, the Sikh Temple also took over the old Gaswork's stables next door which have been converted into the **Sira Guru Singh Sabha Library.** The welcome sight of the **Havelock Arms** at the end of the road, brings you to King Street, formerly called Denmark Terrace.

Platts the Grocers in King Street, 1905.

King Street has developed a definite eastern flavour in recent years. Sarees are now displayed in the shops on the corner of **Western Road** where Platt's the grocers stood at the turn of the century, and the ordinary stores seem very pale and uninteresting compared with the spicey aromas and exotic fruits and vegetables to be found in their Indian counterparts. Why not try some of the delicacies on display? Most shops have a restaurant section, or you could make your selection and picnic on the lawns of the Manor House nearby. The **old St. John's Church,** on the opposite corner of Western Road, was built in 1838 when the expanding population was beginning to outgrow St. Mary's. All the costs of the church, St. John's School (which then stood behind the church) and the vicarage were met by *Mr. Henry Dobbs,* who owned the vitriol factory on the canal bank. The church was made a sub-parish of St. Mary's in 1850, but by 1910, the building had become too small for the large congregation and so the **new church of St. John** was built across the road in **Church Avenue,** in the grounds of what was once a large mansion called **Elmfield House.**

The shops fronting the cemetery in King Street were built on the site of the old parsonage, which was demolished when a new vicarage was built in Church Avenue in 1929. The Rev. J. Jackson and his wife lived here from 1887 until his death in 1895, and it was perhaps to keep herself busy after her husband died, that Mrs. *Edith Jackson* started writing her *Annals of Ealing* which is such a valuable source of reference for local historians today. The old church is now used as a meeting place for various groups, including Asian Christians, while the former **St. John's Hall** next to it has been **The Hindu Temple** since 1979. St. John's Hall opened in 1893 and, like so many other buildings in the parish, was built by *A&B Hanson*, a family of Danish origin who started their firm in the old Workhouse during the 1850's and grew into one of the biggest building contractors in the country. Two marble plaques in the new St. John's commemorate members of the family from 1817-76, but little remains of their building yard in Featherstone Road, which closed down in 1977.

Most of the shops between the Temple and Featherstone Road were built in the early 1900's, although a pair inscribed with the date '1897' stands out from the others. A pond and the stocks used to stand on the corner of Featherstone Road, which is named after one of the old farms that once lined the western side of The Green. The farmhouse was pulled down in the 1870's and replaced by a rather grand residence, **Featherstone Hall,** known locally as 'Welch's Folly' because the high wall that its owner built around it, included the odd feature of a series of windows. The **Dominion Cinema** and adjoining shops were built on the site in 1934 by A&B Hanson, and the cinema was opened the following year by Gracie Fields. Indian films have been shown here in recent years, but it is now closed and a new Community Centre is planned to open on the site in 1985. Before crossing over to the Manor House, we make a swift diversion down **Featherstone Road.**

A view of King Street in 1911 showing the old St. John's Church,
and Alfred Welch's walled 'folly' in the distance.

Cleo Laine, the well-known jazz singer, spent most of her childhood in one of the group of 3-storey houses on the right hand side of the road. Two of the houses are now used by the Sikh Missionary Society and Southall Youth Movement. The **Featherstone Arms** has hardly changed since it was built in 1832 but the 18th century **Workhouse** taken over by *A&B Hanson* is in the process of being demolished to make way for the new **Health Centre.** On the opposite corner stands the 1901 **Drill Hall,** but it is many years since it was used for army purposes. **Featherstone First and Middle Schools** nearby were built in 1895 and 1901 respectively — the former has been considerably modernised, but the old Boys' School (which replaced St. John's School) still provides a solid Edwardian backdrop for the **War Memorial** dedicated to past pupils.

Back to **The Green** again, and the **Victory** (called the King of Prussia until 1914) which was rebuilt during the 1930's. **St. Anselm's First and Middle Schools** incorporate the iron building which served as the original St. Anselm's church from the early 1900's until the new **Church of St. Anselm** was built higher up on the opposite side of the road in 1967. Before the iron church was erected, mass was said in the old tithe barn attached to the Manor House. This was demolished, together with four cottages, when The Green was widened after the First World War. The **Manor House** has been much altered since it was first built early in the 16th century under the name of **'Wrenns'.** *Francis Awsiter* made various improvements when he bought the house in 1587 (the date said to be carved above one of the windows — although I have never been able to find it), and substantial changes were made during the 18th and 19th centuries. The timber-framed house is nevertheless unique in Middlesex, and certainly one of Southall's most interesting features.

a.a.

OLD MANOR HOUSE , SOUTHALL

The house was not included in the sale of the manors to *Agatha Child* in 1756, and remained in the Awsiter family until it was bought by *William Welch* in 1821 — some time after he had aquired the lease of the Merrick's market. (*Alfred Welch*, of Featherstone 'folly' fame was probably his son.) The most noteworthy of its subsequent owners was *William Thomas*, inventor of the lock-stitch sewing machine, who, throughout the winter of 1885, daily provided up to 100 dinners for children whose fathers were out of work because the extreme cold had forced the brickfields to close. The Council bought the Manor House in 1913, and it is now used as offices for the **Southall Chamber of Commerce** who have paid for much of the restoration work, including the fire-place in the central hall attributed to Grinling Gibbons. The very plain **War Memorial** which stands outside is not, in local opinion, considered a fitting tribute to the hundreds of Southall people who lost their lives in the two World Wars; but I am sure everyone will agree that the well laid-out gardens around the Martinware fountain, make a pleasant break in this rather long walk.

Southall-Norwood Hospital, on the corner of Osterley Park Road, was established in 1934 in a large 19th century house called 'The Chestnuts'. The dilapidated **Century Cinema** opposite, was rebuilt during the Thirties on the site of Southall's first electric cinema, The Gem, which opened amidst great excitement in 1910. Until the 1960's, some of Southall's finest mansions were still to be found on this side of the road, all built on the old **Southall Green Farm** which had extended as far as the railway. **The Grange** and a cherry orchard have given way to the 7-storey Phoenix House and Southbridge Way (which originally led to the Western Iron Foundry); a very old house called **The Romans** (thought to have been named after a 16th century family, the Romaynes) became the new cinema and small trading estate behind it; while **South Lodge,** owned by Mr. Baxter, a former chairman of Southall-Norwood Urban District Council, was sold on his death and the new **St. Anselm's church** now stands on the site. Incidentally, the intriguing little house between the church and the entrance to the trading estate, is the electric generator which once provided power to the estate.

The **Three Tuns** on the eastern side of The Green was built in the early 1800's, and it's nice to see plants, instead of the usual litter, filling the old stone drinking fountain for cattle and horses which stands outside the shops nearby. Turning into **Osterley Park Road,** you will find **Southall Library** on the left-hand side. It was built in 1905 and paid for by the Andrew Carnegie Trust. In recent years, the interior has been remodelled to make the most of space and natural lighting, and the beautiful collection of work by the *Martin Brothers* (ranging from buttons to clockcases) is well displayed in an upstairs room — a visit is highly recommended. The **Hortus Cemetery,** built in 1944 at the end of the road will soon lie on the other side of the new by-pass, but it will still be possible to walk left along the Church Path to **Bridge Road,** or Merrick Road as its new name is going to be. The path comes up behind the old **Maypole Institute** to your left, **Otto Monsted's** former margarine factory on the right, and the matching red-brick facade of what was once the Maypole shipping siding, straight ahead — all built by A&B Hanson.

Otto Monsted learnt all about the manufacture of margarine in his native Denmark, before starting his first business near Cheshire in England. Demand for his product became so great, that he planned a new factory in Southall and purchased a 70-acre site from the Earl of Jersey and the GWR. His factory opened with a formal Dinner and Ball for his hundreds of new employees in 1895, and this genuine concern for the happiness of his workers was maintained, with good results, until the firm closed thirty years later. Times had changed: road transport had taken over from rail and the cost of bringing the huge production department in line with modern packaging requirements proved too much. **Walls** now own the front portion of the factory; **Quaker Oats** built on some of the land at the back; and the rest houses a variety of other business concerns. The Maypole Institute, which was built in 1910 as a social club for employees, became a temporary military hospital during the First World War, and now serves as **Southall Community Centre.** Some of the lime trees which were planted on both side of Bridge Road when it was first built as a private road to Monsted's, still survive outside 'The Limes', a very pleasant-looking old people's home which replaced the bowling green and tennis courts of the Institute in 1966.

The Maypole shipping siding was the first section to be axed when the factory announced its closure in 1925, but after years of neglect it has come to life again since the **GWR Preservation Group** established the **Southall Railway Centre** here in 1981. Members have already done wonders towards achieving their aim of recreating the Victorian age of steam, and vistors can see some of the GWR locomotives they have painstakingly restored from scrap to mainline working order, on Bank Holidays and the last Sunday in every month from April to October. A lot of work has also been done on converting the old goods depot to a typical Victorian railway station. Although the gas lamps and wrought-iron work have yet to come, the benches and signal-box look as good as new on the platform where roller conveyers once carried boxes of margarine from Monsted's factory. The arched wall round the siding has weathered well and could still be described as 'one of the finest examples of brickwork in the country', which was the accolade paid to the Hansons when they built it in 1922, to an award-winning design in the 'Architects' Journal'. New members of the GWR Preservation Group are always welcome, and £1 shares can be bought in the locomotives to help towards restoration. The hope eventually to link their 400-ft of track to the adjacent British Rail line, so maybe passengers will steam down to Brentford once again.

Directly opposite the Church Path, a **footbridge** leads over the railway to **Park Avenue.** From the top you can see Southall's 19th century station, with the 320ft high gasometer and castle-like water tower of the gasworks in the distance. Just after the

View of the gasworks and water tower from GWR footbridge in 1951.

gasometer was completed in 1932, it helped raise funds for the Southall-Norwood Hospital when, for a fee of sixpence, people could climb or take a lift to see the view from the top. The gasworks closed in the early 'seventies with the changeover to North Sea Gas and the site is rapidly being reduced to rubble, while work has recently begun on a £1 million conversion of the water tower into flats and bedsits. Another sign of the times is evident in **Villiers Road** (to your right from the footbridge), where the pink corrugated walls of the Mangat Hall stand out against the former Congregational Church, which became the **Guru Granth Gurdwara** in 1969. The 1931 foundation stone of the original church can still be seen near the main entrance.

About 100 yards further along Park Avenue, the **Church Path** reappears as one of the entrances to **Southall Park,** where the tennis courts mark the site of the Merrick family's mansion. During the 1830's, the house was bought by *Sir William Ellis*, then superintendent of the newly-built St. Bernard's Asylum and one of the great reformers in this branch of medicine. After his death, Southall Park was used as another of the private mental homes that were a feature of the parish during the 19th century; **Vine Cottage** in Park View Road (now a Youth Centre), an old house called The Shrubbery further to the north, and Featherstone Hall made similar profitable sidelines for the medical staff at the county asylum. Southall Park was burnt down in a disastrous fire early one morning in 1883, and never rebuilt. The estate was later bought for a public park and footpaths now criss-cross through the trees planted by its earlier owners. You could end your walk here in one of the rose-gardens if you cannot bear the thought of any more sight-seeing but, having come this far, I shall just round off the 'City Tour' with a quick trip down the High Street.

Holy Trinity Church, opposite the lodge-house at the Uxbridge Road entrance to the Park, was built in 1890 on land donated by the Earl of Jersey, and was one of the few buildings in Southall to suffer damage during the Second World War. Further down the High Street stands the **Red Lion,** first built c.1650 and still going strong. The entrance to **Southall Market** lies just beyond the pub, and the traditional livestock sale is still held every Wednesday, with a general shopping market on Fridays and Saturdays. They are very tame affairs compared with the days when Southall was second only to Smithfield for the sale of fat cattle, after William Welch had purchased the lease on Merrick's charter in 1805. Some of the market atmosphere still prevailed in the 1920's, with cattle arriving in droves and gypsies trading horses outside the **White Hart** across the road, where there was a blacksmith's forge in the yard. The modern and rather forbidding **Police Station** on the corner of North Road, was then a simple cottage known as 'Police House', but the cottages behind the shop fronts leading down to the **Three Horseshoes** are the same as when they were first built, together with the pub, in the 1850's. The **George and Dragon** had been serving pints for about 200 years before the **Town Hall** was built in 1897, and perhaps the chap who later added the glass canopy and public convenience to its front, had had a few before doing so. A **Fire Station** was also tacked onto the Town Hall in 1901 (for a mere £175) but its modern counterpart now has premises a few doors down and horses no longer have to be rounded up from the fields to pull the fire-engine. Around the corner in South Road stands the distinctive Chinese-style **Liberty** cinema, complete with dragons. It was rebuilt during the 1930's on the site of the old 'Paragon Palace' and is to change its name yet again in Spring 1982, when it becomes the **Liberty Market Hall.**

Southall fire brigade outside the Town Hall in 1900.

*The tree-lined 'Dutch canal' on Norwood Green at the turn of the century,
with The Grange and Friar's Lawn in the background.*

ROUTE THREE *(Norwood Green to Bull's Bridge via the canal — 2 miles)*
This walk makes an excellent excuse for a pub-crawl on a fine weekend. You could begin with a quick one at **The Plough,** and then set off across the Green towards **Norwood Road.** Few of the ancient elms remain which once lined the 'Dutch Canal' in the photograph, but the Green still has a leafy appearance and, recently, more trees have been planted along the edges. The pond itself became more insanitary than picturesque over the years, and was filled in during the 1930's. Cricket has been played on the Green for over a century and the area is very popular with horse-riders. Norwood Green was declared a Conservation Area in 1969, but rather too late for most of the 'gentlemen's residences' which gave Norwood such a respectable air during the 19th century. Housing developments have replaced **Bridge Hall** (on the site of Norwood Close flats) and its neighbours, **Norwood House** and **Norwood Court** (built by *Josiah Wedgwood*), in Norwood Road on the western side of the Green; to the south, in Tentelow Lane, the lovely old **Rectory** was destroyed by a flying bomb in 1944, and **The Cedars,** another fine old Georgian mansion which stood nearby, was rebuilt as an old peoples' home in 1963. The northern side of the Green has been more fortunate however, and several of the original houses are still standing in Norwood Green Road.

Tucked away behind a screen of trees near the church, lies **Norwood Hall** — built c.1813 for a London cabinet-maker, *John Robins*, who was also responsible for erecting four almshouses (rebuilt 1962) near Frogmore Green. Most of the houses north of the Green (as far as Poplar Avenue) were built on the orchards and meadowland of Norwood Hall when the estate was broken up during the 1920's, and the Hall itself has been used as a Horticultural Institute since the 1950's. Between the Hall and the red-and-blue pantiled St. Mary's Church Hall, stand a tall pair of 3-storey houses, **The Grange** and **Friar's Lawn,** which are said to have been built by *Isambard Brunel* while overseeing the construction of the GWR through Southall. For more detailed information about these and other buildings in the area, I recommend the excellent booklet produced by members of the **Norwood Green Resident's Association** to celebrate their Golden Jubilee in 1982.

Further up Norwood Road, the red-brick police station on **Frogmore Green** was built in 1890 on the site of the old Manor Farmhouse, and some of the farmland has been preserved in **Wolf Fields,** the quiet little park to the left of **The Wolf.** The giant-sized cricket bat displayed outside the pub, was the much-prized trophy in the annual cricket match between regulars of The Wolf and The Lamb. Known locally as the **Battle for the Bat,** the custom began about 1901 and drew large crowds to Norwood Green every August bank holiday. Results of the matches are recorded on the bat from 1938-63, the last year the game was played. The Wolf won on that occasion but there is talk of a revival of the match, so perhaps the bat will be transferred to The Lamb some time in the future. The Wolf is a cosy little inn, filled with photographs of forgotten cricket-teams and pictures of the pub in days gone by, and it seems just as popular with locals today as it was with canal boatmen in an earlier age.

The terraced cottages betweeen the pub and **Wolf Bridge** were the first Council houses in the parish. They were built by A&B Hanson in 1920 and over a thousand more were to follow before the outbreak of the Second World War. **The Lamb** has a beer-garden overlooking the canal, but the towpath is on the other side of the bridge, down the stepped cobbled path once used by barge-horses to turn the boats around. Once under the bridge, you will be walking along the southern border of the borough which the canal follows all the way to Bull's Bridge. On the far side of the canal, the long wharf beside **Southall Timber Yard** played a more active role when *Henry Dobbs'* vitriol factory stood on the same site, soon after the Grand Union opened in 1798.

.. THE WOLF INN, FROGMORE GREEN ..

Adelaide Dock, further up the towpath was built in the 1850's for the steam-powered Norwood Flour Mills, the first big factory in the district. The dock, with the gasometer towering in the distance, has been disused for years but is to receive a new lease of life in Summer 1982, when it becomes a centre for the **Colne Valley Passenger-boat Service,** presently based at Bull's Bridge. The company's traditional canal-boat has been converted to carry up to 70 people on pleasure trips between Rickmansworth and Brentford, and down the Paddington Arm. Eventually they hope to run public day-trips from Adelaide Dock, similar to the ones that set out from Coldharbour Lane Bridge in Hayes throughout August and September.

Well-kept gardens, many with trees overhanging the water or towpath, line both sides of the canal until the **Old Oak Tree** welcomes you to **The Common,** just beyond Regina Road bridge. Here, the view of the pretty pub next to the village shop, with the open green of the large recreation ground beyond, contrasts sharply with the messy dumping ground on the North Hyde side of the canal, where no advantage seems to have been taken of gardens on the water's edge. Further up the towpath, some of the little terraced cottages (one has the interesting inscription 'Industrious Cottages') date from the early 19th century, when brickfields lined the canal banks from Southall to Northolt and many homes were built for the labourers on what was then **Glebe Farm.**

The towpath joins the road after **Western Road bridge,** where you will find the **Grand Junction Arms** — the last pub on this walk, so make the most of their sunny beer-garden. **Bull's Bridge** now lies straight ahead with the British Waterways repair yard across the water at **Willow Wren Wharf.** Houseboats, various pleasure-craft and the more traditional canal boats are moored in what used to be the Grand Union Canal Carrying Company's narrowboat lay-by, made famous by the women who 'manned' and the boats during the Second World War. The peaceful scene is very different from the old days when dozens of working boats with smoking chimneys waited for the loudspeaker call, "All captains to the office for orders", while women washed clothes in the wash-houses and children and animals rushed about.

The 13-mile long lock-free Paddington Arm begins under the white-washed bridge, but if you cross over and follow the old wooden signpost towards 'Birmingham' for a short way, you will find a group of canal cottages and the old siding, known as **Sleeper Depot,** which the GWR built to receive materials by boat from Paddington and Brentford in the 1830's. Most of the timber for sleepers on the London to Maidenhead line was brought here to be treated, and huge tanks were built for soaking the wood in creosote. The first locomotive to use the line was also taken to West Drayton by canal boat. Bull's Bridge depot gradually declined in importance once the railway from Southall to Brentford was opened in 1859, but the wharfs and sidings continued to be used until well into this century.

If you are still bouncing with energy or just want to clear you head after the last few pubs, it is only about a mile up the **Paddington Arm** to the Uxbridge Road and the burnt-out shell of the **Hamborough Tavern,** which is in the process of being reconstructed after the 1981 riots. There is not a lot to see on the way: beyond the old toll-house (the present headquarters of Colne Valley Passengerboat Services) the towpath winds through scrubland, under the railway, and past the sites of Southall's early industrial development to some pleasant terraced houses at **Bankside.** Today, only the iron towpath bridges over a series of private docks, long since filled in, show where the coal-boats once gained entrance to the Gasworks, and Kearley and Tonges jam factory — known as the "jam 'ole" by boatmen. Still, if it's fresh air you're after — there's plenty of it!

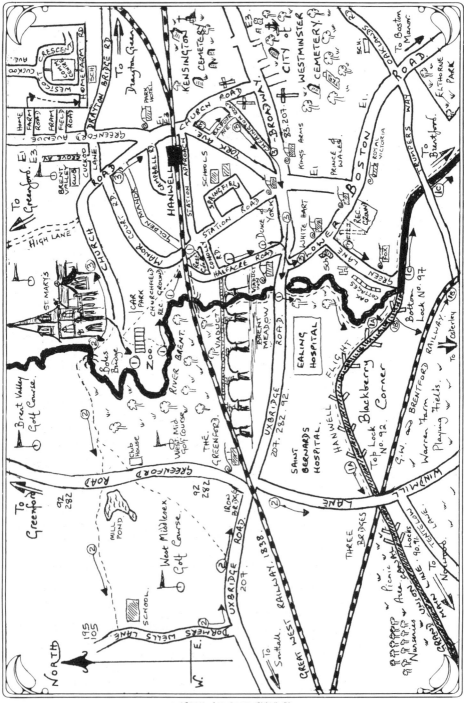

HANWELL 198

CHAPTER XI

The neighbourhood of Hanwell is green and pleasant,
gently undulating, mostly pasture land, with the Brent,
a thin stream, winding through it.

JAMES THORNE, Handbook to the Environs of London (1876)

  owes its development to the three R's of communication: river, road and rail. The latter brought about the greatest changes in this small parish which, although half the size of Greenford and Northolt, had a population of over 19,000 by 1911 — when its neighbours had still to reach the 1000 mark. But huge supermarkets and large-scale industry have yet to encroach on this attractive district and, if local conservationists have their way, never will. Blessed by the rural delights of the Brent River Park and the preservation of numerous 19th century houses (many of them listed buildings), Hanwell retains a strong sense of community spirit and, in my opinion, is the only suburb in the Borough that can still be called a village.

The fresh waters of the Brent and several natural springs, and the protection offered by the high land around the present Parish Church attracted settlers to Hanwell from the earliest times. Hundreds of Stone and Bronze Age implements have been found in the area, and in 1886 the graves and remains of ten 6th century West Saxon warriors were excavated from a gravel pit on the site of the present **Oaklands School** — one of the few discoveries of Early Saxon occupation in Middlesex. These invaders are thought to have died in a battle with the resident tribe of Romano-British on Cuckoo Hill — in a field which for centuries was known as **Blood Croft,** until covered by the houses at the northern end of **Grove Avenue.**

The name 'Hanewelle' (meaning a 'cock-frequented spring') does not appear until 959 AD, however, when *Alfwyn,* the Saxon Lord of the Manor, pawned Hanwell in exchange for £30 of silver from the Archbishop of Canterbury, *St. Dunstan,* so that he could make a pilgrimage to Rome. He returned penniless and was unable to redeem his pledge, but St. Dunstan allowed him to remain on the estate until his death — when he gave the land to the **Monastery of St. Peter** at Westminster. At Domesday, the Abbot of Westminster controlled a manor of around a 1000 acres and 20 or so people, at various levels of servitude. A watermill was mentioned and is likely to have been the one on The Butts at New Brentford in the Abbot's **Manor of Boston,** which was then a sub-manor of Hanwell. There was also a large freehold estate (later known as **La Brome Land**) which lay to the south between the road from Boston and the Brent. During the 12th century, the Abbot sold Boston Manor to *Ralph de Brito* (see Page 54 for its subsequent history) and amalgamated Hanwell with his other manor of Greenford — where the manor courts for both villages were held.

The medieval layout of Hanwell remained much the same until the advent of the railway. The main settlement was around the Church at **Churchend,** with a few more houses dotted around the large green at the southern end of **Cuckoo Lane.** This, together with **Hay Lane,** gave access to Greenford and Northolt. A windmill was built just north of Blood Croft by the Abbot, *Richard de Crokesley* c.1250, but was removed early in the 14th century (possibly replaced by the watermill in what is now Greenford Road), although the site was still known as **Mill Hill Field** 500 years later. The track from the Church continued down to the Uxbridge/Oxford Road, where another settlement (called **Tickhill** on old maps) had sprung up around the junction of the lane to Brentford and the **Middle Ford** over the Brent. From here, another footpath (corresponding to the present Half Acre Road) led back through the fields to the Church. The southern part of the parish was covered by open heath and arable land, and uninhabited except for a farm (later **Park Farm**) in Brome Close, which had been granted to the Abbot by *Joan and William de Langdon* in 1254. **Green Lane** cut across The Warren (later **Warren** or **Trumpers Farm**) to Norwood Green for those who wanted to avoid the toll-gate at the ford. The Abott's **gallows** gave their name to a third bridge over the Brent, which allowed the inhabitants of Little Ealing to cross to Osterley from Thieves' Lane (today's **Hazlemere Avenue**). The **Gospel Oak** formed the boundary between Hanwell and New Brentford, although Hanwell retained jurisdiction over the township until the 17th century.

The three common fields — **Church Field, East Field** and **South Field** — were divided up into short strips, copyholders usually holding a few plots in each field. In 1484, *William Hobbayne* bequeathed his farm to the parish for 'godly purposes'. It consisted of a house and 23 acres of land, scattered around the common fields in separate strips, which the Hobbayne Charity trustees sold or leased over the years to provide funds for the poor, or the maintenance of the Church. The map of old Hanwell reproduced here is based on the Hobbayne Charity map of 1790. (The Charity still owns land in Hanwell and will soon be 500 years old.)

Hanwell and Greenford both passed to the Bishop of London in 1550 (see Chapter VIII for details), but separated into independent manors once again about a century later — although they continued to share the same Manor Court. The Civil War and the Plague seem to have passed Hanwell by, and except for the old tale related on Page 32, neither receive any mention. During Elizabethan times, the woodlands covering Cuckoo Hill were cleared for growing wheat, but as the number of stage coaches on the Turnpike Road to Oxford increased, hayfields began to replace the arable land — although sheep and cattle were still kept. The Brent made Hanwell a natural stopping-place for coaches. Horses could be watered and rested, and the travellers themselves were well provided for by inns like the **Coach and Horses** (now the Viaduct) which offered overnight shelter from the highwaymen who prowled the lonely heath beyond.

Wealthy Londoners began to take an interest in this quiet backwater, and towards the middle of the 18th century several small copyholders in the northern part of the parish sold their land to *Charles Gostling*, who built **Hanwell Park** — the largest house in the parish — on part of the estate. He died in 1766, and Hanwell Park and 286 acres passed to his brothers, *William* and *Henry Berner* — lessee and trustee, respectively, of the Hobbayne lands. (I have not been able to find out why Gostling should have had a different surname from his brothers — perhaps he had married a wealthy heiress, and changed his name to her's.) Following the death of the last of the brothers in 1782, the outlying portions of the estate were sold for two more large houses, **Brent Lodge** and **The Grove,** which set the tone for the air of prosperity this part of the parish was to assume over the next few years. **Hanwell Park** belonged to *Sir Henry MacDonald,* Chief Baron of the Exchequer, at the turn of the century, and by 1816 had passed to *Thomas Willan* of Twyford Abbey and Springfield Park fame.

The opening of the **Grand Junction Canal** along the lower course of the Brent through Hanwell in 1796, seems to have passed unnoticed; but the **Enclosure Act** of 1814 had far-reaching effects on the town's future development. It put an end to the old method of strip-farming, and the resulting increase in land values encouraged more farmers to give up their smallholdings on the hillside, and move further south where 100 acres of heath had been enclosed. Following the establishment of the **County Asylum** and **Hanwell College** in the early 1830's, houses for doctors, teachers and other

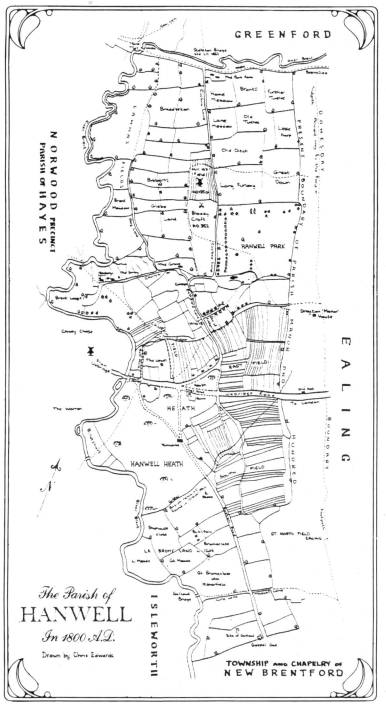

The Parish of
HANWELL
In 1800 A.D.

Drawn by Chris Edwards

professional people began to appear in the lower Church Field, and along the south-western stretch of Church Road.

This north/south division between wealthy middle and working class was accentuated by the opening of the GWR's main line to Slough through Hanwell in 1838. Services from **Hanwell Station** (which then stood immediately east of Brunel's famous Viaduct) were poor to begin with and there was no sudden demand for housing. By the late-1870's, however, the building of closely-packed terraces in new roads south of **Green Lane** was well underway and, within a few years, commuters were flocking to buy the larger houses with gardens on the **Golden Manor Estate** in the north.

Great changes had also taken place at **Hanwell Park.** The estate, covering all the land east of Cuckoo Lane, had been bought by *Benjamin Sharpe* in 1843, but he soon disposed of the 170-acre farm north of the house. **Cuckoo Farm** was further subdivided in 1854, when the London Poor Law Guardians purchased 112 acres to build a residental school for the hundreds of children in the Workhouses, and those who had been orphaned or abandoned. The **Central London District Schools** (better known as Cuckoo Schools) opened in 1857, and the number of children accounted for almost half of Hanwell's total population of 2,687 in 1861.

Cuckoo and Park Farms were the only ones left by the mid-19th century — although the **Stud Farm** (now Gifford Gardens) in Cuckoo Lane was to be established later. Land in the former **East** and **South Field** had been sold to provide **cemeteries** for the built-up areas of Kensington and Westminster in 1855; and new roads were laid out across the remaining farmland as the workmen's trains improved, small local factories increased, and after the final break-up of the **Hanwell Park** estate allowed Cuckoo Lane to be extended southwards in 1886. Gravel for the new roads was dug from extensive pits near the Brent in the extreme south of the parish. There were still large areas of open space, however, and in 1898 the Local Board took the first step towards keeping the hillside and river valley free of building by preserving the remaining few acres of the **Church Field** as a recreation ground. The **Local Board** had taken over from the Parish Vestry in 1885, but even after Hanwell was made an **Urban District** in 1894, Manor Courts continued to be held at the Viaduct Inn until the turn of the century.

By 1901, the year the electric tram service from Acton to Southall began, Hanwell's population had reached 10,000. It was to double again over the next decade as building spread east and west of **Boston Road** following the opening of the tram-link to Brentford in 1906, and increase in the number of trains on the Metropolitan District Railway through **Boston Manor Station** (est. 1883). Developers then turned their attention to the northern slopes of Cuckoo Hill where the Brent Valley Golf Course (with Club H.Q. at **The Grove**) and **Elthorne Heights** had been laid out by the First World War.

Development of the western side of **Greenford Avenue** (the old Cuckoo Lane) continued after Hanwell became part of Ealing Municipal Borough in 1926, but the grounds of **Brent Lodge** were added to the recreation ground after the Council acquired the estate in 1931. **Cuckoo Farm and Schools** (the only large remaining space) closed in 1933, and by the outbreak of the Second World War the LCC had erected 1,592 houses, houses, two churches and three schools on the 140-acre estate. The administration block (and clock-tower) of the old school survived, however, and has been used as a **Community Centre** since 1938.

Post-war building has been concentrated on flats and, except for the development of a small trading estate off **Trumpers Way,** there have been no major changes to Hanwell. **Brent Lodge, The Grove** and some of the older houses at the northern end of Church Road were demolished either before or soon after the War, and others would probably have gone the same way in recent years had it not been for the efforts of the **Hanwell Preservation Society** and the **Brent River and Canal Society** — who realised that

Hanwell was something special and should be kept that way. And when, having walked the length and breadth of the Borough, you finally stumble on this charming little town, I'm sure you'll agree with them.

ST MARY'S HANWELL

The **Parish Church of St. Mary** was first built on the little knoll overlooking the Brent in 958 AD — possibly on the site of an earlier Saxon structure. (When Bishop Mellitus, who gives his name to another Hanwell church, was sent to England by Pope Gregory in Saxon times, he was ordered to consecrate rather than destroy the pagan temples so that local tribes would take more easily to the new religion.) The church was rebuilt in the 12th century — probably around the time that **St. Lawrence's** was erected at **New Brentford** as a Chapel-of-Ease to the mother church. The rector of St. Mary's preached at St. Lawrence's once a month until a curate was appointed to the chapel in 1573, some money having been left for his salary to save New Brentonians the long walk to Hanwell on other Sundays. It has been suggested that, as a compromise, parishioners and rector sometimes met halfway for services under the **Gospel Oak.**

Although New Brentford became independent of Hanwell's administration in the 17th century, the link between chapel and church was not broken until 1744 when St. Lawrence's finally got its own vicar. Once again, the churches were rebuilt within a few years of each other — St. Mary's in 1782 by the same architect as the new St. Lawrence's, *Thomas Hardwick Snr.* This building wasn't big enough to cater for new residents after the opening of the railway, however, and in 1841 *Sir George Gilbert Scott's* plans for the present Gothic-style church were converted into flint and brick under a slender spire. It was one of the first in a batch of six that Sir George was later to describe as 'a mass of horrors', when he looked back on his early attempts at revolutionising church design (Scott's omission of a proper chancel was only corrected in 1898) from the dizzy heights of the Albert Memorial and St. Pancras Station. But most people think he was a little harsh on himself.

No monuments for furnishings from the medieval church were preserved, and the oldest **memorials** date from 1788. The frescoes in the new chancel were painted by the churchwarden, *William Yeames,* creator of that well-known piece of Victorian sentimentality, *'When did you last see your Father?'* These had to be restored after a fire in 1912, which was evidently caused by militant suffragettes — but presumably had nothing to do with their taste in art.

The list of known **rectors** begins in the late 13th century, but the most interesting ecclesiastical personalities are well towards the end — starting in 1781 with *Samuel Glasse,* chaplain to King George III, who has already been mentioned in connection with a school at Greenford (see Page 151). His son, *George,* took over from him in 1785 and was equally well-connected, being Chaplain to the Duke of Cambridge and friend to numerous members of the nobility. George devoted a lot of his wealth and attention to improving the parish — perhaps too much of the former, as £61 was found to be missing while he was Treasurer of Hobbayne's Charity. In 1809, he accidentally left a large sum of money (of unknown origin) in a hackney-cab he'd been travelling in, and, when efforts to retrace it proved fruitless, he committed suicide. A few hours later, the hackney driver returned the money intact.

Derwent Coleridge, son of the poet Samuel Taylor, became rector in 1864. He was responsible for establishing St. Mark's Church in Green Lane to serve the expanding population in that part of the parish. The most recent rector of St. Mary's was *Fred Secombe* who, besides being brother to singer and comedian, Harry, was a keen local historian. Unfortunately he disappeared off to the wilder parts of Wales before I had a chance to question him.

Buried in the crypt of the church lies *Jonas Hanway* (1712-86), another friend of the ill-fated George Glasse, but better known for his philanthropy to chimney-sweeps, waifs and down-and-outs, on whose behalf he tirelessly fought for social reforms. He also founded the Marines, and was the first man in England to use an umbrella — brought back from his travels in Persia to protect his delicate health from the English weather. It also proved to be a useful shield from the unimpressed Londoners who cast doubts on his masculinity — a 'parapluie' at that time only being carried by the 'mincing Macaronies', a set of foppish young men who had travelled in Italy and set London agog on their return by demanding new-fangled Italian food at their club.

In the crowded **churchyard,** which slopes down the hillside behind the church, you'll find the names of *Mr. and Mrs. Benjamin Sharpe, Dr. James Emerton* (headmaster of Hanwell College and also curate of St. Mary's), the *daughters* of the artist, *Thomas Gainsborough,* and a host of others — which you can have fun discovering for yourselves.

(Through Brent Lodge Park to the Grand Union Canal via Fitzherbert Walk, and then a choice of walks to Three Bridges, Osterley or Boston Manor — 1½ to 3 miles) Churchfields Recreation Ground and Brent Lodge Park form part of the 4½-mile long **Brent River Park** which follows the course of the River Brent from Western Avenue in North Ealing, through Perivale, Greenford and Hanwell, down to the A4 in Brentford. The concept of uniting this natural green belt (made up of public and private golf courses, sports fields, allotments and several formal parks) into one continuous park was first proposed by the **Brent River and Canal Society** in 1973, and accepted by Ealing Council the following year. This marked the start of an unusually co-operative working partnership. In 1977, the Society and the Council's Steering Group commissioned *Brian Green*, a landscape architect, to devise a plan for landscaping the area as a whole, and many of his ideas have already been put into practise.

A lot of hard work has gone into creating a network of footpaths that will eventually enable you to ramble over 850 acres of almost uninterrupted open space, following the special wooden signposts through a marvellous combination of river and canalside walks, woodlands and recreation grounds. Much has been done to reduce the danger of

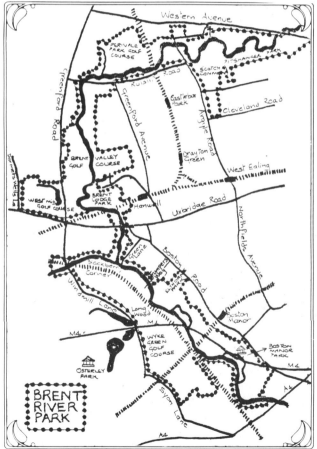

flooding (a threat which had previously preserved this lovely valley from the urban development sprawling round it), and the tree-planting programme to improve the starkness of certain areas is well underway. Other projects can only be started once the GLC's flood-alleviation works are complete, but, considering how much has been accomplished in the first 10 years, it should not be long before all the proposals become reality. You can help by joining the Society and taking an active part in this excellent scheme.

One of the first tasks the Society tackled was to get something done about **Rectory Cottage.** This Grade II listed building beside the main entrance to Brent Lodge Park had been vacant for many years (the owner having gone overseas), and vandals and nature had taken their toll — the roof was falling in, gardens overgrown, windows were broken etc. After prolonged negotiations, instigated by the Society, the neglected cottage was resold to more appreciative owners who have transformed it into the immaculate property you see today. The cottage stands on the site of the 16th century **Church House** in which the Hobbayne Charity Trustees established the first **village school** in 1782. The old building was blown down during a gale a few years later, and rebuilt — but storm clouds soon gathered again, and in 1805 the new schoolhouse was struck by lightning and burnt down. The Trustees then decided to move the school to the Half Acre (where the weather seems to have been better), and *Rev. George Glasse* built Rectory Cottage in its place.

George Glasse had earlier acquired **Brent Lodge** (no wonder he eventually ran short of money), and the path from the main gates into the Park follows the line of the carriageway that once led down to his house. Sadly, the **stables** are the only buildings on the estate to have been preserved — they stand just beyond Rectory Cottage. After Glasse's untimely death, Brent Lodge passed to his son-in-law, *Dr. Hume* (personal medical attendant to the Duke of Wellington in many campaigns), and was later sold to *Alderman Bridge*, a former Lord Mayor of London who retired to Hanwell. By the late-19th century, the house belonged to *Captain John Parsons* whose daughter fell in love with and later married the heir to Hanwell's largest estate — *Montagu Sharpe* of Hanwell Park.

RECTORY COTTAGE

The couple chose to make Brent Lodge their home, however, and lived here until their deaths. Montagu Sharpe rose to become one of the most respected men in Middlesex. He was knighted for his services as a Justice of the Peace and member of Middlesex County Council and, on his retirement, wrote several authorative works on the early history of Hanwell and Brentford. Ealing Council bought the estate for a public park in 1931, but the house was left vacant and eventually had to be demolished after a fire caused by vandals.

Brent Lodge Park is known as the 'Bunny Park' to the hundreds of children from all parts of the borough who regularly visit the splendid little zoo at its centre. Besides huge lop-eared rabbits and the more usual goats and geese, the free open-air farmyeard offers wallabies, llama, and black-and-white Jacob sheep; while the small entrance fee to the glassed-in enclosure allows them to see a satisfying selection of things that wriggle and bite, and to watch the antics of monkeys and other small wild animals. A pictorial history of Brent Lodge is displayed in the animal-house, and refreshments are available from the nearby **cafeteria** — which marks the site of the old mansion.

The path winds past the bowling greens, down to the river and into **Churchfields Conservation Area.** Masses of old trees line the riverbank — their spreading branches just asking to be climbed by older children. In summer, their foliage is so dense that only the noise of high-speed trains reminds you of the presence of the **Wharncliffe Viaduct** which spans the Brent 65-feet overhead. Near the exit into Manor Court Road, the landscaped view down the slope to Brent Meadow and the viaduct gives you a clearer impression of the scale and architecture of Brunel's engineering.

Isambard Kingdom Brunel became Chief Engineer to the GWR at the age of 27 — having already made a name for himself by helping to design the Thames Tunnel and drawing up plans for the Clifton Suspension Bridge across the Avon Gorge. This famous bridge wasn't built until after his death, however, and the 300-yard long viaduct over the Brent at little-known Hanwell was in fact the first of his large-scale designs to be constructed. Work began on the eight huge arches almost as soon as the GWR had obtained parliamentary approval to build their line in 1835. When completed eighteen months later, the viaduct was named after *Lord Wharncliffe* — Chairman of the House of Lords' Committee on the Great Western bill. The young Queen Victoria and Prince Albert made their first ever rail journey a few years after the line opened — with Brunel travelling on the footplate of the special train which carried them from Slough to Paddington in 25 minutes. She was very taken with the view across the Churchfields and is said to have issued instructions for her train to pause for a few minutes on the viaduct whenever she passed that way in future. The viaduct was widened in 1877 — when the present station was built.

Lord Wharncliffe's coat-of-arms are displayed on the southern side of the viaduct, but unfortunately there is no direct access from Churchfields to **Brent Meadow.** The Brent River and Canal Society plan to create two new paths under the viaduct as soon as permission can be obtained from British Rail, but until then you'll have to go the long way round, via Half Acre Road, or take the shorter but rather overgrown route from Church Path on the other side of the railway. From the Manor Court Road exit walk under the arch across **Station Road** (where the bricked-up windows of the original station can still be seen) and turn right into **Conolly Dell** to reach **Half Acre Road;** or take the **Church Path** above the rest-garden and look out for the entrance to a narrow footpath (about 50 yards along on the right) which winds through the trees and undergrowth on the viaduct embankment, and crosses into Brent Meadow by way of a footbridge over the river. The delightful Conolly Dell once formed part of the grounds of **The Lawn,** home of the man who revolutionised treatment of the mentally ill — *Dr. John Conolly.* He was superintendent of the County Asylum (now St. Bernard's Hospital)

WHARNCLIFFE VIADUCT - HANWELL

from 1839-44, and one of the first doctors in his field to abandon the use of restraining instruments. He died in 1866 and is buried in Kensington Cemetery. The Lawn was demolished in the 1880's for Conolly Road and Lawn Gardens.

Half Acre and Station Road were formed from two of the original strips of land that *William Hobbayne* donated to the parish in 1484. Hobbayne's Charity made a great difference to the poor in Hanwell during the impoverished years of the late-18th century. As food prices rose and wages dropped under the combined effects of the Industrial Revolution and England's attempts to extend her empire in India, America and Europe, farm labourers, unable to live on the pittance they were paid, flooded into market towns like Brentford and Southall in search of work — the unsuccessful adding to the poor of surrounding parishes. **Hobbayne's School** was established to teach their children to read and write, and in 1790 the Trustees erected a group of **almshouses** in the Half Acre. But, as the problem increased, the Parish Vestry had to resort to sending some of the children away — to work in a worsted spinning mill in Nottinghamshire.

The magnanimous proprietors of this establishment sent circulars to all the local Vestries offering clothing, maintenance and education for the children's 'occasional attendance' on the factory floor. In reality, the children (aged between seven and twelve) worked six days a week from 3am to 10.30pm, with a break of 45 minutes for food, and slept beside the machines. They were, however, allowed time off for Sunday School. Several local parents wisely refused to let their children go to the mill and, through the efforts of people like *Jonas Hanway*, legislation was eventually introduced to prevent such shameful abuse of child labour. It is to be hope that conditions in the **glove factory** which opened in the Half Acre in 1795 were considerably better — as the owner, *Mr. John Fownes*, was a churchwarden of St. Mary's. He offered work to 'women and children of the poor', but moved the factory elsewhere soon afterwards.

The village **stocks** and **cage** used to stand at the Uxbridge Road end of the Half Acre. It is safe to assume that both saw good service during the years that the parish was invaded by Irish labourers working first on the canal, and then the railway. These inland navigators or 'navvies' (another exploited workforce) often became uncontrollably drunk, and were greatly feared by the districts in which they temporarily resided. A 'desperate affray' took place at the **Viaduct Inn** in 1838, when the constable and mounted police were called in to settle a brawl and 'were attacked with great violence by men and women wielding pickaxe-handles and shovels'. The cage where such miscreants (when finally subdued into submission) were confined until carted off to prison, was taken down in 1844; and the bricks were used to rebuild the western wall of the churchyard.

The beer garden of the Viaduct Inn is comparatively peaceful these days — except for the noise of the express trains whizzing across its namesake. Its predecessor, the **Coach and Horses,** was established in the early 18th century — probably around the time that the Uxbridge Road was turnpiked in 1714. The tollgate stood just before the **bridge** over the Brent, which has been rebuilt several times since it was first erected in the 14th century — the present one dates from 1906.

Brent Meadow has been greatly improved since GLC contractors completed their flood alleviation work between the viaduct and canal. New trees have been planted to replace those lost when the river was widened, and benches put up by the roadside to allow you to rest awhile and enjoy the view before following the new riverside walk under the bridge to the canal. (If the tunnel is too muddy, cross over the Uxbridge Road and pick up the path from there.) **FitzHerbert Walk** is named after the founder of the Brent River and Canal Society, and was opened by the Mayor in 1983 as part of the 10th Anniversary celebrations. The path passes through the grounds of **Ealing Hospital** (which will be less overpowering once the newly-planted trees have matured) and branches into two just before the canal joins the river. The right-hand fork leads to the second lock (No. 96) of the **Hanwell Flight,** while the other carries on to the footbridge near Green Lane. Having refreshed yourselves at **The Fox** nearby, you have the choice of three walks through the Brent River Park.

Route A leads up the Hanwell Flight to **Three Bridges** (½ a mile). The six locks that raise the canal over 53 feet were built between 1793-6, and have been designated an Ancient Monument. It takes a narrowboat 1½ hours to clear the flight — during which time sixty thousand gallons of water are lost. For many years, the Grand Junction Company's plans to build the canal were thwarted by strong opposition from landowners, who claimed that the scheme wouldn't work and that the canal would become 'green mantled pools of stinking water' which would 'contaminate the passing breeze with noxious exhalations'. Foul gases did indeed once rise from the canal at Hanwell — but these were caused by the insanitary condition of the River Brent (described as an open sewer in 1897), rather than the canal. For centuries, the river had been the only form of drainage in the villages on its banks, and as the population grew so the pollution became worse. No fish or even water-rats could survive in the canalised section of the river, and boatmen were practically incapacitated by the stench from the filth stirred up by their barges.

Only the scent of may and hawthorn are wafted by passing breezes today, however, and the walk up to Three Bridges is quite the nicest stretch of canal in the borough. The towpath skirts the lovely old wall around **St. Bernard's Hospital,** which used to have its own private dock. The bricked-up archway can still be seen next to Lock No. 94 — known as Asylum Lock to the boatmen who carried coke to the hospital in the old days. The history of St. Bernard's and Three Bridges (also an Ancient Monument) is related in Route 2, which you can follow back to the Uxbridge Road — or continue along the towpath to Norwood and Southall. Just beyond the lock-keeper's cottage on the other side of Three Bridges, you'll find a secluded picnic area between the screen of trees beside the towpath, and Ealing Borough Nurseries — which provide most of the plants that keep our parks blooming.

It was not possible to show the full extent of the next two walks on the route-map at the beginning of the chapter, but the map of the Brent River Park on Page 20 should prevent you from losing your bearings. Better still, arm yourself with a copy of the Brent River and Canal Society's recently published booklet which clearly illustrates these and other walks through the Brent River Park.

Route B takes you over the bottom lock of the canal and up to **Osterley Park** (1½ miles). **Blackberry Corner,** the new name for the old hay meadow on the southern bank of the canal, was planted with a variety of fruit and nut trees to celebrate the Queen's Silver Jubilee in 1977. Besides blackberries, the autumn harvest includes raspberries, hazel nuts, sloe and elderberries — all free for the picking; while in summer, the flower-filled meadow provides the perfect setting for a picnic. From the stile, follow the footpath over the railway line and turn left at the playing fields, which were created from the pasture land of **Warren Farm** in the late 1950's. The old dairy farm was run by the *Trumper* family during the 19th century, and their name lives on in **Trumpers Way** at the end of the playing fields. Here the path turns up to **Windmill Lane,** and you'll find an entrance into Osterley Park a little way to the right on the other side of the road. (Read all about it in Chapter IX, if you haven't done so already.)

Some time in what the Brent River and Canal Society hope will be the very near future, British Rail is to provide a proper crossing over the railway to Trumpers Way and Wyncote Farm Riding School (see Route C), and will also fence off the railway so that a new path to **Long Wood** can be made on the Osterley side of the line. At present, this ancient stretch of woodland (which abounds in plant and animal life) can only be reached by a path near the M4 on Windmill Lane; although, unofficially, it is possible to gain access by walking across the fields beside the railway — along the line of the proposed new path from Trumpers Way. The railway (part of the old GWR line from Southall to Brentford Dock) is still occasionally used for carrying freight, however, so do be careful.

Route C follows the towpath westward to **Osterley Lock,** then up through fields and woodland to **Elthorne Park** or **Boston Manor** (1¼-1¾ miles). From the peaceful country atmosphere of the Hanwell Flight, the towpath passes through the **Trumpers Way Industrial Estate** — which would be a lot less intrusive if factory-owners were to replace the tatty corrugated iron and barbed wire fencing along the towpath with wooden palings. Some of the industrial bleakness is offset by the open fields on the far side of the canal, where horses graze under the trees — oblivious of the fact that the Council are trying to sell their pasture for a boating marina. Commercial enterprise is not new to this stretch of the canal, however, for today's factories cover the extensive **gravel pits** which helped to build many new roads in the borough last century. The skeleton loading gantries on the old paper warehouse overlook the site of the once busy **Humes Dock,** which lay behind the towpath until filled in during the 1930's.

Beyond Trumpers Way bridge, the scenery improves once you've passed the faded blue sign on the towpath which proclaims the 'Prize Length of Piling' that won a British Waterways maintenance gang the Kerr Cup in 1959. This annual competition for the best stretch of bank-support piling was inaugurated by *Sir Reginald Kerr*, a former chairman of British Waterways. The canal at this point could certainly do with a bit of maintenance work today, as pools of stagnant water have been trapped by the weeds and reeds lining the bank — the whiff being vaguely reminiscent of the old **sewage works** for Hanwell and Southall which used to lie on either side of the canal. But at least you're spared the 'noxious exhalations' which emanated from the **piggeries** opposite Osterley Lock until a few years ago — **Wyncote Farm** is now a **riding school,** and the atmosphere is considerably better for it!

GLC contractors are at present working on the loop of the Brent which plunges over a **weir** just before Osterley Lock, and the Brent River and Canal Society have also been very busy in this corner of late. The burnt-out shell of the old **Lock Cottage** is at last being renovated; a wooden bridge has been built over the lock; and a new footpath created around the riding school and up to the railway (with Long Wood beyond), to join up with Trumpers Way. The path from the canal can be very muddy, however, and is best negotiated in wellies. You can also explore the wooded island behind the lock house which is covered with wild flowers and blackberry bushes — the trees muffling the noise of traffic on the busy motorway bridge nearby.

Where the river rejoins the canal before the M4, a very pleasant picnic area has been created beside the path leading up through the woods to Boston Road. At the top of the hill, another little path branches off into the open space and playing fields which now cover the farmlands of **Park Farm.** Broom, the wild shrub with yellow flowers which gave this area its original name of **La Bromeland,** still flourishes on the steep slopes of the river embankment — where new trees and shrubs have been planted to disguise evidence that this was once a municipal dumping ground. The freehold of the Broomland was bought by Thomas Gresham's widow in the 16th century, and descended with Osterley to the Earls of Jersey. After the 1816 enclosure the remaining 90 acres was called Park Farm and, when this was broken up c.1910, **Elthorne Park** was formed from 10 acres of the estate.

You'll find a gate into the Park near Elthorne School. Hanwell Band frequently plays on the **bandstand** in the Park on Sunday afternoons in summer, and the children's **playground** offers an unusually good selection of swings, roundabouts and wooden climbing frames. When Townholme Crescent was being excavated earlier this century, a **sarsen stone** was discovered in the gravel below the surface and is now displayed at the main entrance to the Park. This large glacial boulder was probably carried down from the frozen north during the Ice Age.

Boston Manor Park lies about half-a-mile to your right, if you follow the path from the canal straight up to Boston Road. Although the Manor stands very close to the canal, it cannot, as yet, be approached from the towpath as this is fenced off at the obvious point of access — across the playing fields beside **Gallows Bridge.** The Brent River and Canal Society are working on getting this far more pleasant route opened up to the public in the near future, however. The cast iron Gallows Bridge (erected in 1820) takes the towpath across to the far side of the canal for the rest of the journey to Brentford.

ROUTE TWO *(Through the Brent River Park to Dormers Wells Lane, and then on to the canal via Windmill Lane — 2 miles)* Walking towards Brent Lodge Park from the Church, turn right down the footpath just before the Park entrance. This takes you across Bole's Meadow to **Bole's Bridge** — once, as you can see from the photograph, a nice old wooden bridge, but since rebuilt in ugly iron. The northern stretch of the Brent from the bridge was considerably straightened in the 1920's, and the wigglely bit behind the Church was cut off, but not filled in. It now promotes the growth of a large variety of wildlife, as well as providing a water obstacle for golfers. Bole's Bridge is thought to have been named after a Mr. *Bowle,* the reeve or steward who supervised Lady Dacre's **Dormers Well** estate in Elizabethan times.

Bowles Bridge (also called Bull's or Bole's) c.1900, with St. Mary's in the background.

Don't be put off by the closed gates which block the entrance to the **West Middlesex Golf Course** beyond the bridge. There is a public right of way across the golf course (even if the path is not very well defined) so you won't be trespassing if you follow the path around to the left of the gates, and continue across the course to the tall hedge around the club house. To the right of the hedge you'll find some steps leading up to **Greenford Road.**

The golf course was the first to be established in Middlesex, and will be celebrating its centenary in 1990. The land once belonged to **Mill Farm** and, if you want to reduce your walk by about a mile and take a short cut down Greenford Road to the canal, you'll pass one of the old farm cottages just beyond the club house and sports centre. (In case you wonder — W. Hanson, the timber and builders' merchants at the end of the road, does not, according to the present owner, have any direct connection with the Hansons of Southall.)

In the days before the creation of Greenford Road turned the old Windmill Lane into a speedway, one of the windmills (or, in this case, a watermill) which gave the road its former name stood directly opposite the steps. Across the road and a little to the right, you'll find a gap in the hedge and a path leading down to the old **millpond** of Hanwell or **Overshott Mill.** The origin of this mill is uncertain. It appears on John Seller's map of 1680, but may have existed long before that as part of the Dormers Well estate — where the moated **Manor House of Southall** stood until the 17th century. The mill ceased operation towards the end of the 18th century, however; the waterwheel and millstones were removed, and the last pieces of machinery were cleared away when Greenford Road was built in the 1920's.

The millpond is now used for fishing and is unfortunately fenced off from the general public, but you can still enjoy the walk through the overhanging trees and natural shrubbery around it. The path follows the stream at the northern edge of the golf course, up to the paved path beside **Dormers Wells School.** The allotments on your right were once part of **Dormers Wells Farm,** where watercress was grown for the London market earlier this century. The farm lay roughly on the site of the old Manor House, until demolished in 1963. Saxon pottery and large quantities of 17th and 18th century material were found on the site.

The history of the early owners of the Manor House has already been told in the previous chapter, and there's not very much I can add here. *Lord and Lady Dacre* were the last manor lords to live in the moated house. He died in 1594 and she then moved to Chelsea — leaving **Dormans Well** (as it was originally called) in the care of *Mr. Bowle* until her death the following year. Southall's next Lord of the Manor, *Francis Awsiter*, preferred to live in his own house on Southall Green, and it's not known what happened to the moated house after that. The well which gave the house its name has been filled in, but it was once renowned for the strength-giving properties of the iron it contained.

If you feel in need of a little energy booster yourselves, the appropriately-shaped **Beehive** pub awaits you around the corner at the northern end of Dormers Wells Lane. Our route continues southwards down to the Uxbridge Road, where you turn left and carry on to the **Iron Bridge** and the unattractive pub, **The Greenford.** The path back through the golf course from the Uxbridge Road (just before the garage) is part of the old footway from Hanwell to Southall. Also look out for the old **waterpump** near the bus-stop opposite Lyndhurst Road.

The construction of the GWR bridge over the Uxbridge Road caused a lot of headaches for *Brunel*, as Windmill Lane then intersected the main road at the same point. The cast-iron girders of his first bridge were supported by two rows of eight pillars — separating the main road from the footpaths — but still allowing access. The spaces between the girders were initially filled with brick (until one of the girders collapsed under the weight in 1839), and then planks — until these caught fire and cracked all the girders in 1847. The present wrought-iron bridge was then constructed, but one of the original cast-iron pillars can still be seen. The Uxbridge Road end of the lane from Greenford to Brentford was realigned when Greenford Road was built.

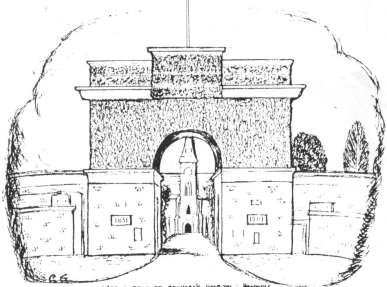

MAIN GATE : ST. BERNARD'S HOSPITAL : HANWELL

Cross under the bridge to **Windmill Lane,** and follow the wall around St. Bernard's Hospital to Brunel's Three Bridges, to join up with towpath-route 'A' in the first walk. The **County Asylum** opened in 1831 and was one of the first mental hospitals to treat patients as human beings, instead of sources of amusement for the more fortunate. This enlightened attitude owed much to the pioneering work of *Dr. William Ellis* of Southall Park, who was the first superintendent of the 500 inmates. *Dr. John Conolly* took over on his retirement in 1838. The hospital was continually repaired and extended during the 19th century — the number of patients in 1880 (as now) being in the region of 2,000. The fine old archway at the Uxbridge Road entrance (with rooms for the former gatekeeper above); the lodges beside the main gate; and the hospital chapel are all listed as being of special architectural interest. Prior to the hospital being built, a large area of heath known as **Cheavy Chase** covered the site.

The old coach-building works on the opposite side of Windmill Lane have been shared by Impac and London Transport since **AEC** ceased production in 1981. The firm opened in 1927 and was once responsible for building all of London's buses. Before walking down to the towpath, take a closer look at Brunel's extraordinary feat of engineering from the road bridge.

The road bridge was first built in the 1790's when the canal was cut, and when Brunel realised that the GWR goods' line from Southall to Brentford Dock had to cross the canal in the same place, he temporarily diverted the water through the Asylum grounds while a new iron channel was made for the canal, and then dug out a path for the railway underneath it. (Simple when you know how, really.) **Three Bridges** — as this masterpiece is popularly, but incorrectly, known — was Brunel's last undertaking; he died a few months after the new railway line opened in July, 1859. The proper name for it is **Windmill Bridge** — after **Southall Mill,** which stood on the south-western side of the canal bridge when *J.M.W. Turner* painted it in 1806. (A photograph of the painting can be seen at Southall library.)

Cart and barge crossing the railway at Three Bridges c.1905.

THE HERMITAGE

ROUTE THREE *(Through the old village to the canal, via Church Road and Green Lane — 1½ miles)*
All the houses on the northern side of Church Road (between the Church and High Lane) stand on the 25 acres of **Glebe** which once belonged to the rectors of St. Mary's. There were just four houses in 1887 — the old **Rectory,** next to the Church; **Madge Hill,** on the corner of Hay Lane; and **The Hermitage** and **The Spring** inbetween. Today only The Hermitage is still standing. The Rectory and The Spring were both demolished before the War and replaced by flats (Glebe/Brent Court and Spring Court, respectively) and Madge Hill was rebuilt as part of a new group of houses in the 1930's.

    The Hermitage, with its neat thatched roof, was built in 1809 on the site of an old house called **The Elms** — home of the *Berner* brothers before they moved to Hanwell Park. The Elms was then sold to the churchwarden, *John Fownes* (owner of the glove factory), and he in turn sold it to the Rector, *George Glasse*, who built the present cottage shortly before his death. While *Mark Webb* lived here during the 1920's and 30's. the Hermitage was the headquarters of the **Selborne Society,** who were responsible for preserving another feature of the Brent River Park — Perivale Wood. One of the springs (known locally as **Caesar's Spring**) which first attracted settlers to the hillside, still bubbles out in the garden behind The Hermitage and Spring Court.

    The age of the pretty **White Cottage** on the western side of The Hermitage is uncertain, but it may be the oldest building in Church Road. It is not listed in the early Kelly's Directories as it was formerly used as stables (possibly for The Spring) with housing for the coachman above, and was only converted into a cottage in the 1920's. Despite the many architectural changes, this part of the old village still retains a rural atmosphere — thanks to the number of trees and the green expanse of Churchfields Recreation Ground. And Hay Lane or **High Lane,** the old bridle-path to Greenford, hasn't changed a bit (except in name) — it's still muddy in winter and banked with bluebells in spring.

On the opposite side of the road, between High Lane and the curve of Church Road, you'll find **Spring Cottage** — another early 19th century house which has been saved from demolition by the Hanwell Preservation Society. This was once the home of *G.L. Dickinson*, philosphic writer and ardent pacifist, whose brainchild was the League of Nations which President Woodrow Wilson helped to found in 1919 — although the USA's refusal to join was one of the reasons it later failed.

The large **Village Green,** which once extended as far as Greenford Avenue, began to shrink after **The Grove** was built in the late 18th century. The old mansion became the Club House of the **Brent Valley Golf Course** in 1910, but was rebuilt after the last War. **Grove Lodge,** the little Gothic-windowed cottage on the corner, still marks the entrance to the estate, however. Two larger 19th century houses also survive — **Crossways** (formerly St. Vincent's Lodge), on the southern corner of Cuckoo Lane; and **Elm Grove** (now flats), further down the Green on the same side of the road. This corner of the Green was called **Round Town** on the 1890 map — but I have not been able to find out why.

Should you wish to make a short **detour** from the main route to visit what remains of the **Central London District Schools,** then continue along Cuckoo Lane and turn left into Greenford Avenue. **Hanwell Park** was the only house in the road at the turn of the century. After *Benjamin Sharpe's* death in 1883, the house passed to his son, *Montagu,* who sold it the following year — perhaps already with a view to taking over Captain Parson's daughter and Brent Lodge. The grand old building had been demolished by 1905, leaving behind a large field of buttercups and daisies (known as **Sharpe's Park**) between the new Framfield and Drayton Bridge Roads. **Drayton Manor High School** has covered the site since 1930. The first houses in **Framfield Road** (or Graham Gardens, as it was called originally) are said to have been built for railwaymen working on the **loop-line** from West Ealing Station through Greenford to the GWR's main Birmingham line, which led to the opening of **Drayton Green Station** in 1905.

Southern side of Hanwell Park House in 1881 during Capt. Benjamin Sharpe's ownership.
The ballustrading at the top hides the servants' quarters.

Cuckoo Schools, Hanwell.

The colonnaded Administration Block (now Hanwell Community Centre) of the Central London District Schools. Dormitory Blocks D (for infants) and E (for girls) are to the left, and Boys' Dormitories B and A on the right. (Charlie Chaplin slept in B-block).

Turn right into **Homefarm Road** and continue up **Westcott Drive** — once the main driveway to the old Cuckoo Schools. The administration block (now **Hanwell Community Centre**) was the first port of call for all new entrants, and thousands of children (some as young as three) passed through its Italianate colonnade between 1856 and 1933 to have their names recorded on the Admission Register. From here they were sent to the isolation block for three weeks, to ensure that no diseases were brought into the school. In the early days, children were given an education 'suitable for their station in life' — manual and agricultural work for the boys, and laundering and cooking for the girls; but academic subjects were later introduced. Boys and girls were strictly segregated (even brothers and sisters were only allowed to meet for one hour once a week), and the school itself was isolated from the Hanwell community and completely self-sufficient. Meat and produce were supplied by **Cuckoo Farm,** and other external needs were met by the private chapel, gasworks and sewage farm.

Charlie Chaplin was seven when he came to the school in 1896 — soon after the death of his actor-father had left the family in straitened circumstances. Already a seasoned stage-performer, he received his first formal education during the two years he spent at Hanwell and his autobiography records the harsh discipline and corporal punishment he experienced. Conditions gradually improved, however; and the grand day when this famous Old Boy hired a fleet of buses so that the whole school could see one of his films, features among the many happy memories related by former pupils in a series of fascinating booklets produced by the **Hanwell Community Association** (see Bibliography).

From the impoverished, we return to the main route and a school for the privileged — **Hanwell College,** which used to stand on the site of the present Rectory on the corner of **Manor Court Road.** It was established c.1820 by a *Dr. Bond*, but achieved renown as a private boarding school under the subsequent headship of *Dr. Emerton,* curate of St. Mary's. The school prepared boys for Sandhurst and the Indian Service, where they must have excelled at long-distance marches — according to the diary of *Charles Burton* (a former pupil who later became churchwarden of St. Mary's), the lads frequently walked to London and back on educational day-trips. The school closed in 1882 and was used as a convent by the Sisters of St. Joseph until replaced by the new Rectory in the 1920's.

The western end of Manor Court Road boasted several celebrated residents in the late 19th century. *Montagu Sharpe* lived there, as did *James Wheeler* (the sporting artist who painted most of the famous race-horses of his day), *Henry Tuke* (whose paintings of nudes lounging on the sea-shore caused much muttering in Victorian times) and his father, *Samuel Tuke*, a distinguished doctor in mental disorders. Despite the names, neither Manor Court nor Golden Manor Road has any connection with a Manor House, as Hanwell shared Greenford's and never had one of her own. This stretch of Church Road was known as Eastfield or **Snape's Lane** in the 18th century — probably after *Thomas Snape* who was Constable of Hanwell in 1721. It still resembles a leafy lane and the ivy-mantled wall lining the eastern side looks considerably older than the 1930 bungalows behind it; but houses get larger and more modern as the road approaches the triangular green at the junction with Greenford Avenue.

Even if railways are not high on your list of interests, do make a short diversion up **Campbell Road** to visit **Hanwell Station** (closed on Sundays). Thanks to the efforts of the Victorian Society and Hanwell Preservation Society, British Rail lost their appeal to modernise this Grade I listed building in 1971, and instead have restored the station to its former Victorian splendour — complete with old gas lampstands and 'GWR'-inscribed benches. The station was moved here from its original site at the top of Station Road after the viaduct was widened in 1877, and was renamed **'Hanwell and Elthorne'** by the GWR in an attempt to satisfy both protagonists and antagonists of a movement to change the name of the village to 'Elthorne'.

The cause of this controversy was the County Asylum which, although it actually stood in the Precinct of Norwood, was always referred to as **Hanwell Asylum** — an association which developers felt would not attract new house-buyers. Outraged residents held a public meeting to protest against getting the 'historic name of Hanwell obliterated by the new fancy name of Elthorne' and the matter was eventually dropped — but the signboard on the station remains. (The Asylum, incidentally, has only been called St. Bernard's Hospital since the Second World War.) It has been suggested that as a result of the new vistas opened up by the Brent River Park scheme, the name **'Hanwell-on-Brent'** would be more appropriate — but whether this delightful idea is ever officially adopted remains to be seen!

The **Park Hotel** faces you across the green on your return to Church Road. It was built c.1890 on the site of *William Hobbayne's* farmhouse, and was recently put up for sale by Watneys. Conservationists have managed to forestall plans to turn this grand example of Victoriana into a bingo hall, but a use for the building which will be both profitable to the brewers and acceptable to the local community has yet to be found. The auditorium, stage and procenium of the **Park Hall Theatre** which occupied the ground floor and basement early this century are still to be seen; and it was here in 1916 that *Ivor Novello's* famous song *'Keep the Home Fires Burning'* was given its first public rendering by *Mrs. Frebaim-Smith* of Golden Manor Road, who was the lead singer in Madame Novello's choir. Although the backstage dressing-rooms were converted into loos when the Hall became a cinema, the remains of the theatre have been well preserved and could be restored to their original use. The **Park Tavern,** meanwhile, is open for business until the fate of the old building has been decided.

The little group of shops and houses on the western side of the green was called Cambridge Gardens when the poet and journalist *Richard Le Galliene* lived here in the 1890's. He and his wife were joined by the composer *Frederick Delius* in 1892 and their house (now No. 33 Church Road) was frequently visited by some of the more illustrious literary and musical figures of the day. Delius later moved to France and Le Galliene to New York — where his daughter, Eva, founded the Civic Repertory Theater in 1926.

Church Road continues under the arch of the railway bridge — known as Haffenden's Bridge in the days when **Bridge House** (on the corner of York Avenue) was owned by the Haffenden family. *Rev. Richard Barham* is said to have written some of his amusing 'Ingoldsby Legends' (published in 1840) while staying with the family, but the earliest mention I have been able to find of the Haffendens occurs in 1864, when *John Haffenden* donated one of the stained glass windows in Christ Church, Ealing, in memory of his wife — who was only 23 when she died. At the turn of the century, Bridge House was occupied by the 'Misses Haffenden' (presumably John's sisters), who were well-known for their generosity and good works in the parish.

For almost a century, the fine old building (now occupied by York House Graphics) to the right of Bridge House was renowned for the violins produced here by **W.E. Hill & Sons** — *William Ebsworth Hill* having built the workshop in 1890 after he came to live at Heath Lodge in Cherington Road. The first in this great dynasty of instrument makers may well have been the Mr. Hill whom Samuel Pepys consulted about 'ye altering of my Lute and my Vial' in 1660; but the history of the present firm begins a century later when *Joseph Hill* (William's grandfather) opened his own business in the Haymarket. The firm expanded with the Hill family's growing reputation for fine craftsmanship and restoration work, and moved to larger premises in New Bond Street shortly before the Hanwell workshop was built. William's sons and a nephew ran the business after his death in 1895, and apprenticed several local men as bow-makers in the Hanwell workshop — among them *Jack Yeoman* (whose son, aged 75, still lives in Hanwell) and *William Retford*.

The Hill brothers died fairly young, but the family tradition was maintained by their cousin, Phillip, and his son, Desmond. In 1979 they decided to close the Hanwell workshop and move to Great Missenden — where a large Georgian Manor House had been acquired a few years earlier with a view to expanding the Hanwell and London branches under one roof. Phillip remained actively involved in the restoration of old violins until his death in 1981 (at the grand age of 98), and saw two of his grandsons through their apprenticeships — the 6th generation of Hills to enter the family business. The **Hill Collection,** a magnificent assembly of antique instruments donated by William's son, Alfred, can be seen at the Ashmolean Museum in Oxford; while examples of the work of bow-maker *William Retford*, and some of the equipment he used at the Hanwell workshop, are displayed in the Faculty of Music at Oxford University.

On the right hand side of York Avenue stand **St. Ann's** and **St. Joseph's Schools,** built in 1902 and 1908 respectively on the sites of two large houses which stood behind the well in the Church Field where villagers once drew their water — hence **Springfield Road.** The spring is now covered by a concrete slab in the playground of St. Ann's. Follow Balfour Avenue down to **Cherington Road** which, as you can see from the 1800 map of the parish, used to form the southern end of Church Road. The four large houses which then stood on the edge of the triangular piece of heath above the Uxbridge Road were called (from left to right): Highfield, Cherington House, Bydorp House and Heath Lodge; but only **Cherington House** remains. It became the offices of Hanwell Local Board in the 1890's, around the time that the adjacent **Fire Station** was built — both buildings are now used by Ealing Health Authority. The Hill family's **Heath Lodge** (occupied by *Alfred Hill* until 1935) was demolished in the 1960's for the Old Age Home on the corner of Church Road.

The three churches dominating this end of Church Road are slightly off our route, but worthy of mention. The **Methodist Church** opposite Cherington Road was built in 1904 to replace a small chapel established 30 years.earlier in the Lower Boston Road (now the Salvation Army Citadel); **St. Mellitus** was designed by Sir Arthur Blomfield and Sons and opened in 1910 — the third C. of E. church in the parish; while on the other side of The Broadway, in bold contrast to its Gothic-style neighbours, stands the modern Church of **Our Lady and St. Joseph** — built in 1965 on the same site as its 100-year old predecessor. Many Irish labourers settled in the parish after helping to build the railway, and Mass was first held in the adjacent **Clifton Lodge** in 1853.

Continue down Cherington Road to The Broadway. The southern side of the road only began to be developed in the 1890's, but several labourers' cottages were built west of Cherington House after the Heath and Church Field were enclosed in 1816. Few of these survive in recognisable form — most were converted into shops (like the quaint **Ye Olde Hanwell Stores** at the end of the road) as the village grew, and two combined to form the **Grand Theatre** (later cinema) early this century. Today, ornamental facade replaced by steel roller-doors, the Grand presents a very different picture as a video warehouse. The **library** next door to Cherington House was funded by *Andrew Carnegie* and opened by *Lady Jersey* of Osterley House in 1904.

Architecturally, **The Broadway** has changed very little since the 1880's when the London & South Western Bank (now Barclays) and other larger buildings such as Vaux's Stores (now Taplin's) and the Police Station were built. In the old days, shops stayed open until midnight on Saturdays and practically everyone in the village would promenade along The Broadway, listening to the music of the Salvation Army Band. The shops have changed hands many times since then, of course, and closing times are less flexible; but you'll still find service-with-a-smile — quite different from the impersonal atmosphere of the big supermarkets further down the road. The **clock** on The Broadway was erected in 1937 to commemorate the coronation of George VI.

CLOCK TOWER · HANWELL BROADWAY

Hanwell Broadway c.1870. Note the original Duke of York Inn behind the lampstand, and Symond's ivy-covered grocer shop — now Ye Olde Hanwell Stores.

Looking towards 'Hanwell' Asylum from the corner of Westminster Road in 1881. The Duke of Wellington pub can be seen on the left.

Stage-coaches from London to Oxford stopped at the **Duke of York** from the early 19th century, and the Manor Courts were held at the **Kings Arms** when they first transferred from Greenford in the 18th century. The latter is possibly the oldest pub in Hanwell as it was formerly called the **Spencer Arms** — after *Sir Edward Spencer,* Lord of the Manor of Boston during the Civil War. Both hostelries have been rebuilt in modern times. A third inn, the **Duke of Wellington,** used to stand just beyond Westminster Road — but had disappeared by 1920. Those who imbibed too liberally in the local inns would wake up to their morning-after headaches in the **Police Station** across the road — still standing, but now used as a training centre for traffic wardens.

Continue westwards along The Broadway and turn left up **Lower Boston Road.** The two large 18th century houses (**Kent Lodge** and **The Heath**) on the eastern side have disappeared under road-widening, but numerous 19th century cottages survive. Older Hanwell residents may remember the **Brent Hill Collegiate School** which occupied two of the cottages on the western side of the road earlier this century; **Bennett & Sons market garden** just before St. Mark's Schools; and the fair which used to be held on the little green beside the **White Hart.**

St. Mark's School opened as the National Schools in 1855 and replaced the old schoolhouse in the Half Acre run by Hobbayne's Charity. Opposite stands the **Church of St. Mark** which the *Rev. Derwent Coleridge* arranged to have built in 1879. Many alternative plans have been proposed for the church since it became redundant several years ago, but so far none has met with the approval of Ealing Council. The cost of converting the building and overgrown churchyard for other purposes becomes greater every year that the church stands derelict and prey to vandals — although the once-proud banner announcing its centenary still flutters above the entrance.

Turning aside into **Green Lane,** you will find a small **rest-garden** beside the church covering the site of the four **almshouses** which *Katherine Buchan* of The Grove gave to the parish in 1876. On the southern side of St. Mark's, another recreation ground, called **St. George's Field,** was created out of the portion of Hanwell Heath that had been allotted to the poor in compensation for their rights of common when the Heath was enclosed. The income from renting out the field was distributed each winter in the form of coal — but children will probably be much more interested in the swings and slides which now occupy the site.

Hanwell Cottage Hospital c.1910. This memorial to Queen Victoria's Diamond Jubilee is soon to be demolished for flats.

Another late-lamented local landmark is to be found further down on the northern side of Green Lane. **Hanwell Cottage Hospital** (or, to give its full title, The Queen Victoria and War Memorial Hospital) was erected by public subscription in 1900 as a permanent memorial to the Diamond Jubilee celebrated by Queen Victoria three years earlier. Voluntary contributions from local residents continued to sustain the hospital until 1948 (when the NHS took over); but with the opening of the new Ealing Hospital across the Brent in 1979, 'The Cottage' — like other small hospitals in the Ealing area — had to close. An application to build two 3-storey blocks of flats on the site has recently been approved.

Green Lane continues down to **The Fox** and **Oak Cottages** — an attractive little corner which could be even nicer if access at this end of the lane was limited to pedestrians only. The local hunt used to meet here earlier this century, and fox-hounds were bred by the appropriately-named *Mr. Gunnings* who lived in one of the houses beyond The Fox in the 1920's. **Billetts Hart Bridge** across the Brent was replaced by lock-gates when the canal was built, but the name has been preserved in the **allotments** behind Oak Cottages. Relax in the beer garden behind The Fox, or on one of the benches in the **waterside garden** created by the Brent River and Canal Society at the end of the lane. From here you can follow one of the walks outlined at the end of Route 1, or return to the Uxbridge Road via **FitzHerbert Walk.** If you're feeling particularly athletic, you could always stride out along the towpath to Brentford — and the final chapter.

Hounds and riders preparing to go in pursuit of the 'uneatable' outside The Fox c.1910.

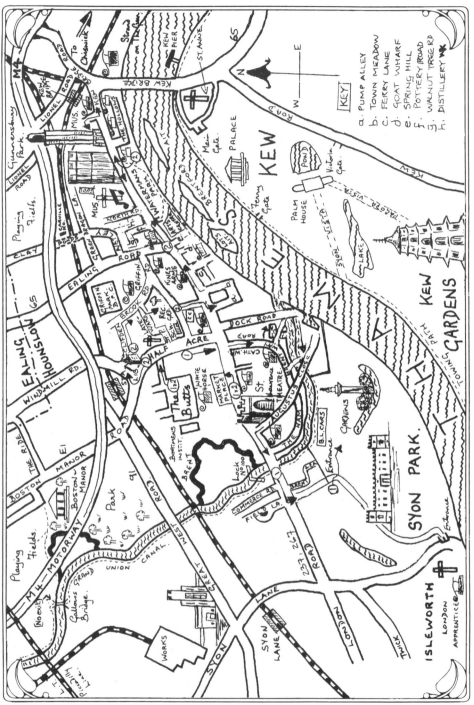

KEY

a. PUMP ALLEY
b. TOWN MEADOW
c. FERRY LANE
d. GOAT WHARF
e. SPRING HILL
f. POTTERY ROAD
g. WALNUT TREE RD
h. DISTILLERY

CHAPTER XII

Brentford, tedious town
For dirty streets and white-legg'd chickens known.

The poet JOHN GAY'S impression of the town in 1716

 strictly speaking, has no place in a book about the modern Borough of Ealing; but anyone who has read this far will appreciate that although the town's links with Ealing and Hanwell were severed over a century ago, it is much too soon to discount their role in the Borough's development — geographically, Brentford now lies in Hounslow, but its early history belongs with Ealing's.

Unlike many of its neighbours, Brentford has never had pretensions to be anything other than a working-class town. Royalty frequently passed through it en route for Hampton Court, Windsor or Kew; the nobility lived on the outskirts at Syon, Boston Manor and Gunnersbury; but the 'gentry' in the town itself was composed of solid working men — tradesmen, brewers and market-gardeners — who took advantage of the excellent river and road connections between London and the western counties to develop the small market town into the most prosperous commercial centre in Middlesex. But all that glisters is not gold — dirt, poverty and living conditions for the ordinary labourer worsened with the industrial growth which followed the opening of the Grand Junction Canal, and it wasn't until after the Second World War that new Council housing enabled the last of the slums to be cleared. By the 1960's most industry had moved out to less crowded areas — leaving disused wharves and derelict factories to add to the atmosphere of neglect under which Brentford languished for many years. But recent redevelopment has made sweeping changes and although old and new still stand somewhat uneasily together, imaginative planning is rapidly turning the riverside into a delightful recreational centre.

Discoveries of the remains of elephants, hippopotami, and numerous Stone, Bronze and Iron Age implements in the area show that the wooded banks at the meeting-point of the River Brent and the Thames were well populated in prehistoric times. Julius Caesar is popularly believed to have defeated the armies of Cassivelaunus at the natural crossing-place over the Thames at Brentford in 54BC; but there is little archeological evidence to support this theory beyond a large number of defensive wooden stakes (similar to those described in Caesar's version of the battle) which were found embedded in the Thames near **Old England** — the name given to the delta between the two rivers. Modern archeologists believe that even these are more likely to have been the remains of medieval fisheries. Brentford High Street roughly follows the line of the old Roman road to Silchester, however, and there was certainly a Roman settlement here from about the 1st century AD.

The town seems to have been abandoned soon after the Romans left, and only one site (near the present County Court) has revealed traces of Saxon occupation. Nevertheless, it was during Saxon times that the town's early name of 'Breguntford' was first recorded — as the place where the Kings of Essex and Wessex met in 705AD to settle a dispute; and again in 780 when the town was selected for a council held by Offa the Mighty, King of Mercia. The name is generally thought to have referred to a ford over the Brent (or 'holy water'), although it could have originated in the Thames crossing — which was of greater strategic importance, and the scene of a great battle in 1016 when Edmund Ironside defeated Canute's Danes on the southern bank of the ford. (The chap who later did away with Edmund — thinking he was doing Canute a favour — was told by the Danish King that he would be rewarded by 'being placed higher than any of the English nobility'. And he was — his head was hung from the highest tower in London!)

Brentford was very sparsely populated (chiefly by fishermen) until about the 14th century. Whatever small settlement existed at Domesday seems to have been concentrated in the area later known as **Old Brentford** (from the Half Acre eastwards), which had been included in the grant of Ealing to the Bishop of London several centuries earlier. **New Brentford** (between the Brent and the Half Acre) doesn't get a mention until 1157, by which time it was already part of the Abbot of Westminster's Manor of Hanwell. The district apparently developed from a farm called Bordwadestone, which later became the Manor of Boston; but the farm- or manor-house was probably the only building until the Lord of Boston built St. Lawrence's Chapel and hospital c.1175. The division between New Brentford and the rest of Hanwell lay roughly along the line of the railway west of Boston Manor Station.

Throughout the Middle Ages, a large common called **The Ham** (from the Anglo-Saxon for a piece of flat land beside the river) surrounded New Brentford on three sides; more fields lay north of the highway through Old Brentford; and, to the south, marshy meadows led down to the Thames. Such houses as there were stood along the High Street — the only other road being the Half Acre, which was just a narrow trackway leading through the fields to Hanwell. However, Brentford and Uxbridge were the only two townships in Middlesex to be represented at Edward I's Parliament in 1295; so the town must have been of some importance even before the weekly **Market** was established at New Brentford in 1306.

River and road traffic increased steadily after the Market opened. Fishing remained the chief occupation, but the two rivers soon produced basket-makers and watermen; while inn-keepers and carters began to ply their trade on the highway. At this stage the two settlements were still known as East and West Brentford — Old and New Brentford probably being adopted after the derelict wooden bridge over the Brent was replaced by a new stone one in 1446. This led to the development of another settlement, called **Brentford End,** between Syon Abbey (founded by Henry V) and the west bank of the Brent.

By the end of the 16th century, the linear plan was beginning to change. Buildings lined both sides of the High Street as far as the present Kew Bridge, but in Old Brentford the whole riverside had been taken up by wharves which were connected by narrow passages lined with cottages and inns. A new back lane (now part of Albany Road) skirted the fields east of the Half Acre, and many High Street tenements extended back to it. Old Brentford thus had more houses, but was much poorer than New Brentford. Inns, houses and the new Market Place had also severed The Ham from the archery butts which had been built on the common west of the Half Acre during the reign of Henry VIII. In 1558, 'Bloody' Mary ordered six Protestants to be burnt at the stake on **The Butts.** None of them came from Brentford, but perhaps she chose this site as a warning to any locals who had supported the Duke of Northumberland's bid to make Lady Jane Grey queen instead of her. (Read all about the plot in the story of Syon in Route 1.)

The first half of the 17th century saw the development of extractive industries such as gravel-digging, lime-burning, and brick- and tile-making. Arable land was gradually taken over for orchards and market-gardens, and most of the open fields were under grass for hay-making. But the Civil War had a devastating effect on the town's rising prosperity, and set the tone for several decades of misfortune.

The bloody **Battle of Brentford** took place on 12th November, 1642 — apparently as the result of a snarl-up in communications. It seems that as the Royalists were advancing on London after successful battles at Edgehill and Reading, the 10th Earl of Northumberland (owner of Syon House) and a deputation from Parliament met the King at Colnebrook with an appeal for peace. The King agreed to negotiate, and suggested Brentford as the meeting-place for discussions. Lord Essex, head of the Parliamentary forces on Acton Green, was then instructed to cease hostilities — but, before a message could be delivered to the King to keep his part of the truce, the Royalist army under Prince Rupert had taken advantage of a thick mist to carry out a surprise attack on the Roundhead garrison at New Brentford bridge. The unprepared defenders put up a stiff fight, but the Cavaliers eventually took possession of the town — whereupon they went on the rampage, plundering whatever they could lay their hands on and pouring any beer or wine they were unable to drink into the cellars of the inns. Perhaps hangovers were the cause of the Royalists' unexpected retreat from the massed Parliamentary forces on Acton Green the next day?

After the war, came the Great Plague — scarcely a day going by without a burial in August and September of 1665. Then, in 1682, a disastrous flood put most of the town under water so that boats were the only way of negotiating the High Street. But normal business gradually resumed and the last decade of the 17th century showed expansion in all directions. Fine houses were built on The Butts (where the Middlesex elections were held from 1701), and the first breweries, malthouses and distilleries were established as a result of the flourishing Corn Market.

Coaching inns thrived on the heavy traffic along the High Street, but the mud or dust churned up by the wheels were already giving Brentford a reputation for dirtiness. However, nothing could detract from the obvious commercial success of the town — which prompted an incredible proposal in 1730, when a group of Jews offered to pay £500,000 (and would have made it a million) if the Government would 'allow them to purchase the town of Brentford with leave of settling there entirely, with full privileges of trade etc'. Needless to say, the offer was not accepted.

Housing never kept pace with the spread of industry. By the end of the 18th century, the town boasted a large distillery, flour mill, and extensive brick, tile and pottery works; but the thousands of labourers who kept these concerns going lived in overcrowded, overpriced slums — barely able to breathe over the stench of sewage and refuse. As the brickfields and potteries declined, new industries — encouraged by the completion of the canal from Brentford to Braunston in 1805 — replaced them; but there was no improvement in living conditions for the workers, many of whom tried to drown their sorrows in some of the 40 local inns. In 1867, no town in England was thought to have more poverty in relation to its size, and the lack of a sewerage system associated Brentford with everything 'stagnant and disgraceful'.

In 1874, New Brentford (which had been governed by its own Parish Vestry since 1621) and Old Brentford (which Ealing had finally managed to rid herself of in 1863) were united into one district with a population of around 11,000 under a new Local Board. As market-gardens declined and more land became available, systematic slum clearance accompanied the building of new houses. Industry began to move out less crowded areas with the coming of the railways, so that the gasworks, waterworks and soap factory were the chief employers by the end of the century. Most of the small breweries had closed, and fishing had been completely destroyed by steam boats and pollution from sewage and the gasworks.

But the biggest blow to local industry came with the opening of the **Great West Road** in 1925, and the development of the 'Golden Mile' of new factories. The influx of workers created further housing problems, but private and Council housing progressed steadily and Brentford was almost completely built up by the Second World War. In 1927, the 17,000 inhabitants became part of Brentford and Chiswick Urban District (later Municipal Borough) which, in turn, was absorbed into the London Borough of Hounslow in 1965. During the Sixties Brentford Dock, the gasworks, waterworks and soap factory all closed followed by Brentford Market in 1974; which left only small businesses in this once thriving industrial town.

But the future looks bright. Few towns are given the opportunity of a fresh start this late in life, and it's heartening to see what good town-planning and private enterprise can accomplish — especially when it incorporates the best of the old. Gloomy factories are being replaced by attractive office-blocks and a well-designed Arts Centre; the waterfront is at last being opened up by public footpaths and a much-needed park; the two former parish churches have been saved from demolition and converted into a theatre and unique musical museum; The Butts still contains the finest group of late-17th century houses you're likely to find in any London Borough; and you cannot walk ten yards without falling into another pub — which can't be a bad thing!

The former **Parish Church of St. Lawrence** has not seen a congregation since 1961 and many changes have been made to the building since it was leased to the St. Lawrence Brentford Trust in 1979. But none of this alters the fact that from the 12th century onwards the church played an important part in the lives of New Brentford residents — and is therefore the logical place to begin an exploration of the town.

An old print of St. Lawrence's showing the 17th century Church House donated by Sir Edward Spencer, and part of Sir William Noy's house (on the left) — both demolished in 1889.

Although ecclesiastical synods were held at Brentford in the 8th century, there is no record of any church until *Ralph de Brito*, Lord of the Manor of Boston, founded **St. Lawrence's Hospital** and adjoining **Chapel** c.1175. In those days a hospital was a charitable institution for the needy, rather than a place for treating the sick — St. Lawrence having been the deacon in charge of orphans, widows and the poor of Rome in the 3rd century. (When summoned by Emperor Valerian's praetor to deliver up the treasures of his church, Lawrence produced the poor in his care and said: "These are the church's treasures" — for which brave statement he was martyred by being roasted on a gridiron.) Nothing more is known of de Brito's hospital, but St. Lawrence's Chapel survived — remaining under the jurisdiction of St. Mary's, Hanwell, until the mid-18th century, when New Brentford was at last considered fit to be made a separate parish with its own vicar.

The most famous of these was *John Horne Tooke* who gave up his earlier ambitions to become a lawyer and entered the church to please his father — St. Lawrence's being his first and only appointment from 1760-1773. Soon after taking up his position, the church (which had been enlarged several times during the Middle Ages) was found to be in danger of collapsing, and Horne Tooke arranged for services to be held in a room at the **Red Lion Inn** while St. Lawrence's was being rebuilt. During this period he took some time off to travel abroad, where he developed a lasting concern for parliamentary reform after a meeting with the outlawed *John Wilkes* in Paris (see Route 1). These political interests augmented his belief (considered, at the time, to be a trifle eccentric) that the social welfare of his congregation was just as important as their spiritual well-being; and on his return to the new church he studied medicine so that he could help those parishioners who could not afford a proper doctor.

Wilkes and Horne Tooke had a violent difference of opinion in 1770, which ended their friendship but not the clergyman's involvement in politics. After resigning from St. Lawrence's he resumed his legal studies and, although never admitted to the Bar, used his knowledge to fight for parliamentary and social reform. His spirited opposition to an enclosure bill earned him the undying gratitude of a *Mr. Tooke* of Surrey whose name Horne added to his own after the wealthy landowner left him £8,000 in his will. But Horne Tooke was less fortunate in other matters: he was imprisoned for taking up a collection for the Americans 'barbarously murdered' during the War of Independence; tried for, but acquitted of, high treason when George III took exception to some of his writings; stood unsuccessfully for Westminster on two occasions and, when he finally gained a seat for the 'rotten borough' of Old Sarum in 1801, had to resign when an Act was passed disqualifying clergymen from being MP's. Even his final wish to be buried in the garden of his cottage in Windmill Lane was not granted and despite his having inscribed his own memorial stone with the words: 'John Horne Tooke, late proprietor, and now occupier of this spot. Content and grateful.' — he was buried in St. Mary's, Ealing, in 1812.

The exterior of St. Lawrence's hasn't changed much since Horne Tooke's day. The main body of the church was completely rebuilt in London stock bricks by *Thomas Hardwick Snr.* in 1764; but the Kentish ragstone **tower** dates from the 15th century and was erected as a parochial fortress during the Wars of the Roses. After the parish of St. Lawrence amalgamated with St. George's and St. Paul's in 1961, pigeons and vandals speeded up the natural process of decay, and the abandoned church was in a sorry state when discovered by the actress, *Pamela Mandell*, who founded the **St. Lawrence Brentford Trust** to save it. In 1979, after battling with the authorities for two years, the Trust managed to buy a 99-year lease on St. Lawrence's with the aid of a Dept. of Education and Science grant; and then set about the mammoth task of finding the money to convert the church into a theatre and community centre, with facilities for a bar, restaurant and business conferences.

Fund-raising activities, Council grants and donations from local firms, residents and a galaxy of theatrical stars (such as Lord Olivier, Janet Suzman, Tom Conti, Glenda Jackson, Donald Sinden and Leonard Rossiter) have helped to raise more than half the £300,000 needed for this ambitious project; and the Grand Opening of the **Brentford Dock Theatre** should take place in Summer, 1983. The conversion has been carefully designed to fit in with the original architecture and will incorporate the splendid wooden Gothic columns of 1889. Most of the Church's monuments and memorials were removed for safe-keeping during restoration work, but will be displayed again when the building re-opens — some as exhibits in the new **art gallery.**

One of the most interesting memorials is the coat of arms of *Maurice de Berkley*, who made a considerable contribution towards the cost of building the original chapel — where he was buried in 1189. The oldest brass in the church perpetuates the name of another early benefactor, *Henry Redman*, master mason to Henry VIII, who in 1528 left endowments towards the salary of the badly paid curate. (For centuries the curates of St. Lawrence's were appointed by the Rector of Hanwell who appropriated all the tithes and collection money — leaving the poor curate to rely on wealthy residents for his income.) Wall tablets and monuments, spanning two and a half centuries, commemorate the Clitherow family of Boston Manor — *Col. James Clitherow* being especially remembered for his generous donation towards rebuilding St. Lawrence's in the 18th century. *Lady Spencer* (formerly Lady Mary Reade), an earlier owner of Boston, was buried in St. Lawrence's in 1658. She also left money to the parish, and her husband, *Sir Edward Spencer*, donated the **Church House** shown in the picture.

As you can see, St. Lawrence's has relied on benefactors throughout its history — and they are just as necessary today. The names of 20th century contributors to the new theatre will be inscribed in the foyer, and yours could be among them if you are willing to covenant £25 a year to this worthwhile project — which, besides prolonging the life of the old church, will also enrich the lives of the community.

I have devised two walks for seeing the best of Brentford today — the first concentrating on what was once **New Brentford** and the second, **Old Brentford**. Both begin at the church and follow the same route through The Butts as far as the Half Acre — the old boundary between the two parishes — where they diverge.

ROUTE ONE *(St. Lawrence's to Syon Park via The Butts and canal — 1½ miles)* The old **Vicarage** on the eastern side of the High Street was built in 1889 on the sites of the ancient **Church House** (traditionally occupied by the curate or the poor — depending on whose need was greater at the time) and another, more substantial, dwelling where *Sir William Noy*, Attorney General to Charles I, resided before being buried at St. Lawrence's in 1634. (It wsa Noy's idea to introduce the Ship Money Tax which made the King so unpopular.) During the 18th century, Noy's house was occupied by *Hugh Ronalds*, Brentford's leading market-gardener, whose principle nursery between the church and the Brent continued to flourish until the 1860's.

The original **Magpie and Crown** began serving travellers in the late-17th century, when this section of the High Street was filled with similar establishments. Older inns like The Plough and Boar's Head were divided into small shops and cottages c.1720, although their names lived on in some of the crowded yards and alleys which soon covered their land between the High Street and waterfront. We'll be returning to explore this area later in the walk, but first let's cross over the High Street to visit a much older commercial centre — the **Market Place.**

Market Place in the early 19th century showing the Three Pigeons Inn on the left the Red Lion stood on the far right, out of the picture and old Market House. The weather vane has adorned Perivale Church since the Market House was demolished for the present Magistrates' Court in 1847.

The orderly square presided over by **Brentford Magistrates' Court** today, is a far cry from the bustling, bawdy Market Place which, for centuries, was practically a byword for the town. It was the nuns of St. Helen's Priory at Boston Manor who obtained the first licence for a weekly market at Brentford in 1307. This took place somewhere along New Brentford's narrow High Street and was probably intended to serve as an outlet for the produce grown on their own extensive estate. However, by the time the Priory was dissolved in the 16th century the market had become the main depot for the City of London's corn-buyers, and the cause of regular traffic-jams on the road from London to the West. One of the local landowners who subsequently leased the rights for the market, sensibly moved it to the present Market Place in 1560 — in what was then an orchard behind two leading inns, the Three Pigeons and the Red Lion.

The **Three Pigeons** stood at the south-western corner of the square, and had replaced an earlier alehouse called The Crown — first mentioned in 1436. The inn held a rather 'loose reputation' in Elizabethan times and Londoners frequently travelled by water to Brentford to participate in or observe the fun. *Ben Jonson* mentions the tavern in his comedy, 'The Alchemist', and it is quite likely that he was accompanied by his close friend, *William Shakespeare*, on some of his forays as Falstaff is disguised as the fat **Witch of Brentford** in the Bard's 'The Merry Wives of Windsor'. (This character would appear to have had some substance, as the Chapel Warden's account books for 1634 record the sum of 11 shillings paid to 'ye Constable for ye conveying away of the Witches'.)

John Lowin, the first actor to portray Falstaff, became landlord of the inn when theatres were closed during the Civil War and was no doubt visited by many of his cronies. At any rate, from the number of literary references made to the Three Pigeons over the years, it is safe to assume that the inn continued to provide inspiration for a variety of writers, poets and dramatists for several centuries. The inn was used as a Sessional Court in the time of James I, and offered stabling for 100 horses during the coaching age — but all good things must come to an end, and in 1916 the pub closed its doors for the last time and was used as shops and offices until demolished in 1950. A used-car-dealer's premises now occupy the historic site.

in the time of James I, and offered stabling for 100 horses during the coaching age — but all good things must come to an end, and in 1916 the pub closed its doors for the last time and was used as shops and offices until demolished in 1950. A used-car-dealer's premises now occupy the historic site.

The **Red Lion,** at the opposite corner of the Market Place (in which Henry VI held a Chapter of the Garter in 1446), and the other great coaching inn, **The Castle,** which lay further to the east, suffered similar fates and were replaced by shops after the First World War. These were demolished when the present shopping parade was built in the late 1960's. However, a later version of the 17th century **White Horse Inn** survives behind the Magistrates' Court, and you can mourn the loss of its more historic counterparts in the attractive beer-garden overlooking a small weir on the River Brent, where the Bishop of London had a fishery in medieval times.

The house west of the White Horse stands on the site of a cottage where the great English landscape painter, J.M.W. Turner, lived as a boy with his uncle, a local butcher, in the 1780's. He was sent here from London at the age of ten, in the hope that the change of air would improve his health; and attended a small school in the High Street, opposite the Three Pigeons, until his obvious artistic talent secured him a place at the Royal Academy when he was fourteen. (The fact that he remained almost illiterate throughout his life, does not say much for educational standards in Brentford at the time!)

A rough sort of justice was meted out in the Market Place long before the present Courthouse was built c.1850 on the site of the quaint old **Market House** shown in the picture. The cage, stocks, pillory and whipping post for New Brentford stood here under the stern gaze of the Beadle in his watchbox, and the punishment of those unfortunates sentenced to flogging or spending a few hours in the pillory, was traditionally carried out on market days — their cries adding to the general din made by the crowds and traders.

But these were tame affairs compared with notorious noise and vulgarity of the annual 6-day **Fair,** for which Edward I had granted permission in his market charter to the Priory. This riotous event originally took place around the Feast of St. Lawrence (10th August) until James I issued a new licence for two week-long fairs to be held in May and September each year — much to the delight of the rabble who came from far and wide to enjoy the spectacle, and the horror of respectable townsfolk whose demands for closure of the fairs went unheeded for another 300 years.

In the Middle Ages, the annual Fair served an important commercial purpose. The weekly markets were specifically for local traders, but these restrictions did not apply to fairs which brought merchants from all over Europe bearing wine, furs, lace, salt and spices to exchange for English wool and cattle-hides. But, as trade improved on a national scale, fairs gradually became an excuse for the whole town to go on the razzle, and most of the business was conducted by local inn-keepers or the organisers of entertainments such as bear-baiting, which *Samuel Butler* records at Brentford Fair in his poem, 'Hudibras', of 1663.

The old **Market House** is though to have been built during the reign of Charles II, when there was an extensive trade in cattle, sheep and pigs. By 1679, both Fair and Market had spilled over into **The Butts** which extended from the Brent to the Half Acre. The practise of archery had declined as guns and muskets gradually replaced the bow and arrow as weapons of war, and from the mid-17th century the land around the former shooting-range had begun to be divided into large plots for new houses — although the 'L'-shaped space in the middle was kept open. Building began in 1690 and within a few years The Butts had developed into a very select residential area — as you can see for yourselves by following the little alleyway next to the White Horse.

Not even the fact that a car-park now covers the central square can detract from the overall elegance of the late-17th century houses around it — no wonder their original occupants fought against the bi-annual invasion of the Fair! But one has to sympathise with the local community as well, for although The Butts had officially belonged to the Lord of the Manor of Boston prior to being sold for building, the square had traditionally been used by the general public for various games and festivities — especially those held on holidays such as May Day and Whitsun. One of the most popular events involved the 'maidens' of the parish who, with hands tied behind them, had to chase after a fat ox (provided by the church authorities) until one of them succeeded in getting a grip on the beast with her teeth! This earned her the title 'Lady of the Ox' for the day, and the right to lead the procession to Butts Common to which the unlucky animal, killed and cleaned, was carried on a long pole. There it was baked and boiled, and shared out between the merrymakers amidst music and Morris dancing.

But, by all accounts, these boisterous games had nothing on the amazing scenes at the **Middlesex Elections,** which took place on The Butts from 1701 to 1885. 'Riotous', 'disorderly', and 'tumultous' are some of the milder adjectives used to describe the political antics of so-called civilised society when the famous libertarian, John Wilkes, repeatedly contested the Middlesex seat from 1768 to 1774. The events leading up to these exciting elections began in 1762 when Wilkes, then MP for Aylesbury in Buckinghamshire, started a weekly periodical called the 'North Briton' which criticised the Whig government of Lord Bute, a close friend and disciple of King George III.

Bute's administration was universally unpopular, however, and he was forced to resign as Prime Minister shortly before publication of the contentious 45th issue of Wilke's newspaper, which impugned the truth of the King's speech at the opening of Parliament. For this sedition, Wilkes was imprisoned in the Tower of London and the renowned 'No. 45' was ordered to be burnt by the Common Hangman. But the Lord Chief Justice ordered Wilkes' release on the grounds that an MP could not be arrested for libel — whereupon he promptly charged the Government with illegal arrest, secured £1000 damages, and became the hero of the hour as the 'champion of liberty'. The House of Commons expelled him nevertheless, and succeeded in prosecuting him for printing an obscene poem which the Earl of Sandwich read out in the House of Lords.

At this point, Wilkes retired discreetly to Paris — but not before he'd exchanged a few choice words with the unsavoury Earl of Sandwich, the corrupt politician who is best remembered for inventing 'sandwiches' so that he could eat without having to leave the gaming table. In reply to the Earl's comment that he did not know whether Wilkes would die on the gallows or of the pox, the swift-thinking Wilkes retorted: "That, my Lord, will depend on whether I embrace your principles or your mistress"! The Earl was no doubt one of the chief witnesses at the trial which later found Wilkes' guilty of 'obscene libel' and outlawed him for non-appearance in court.

Meanwhile, Wilkes had met up with John Home Tooke who was tutoring in Paris, and decided to stand for Middlesex at the next election. On the day, 28th March 1768, the roads to Brentford were lined with riotous mobs who allowed no-one to pass unless the number '45' was prominently displayed about their person. Cries of "Wilkes and Liberty" rang out over the town at the announcement that Wilkes had polled 6-1 more than his opponents — but, despite this large majority, Parliament refused to admit him and declared the result void. However, the electors kept nominating him as their candidate, and Wilkes was re-elected three times in succession until finally, in 1774, he was allowed to take his seat without further opposition. By this time he had also been elected Lord Mayor of London, and went on to become Chamberlain of the City before retiring from politics at the age of 73. The present liberty of the press owes much to his efforts.

In the early 19th century elections, the liberal attitudes of the Ealing-born candidate, *Sir Francis Burdett*, caused further disturbances as crowds flocked to vote for this popular politician whose opposition to the war with France and advocacy of parliamentary reform, freedom of speech, Catholic emancipation etc made him anything but popular with the repressive government of the time. He was narrowly defeated by Wilkes' former colleague, *George Byng*, in the 1802 election, but was successful in 1804. This result was declared void by Parliament, however, and involved Burdett in four years' costly and fruitless litigation — although money was hardly a problem, as he was married to *Sophia Coutts* of the great banking family. Their daughter, incidentally, inherited the family fortune at the age of 23, and devoted the rest of her life to relieving poverty in England and financing a wide range of philanthropic schemes — such as David Livingstone's explorations. (If you'd like to know more about this unassuming benefactor, a biography of *Angela Burdett-Coutts* entitled 'Lady Unknown' has been written by none other than *Edna Healey*, wife of the former Chancellor.)

But now, having advanced several pages but only a few yards into this walk, I think we'd better return pretty swiftly to the 20th century before gangrene sets in. As you make your way round the car-park towards the Half Acre, you will pass the **Boatmen's Institute** at the western end of The Butts. This was built on the site of a ruined 18th century mill in 1904 and served as a school, church and maternity hospital for the boat people until it transferred to the former St. Lawrence's school in The Ham c.1950. The old Institute has now been converted into a private home, although it still bears the legend 'London City Mission: Boatmen's Institute' across the front. (The building inspired local writer, *Robert Rankin*, to make it the scene of some very odd goings-on in his recently published paperback, 'The Antipope' — a very funny blend of historical fact and modern fiction about everyday folk in Brentford.)

BOATMENS INSTITUTE, THE BUTTS, BRENTFORD.

Brent House, a large mansion in which the celebrated *Nell Gwynne* is said to have lived, used to stand just north of the Institute. A strange horseshoe-shaped mark on the old oak staircase gave rise to the tale that *Charles II* was in such a hurry to see his mistress one night that he neglected to dismount from his steed beforehand. However, modern research — that killer of all good stories — reveals that the house was not built until 1694 (several years after the deaths of the happy couple), although a family of Gwynnes did live in the vicinity in later years. There is no way of checking the evidence anyway, as the house was demolished in 1909 — lock, stock and staircase.

Practically all the surviving houses in the square were built before 1720 — those on the eastern corner being a few years older than the group on the north side and Upper Butts. Nos. 24 & 26 (at the eastern entrance to the square) were used as the **Brentford Dispensary Cottage Hospital** from 1891 to 1928, when patients were transferred to the new Brentford Hospital in Boston Manor Road. (This closed in 1977 and is now a home for the elderly.) In 1880, two more houses towards the Half Acre were taken oven by **St. Mary's Convent** which later incorporated **St. Raphael's Home** for mentally retarded girls and, as you can see, gradually expanded to cover the whole corner at that end of the road.

Until Victorian times, there were few houses on the northern side of the road leading to the square as this was the site of a large orchard and market-garden — described in 1774 as 'resembling the seat of paradise'. Here, **Hugh Ronalds & Sons** grew mulberries, cherries, asparagus, strawberries and 300 varieties of apple, as well as numerous plants and shrubs — some of which went to stock Kew Gardens in the early 1800's. The firm later transferred to their main nursery near St. Lawrence's church, however, and new houses soon began to blossom in The Butts' orchards instead. The stone plaque in the wall on the corner of the Half Acre marking the entrance to 'The Butts Estate', was probably erected around this time.

Towards the end of the century, the weekly Market also declined as market-gardeners set up their stalls around the fountain at Kew Bridge. This caused such traffic congestion that the Local Board eventually built an enclosed market in Kew Bridge Road. Middlesex County Council acquired the licence for the old Market in 1891 and although they resisted pressure from Brentford District Council for many years, they finally yielded and closed the Market in 1933 — having abolished the Fair the previous year. And so ended another era in Brentford's history.

And now we leave The Butts and turn right into the **Half Acre.** Most of the original buildings on the eastern side were demolished in 1905 when the road was widened for the new electric tram route from Hanwell; but a few still survive on the western side. The **Youth Centre,** for instance, occupies the former **St. Lawrence's School for Girls** which moved here from The Butts in 1840 — finally closing in 1931. The adjacent pair of 1852 cottages abut another well-preserved old residence, **Half Acre House;** but the group of shops at the end of the road are part of the 1970 redevelopment of the High Street. Tucked away behind a block of flats on the eastern side, stands **St. Paul's Church** — since 1961 the principle Anglican church of the united parishes of Brentford.

The ragstone building with its distinctive tower and spire was erected in 1868 on a plot of land originally intended for the new St. George's church (see Route 2), and had to be quite extensively restored in the 1950's after War damage. Its most interesting relic is a painting of 'The Last Supper' by *John Zoffany,* who lived in Strand on the Green for several decades before his death in 1810. Zoffany actually painted the picture for St. Anne's church on Kew Green, but presented it to St. George's Chapel after objections to the fact that he had modelled the faces of the apostles on local fishermen! St. Paul's inherited the controversial picture in 1968, following the closure of St. George's.

Brentford **Police Station** was built in 1966 on the site of the old **Vestry Hall.** This opened in 1899 and was used as the County Court until made redundant by the new Court in Alexandra Road. Further down the road, a huge supermarket for International Stores is nearing completion — the latest in a long line of stores since this now country-wide chain opened its very first shop near Pottery Road in 1878. The **Beehive,** on the corner, brewed its own beer early last century — the brewery later moving from the High Street to Catherine Wheel Yard (now Road) where *William Gomm & Sons* continued to produce fine ales until their business was taken over by Fuller's and the premises put up for sale in 1908.

Catherine Wheel Yard came into existence during the late-17th century and was the first of many riverside developments in New Brentford. The name probably originated in some long-vanished inn to which a **malthouse** was attached in 1679 — a forerunner of the brewing and allied trades which were to flourish for the next two centuries. Other yards and alleys sprang up as the land behind High Street properties was divided up for building; and by the time work began on the Grand Junction Canal in 1793, the whole of Brent Creek waterfront — from Catherine Wheel yard to The Ham — was filled with cottages and new industries. Besides coal, corn and malting businesses, Catherine Wheel Yard boasted a turpentine factory and a coke-powered starch mill — which were joined by a large flour mill after the canal opened.

As these industries declined, others took their place and today, although most of the old cottages and yards have gone, a variety of manufacturing businesses still line the cobbled lanes of the **Brentway Trading Estate** — as the area is now called. Not all the traders are new ones — the family firm of *H. Band & Co.* have been making parchment in Brentford since 1845. Although the address of their tannery in **Old Plough Yard** has now become Brentway, many of the original vats, wooden frames for stretching the skins, and other traditional tools of their trade are still being used to produce parchment and vellum for worldwide export.

No breweries have survived the passage of time, but beer still flows at **The Brewery Tap** at the end of Catherine Wheel Road. From here, a footpath leads eastward over the disused flood-gates known as **Dr. Johnson's Lock** (after *Dr. William Johnson,* proprietor of the 18th century starch mill), then bridges a backwater basin and weir, and finally emerges at the hydraulic **Thames Locks** below Dock Road, which mark the start of the Grand Union Canal. When the first section of the 93-mile canal from Brentford to Braunston was opened as far as Uxbridge in 1794, boats still had to navigate the tidal **Brent Creek** before they could reach the Thames. It took several years of argument with millers and brewers using the water in the creek, before the Grand Junction Company was able to canalise this last stretch of the Brent, and construct Thames Lock.

If you leap nimbly (and carefully!) across the iron footway over the lock-gates and up to **Dock Road,** you'll get a good view of some of the old wharves and any boats waiting for the tide. The junction with the river used to be dominated by the warehouses of **Brentford Dock,** which was designed by *Brunel* on the Old England delta in 1855 to provide river barges with a direct link to the Great Western Railway. But the goods yard closed in 1964 and has since been redeveloped into a large Council housing estate — although part of the old dock on the far side has been preserved as a marina for pleasure-craft. Follow the 'canalway' sign back down to the towpath and, a little way before the Augustus Close footbridge, you will find some steps leading up to the road.

As you cross the bridge towards the High Street, the statue of Flora in the gardens of **Syon Park** can be seen to the west; and further on you can look down on the messy conglomeration of industries in **The Ham** — the name being all that survives of the huge common which covered most of New Brentford until the 17th century. We'll be passing the entrance to The Ham later in this walk — but as there are only two structures of any interest in this unattractive road, I may as well tell you about them from here.

The dilapidated building in the curve of The Ham bears a plaque which proclaims it to be 'Brentford Free School, erected by voluntary contribution, 1815'. This is the old **St. Lawrence's School for Boys** which closed in 1931, and was later used as a school for the canal boatmen's children. There were 100 of these itinerant children on the roll in 1950, but the maximum attendance was only 18 — a figure which decreased steadily with the decline of the canals and forced the school to close in 1957. Further to the right, landscaping hides the overgrown remains of the **railway bridge** which from 1859 to 1964 helped carry the GWR's line from Southall across to Brentford Dock. The main bridge over the canal was demolished when the Dock closed, but the abutments still stand beneath your feet, under Augustus Close.

Back on the High Street again, you turn left towards the **Six Bells** — possibly so-named in honour of the six bells in St. Lawrence's tower, which used to ring out triumphantly whenever royalty passed through Brentford, to and from Windsor Castle. (From the regular payments to bell-ringers recorded in the old parish account books, it would seem that their's was a far more profitable occupation than the poor curate's.) Beyond The Ham, a group of 18th century weather-boarded houses await demolition. No. 152 is in slightly better condition than the others and was once the **Magnet Beerhouse.**

The **canal** now comes into view again as you reach **Brentford Bridge.** This was built by Middlesex County in 1824, and is about the fourth bridge on the site since a new stone bridge replaced the 13th century wooden one (which lay further downstream) in 1446. The earlier bridges were not very well constructed and were in a constant state of disrepair. Tolls were imposed from time to time to help pay for their upkeep, but the ever-increasing volume of traffic along the High Street made proper maintenance impossible. Accidents were also a serious problem as the bridges had to be placed at a very awkward angle across the river to allow for the numerous houses and shops lining the approaches. The authorities straightened things out when they built the present bridge, however, and the offending buildings were speedily removed.

From the northern side of the bridge, you can see the paired **Brentford Gauging Locks** at the entrance to the British Waterways Board **Brentford Depot** — still a busy freight terminal for export goods brought in by road, to be carried down to London Docks in Thames barges. The towpath lies on the western bank of the canal and passes through a huge canopied warehouse, where narrowboats once deposited and collected their loads. When Gallows Bridge is eventually opened to allow access to **Boston Manor** (see Chapter II), the canal will make a lovely walk to this historic house — which really ought to have been included in this chapter, but had to be relegated to Ealing for want of a better way of getting there.

Continue westward along the High Street, through the part of town formerly known as **Brentford End.** This settlement grew up around the **Chapel of St. Michael and All Angels** — a friary, associated with Syon Monastery, which was built on the northwestern side of the new bridge during the reign of Henry VI. The chapel disappeared some time after the mid-17th century, but the inns and shops of Brentford End remained — and even had their own station (off today's Commerce Road) on the GWR's Southall to Brentford line until the passenger service ceased in 1942. The village has now been absorbed into Isleworth and of the old buildings only the **George and Dragon** survives — in name, at least. This was possibly the site of the inn called 'The George' which *Henry Redman* bequeathed in 1528 to pay the curate's salary.

The large wall on the northern side of the road has been extensively rebuilt in modern times, but once surrounded the school which the poet, *Percy Bysshe Shelley,* attended before going to Eton in 1804. By all accounts, Shelley did not enjoy his stay at **Syon House Academy** — where he was bullied; but his fellow-pupil, *John Rennie* (later knighted for his contributions to the field of engineering — which included the construction of London Bridge), relates in his autobiography some of the poet's rather eccentric attempts to liven up the school — such as blowing up the palings of the playground with gunpowder, and also the lid of his desk! The school became a private residence in 1820, and was demolished during the 1950's for the housing estate around Field Lane.

Directly opposite **Field Lane,** you will find a footpath leading to **Syon Park** and the Tudor mansion which has been in the *Percy family,* Earls and Dukes of Northumberland, since Elizabethan times. The history of the estate goes back much further than that — to the reign of *Henry V,* who founded **Syon Monastery** for the English Bridgettines, an order of nuns established by St. Bridget of Sweden in the 14th century. The original monastery was near Twickenham, but in 1431 *Henry VI* granted permission for the nuns to move to a larger building on the present site — where they remained until their peaceful existence was brought to an abrupt end by *Henry VIII* in 1539.

The Monastery was used to imprison the King's fifth unfortunate wife, *Katherine Howard,* for four months before she was rowed down river to the Tower to be beheaded in 1542; but otherwise lay vacant until the King's own death in 1547 — when it played a macabre role in fulfilling the prophesy of a Franciscan monk who, angered at the King's eviction of the nuns, had declared that: "... the dogs would lick his blood as they had done Ahab's". During the night that the King's corpse rested at Syon on its way from Westminster to Windsor, the coffin burst open and ... a pack of dogs refreshed themselves on parts of Henry that only his funeral bier should have been able to reach!

SYON HOUSE, SYON PARK, BRENTFORD.

A few months later, *Edward VI* granted Syon to his 'Protector', the *Duke of Somerset,* who pulled down most of the monastery and built a grand Tudor house — which forms the major part of Syon House today. But, as you know, Somerset was not without faults — or enemies — and in 1549 was forced to resign the Protectorship in favour of his main adversary, *John Dudley,* Earl of Warwick, who had been created *Duke of Northumberland* by Edward VI. (It should be noted that the Percy family, Earls of Northumberland since the 14th century, had temporarily fallen from grace and lost their title.) But as long as Somerset was alive, he presented a threat to Northumberland who, in typical Tudor style, 'arranged' his execution three years later — collecting Syon House as part of his• spoils.

Then, under the pretext of upholding the Protestant religion, Northumberland persuaded the dying King to name as successor his 15-year old cousin, *Lady Jane Grey* — who was immediately married, against her wish, to the Duke's own son. At Syon House on 9th July 1553, Lady Jane Grey unwillingly accepted the crown. Ten days later, her brief reign over, she was imprisoned in the Tower of London — where she, her husband and the wicked Duke were later executed on Queen Mary's orders. Mary then restored Syon to the Bridgettine nuns, and the Earldom of Northumberland to the Percys. However, forty years later, her sister Elizabeth (a Queen after Henry VIII's own heart) banished the long-suffering nuns once again — and granted Syon House to Henry Percy, the *9th Earl of Northumberland.* (Whew! Have you got it?)

The Percy family get mixed up with the Somersets again, further down the line — but I don't think we'll confuse the issue any further. Suffice to say that the male line became extinct after the death of the 11th Earl and the title skipped several generations until the Percy heiress married a Yorkshire baronet, *Sir Hugh Smithson,* who changed his name to her's and succeeded to the Earldom. He then asked King George II for the Garter, saying he was the first Earl of Northumberland not to be given this honour. The King replied that he was the first Smithson to ask for it — but he was later granted the Order and in 1766 was created *1st Duke of Northumberland.* The Duke employed the best men available to create the Syon Park you see today: *'Capability' Brown* was responsible for landscaping the magnificent gardens, and *Robert Adam* transformed the interior of the house to its present splendour.

Besides these important features, the 55 acres of parkland open to the public offer a number of 20th century attractions which are well worth seeing. But, in common with many other stately homes still occupied by the nobility, entrance fees have to be imposed to help towards the high cost of maintaining a private estate this size (300 acres overall) — so the 'grand tour' could be quite expensive for a family outing. There are reductions for children and OAP's, however, and a combined House and Garden ticket only costs £1·30 per adult — which includes admission to the aviary and aquarium in the Great Conservatory.

The footpath from the High Street emerges at the garden entrance to the Park, where you have the choice of heading **south** along the perimeter path to the **British Leyland Heritage Collection** of motor-cars over the ages, or following one of the lovely tree-lined walks beside the ¼-mile long **lake** (created by 'Capability') to the broad expanse of **Flora's Lawn** — overlooked by the statue of the Roman goddess of flowers, on her 55ft column, since the 18th century. You'll find a small **playground** for children at the far end of the lake, near the riverside. To the **west,** the garden path takes you to the **Great Conservatory** (built by *Charles Fowler* for the 3rd Duke in 1827, and later used as a model for the Crystal Palace) which contains about 200 varieties of plants, as well as a **Tropical Birdhouse and Aquarium.** The birds are not caged and fly around freely in the west wing.

The main path outside the garden entrance, leads past the restaurant, bar, cafeteria and shop (where you can buy detailed guides to the house and gardens), to the **Garden Centre** in the former stables. Here budding 'Capabilities' will find all the plants and equipment they need for indoor or garden use. Do visit the free **Art Gallery** (beside the Centre) which is housed in one of the oldest buildings in the Park — an original Tudor barn. The **Butterfly House** at the southern end of the adjacent car park is a recent addition to Syon, and a must for lepidopterists.

Further west, two early 17th century **garden lodges** mark the entrance to **Syon House**. Don't be put off by the barrack-like walls with which the 3rd Duke recased the original house — they protect a sumptuous interior, brilliantly decorated and furnished by Robert Adam, and filled with antique treasures. The 6-acre **Rose Garden** on the western terraces makes a perfect ending for your tour, and is a breathtaking sight in summer when the thousands of roses of every variety come into bloom. The main gardens and Garden Centre are open all year round, but the house and conservatory are closed in winter. Opening times and admission prices for these and other attractions in the Park can be checked through the phone numbers given at the back of this book.

ROUTE TWO *(The Butts to Kew Bridge via Watermans Park — 1¼ miles)* From The Butts, cross over the Half Acre towards the pineapple-topped gateposts of the former Congregational Chapel, or 'New Temple' as it was called when first erected in 1783 — Congregational meetings having been held in the district for over a century before. The church was partially rebuilt after bomb damage in 1944, and was joined by the Presbyterians to become the **United Reformed Church** in 1972. Continuing northwards, you come to another fine old house which was built c.1800 in the Greek Revival style. Beyond that stands the **Public Library,** opened in 1904 by the Scottish/American philanthropist, *Andrew Carnegie,* whose Trust Fund paid for several other libraries in the Borough — not to mention the rest of Britain and the USA. Born in Dunfermline, Carnegie later emigrated to Pittsburgh where he established what was to become the largest iron and steel works in America. He retired in 1901, a multi-millionaire, and donated much of his wealth to various educational causes.

It was largely due to the efforts of the first librarian, *Fred Turner* (author of 'History and Antiquities of Brentford'), that the new building was erected — thus enabling the library to move from the small room in **Clifden House** where it had been established 15 years earlier. This large Georgian mansion then stood on the corner of Boston Manor Road now covered by Clifden Road, and was occupied by Henry Agar, *Viscount Clifden,* during the early 19th century. It later became a school, and from 1890-1927 was used as offices for Brentford District Council — finally being demolished in 1953.

If you were to carry on up **Boston Manor Road** for about half a mile, you would come to **Boston Manor** itself. But, although New Brentford was once part of the Manor's demesne, the history of the house and its owners has been told in Chapter II — simply because the walk from Ealing is more attractive. You could, of course, jump on an E1 bus from here (which will take you right to the entrance), but those bound for Kew Bridge should turn right into **Clifden Road.** Two further snippets of information before we leave this area — **Brentford Central Station** opened in 1849, and **Windmill Road** (the old lane to Little Ealing) takes its name from a windmill on the Boston Manor estate which stood at the entrance to what is now **The Ride** until late last century.

Clifden House (then used as Council Offices) and the new Library in 1904.

Clifden House flats, on the corner of Clifden Road, stand on the site of the ornate, Gothic-style **Wesleyan Church** which was replaced by a new building, further down the road, in 1964. (John Wesley, the founder of Methodism, frequently preached in Brentford in the mid-18th century.) Opposite the new church are the **Public Baths** designed by the Town Surveyor, Nowell Parr, and opened in 1895. Behind the houses lining the right-hand side of the road, lie the grounds of **Brentford School for Girls** — which was built as a mixed Secondary Modern in 1930, but changed status when overcrowding and the introduction of the Comprehensive system caused the boys to be moved to Syon School, Isleworth, in 1968.

The far end of Clifden Road is dominated by the spectators' stands of **Brentford Football Club** — established in 1888 as the sports' club of the old Wesleyan Chapel. The **Griffin Park** ground (subsidised by the Griffin brewery of Fuller, Smith & Turner at Chiswick) opened in 1905 and the Club soon established a name for themselves — winning every home game of the 1929-30 season, a record which has yet to be beaten. Brentford is in the 3rd Division at the moment, but very optimistic for the future. Perhaps they'll repeat another of the records they once held — for the fastest promotion from 3rd (1933) to 1st Division (1935)?

Critics of the game may be interested to know that the football hooliganism which receives so much coverage in the press these days (not, I hasten to add, necessarily connected with BFC), is by no means a modern invention. The earliest mention of football in Middlesex occurs in the records of the Justices of the Peace in 1576, when five men from Ruislip and seven from Uxbridge 'with unknown malefactors to the number of a hundred played a certain unlawful game, called football, by reason of which there arose amongst them a great affray, likely to result in homicides and serious accidents'! The game had in fact been banned by Henry VIII in 1541 (along with milder pastimes such as bowls, quoits and tennis) because it interfered with the practise of archery.

Brook Road was built in the 1850's over the little stream which now flows underground from Castlebar Hill, through Little Ealing, and down to the Thames near Ferry Lane. According to the landlord of **The Griffin** pub (which lies to the right in Brook Road) the stream still occasionally makes an appearance in his cellars, but this has not prevented the pub from being granted the Best-Kept-Cellar Award by Fullers Brewery — so it would seem a good place to pause for a while and enjoy a pint of draught.

Carry on southwards from the pub and turn right into **Lateward Road,** where neat terraces of late-19th century cottages overlook **St. Paul's recreation ground** — one of the few open spaces in Brentford. The inscription ón the obelisk near the ornate drinking-fountain describes how the park was built to celebrate Queen Victoria's Jubilee in 1887 — not that the majority of Brentford's inhabitants had much to celebrate at the time as the new houses north of the park contrasted sharply with the vast slum area to the south, where hundreds of dilapidated, weatherboarded cottages were crammed into a maze of yards and alleys between Back Lane/Albany Road and the High Street.

Troy Town, as it was called (from the Cornish expression for a labyrinth of disorderly streets), started in the mid-18th century as a handful of cottages which, like so many of Brentford's slums, grew to keep pace with the demand for labourers in the breweries, and soap, water and gasworks. Few houses were kept in a reasonable state of repair; none had adequate sanitation; and yet the need for housing was so great that high rents could be charged for these miserable hovels. Lack of land made it difficult for the Council to provide alternative accommodation, and it wasn't until 1910-12 that some of the worst alleys began to be cleared — the last derelict cottages only being demolished in 1958. The phased scheme to rebuild the northern side of the High Street (from St. Paul's to North Road) began the following year, and was completed by 1978.

At the western end of the park stands part of the original **St. Paul's School** which opened in 1873 and was largely rebuilt in the 1920's. Further extensions were added after the money from various educational charities and legacies to the former St. Lawrence's School were transferred to St. Paul's in 1953, and the school became known as St. Lawrence's with St. Paul's. Leave the park by the gate near the children's playground and turn right into **Albany Road,** and then first left into **Alexandra Road.** The **Health Centre** lining the eastern side of the road was built in 1938 on the site of the old Brentford British School — considered one of the best schools in London in 1872. The school was financed by subscriptions, especially from the Rothschild family, and was later renamed the **Rothschild School.** It closed in 1930 when the new Secondary Modern school (now Brentford School for Girls) was opened in Clifden Road.

At the **County Court** (opened 1963), cross over the High Street to where smart red-brick office blocks cover the sites of some of Brentford's earliest industries — such as the 18th century **tile-making works** of Messrs. *Trimmer & Clarke* near Dock Road, and the large **timber yard** and sawmills of *James Montogomery & Son* whose wharf (now occupied by Heidelberg) was a constant flurry of activity from 1806 to 1911. Turn down into **Pump Alley** which is lined with some attractive old cottages — probably built when the **Town Meadow** was taken over for Brentford's much-needed **Drainage and Sewage Works** in the 1880's. Sewage was collected here and pumped to the sewage farm in South Ealing Road (established by Ealing's Local Board in 1863), until a new disposal system for West Middlesex opened at Isleworth in 1936. The old wharf buildings are now used by Hounslow Borough Works Depot.

The air in Town Meadow during the 19th century, could not have been much improved by the fact that *T.B. Rowe & Co.* were boiling up vast vats of fat at their soap-making works on the riverside between Town Meadow and Ferry Lane. The site was acquired in 1800 and within a few years the factory had become the biggest producer of hard soap in south-eastern England. The company was later taken over by Lever Brothers, but closed in 1933. Employees then opened the **Brentford Soap Company** in Catherine Wheel Yard, which finally shut down in the 1960's.

Follow the alley round to the High Street, where the old shops on the northern side have given way to flats and a landscaped area. Between them stands a lone survivor — the former **King's Arms Inn,** now used as offices for Brentford Housing Association and the **West London Archeological Field Group.** The latter was initiated by the Museum of London in 1966 and their excavations in the area have produced a number of interesting finds. By digging trenches prior to redevelopment between the Half Acre and Alexandra Road, they were able to establish the line of the old Roman road north of the present High Street; and evidence of what was probably a small Roman trading post or — judging by the number of gaming counters — a place of relaxation. Traces of a Saxon hut were found near the County Court in 1970; and the rare discovey of a particularly well-preserved clay pipe kiln was made in 1977, when nearly a thousand pipes made by *William Heath* in the early 18th century were unearthed from his kiln behind Nos. 240-246 in the High Street. Nothing has yet been found to substantiate the theory about Julius Caesar's crossing — but who knows what will turn up next?

Turn right into the High Street, past the disused **Fire Station** (built late last century), and down **Ferry Lane.** A beautiful magnolia tree graces the small rest garden on the opposite corner, where the stocks and cage for Old Brentford once stood. Gone, too, are the adjacent **almhouses** established by Queen Elizabeth in 1573 and demolished after closure in 1949, and only the **Waterman's Arms** (first mentioned 1790) survives of the several inns which once lined this busy thoroughfare to the **Kew Ferry.** *William Penn,* founder of Pennsylvania, helped to establish a Quaker Meeting House in a barn in Ferry lane during the time he lived in Brentford (1706-10), but this moved to Brentford End towards the end of the 18th century.

The former **Ferry Hotel** (or Bunch of Grapes as it was called when erected c.1880) can be seen at the end of the lane. Used as offices for Clements-Tough lighterage company from 1922 and recently taken over by a property development group, the building is no longer accessible to the public — although, officially, a public right of way

Ferrymen outside the Ferry Hotel (then run by Mr. Johnny East) c.1905. The ferry service ceased in 1939.

still exists down to the ferry steps. Ferrymen were appointed by the King in medieval times — a privilege which was jealously guarded by the chosen few. From time immemorial Brentford residents had been granted free passage on the ferry to Kew, but with the appointment of *John Hale* as keeper in 1536, local pedestrians and horsemen were charged for this service. Hale and his successors also prevented rivals from carrying horses and vehicles across the river until 1659 — when *Robert Tunstall* succeeded in establishing a cheaper ferry service from his lime-kilns in **The Hollows,** further east. This eventually passed to another Robert Tunstall (possibly a grandson), who opted for the easy life by getting permission to build the first **Kew Bridge** in 1757. However, the old Ferry Lane service continued to operate until the outbreak of the Second World War.

Tucked away in a litter-strewn alcove at the end of Ferry Lane, a stone **monument** commemorates the three battles against the Romans, Danes and Roundheads which supposedly took place at the natural ford over the Thames nearby. Erected by Brentford Town Council in 1909, the monument also records the Synod held by Offa the Mighty in 780 AD and the discovery by *Sir Montagu Sharpe* (then Chairman of Middlesex County Council) of the oak pallisades buried in the bed and bank of the river.

Back on the High Street again, you are faced with a pleasant view across the landscaped area to some of the 19th century terraced cottages and the **Albany Arms** pub in Albany Road. To your right, a DIY supply store stands on the site of the old **police station** and, further east, the warm red-brick of Thameside House marks the first completed phase of the **Brentford Riverside Scheme.** From 1881 until 1965 the **Thames and General Lighterage Company's** boat-building yard covered this site, which was enlarged by slipways on Lot's Ait in 1926. The yard was used for maintenance after boat-building ceased, and remained active until the recent redevelopment began. More office development is planned above the disused **Goat Wharf,** from which the malthouses of *William Jupp*, Brentford's leading maltster in the 19th century, once stretched westward towards Ferry Lane. Uninspiring 1960's shops and flats line the northern approach to **Ealing Road** — known as Drum Lane until the old **Drum Inn** was demolished in 1922 for road widening. The **Red Lion** pub now stands on the corner site.

From here on, the northern skyline is dominated by the gas holders, water tower and six tower blocks of council flats; while the southern side of the High Street offers the welcome refuge of the newly-built Watermans Park and a riverside walk to Kew Bridge. To save confusion, I shall relate the history of each side of the road in turn — and leave you to decide the best way of getting to the places which interest you.

Northern side: The names of **Pottery Road** and **Distillery Walk** give you an idea of some of the industries carried on here during the 18th and 19th centuries. The pottery lay roughly in the angle of today's **Netley Road** and belonged to Sir *Thomas Edwardes* in 1766. It later passed to his son-in-law, *John Hope*, and was subsequently taken over the *Trimmer* family until bought by *George Robinson*, who managed the tile kiln and brickfield near the Potomac pond at Gunnersbury. It eventually closed in the 1870's. The distillery was established by *David Roberts* in the latter half of the 18th century to augment his already extensive premises south of the High Street — but its actual site is less easy to pinpoint. As far as I can make out from old maps of the period, it lay almost opposite the pottery, on the south-eastern side. It was sold to the London distiller, *Felix Booth*, in 1817, and in 1845 was described as the most self-contained distillery in the world — producing nearly a million gallons of spirit a year despite a disastrous fire a few years earlier. This thriving concern was bought out by *Messrs. Haig* in 1851 — but for some reason ceased production within eight years, and the site was later sold for housing. Nearer the High Street in **Walnut Tree Road,** the jam factory of *T.W. Beach* (the so-called 'father of the jam trade') also provided work for many locals from 1886 to 1930.

North Road Baptist Chapel opened in 1840 but, a century later, was damaged by a bomb probably intended for the gasworks, and has been extensively restored. Nonconformist residents of Old Brentford had a considerably wider choice of local churches than their C. of E. counterparts — who, you may remember, were tied to Ealing parish until 1828. (Clayponds Lane and Avenue now cover the well-trodden **Church Way** between Old Brentford and St. Mary's, Ealing.) To get round the problem, prominent inhabitants led by the *Trimmer* family raised subscriptions to build **St. George's Chapel** in 1762. It was designed by *Sir Joshua Kirby* whose daughter, *Sarah*, subsequently married *James Trimmer* and became something of a pioneer in technical education. In 1768 she helped the vicar of Ealing, Rev. Charles Sturgess, to found a **Sunday School** — in the building which still stands next door to the present church —

St. George's Chapel prior to being rebuilt in 1867.

and went on to establish a School of Industry for girls and, less successfully, boys. *Queen Charlotte* was so impressed with her work that she summoned Mrs. Trimmer to Windsor to advise on a similar institution in the Royal Borough.

St. George's Church, although unconsecrated until 1828, also went from strength to strength and was too small by 1851, when a new site was bought off the Half Acre. This, as you now know, was taken for St. Paul's instead; and in 1867 the present rather gloomy-looking church was rebuilt by *Sir Arthur Blomfield* on the original site — in the shadow of the **gasworks**. These had opened in 1821 to light the turnpike road through Brentford to Kensington — oil lamps having been the only illuminant in the High Street since 1767. But *J&G Barlow*, the private firm of engineers who constructed the works, got into financial difficulties almost immediately and were superseded by the **Brentford Gas Company** — under the chairmanship of *Felix Booth*, the wealthy distiller. By the time St. George's was rebuilt, the company was supplying gas to all the parishes between Hounslow and Notting Hill; had taken over the site of Booth's former distillery south of the High Street; and was provoking numerous complaints about pollution of the air and river. The Gas Light and Coke Company gained control in 1926, and was succeeded by the North Thames Gas Board until the works closed in 1963.

St. George's closed in 1959 and since 1963 has housed the **National Musical Museum** — where you can not only trace the history and development of the piano and all kinds of automatic playing instruments, but also see and hear them in action. The museum is open at weekends from 2-5pm, April to October, and the small entrance fee covers a 1½-hour guided tour and demonstration of some of the 200 instruments (ranging from pianolas to phonographs) which have been lovingly restored by *Frank Holland MBE*, creator of this fascinating collection. The stained glass windows and high, vaulted ceiling of the old church enhance the atmosphere; and whether it's the sound of the humble hurdy-gurdy or mighty WurliTzer organ that turns you on, you can be assured of a unique experience.

The Musical Museum is not really suitable for very small children — but around the corner at the **Living Steam Museum** in Green Dragon Lane, junior's cries will barely be heard above the noise of the huge Victorian beam engines as their pistons thunder up and down, steam hissing and brasswork gleaming. The Grand Junction Water Works Company opened the **Kew Bridge Pumping Station** in 1838 to supply clean drinking water to central London, Paddington and Kensington — a territory which gradually expanded to include the whole of Ealing, Brentford, Acton and Chiswick. In 1944, however, these five magnificent 'dinosaurs of the industrial revolution' were made redundant by the electric pumps of the Metropolitan Water Board, and lay idle until the newly-formed **Kew Bridge Engine Trust** set about restoring them in 1993. Now (on weekends and Bank Holiday Mondays from 11am to 5pm) members of the public can wander through engine rooms and boiler houses, over cylinder stages and beam floors, and marvel at the spectacular sight of these powerful engines in action.

The collection includes other rare steam engines and a display of models which illustrate how some of the engines work. Traction engines belonging to friends of the Trust can also sometimes be seen receiving a final tune-up in the yard, before steaming off to various rallies around the country. Beyond the shop and pay-office (where you can buy a brief guide to the engines), lies the **Tea Room,** and Victorian **forge and machine shop** — still used by restorers. The familiar landmark of the 235-ft. **water tower** was built in 1867 to house the four stand pipes which once provided the pressure in our water mains; while the now equally familiar **Council tower blocks** in the background (named after some of the engineers who designed the old Cornish pumping engines) were built over the former filter beds of the waterworks just over a century later.

MUSIC MUSEUM BRENTFORD.

THE LIVING STEAM MUSEUM.

Green Dragon Lane takes its name from a 17th century inn, and used to extend much further northwards (along the line now taken by Lionel Road) until its course was altered by the building of the London and South Western Railway in the 1840's. During the Great Plague, victims from Ealing and Brentford were buried in a field known as **Dead Men's Grave** which lay north of Green Dragon Lane. In later years, market gardens covered the area between the waterworks and railway line and were gradually taken over for housing from about 1885 onwards. Most of these old cottages are still standing — in various stages of dilapidation and restoration. All the development along the northern side of **Kew Bridge Road,** between Green Dragon Lane and the motorway, has taken place on the lands of **London Stile Farm** — once the largest market garden in Ealing. (Would that just a few of the fruit trees covering its 96-acres had survived to brighten up this shabby stretch of highway.)

Kew Bridge Station opened in 1849 on the L. and S.W.R's loopline through Chiswick to Hounslow, and was joined by the North and South-Western Junction Railway Co.'s line from Acton in 1862. Further up, on the western side of the road, building work is in progress on the site of **Brentford Market** which replaced the stalls around Kew Bridge fountain in 1893. A large yellow-brick market house was built here in

1905 and remained in use until 1974, when traders moved to the Western International Market at North Hyde. After serving as a Sunday market and skateboard park, the old market buildings were finally demolished in 1982 to make way for offices, warehouses and a large leisure centre. The elevated section of the **M4 motorway** ahead was completed in 1965 and opened by filmstar, *Jayne Mansfield* — an interesting choice of personality compared with the opening of the A4 by *King George V*, forty years earlier!

Southern side: A long overdue transformation is at last taking place on this stretch of the riverside which, even before the industrial expansion of the 19th century, was described as an eyesore from the Surrey side of the Thames. An overgrown passage down to the river is, at present, all that remains of the notorious **Smith Hill** — once the centre of another of Brentford's insanitary slums — but even this is soon to be given a new lease of life as the starting point for a public footway through the adjacent **Brentford Arts Centre** and **Watermans Park.** By Summer 1984 (if building work keeps to schedule), you will be able to take tea on the terrace of the new Arts Centre, wander round the art gallery, or enjoy a show at the small cinema and theatre on the lower tier — a vast improvement on the ramshackle huts which occupied the same site a century ago.

Smith Hill developed as a result of the number of breweries in this vicinity — the first cottages being erected a few years after *David Roberts* acquired a Thameside malthouse in 1773, which rapidly expanded over most of the area now covered by Watermans Park. From about 1790 Roberts seems to have concentrated on his principal distillery north of the High Street, leaving the riverside brewery in the hands of his partners, *Smith and Harrington.* They also sold out to *Felix Booth* c.1817 — but Thomas Smith's name continued to be associated with the rows of workers' tenements which by then lined the High Street as far as Pottery Road. When production ceased in the 1850's, Booth converted the premises to the use of his Brentford Gas Company; but retained his interest in the 18th century **Red Lion Brewery,** which stood next to an old **watermill** almost opposite Pottery Road — forming a barrier between the slums and the gasworks.

In 1829 its name was changed to the **Royal Brewery** to commemorate a visit by *King William IV,* who came to discuss an expedition to the Polar Sea which Felix Booth was financing. Booth contributed £17,000 to *Sir John Ross'* Arctic voyage — in which the peninsula of 'Boothia Felix' was discovered — and was made a baronet in 1835. (One can't help feeling that the money would have been better spent on providing decent accommodation for his workers — but perhaps that sort of philanthropy didn't carry a knighthood.) The Royal Brewery closed in 1923 and the site was soon gobbled up by more extensions to the gasworks.

The gasholders remain, but the so-called 'King of Brentford' no longer rules the eastern end of the High Street. Its fortress-like walls have been lowered at last and the new **Watermans Park** provides visitors with their first clear view of Brentford's other highway — the Thames. This famous river owes its present-day pronunciation to the gutteral accent of King George I, who never bothered to learn English and had trouble with his aitches — "te Temmes" being the closest he could get to the original name (which sounded like 'same'-s, with a lisp). This solecism was probably mimicked by his mocking English courtiers to begin with — but the new pronunciation eventually stuck. George I was purported to be very fond of Brentford because it reminded him of his beloved Hanover — from which he seldom strayed throughout the 13 years of his rule. He even made one of his two mistresses (who always accompanied him on these reluctant visits to England) *Baroness of Brentford* in 1722 — having divorced his wife for infidelity some years earlier!

From Watermans Park, you have an unspoilt view across **Brentford** and **Lot's Ait** to Kew Gardens. Osiers — a type of willow used in basket-making — were cultivated on this little group of islands from the 14th century until demand for the baskets ceased with the decline of Brentford's market-gardens. The slipways of the now defunct Thames and General Lighterage Company later encroached on Lot's Ait — where a housing scheme is to be built some time in the future — and the other osier-beds and site of the 18th century **Three Swans Inn** (on the island nearest Kew Bridge) are all pleasantly overgrown and filled with birdlife. The days when canal boats and Thames sailing barges (glorious under their red-brown canvas) jostled for position on the river are gone, and few working boats operate on this stretch of the waterfront today. However, pleasure craft and rowing crews provide plenty of entertainment as you wander along to the exit near **Victoria Steps** (another disused wharf), or wait for the children to have their fill of the excellent **playground** in the park.

Turning right into the High Street, you will find a public footpath just beyond the **Royal Tar** pub (est. 1892) which leads down to **The Hollows** — one of the first wharves to be built. The *Tunstall* family owned several lime kilns here during the 17th and 18th centuries — leasing two to *James Trimmer* in 1791. Limestone was brought in by boat and burnt to make slaked lime — used in mortar and cement, and to neutralise acidic soil. Coal for firing the kilns was probably stored in a warehouse nearby; but today the only smoke to be seen comes from the chimneys of the houseboats which line the bank as far as Kew Bridge — the third on the site since Robert Tunstall decided there must be an easier way of getting people and their paraphernalia across the river than ferrying them.

Tunstall's bridge opened with a grand celebration on Kew Green on the 4th June 1759 — the birthday of the *Prince of Wales*, then living at Kew Palace. Tradition has it that the bridge marked a far more important milestone in Prince George's life — for it was while riding over the bridge with Lord Bute the following year that he supposedly met the messenger who announced the death of his grandfather, and proclaimed him George III. Kew Palace remained the favourite residence of this very popular King, however, and the receipt books for the Toll House record his frequent passage over the bridge. Although toll fees produced a substantial income, Tunstall never made much profit as the wooden frame of his bridge required constant repair work, and had to be replaced by a stone bridge 30 years later. This bridge lasted until 1898 — finally being freed from tolls in 1873. The present bridge was erected by Middlesex and Surrey Councils and opened by *King Edward VII* in 1903.

The footpath winds round the **Horseferry Boat Club** and emerges in Kew Bridge Road, which is laden with a slightly smoother flow of traffic than in the days when market-gardeners stalls and wagons jammed the crossroads. The Midlands Bank on the corner site was built over the house which *Thomas Layton*, chairman of the library committee and a serious collector of books and antiquities relating to Brentford, left to the town in 1911. This disorderly treasure-house of prehistoric implements, coins, pottery and engravings was catalogued and classified by the librarian, *Fred Turner*, who arranged for their removal to the library as the house was in such a ruinous condition. Today, the bulk of the **Layton Collection** is stored at Chiswick Town Hall, and the artefacts are displayed at the Museum of London and Gunnersbury Museum.

A wide choice of inns await your pleasure at the end of this walk. The **Plough** and **Waggon and Horses** were first established in the 17th century — the latter is thought to have been the waterside inn which *Samuel Pepys* visited in 1665. This and the **Star and Garter** were among the larger coaching inns serving travellers from the 1750's, while the **Express Hotel** dates from the advent of the railway. Electric trams were introduced by London United Tramways in 1901, and ran from Kew Bridge along the High Street — linking up with LUT's Acton to Southall service via Boston Road and the Half Acre in 1906. Trams were replaced by trolleybuses in 1935, which ran daily until 1962.

A view from the drinking fountain at Kew Bridge in 1892, looking towards the familiar landmarks of the gasworks and water tower. The fountain was resited inside the gates of the Western International Market when Brentford traders moved there in 1974.

And now we've come to the end of the trail. To the east lies the historic village of **Strand on the Green;** over the river, **Kew Gardens** beckon; while on Kew Green stands the **Church of St. Anne** where ... but that's another story — one can only stretch the boundaries of Ealing so far!

THE END

 ACKNOWLEDGEMENTS

Many people have given me help and encouragement during the long gestation of this book, and while it isn't possible to acknowledge each and every one by name, I feel that the book would be incomplete without mentioning a few at least. The staff of the local history departments at Reference Libraries in and around the borough have been an enormous help in tracking down elusive facts and figures for this book, and I should like to thank Maureen Gooding and Mr. Skoles of Ealing Central Library, Liliane Anderson of Southall, Andrea Cameron of Hounslow, Mrs. Hammond of Chiswick and, especially, Ann Balfour Paul of Gunnersbury Museum for giving me so much of their time and knowledge.

I am further indebted to Andrea Cameron and Ann Balfour Paul for checking the Brentford and Gunnersbury chapters, and also to Peter Hounsell for reading through North and South Ealing, his wife, Frances, for her assistance with Greenford, and the same service rendered by Mr. R.N.G. Rowland for Acton, Mr. C.H. Keene for Northolt, and Mr. Tom Greeves for Bedford Park. Besides removing the worst errors from my manuscript, they all offered much useful advice — most of which I tried to follow, but any mistakes that have persisted are entirely of my own making.

A great deal of information has also been made available to me by the many local history societies in the area, either personally or through their various publications. Specific thanks is due to Jay Cayley and Gordon Pedley of the Hanwell Preservation Society, Jenny Vallance of the Brent River Park Society, and Peggy Ivie of the Ealing Museum, Art and History Society who were particularly helpful in answering my innumerable queries.

I am also very grateful to the following people for the material they contributed: Alan Gillett, who somehow managed to produce 41 original illustrations in his very limited spare time; David Gordon for his help in researching the Acton chapter; Carol Fisher for preparing the bibliograpy and trying to correct my terrible punctuation; Roger Lake for helping me to find my way through the maze of the introductory chapter; Tim Baker of the Institute of Historical Research, and Bryn Brookes and Liz McDowell of the BBC for lending me pre-publication proofs of the *Victoria County History, Vol. VII* and *History on Your Doorstep*, respectively; Michael Moss, the Borough Librarian, for allowing me to reproduce numerous photographs from the library's local history collection; Messrs. John Murray for permission to use quotations from Sir John Betjeman's poem, *Middlesex*; and to Sir John himself, my very special thanks for the enthusiasm with which he responded to my request for a Foreword, despite not being very well at the time.

During the course of my perambulations around the borough, I've been given so much help of one sort or another by local people I stopped in the street or who answered my unexpected telephone calls or knock at their door, that I can only add to their number the army of anonymous company information officers, clergymen, British Waterways engineers, and workers in the planning, conservation and mapping departments at the Town Hall — and offer one big 'thank you' for their individual responses to my oft-repeated opener: 'Sorry to bother you, but I'm writing a book about ....'. My only regret is that I was unable to make more use of all the information and reminiscences they shared with me but this was meant to be the portable edition.

For all the help given to me in researching the book, the greatest credit must go to those who made it possible for me to convert the superabundance of information into its present form. First in line for the Grand Salute is Alistair Chisholm, my Chief Mate and mainstay throughout the rough 3-year passage. Between bread-winning expeditions, he created order out of domestic chaos by slotting into the role of cook, dishwasher and babyminder, not forgetting cartographer; and displayed remarkable self-control at almost all times — particularly when returning home after guiding tourists around the archeological sites of Ancient Greece and Egypt, to find me still stuck in some forgotten corner that is forever Ealing. However, no working mother with an itinerant mate can survive without the support of friends and relatives, and I am deeply indebted to Monica and Rob Munro, 'Deda' Kordic, Shirani Dassanaike and, especially, Jenny Chisholm, Peter's grandmother, for the many hours they have spent entertaining my son while I worked; and to Anne and Phil Tracy for providing me with a peaceful refuge when my own home was under invasion. A large dollop of loving appreciation also goes to Peter, for keeping maternal guilt to the minimum by happily adjusting to the changes in his environment and my frequent absences; and to my parents, who provided moral support from 6,000 miles away through a steady flow of encouraging letters — none of which ever complained about the long gaps between my replies.

On a less personal but equally practical level, I should like to thank Antony Jay and Alan Gillett for backing me from the start — both financially and by giving me advice; my accountant, Elizabeth Bingham, for pointing out the potholes in my mathematics; Tim Boyle and Kate Gellately-Smith for providing a temporary filling for some of the gaps; and those individuals and companies who responded so generously to my last-minute appeal for financial help when it became obvious that, without it, the overall cost of producing an illustrated book of this length could not be met unless it was sold at a price that would put it right out of the reach of the average resident, and thus defeat the whole object of writing it.

And finally, a tribute to the man who had the unenviable job of putting it all together — my printer/publisher, Nick Wheatley. Deadlines came and went, but his patience, sense of humour and belief that the book would, one day, be finished never outwardly faltered, and kept me going from week to week — and year to year. To him I offer my heartfelt gratitude and the words of the 17th century historian, Thomas Fuller: 'Learning hath gained most by those books by which the printers have lost' — and hope that they may be of some consolation.

⬤⬤ LOCAL SOCIETIES ⬤⬤

A — archeology   C — conservation   G — general history   L — local history
                   N — natural history   R — railways

Information about the various societies may be obtained from the Membership
Secretaries whose names and addresses are given below. Ealing Arts Council also publish
a useful guide to all the organisations in the borough, which is updated annually and
available from libraries or the Town Hall.

1895 ASSOCIATION OF ACTONIANS (L)
Miss D.M. Rham, 87 Shakespeare Road, Acton W3.
BEDFORD PARK SOCIETY (C,L)
The Membership Secretary, 16 Woodstock Road, Bedford Park W4.
BRENTFORD & CHISWICK LOCAL HISTORY SOCIETY (C,L)
Miss W.M. Heard, 12a Bracken Gardens, Barnes SW13 9HW. Tel: 748 5838
BRENTFORD RIVERSIDE ASSOCIATION (C)
Mrs. Betty Colman, 59 Strand on the Green. Tel: 994 3437
BRENTHAM SOCIETY (C,L)
Mr. C. Strachan, 26 Holyoake Walk, Brentham W5. Tel: 997 1904
BRENT RIVER & CANAL SOCIETY (C)
Mary Hall, 72 Half Acre Road, Hanwell W7. Tel: 579 7594
EALING ARTS COUNCIL
Mr. D. Sellwood, 1 Cleveley Crescent, Ealing W5. Tel: 997 9060
EALING CIVIC SOCIETY (C)
The Membership Secretary, 5 Fosse Way, Ealing W13.
EALING MUSEUM, ART & HISTORY SOCIETY (G,L)
Mr. A.W.D. Fryer, 16 The Orchard, Montpelier Road, Ealing W5. Tel: 997 3951
EALING NATIONAL TRUST ASSOCIATION (C)
Mrs. Sonia Pearson, 21 Creffield Road, Ealing W5.
FRIENDS OF GUNNERSBURY PARK & MUSEUM (C)
Mrs. J. Catterall, 39 Lionel Road, Brentford. Tel: 560 4262
FRIENDS OF ST. MARY'S, PERIVALE (Cultural Community Centre)
Miss A. Mansell, 33 Langdale Gardens, Perivale. Tel: 997 0478
GREENFORD SOCIETY (C,L)
Mr. N.S. Tams, 15 Farndale Crescent, Greenford, Middlesex.
GREAT WESTERN SOCIETY (R)
Mr. Tony Bayliss, 25 Chalfont Way, Ealing W13. Tel: 567 7178
GWR PRESERVATION GROUP (R)
Mr. R.A. Gorringe, 16 Grange Close, Heston, Middlesex TW5 0HW. Tel: 574 1529
HANWELL PRESERVATION SOCIETY (C,L)
Lucy Brown, 93 Church Road, Hanwell W7. Tel: 567 2758
HISTORICAL ASSOCIATION, EALING BRANCH (G)
Miss M. Palmer, 44 Kingfield Road, Ealing W5 1LB. Tel: 997 2640
KEW BRIDGE ENGINES TRUST (C)
The Secretary, Living Steam Museum, Green Dragon Lane, Brentford. Tel: 568 4757
LONDON WILDLIFE TRUST (N,C)
The Secretary, 1 Thorpe Close, London W10. Tel: 968 5368/9
NORWOOD GREEN RESIDENTS ASSOCIATION (C,L)
Mrs. Peggy Ivie, 207 Tentelow Lane, Norwood Green, Southall. Tel: 574 4642
ROYAL SOCIETY FOR PROTECTION OF BIRDS, WEST LONDON GROUP (N)
Mr. R. Williams, 63 Cumberland Road, Hanwell W7. Tel: 579 6008

ST. LAWRENCE BRENTFORD TRUST (Theatre and Community Centre)
Pamela Mandell, 171 Boston Manor Road, Brentford, Middlesex. Tel: 560 8821
SELBORNE SOCIETY (N)
Mr. R.J. Hall, 89 Daryngton Drive, Greenford, Middlesex. Tel: 578 3181
SOUTHALL LOCAL HISTORY SOCIETY (L)
Paul Partridge, 5 Church Road, Heston, Middlesex. Tel: 572 4575
VICTORIAN SOCIETY (C,G)
The Secretary, 1 Priory Gardens, Bedford Park W4. Tel: 994 1019
WEST LONDON ARCHEOLOGICAL GROUP (A,L)
John Cotton, 273 High Street, Brentford, Middlesex. Tel: 560 3880
WEST MIDDLESEX RAILWAY SOCIETY (R)
Colin Derry, 56 The Alders, Heston, Middlesex. Tel: 571 5450

PLACES OF INTEREST

Opening Hours
(An admission fee is charged unless otherwise stated)

BOSTON MANOR
House: May to September — Saturdays only 2-4.30 (free)
Park: Daily (free)
Tel: 570 7728
GUNNERSBURY
Museum: March to October — Mondays to Fridays 1-5
(free) — Weekends and Bank Holidays 2-6
November to February — Monday to Friday 1-4
— Weekends and Bank Holidays 2-4
Park: Daily (free)
Tel: 992 1612
KEW BRIDGE ENGINES TRUST (Living Steam Museum)
Weekends and Bank Holiday Mondays 11-5
Tel: 568 4757
NATIONAL MUSICAL MUSEUM
April to October — Weekends only 2-5
Tel: 560 8108
OSTERLEY
House: April to September — Tuesday to Sunday & Bank Holiday Mondays 2-6
October to March — Tuesday to Sunday & Bank Holiday Mondays 12-4
Park: Daily (free)
Tel: 560 3918
SYON
House: April to September — Sunday to Thursday 12-4.15
October — Sundays only 12-4.15
Tel: 560 0881/4
Gardens and Great Conservatory: 21st March to 23rd October 10-6
Gardens only: 24th October to 20th March 10am-dusk
Garden Centre: Summer — Monday to Saturday 9.30-5.15 (4.45 in Winter)
Tel: 568 0134 — Sundays 10-5.45 (4.45 in Winter)
B.L. Heritage Motor Museum: Daily 10-5.30
Tel: 560 1378
Butterfly House: Daily 10-5 (3.30 in Winter)
Tel: 560 7272

PRESERVED BUILDINGS

Buildings in the Borough statutorily listed as being of special architectural or historical interest. Grade II except where indicated. An asterisk signifies that the structure has a higher value than a Grade II, but less than a Grade I.

ACTON
Obelisk in Acton Park
Goldsmiths Almshouses* in East Churchfield Road
Acton Hill Methodist Church, George and Dragon PH, and No. 185 in the High Street
Church of St. Mary in King Street
Gate, posts and railings behind Nos. 13 and 15 Newburgh Road
Berrymead Priory in Salisbury Street
West Lodge and The Elms in Uxbridge Road
356 houses in Bedford Park (full list from Council or B.P. Society)

EALING
Nos. 28 and 30 in Castlebar Road
Ealing Abbey in Charlbury Grove
Nos. 1 and 15 in Church Lane
St. Mary's (GPO building), Morgan House, Wrexham Lodge and Willow House on Ealing Green
Thorncote in Edgehill Road (built 1890)
All Saints Church in Elm Grove Road
No. 36 (chemist) on Haven Green
Rochester House in Little Ealing Lane
No. 86 and the Church of St. John in Mattock Lane
Brentham Club House in Meadvale Road
Church of St. Peter* and The Vicarage (no. 56) in Mount Park Road, and lamp standard at junction with Park Hill
Christ Church* and Town Hall in New Broadway
Coronet Cinema in Northfield Avenue
Nos. 19, 21, 94 (Westfield House) and Church of St. Mary* in St. Mary's Road
Church of St. Stephen in St. Stephen's Road
Nos. 6 to 9 on The Common
Nos. 42, 43, and Nat. West. Bank in The Mall
Nos. 17 to 26 in The Park
No. 2 (fish shop) in Uxbridge Road W5, and mile post at junction with The Common
Mile post outside No. 173 in Uxbridge Road W13
Pitshanger Manor (Grade I), entrance archway and gate to Manor (Grade I), Lodge, stone bridge* and bench, brick wall forming northern boundary of Walpole Park
Ealing Broadway Methodist Church and Memorial Hall in Windsor Road
Lamp standard at junction of Woodville and Aston Roads

GREENFORD
Holy Cross New Church in Ferrymead Gardens
Holy Cross Old Church (Grade I) and Betham House* (No. 162) in Oldfield Lane

GUNNERSBURY
Gunnersbury Park House (large mansion)
Gunnersbury House (small mansion)
Conservatory
Archway at east end of terrace behind large mansion
Archway to south-west of large mansion

Temple
Gothic outbuildings east of small mansion, including Princess Amelia's Bath House
Gateway near Bath House
Archway next to east entrance lodge to Gunnersbury Lane
North Entrance gateway to Park
Three iron lamp standards in front of large mansion
North and East Lodges
Stables
Boathouse and Pavilion on Potomac Pond
Gothic ruins on borders of former Japanese Gardens
Remains of stone fountain near cafeteria
Kitchen garden wall

HANWELL
Church of St. Mary*, Spring Cottage, Rectory Cottage, No. 134, and The Hermitage in Church Road
Stable block in Brent Lodge Park
Wharncliffe Viaduct (Grade I)
Hanwell Community Centre in Cuckoo Avenue
Hanwell Railway Station (Grade I)
Railing and gates to City of Westminster Cemetery, and Bridge over Brent in Uxbridge Road
Lock keepers' cottages at Locks 92, 93, 95 and 97 on Grand Union Canal
Hanwell Flight and brick boundary wall of St. Bernard's Hospital (Ancient Monuments)

NORTHOLT
Church of St. Mary (Grade I)
16th century timber-framed barn behind Smith's Farm in Kensington Road
White Hart PH in Ruislip Road
Moated site at Down Barns Farm in Sharvel Lane (Ancient Monument)
Moated site in Belvue Park (Ancient Monument)

PERIVALE
Lych gate, and Church of St. Mary (Grade I) in Perivale Lane
Main block, canteen block, four sets of gates, posts and railings of Hoover Factory in Western Avenue. Also Bideford Avenue frontage
The Sudbury Stone (sarcen) behind Sudbury Golf Club in Whitton Avenue East
Moated site on Sudbury Golf Course (Ancient Monument)
Iron Age site on Horsenden Hill (Ancient Monument)

SOUTHALL
No. 13 Allenby Road
Grand Union Canal Lock and Bridge No. 90 off Glade Lane
Red Lion PH in High Street
Grove House (No. 77) in North Road
Nos. 196 and 198 in Norwood Road
The Grange and Friars Lawn in Norwood Green Road
Roman bridge* in Osterley Park
Frontage of former Liberty Cinema in South Road
Church of St. Mary*, No. 15 and The Plough PH in Tentelow Lane
The Water Tower in The Crescent
Southall Manor House in The Green
Church of St. George in Tudor Road
Gateway, lodges, chapel and West Lodge of St. Bernard's Hospital
Water pump in Uxbridge Road (opposite Lyndhurst Avenue)

Bulls Bridge at junction of Grand Union and Paddington Canals
Windmill Bridge or Three Bridges in Windmill Lane (Ancient Monument)
WEST TWYFORD
Church of St. Mary in Brentmead Gardens
Twyford Abbey and wall to garden in Twyford Abbey Road

This list was correct at the time of going to print, but the Local Planning Authority
should be consulted to ensure that no changes have taken place since.
For a list of the sites of early settlements, burials, defences and industry — see *Field
Monuments in the London Borough of Ealing* which was compiled by Mr. C.H. Keene for
the Council's Technical Services Group in 1975.

BIBLIOGRAPHY

Sources: Most of the books in this extensive list have been studied during long hours
spent at Ealing Central Reference Library. A few are available from the Lending Library;
the more recent ones can still be purchased; but many are out of print — and some never
made it past the manuscript stage (these are indicated by the letters MS). A wealth of
useful information has also been culled from old maps (especially the *Ordnance Survey* 6
inches to a mile sheets from 1863 onwards), newspapers (Ealing Library has microfilms of
the *Middlesex County Times* from 1866 to 1974), *Kelly's Directories* (1887-1940), and various
back issues of the *Local Historian* — produced by the former Ealing Local History Society
and made available to me by Ealing Museum, Art and History Society. Gunnersbury
Park Museum has been another valuable source of reference material and I recommend
their excellent local history collection to other researchers.
GENERAL BACKGROUND
Daniel Lysons, *The Environs of London* (1795-1800)
James Thorne, *Handbook to the Environs of London* (1876)
W.J. Hardy and W. le Hardy, *Middlesex County Records Reports 1902-1928* (1928)
Cyril M. Neaves, *A History of Greater Ealing* (1931 edition — reprinted 1971)
Michael Robbins, *Middlesex* (1953)
K.J. Allison, *Ealing in the XVII Century* and *Ealing in the XVIII and XIX Centuries* (1966)
— Ealing Vestry Minutes and Hearth Tax Assessments for Ealing, Hanwell and
Greenford
Norman Crossley, *Public Houses and Coaching Inns* (MS 1968)
The Victoria County History of Middlesex, Vol. III (1962) — includes Hanwell and
Greenford; *Vol. IV* (1971) — includes Northolt, Perivale and Southall; *Vol. VII* (1982) —
includes Ealing, Brentford, Acton and West Twyford
C.H. Keene, *Field Monuments in the London Borough of Ealing* (1975)
Maureen Gooding, *London Borough of Ealing Historical Notes and Tables* (typescript, 1975)
Derek Pratt, *Discovering London's Canals* (1977)
Ealing Museum Art & History Society, *Art, Architecture and History of Ealing's Churches*
(1977)
Geoffrey Hewlett, *A History of Wembley* (1979)
Ealing History Workshop, *Dipping into the Past* (1980)
Geoff Elwin and Cathleen King, *Braunston to Brentford* (1980) — a guide to the Grand
Union Canal (1980)
London Borough of Ealing Official Guide (5th edition 1981)
Ealing Borough Draft Plan (1982) — projected Statutory Land Use Plan for the next 15
years (to be endorsed following public enquiry in 1984)

ACTON

P. Jolliffe, *Acton and its History* (1910)

W.K. Baker, *Acton, Middlesex* (2nd edition 1912)

H. Mitchell, *Records and Recollections of Acton* (1913)

R.N.G. Rowland, Historical plans and notes for a series of rambles by the 1895 Association of Actonians (MS): *Part of North Acton* (1965, revised 1972), *Central Acton and Berrymead in the 1860s* (1973, revised 1980), *East Acton* (1974), *Mill Hill Park and Acton Hill* (1975), *The Church Field* (1980); *Street Names of Acton, Middlesex* (1977 — new edition being prepared); *St. Dunstan's Church, East Acton: A Centenary History 1879-1979*

J. Wigley, *A Short History of the Haberdashers' Aske's School* (1980)

LBE Library Service and R.N.G. Rowland, *Acton As It Was* (1981) — annotated photographs

BEDFORD PARK

T. Affleck Greeves, Articles in *Country Life — London's First Garden Suburb* (7th Dec. 1967), *The Making of a Community* (14th Dec. 1967) and *100 Years of Bedford Park* (27th Nov. 1975). Also *Bedford Park, A Pictorial Survey* (1975) and *A Guide to Bedford Park 'The First Garden Suburb' in the Form of Two Walks* (1983)

Margaret Jones Bolsterli, *The Early Community at Bedford Park* (1977)

BRENTFORD

T. Faulkner, *The History and Antiquities of Brentford, Ealing and Chiswick* (1845)

Montague Sharpe, *Bregantforda and the Hanweal* (1904); *Some Account of Bygone Hanwell and its Chapelry of New Brentford*

Fred Turner, *History and Antiquities of Brentford* (1922)

Brentford and Chiswick Local History Society and Hounslow Library Services, *Brentford and Chiswick As It Was* (1978, 2nd impression 1979) — annotated photographs

Brentford and Chiswick Local History Society *Journals: Vol. I* (1980), *Vol. II* (1981)

John Yates, *A Guide to Kew Bridge Engines*

Guide to The Musical Musical Museum

The Guide to Syon Park

Syon House — A Brief History and Guide

EALING

T. Faulkner, *The History and Antiquities of Brentford, Ealing and Chiswick* (1845)

Ealing Illustrated (1893)

Edith Jackson, *Annals of Ealing* (1898)

Charles Jones, *Ealing from Village to Corporate Town* (1902)

Mrs. Basil Holmes, *The Home of Ealing Free Library* (1902)

The 'Borough' Pocket Guide to Ealing (1910)

M.J. Elliott, *Castlebar Hill and the Duke of Kent* (MS 1973) — project undertaken whilst pupil at St. Benedict's School

Bernard Johnson, *Brentham — Ealing's Garden Suburb* (Brentham Society, 1977)

Hector Smith, *A Perambulation at Ealing in 1766* (Ealing Museum, Art and History Society, 1980)

LBE Library Service, *Ealing As It Was* (1980) — annotated photographs

J.R. Ravensdale, *History on your Doorstep* (BBC Publications 1982)

GREENFORD

Albert Blount, *History of Greenford* (MS 1969) — based on material collected by John Lawson Pettingale in whose memory The Greenford Society was founded

C.H. Keene, *The Life Story of F.W. Crees* (1979)

Frances Hounsell, *The Suburban Development of Greenford* (MS 1981) — thesis presented for University of London Diploma

GUNNERSBURY
T. Faulkner, *The History and Antiquities of Brentford, Ealing and Chiswick* (1845)
Edith Jackson, *Annals of Ealing* (1898)
Fred Turner, *History and Antiquities of Brentford* (1922)
A History of Gunnersbury, Its Park and Museum (2nd edition, 1974 — new edition being prepared)
Roger White, *'As finely finished as anything'* (Country Life, 11th Nov. 1982)
Friends of Gunnersbury Park & Museum, *Newsletters Nos. 1-7*
HANWELL
C.S. Burton, *Hanwell in Olden Times* (1900)
Montagu Sharpe, *Brengantforda and the Hanweal* (1904); *Some Account of Bygone Hanwell and its Chapelry of New Brentford*
A. Beasley, *Ancient Hanwell, Peeps into the Past* — lecture reprinted in *Middlesex County Times* (9th Dec. 1911)
J. Troy, *(Old Hanwell* (MS 1960)
Brian Green, *The Brent River Park* (1977) — report of landscape proposals
Geoffrey Lee, *A New Park for London* (Country Life, 16th Nov. 1978)
Susan Stewart, *The Central London District Schools* (1856-1933) — published by Hanwell Community Association
Tim Leonard and Susan Stewart, *Hanwell Remembered — Book I* and *Book II* (Hanwell Community Association, 1980)
Jenny Vallance, *Walks in the Brent River Park* (Brent River and Canal Society, 1983)
NORTHOLT
K. Cochrane-Holroyd, *A History of Northolt Parish Church* (1930); *The History of Northolt* (1938)
C.H. Keene, *St. Mary the Virgin, Northolt, Middlesex* (1976); *A History of the Manor Houses and Manor Lords at Northolt and Down* (1978); *The Life Story of F.W. Crees* (1979)
PERIVALE
J.A. Brown, *The Chronicles of Greenford Parva* (1890)
The Parish of Perivale, A Short History (Church Publishers, 1976)
SOUTHALL
S.G. Short, *Southall and its Environs* (1910)
Paul Kirwan, *Southall — A Brief History* (1965, reprinted 1980)
Richard J. Meads, *Growing Up in Southall from 1904* (1978); *The Maypole and Southall Green* (1980)
May Barnett and Douglas R. Lewis, *A Story of Norwood Green — Its Residents and Environs* (Norwood Green Residents' Association 1982)
Guide to Osterley Park (V&R Museum, 1977)
WEST TWYFORD
Mrs. Basil Holmes, *Notes on the History of the Parish from the Time of the Domesday Survey* (1936)
Brother Cornelius Kearney, *List of Owners and Tenants of Twyford Abbey from 1085-1977* (typescript, 1979)

INDEX

Please note: **Railway Stations, Churches, Hospitals, Inns and Public Houses,** *and* **Schools and Colleges** *are listed collectively under the initial letter of these headings.*

Railways 21-22
— Bakerloo 127; British Rail Suburban Service 154; Central Line 69,105,137,154,166; District 34,50,69,114,125,129; Ealing & Shepherds Bush 105; Ealing & South Harrow 125,129; Great Western 34,66,69, 96,127,131,142,154,161,166,176,197,202, 207,210,213,214,216,218,236-7,240; GWR Birmingham 127; London & South Western 114,248; Metropolitan/District 125,202; Midland and South Western 127; North London 96,103,127; North & South-Western Junction 248; Piccadilly 120,125;
— Stations
Acton Central 96; Acton Main Line 96; Boston Manor 202; Brentford End 237; Brentham Halt — see Hanger Lane; Castlebar Park 66; Drayton Green 66,216; Ealing Broadway 69; Ealing Common 58; Greenford 154; Hanger Lane 66; Hanwell 202,207,218; Haven Green 61,69; Kew Bridge 248; North Acton 105; North Ealing 129; Northfields 50; Northolt 166; Park Royal 120,125,127; Perivale 137; South Greenford 154; Southall 176; Turnham Green 114; Twyford Abbey — see Park Royal; West Acton 120; Willesden Junction 127
Ranelagh Road 40
Rankin, Robert 234
Rann, John 91
rates 13,24,
Ravenor family 146,150
—, House 150
—, Park 151-2
Rawlinson, Dame Jane 39,44
—, Sir Henry 41
Reade, Sir William 54,183
—, Lady Mary 54,55,230
Rectory Cottage 206
—, Houses 40,102,146,153,165,215,218
Redman, Henry 230,237
reeve 4
Reformation 11,12
Relton, Rev 39
Renaissance 11
Rennie, John   ,238
Restoration 15
Retford, William 219
Revolution, 'Glorious' 15
'ribbon development'   ,161
Richard II 9,11,83,160,169
Richardson, Sir Albert 144
Rigg family 148
Ridley, Nicholas 12
Rivers, Earl 42,85,139

—, see Brent, Colne, Lea and Thames
roads, condition of 20,44,45,227
Roberts Alley 56
—, David 245,249
Robins, John 195
Robinson, George 91,245
Rochester, Bishop of 40,52
—, House 52,53
Rochford, Countess of 42
Rock House 45
Rockware Glass factory 145,154
Roe, Sir Thomas 146
Romano-British finds 4,65
Romans 2,4,225
Roman roads 4,160,225,243
Ronalds, Hugh 230,235
Ross, Sir John 249
Rothschild, Leopold 57,62,78,86,87,109
—, Lionel 22,86
—, Nathan Mayer 86,87
Round Town 216
Rous, Sir Francis 94,99,102
Rowland, R N G 117
Roy family 148
Royal Academy 46,232
—, Agricultural Society 120
—, Exchange 182
rubbish disposal 172
Rupert, Prince 94,227
Russell, Lord John 94
—, John, 2nd Earl 113
Ryves, Dr Bruno 99

S

Sadler Collection 88
St Augustine 5
—, —, Priory 76
St Bartholomew's Priory 11,94
St Bernard's Hospital — see Hospitals
St Bridget 238
St Catherine's Court 117
St David's Home 73
St Dunstan 104,199
St Helen's Priory, Bishopsgate 9,55,231
St Lawrence 229
St Lawrence Brentford Trust 229
St Mary's Convent 235
St Mary's Court 41
St Mary's-on-the-Green 45
St Mary's Place 41
—, —, Square 36,49
St Paul's Cathedral 5,8
—, —, Canons of 119
—, —, Deans of 11,146
—, —, School 11,31,39
St Peter's — see Westminster
St Raphael's Home 235

NOTES